D1084855

THE
COOL
SCHOOL

THE COOL SCHOOL

writing
from
america's hip
underground

edited by
glenn o'brien

A Special Publication of
THE LIBRARY OF AMERICA

Some of the material in this volume is reprinted by permission
of the holders of copyright and publication rights.
Sources and acknowledgments begin on page 465.

The paper used in this publication meets the
minimum requirements of the American National Standard for
Information Sciences—Permanence of Paper for Printed
Library Materials, ANSI z39.48—1984.

Distributed to the trade in the United States
by Penguin Group (USA) Inc.
and in Canada by Penguin Books Canada Ltd.

Library of Congress Control Number: 2013941522
ISBN 978-1-59853-256-2

First Printing

Printed in the United States of America

Contents

Introduction

1.

I'm hip.

That means "I know."

My friend Eric Mitchell says Hip comes from the West African word "hipi" meaning "to open one's eye." (Some philologists disagree but Eric is hip.)

If you're hip your eyes are open, all three of them.

Hip is kind of like being gnostic. How do I know? I don't know, I just know.

2.

Hipness is a pre-existing condition, something you discover in yourself by yourself.

To be hip is to be an outsider who connects with other outsiders to become insiders of a sort.

To be hip is to belong to an underground, a subculture or counterculture, an elective tribe located within a larger community, outsiders inside. It is detached from the main thing and proud of its detachment. Hip is not always an option but it is always optional.

To be hip is to be Other. (Rimbaud: "I is another.") We all feel other sometimes and some feel it all the time. The other is the outsider within: the shunned, the excluded, the non-conformist, the escapist, the oddball, the misfit, the square peg, the freak. One of "us" gone rogue, gone haywire, gone wrong trying to get right.

The hipster is either the next step in evolution or the type next destined for extinction.

3.

Cab Calloway defined hep cat as "a guy who knows all the answers."
Thus hep cats date back to Socrates (470–399 B.C.E.), who knew all
the questions.

So Socrates was probably the first historical hipster. The first real
beatnik might have been Diogenes (412–323 B.C.E.), the philosopher
who lived in a barrel in Athens during the time of Plato. When Alexander the Great asked him if he wanted anything, he said "Yes, don't
block my sunshine." He was a dropout.

4.

The original hipster was an underground figure: an outlaw, an outsider, an outcast, an exile, a heretic, a Bohemian, a misfit, a pariah,
a fugitive—a street person, a criminal, a sexual outlaw, a madman.
America had known many such.

"So it is no accident that the source of Hip is the Negro for he has
been living on the margin between totalitarianism and democracy
for two centuries."—Norman Mailer, "The White Negro"

In the early twentieth century black culture, rooted in jazz with its
free sexuality and use of marijuana and other drugs, was an outlaw
culture that required an opaque language and a speakeasy limited
access to survive.

"And Newark always had a bad reputation, I mean, everybody
could pop their fingers. Was hip. Had walks."—Amiri Baraka

5.

The hipster is identified by language reflecting an alternate set of
values—a lingo or slang not understood by the mainstream. It is a
language whose meaning may be multileveled and whose surface
may be deliberately misleading. Thus, to understand—to catch the
deliberate drift—is to dig.

"**Dig**: Understand, appreciate . . . Often used as interjectory verbal
punctuation, to command attention or to break up thoughts. 'Dig. We
were walking down Tenth Avenue, you dig it, and dig! Here comes
this cop. So dig, here's what we did."—Del Close

Hip language is a living medium. The dictionary of hip is unprintable as it is always mutating faster than fruit flies, too fast for the squares to catch on.

"By the time they catch us we're not there."—Ishmael Reed, "Foolology"

To get it you have to have, like Jesus put it, "ears to hear." Like Antony said, "Lend me your ears." Like Lord Buckley said, "Knock me your lobes."

The hipster spoke jive talk. Jive was jazz talk. A 1928 dictionary defined it as "to deceive playfully" (v.), also "empty misleading talk" (n.). It was ironical language copped from blacks and Jews, gays and jazz musicians and junkies, bootleggers and second story men. Jive was an underground, initiatory language existing, the vernacular as survival strategy, a way of speaking in front of the enemy without being understood. It is the language of the marginalized—although sometimes it isn't simply a way of excluding people outside the group from understanding, but also of bonding and affirming status within the insider/outsider group: converting exclusion into exclusivity. Can you dig it?

6.

"As he was the illegitimate son of the Lost Generation, the hipster was really *nowhere*."—Anatole Broyard

In "The White Negro" Norman Mailer explained the hipster as a result of existentialism hitting the melting pot. Mailer's hipster is a white man who removes himself from the culture into which he was born because of existential dread. Dread from the A-bomb's threat of mass extinction or the corporate world's mass identity extinction.

"One is Hip or one is Square . . . one is a rebel or one conforms, one is a frontiersman in the Wild West of American night life, or else a Square cell, trapped in the totalitarian tissues of American society, doomed willy-nilly to conform if one is to succeed."—Norman Mailer, "The White Negro"

7.

The hipster is cool because he is detached, or semi-detached. He is independent. He is non-invasive and self-contained. A group of hipsters might be called an archipelago.

Cool isn't something invented recently. It was probably cool in the caves where the original underground cats dwelt. When the tribe was having a war dance, the cool one wasn't dancing, but he might have been playing a drum in the corner. Syncopated.

Cool cannot be faked. Someone trying to be cool is generally more uncool than somebody who is not trying at all.

Cool is like grace. It can be sold but not bought.

Cool is provisional. Cool wants to think it over and get back to you.

"There is a cool spot on the surface of Venus three hundred degrees cooler than the surrounding area. I have held that spot against all contestants for five hundred thousand years."—William S. Burroughs

"Nothing gives one person so much advantage over another as to remain always cool and unruffled under all circumstances."—Thomas Jefferson

8.

"By 1948 it began to take shape. That was a wild vibrating year when a group of us would walk down the street and yell hello and even stop and talk to anybody that gave us a friendly look. The hipsters had eyes."—Jack Kerouac

"All the people who, like me, had hidden and skulked, writing down what they knew for a small handful of friends . . . waiting with only a slight bitterness for the thing to end, for man's era to a close in a blaze of radiation—all these would now step forward and say their piece."—Diane di Prima

As the Beats got exposure, their bohemian enclaves supplied the big city with some excitement, and gave youth somewhere to rebel to. It was hang in the enclave or hit the road—and it was no coincidence that the Genesis of Beat was *On the Road*. Already the scene was not a place but a trip.

9.

To the latter day hipsters of my baby boom generation hipness was redefined as a kind of religion, a trans-apocalyptic cult that burned cool, that fluoresced around us, threatening to erase official history in a spontaneous rhythmic carnal uprising, a revolution of the mind, an eruption of eros, and enlightenment. It was where we came in.

The whole scene morphed from cool detachment to swirling total immersion, from nihilism to nirvana.

It became a spectrum of otherness: Hippies and Yippies, Panthers and Diggers and Merry Pranksters.

We weren't Americans anymore. The hipster had become a cosmopolite, an organism that occurs in most parts of the world. The hipster feels at home or not at home everywhere equally.

But finally every hipster is the citizen of himself.

"The hipster has usually been associated with being a number, a hot card, something oddly independent, responsive to whatever circumstance he finds himself in, disaffiliated but sovereign to whatever turf he finds himself wise to."—Richard Prince

10.

A funny thing happened on the way to nirvana. Handfuls of demonstrators turned into "the armies of the night." The counterculture grew so large it became a sort of co-culture. The success of the hip changed the trip. It was no longer Route 66 but the Interstate, no longer boxcars but tour jets.

For true believers in rebellion as a conspiracy against fascist control and the status quo, the end of the twentieth century proved a disappointment as the counterculture was absorbed nearly whole by the mechanisms of consumer culture. The radical ideas of the sixties went into business for themselves. It wasn't only that boundary-breaking genres were co-opted. They were embraced and enthusiastically marketed to such an extent that it was increasingly difficult to maintain a serious posture of opposition. Fashion raided the archives of the underground and began selling a simulacrum of rebellion.

The crazed hippies intent on destroying the system sold like hot-cakes. Cool hotcakes. They became product despite themselves, to spite themselves.

11.

But sometimes a simulacrum gives you a taste and you want more. You want the real thing. The appearance of rebellion could still supply a frisson to bored youth who saw the youthful antics of predecessor generations as exciting.

There was little to revolt against except ennui, but that was something.

The young began dressing like pictures they had seen of rebels past, rebels who seemed to be having a wild time that was no longer accessible.

12.

Today if you use the term hipster it's usually referring to a kind of look. The online urban dictionary actually says "The 'effortless cool' urban bohemian look of a hipster is exemplified in Urban Outfitters and American Apparel ads which cater toward the hipster demographic."

I had noticed the new class hipsters but I didn't pay them much mind except to admire their fedoras, beards, and tattoos. Looking or simulating interesting may be the first step toward being that way. They certainly looked more interesting than the power-suited yuppies of the eighties, but their focus seemed more about craft beers and artisanal cheese than more profound cultural involvement.

Then I was browsing at a bookstore in Berlin and I came across a book the title of which intrigued me: *What Was the Hipster?* It had been put together by a bunch of young Brooklynite intellectuals, apparently neither bearded nor tattooed. The book's premise was that the hipster was a fairly recent phenomenon and that it was over, and in retrospect it wasn't anything that anyone would have genuinely wanted to be anyway. I found that puzzling as I had always wanted to be a hipster from slightly before the moment that I figured out what a beatnik might be.

I realized that the word had changed meaning while I was dozing in the sun or strolling on a golf course. According to the leader of their panel of experts, Mark Greif: "... the contemporary hipster seems to emerge out of a thwarted tradition of youth subcultures, subcultures which had tried to remain independent of consumer culture, alternative to it, and been integrated, humiliated, and destroyed."

"Oh wow!" I thought, in the words of Maynard G. Krebs, the cat who had me playing bongos when I was twelve. Humiliated and destroyed by consumer culture! Not again! This generation sure went down in flames a lot easier than the hippies and the punks.

13.

Finally I figured out what these guys were talking about. One of their definitions of this new hipster was "rebel consumer"—"the culture figure of the person, very possibly, who understands consumer purchases within the familiar categories of mass consumption . . . like the right vintage T-shirt, the right jeans, the right foods for that matter—to be *a form of art*."

That rang a bell and it sounded like Richard Prince's fault. I had seen the hip career choice change from rock musician or painter, to DJ or curator. Life had become a matter of selecting among readymades. Greif concludes his essay: "The 2009 hipster becomes the name for that person who is a savant at picking up the tiny changes of consumer distinction and who can afford to live in the remaining enclaves where such styles are picked up on the street rather than, or as well as, online."

I could actually dig that analysis. It took me back to the early nineties when I was asked the definition of Alternative Music, then a principle category in music, and I replied "mainstream." I had once asked Madonna why her music was categorized as Pop while Elvis Costello's was Alternative and she said, "Because he's not good looking."

14.

The scary thing about this project is that you begin to realize that the underground as we used to know it really doesn't exist anymore except in our nostalgia for it. Burroughs was always quoting Hassan i Sabbah, the Old Man of the Mountains, the founder of the assassin order, the first terrorist: "Nothing is true. Everything is permitted."

And never was this more true. Or permitted. Marketing has simply turned the forbidden, the underground, the enemy even, into something marketable. What once made artistic products underground was either censorship or cultural disapproval enforced by the guardians of the marketplace. If a book or a band was too outrageous it wasn't considered for production. But in the digital age the gatekeepers are out of business.

Lately I sensed that something else was stirring out there. Every now and then a group of Occupy others march past my house and I can't help cheering out the window.

The underground seems to be trying to come around again. I can dig that and I sincerely hope that these cool artifacts aid and abet a cool front moving in.

I don't mind if it starts out totally fake, with a beard and a tattoo and a copy of Kerouac carried for effect. Hey I started with Maynard G. Krebs and his goatee and it worked for me.

"Work?!"

15.

In a way this volume is a compendium of orphans.

It's not really an anthology as much as a sampler. A few tasty morsels from the bebop scene, some ancient history of the pre-wiggers, the Beats both beatific and downtrodden, some gonzo and gonzo-esque journalism, even a bit of punk picaresque. It's really a louche *amuse bouche* and possible textbook for Outlier Lit 101.

My guiding principle in selecting was filtered randomness. My only agenda was to provide a primer and inspiration for future thought crime and written rebellion. This volume is by no means definitive in terms of the writers selected or the examples chosen. It could have been almost entirely composed of different authors, except for a few prime mover usual suspects. I may have given shorter shrift to the greener, more Big Sur Zen garden end of the spectrum in favor of urban grit, but that can easily be rectified—get with Gary Snyder and he'll do the rest.

What is collected here is just a little taste to whet cool appetites.

Glenn O'Brien
New York 2013

THE
COOL
SCHOOL

Mezz Mezzrow
(1899–1972)
and
Bernard Wolfe
(1915–1985)

Really the Blues—*Mezz Mezzrow's memoir of the early days of jazz, cowritten with novelist Bernard Wolfe—came out in 1946 and was an instant counter-cultural classic. Henry Miller applauded its "unadulterated joy." For Allen Ginsberg it was "the first signal into white culture of the underground black, hip culture that preexisted before my own generation." Hip came out of jazz and no hepcats put more effort into attaining and practicing hipness than the white players on the jazz scene. Mezzrow was a reed man better known as a weed man. At one point "the mezz" meant the highest quality weed. He was so hip, when he was sent up to Rikers Island he told the judge he was black so he could be locked up right. In this episode Mezz recounts the struggle of Chicago musicians—including such legends as Eddie Condon, Frank Teschemacher, Joe Sullivan, and (briefly) Gene Krupa—to make it in New York. The propulsive jive-talking prose remains irresistible.*

If You Can't Make Money

I'd rather drink muddy water, Lord,
    sleep in a hollow log,
I'd rather drink muddy water, Lord,
    sleep in a hollow log,
Than to be up here in New York,
    treated like a dirty dog.

JACK TEAGARDEN sang that lament on a record of ours called *Makin' Friends*, and it should have been the theme-song of the Chicagoans. The panic was on. When we bust in on our pals we found them all kipping in one scraggy room, practically sleeping in layers. They should of had the SRO sign up. Eddie Condon was out scooting around town with Red McKenzie, trying to scare up some work. There wasn't a gas-meter between them all, and they couldn't remember when they'd greased their chops last. "Wait'll you get a load of this burg—don't lose it," Tesch mumbled in his signifying way, cocking his sorrowful eyes over those hornrimmed cheaters.

They'd had a job all lined up when they first breezed in, but when they made the audition the boss got one earful of Chicago music and yelled "Get those bums out of here!" That was how jazz hit the tin ears of Tin Pan Alley. After one week at the Palace, where they played slink-and-slump music behind a team of ballroom dancers, they all holed up in this cubby, singing those miss-meal blues like Doc Poston had predicted. They picked up on some vittles once today and then again the day after tomorrow.

Well, we all laid around in that fleabag-with-room-service for a couple of gripy weeks, and then, through a fiddle-stroker who was crazy about hot music, I landed a job in a roadhouse called the Castilian Gardens, out in Valley Stream, Long Island. Gene, Eddie, Sullivan and Billings made a beeline for the suburbs with me. Soon Gene left for Chicago. Then we eased our guitar player out and moved in Eddie with his long-necked banjo; next the piano player quit, by request, and Sullivan took over his place; finally our tenor sax player said, "Milton, Tesch needs to be in this band, and I can go with a straight dance band, so I'll gladly leave if only you'll teach me how to play jazz," so in a few days we began to sound like something. Talk about infiltration tactics—we just surrounded that band from within. The trumpet player quit soon after because he didn't know a single tune we played, as we kept reminding him, and right after that our leader got a bigtime offer somewhere, so he turned the whole band over to me. The boss wouldn't hire Tesch, and I couldn't get Gene and Bud back from Chicago, but still, out of seven men we were left with four and three of them were Chicagoans, so the band didn't sound so bad.

One night Jack "Legs" Diamond fell into the joint with scumpteen of his henchmen and ordered the doors closed, and Jim, it was on. Our music hit Legs' girl friend so hard, she jumped out on the dance floor and began rolling her hips like she was fresh in from Waikiki, with ball-bearings where her pelvis should of been; then she pulled up her dress till it was more off than on, showing her pretty linens or what she had of them. I nearly swallowed my horn, gunning Legs to see how he felt about it. I was all set to stop the band as soon as he batted an eye. The boss almost shook his wig off giving me the office from behind a post—he knew Legs wasn't so well liked in the under-world, and the last time this gang was in they almost wrecked the place. But the moment the music stopped this grave-bait ran pouting to her daddy, and Legs motioned to us to keep on playing. Before his finger stopped wagging we were halfway through the second chorus.

We were at the Castilian Gardens for about three months, right through the summer season. While we were out there Tesch left to go with Sam Lannin's orchestra, and I never did get to see him again before he got killed in 1932. Then, one night after Labor Day, when we all came to work togged in our tuxedos to open the fall season, we found a brand-new padlock on the slammer and we couldn't get in. The boss showed up and sighed, "Well boys, this is it—I couldn't pay the rent so the landlord closed me up, and just when I got an icebox full of ducks for the week-end dinner crowd." He was so bad off he couldn't even get up our back pay, which was a bringdown to me because my wife and her son had just come in from Chicago. Well, we broke open a side window and climbed in to get our horns, and at the boss' suggestion we trucked into the refrigerator and loaded ourselves with all the fowl we could carry, and that's how we wound up at Valley Stream getting paid off in ducks instead of dollars. "We ask for our salary and get the bird," said Joe Sullivan, but nobody even cracked a smile.

WALKING DOWN Broadway one afternoon, minding my own busi-ness, I was surprised to find the sidewalk heaving up into my face and the buildings beginning to jig and teeter, getting ready to crash-land on my skull. All mush behind the eyeballs and my muscles turned to jelly, I grabbed a lamppost and hung on. Sweat squirted from my face; my stomach was practising sailor's knots, there was a pain big as a baseball buried in the nape of my neck, and my scalp stretched so tight I was afraid it would split right down the middle. I held on, frantic, while The Apple melted down to churning applesauce and I bobbed in and through it all. My prayerbones played knock-knock. Jack, I was bad off. One look at me just then would have scared Doc Freud right back into the pill business.

I watched the people fly by. The men all had snap-brim Capone hats pulled down low over their eyes, their coat collars were all turned up, they had their shoulders hunched and their hands buried deep in their overcoat pockets. I could tell that every one of them had a handful of Colt .45. From the way they eyed me, I knew they all meant to get me, now or five minutes from now. That was the reason behind all their scampering and scurrying around; they were laying their plans, getting ready to ambush me. I saw clear that they were one big race of torpedoes, plug-uglies, and murder merchants. They had me surrounded and they were closing in. Any minute now all those automatics would start barking from all those overcoat pockets—in my direction. My stomach started to do flip-flops.

I knew I was more complexy than the whole Bellevue psycho-pathic ward, and that my nervous system had been building up to this breakdown for a long time. I first began switching to the psycho kick when I landed a job out at the Woodmansten Inn, on Pelham Parkway in the East Bronx. That's where my neuroses started sprouting neuroses. A drummer named Johnny Powell was leader of the band out there, and Eddie Condon and Joe Sullivan were playing alongside me, in addition to a fiddle player. It was early Fall by the time we went to work but the weather was still balmy, so we played in a very large screened-in open-air café, loaded up with the usual palm trees and Chinese lanterns.

Now you couldn't ask for a sweeter guy than Johnny Powell—a tall spry French-Canadian, with one of them twirl-away moustaches.

He worshipped the ground we Chicagoans walked on, and he was dying to learn the jazz technique on the drums because he knew that Gene Krupa had come up under our tutelage. But we were allergic to him. For one thing, he drove us crazy with his habit of always using the word "interpolate." "How can I interpolate that beat?" he would ask, and we all winced. "Do you guys think we ought to interpolate now or later," he wanted to know. Johnny was a very studious guy, all wrapped up in his drums, but he just didn't have it in him, interpolate or expectorate, and we suffered the agonies of the damned because his foot was so heavy and he dragged time till it drove me and Joe out of our minds. It was his gimpy tempo that first brought on my nervous indigestion.

The violin player got on our nerves too. He played sweet, with a full round tone, and he had plenty of technique, but there was that inevitable pulling back of the time again. Way back there, Bix and I used to talk about the dragging violins. We often wondered if maybe it wasn't the large number of them in the symphony that made them lag behind, but here we were playing with only one violin and still we kept getting tangled up in its strings. That violin, added to the straggling drums, began to give us nightmares. Joe would take drink after drink and almost break his fingers on the keyboard, and I would blow until I was blue in the face, trying to get those slow-motion artists in step, but we might as well have tried to budge a couple of hungry mules. It was worse than the Chinese water torture, where they tie you up and let water trickle on your forehead drop by drop. Guys go howling mad and make a meal of their tongues, waiting for the next drop, and that's just what happened to us every time Johnny debated with himself whether he should interpolate now or later. In that fraction of a second while we waited for those two guys to catch up with our chord, I would sweat a bucket of blood and my ticker just gave up and quit altogether. It was like waiting for the accentuated beat of your heart when you're on a reefer jag, and you wait and you wait and the beat doesn't come and you think you've stopped living. I swear, after a few weeks I began to wonder if Johnny Powell wasn't using my head for a gong, conking me with delayed-action sledgehammers, while the violinist bowed across all my raw nerves with a hunk of jaggedy glass. It was an effort to keep from screaming, It's all right, beat me to a pulp, cut me to ribbons, only keep time, for Christ's sake, *just keep in time.*

With that waxed soup-strainer of his and that slick hair, Johnny took on some grotesque features in my hot mind. I'd look and look at him and begin to see him as Dirty Dan Desmond himself, cool and suave on the outside but with a heart full of evil and larceny. Sometimes I got to thinking that he was deliberately, cold-bloodedly trying to wear me down, make me blow my top. There was a conspiracy in Manhattan, headed by him, to give all Windy City musicians the heebies until they were ready to be bugged.

He was the kindest, gentlest, most considerate guy alive, was Johnny Powell, and I was beginning to despise him. All day long I shook like I had the palsy, dreading the hour of doom when I would have to face him again. I guess I was a little on the sensitive side just then. It came from being all bottled-up musically, and from seeing the Chicagoans getting lost in the stampede of the squares. I saw nothing ahead for us but yawning oblivion, and Johnny was greasing the way for us with that better-late-than-never beat of his.

To keep one jump ahead of the straitjacket squad, we used to drive down to Harlem after work on the hunt for some decent music, but it was nowhere to be had, even in the world's greatest Negro community. I missed the South Side plenty; New Orleans–Chicago jazz hadn't hit New York yet, so in Harlem too we were starved for our musical daily bread, cut off from the source of life and spirit. I felt like an alien here, an outsider who just came along for the ride, because I was advocating and signifying in an idiom that hadn't yet caught on in these parts. It was a feeling I never got on the South Side, and it didn't help my morale none. Harlem wasn't any nerve-tonic for me. What made me feel even more like a foreigner was that most of the Harlem spots we hit were controlled by white hoodlums. The whole area was overrun with fay gangsters who got fat on the profits they raked in from the big nightclubs and speakeasies and from the numbers racket. I began to feel that the conspiracy against us, the white man's conspiracy, had reached up into Harlem too.

I'd had a bellyful of gangsters and muscle men by that time. They'd always been luring me on, trying to win me away from the music to their loutish way of life—all of them, from the gamblers and pimps in the Chicago syndicate to Frank Hitchcock's boys at Burnham and the hophead mugs over in Detroit. Our whole jazz music was, in a way, practically the theme-song of the underworld because, thanks to prohibition, about the only places we could play like we wanted were illegal dives. The gangsters had their dirty grabbers on our music too, just like they kept a death grip on everything else in this booby-hatch of a country. If I resisted their come-on even a little, it was only because of my obsession with the music. Every time I got in trouble, it was because I strayed away from the music. Whenever I latched on solid to the music, I flew right. I was beginning to sense a heap of moral in all this, but my hot instincts to stick with the music and keep straight were all frustrated now. I saw these white gangsters ruling the roost in Harlem, so I blamed them for it. I kept sinking lower and lower. Every night I would wind up in Harlem with nothing to do but wolf down a mess of barbequed ribs smothered in red-hot tabasco sauce and swill terrible rotgut by the barrel. That didn't soothe my jumpy stomach much either. At first my digestion was just nervous; pretty soon it stopped altogether.

I even made myself lose that Woodmansten Inn job, along with Eddie Condon and Sullivan, but still the jitters wouldn't quit me. The last night there I was blowing real hard, really reciting out in front of the band, when suddenly I went all shatter-brained. A bunch of ugly-looking gangsters had taken the joint over for a big party, and they were all wobbling around the floor with their floozies, so drunk they could hardly stand. One of these mugs danced right up under the bandstand and just stood there, staring at me. When I swayed, he swayed. When I stomped, he stomped. Suddenly I began to shake so bad I could hardly hold my clarinet. I had just remembered something that froze my spine. Joe E. Lewis had been working in a Chicago nightclub run by some gangsters, and one night he mentioned to his bosses that he was thinking about changing jobs because he had got a much better offer. Those hoodlums didn't argue with him. They didn't bargain. They just smiled, and paid him a visit and slit his throat from ear to ear. It happened in his hotel, just around the corner from where I was living.

I watched that yegg while my clarinet weaved a spell around him, and I thought, Jesus, this music sure has got a hold of him. Suppose he owns some club and likes my playing so much he wants me to go to work for him? Maybe he's thinking it over right now, while he's casing me. If I have to work for him I'll really be under his thumb, and if I try to make a move they'll just cut me open like they did poor Joe E. Lewis. . . . Right quick I changed the phrasing and meter of my improvisation, fading all the way into the background. The audience felt the let-down and yelled, "Come on, get hot," but I didn't feel like reciting any more—I'd lost all voice for it.

That same night I quit the job and rushed home. I sprinted all the way from the bus stop to my house, and took those stairs three at a time. I heard footsteps dogging me all the way, right up the stairs and into the house. They were slow and dragging, in gimp-time. They sounded like Johnny Powell's drums.

MY MIND was a cistern, clogged with maggoty memories. I remembered that just before I left Chicago, in the same apartment house where Tesch and I lived, right over my head, some dame had been strangled with a lamp cord. Then came the Saint Valentine's Day massacre, when a bunch of Capone's gangsters got dressed up like cops and drove up in a police wagon and lined another mob against the wall and mowed them down with machine guns, leaving the mangled bodies all crumpled up on the floor like some soggy lumber. Then, right after I hit New York, Arnold Rothstein the gambler was strolling down the stairs at the Park Central and came somersaulting down with a load of lead in his hide. And there was that subway train that got derailed at Times Square, leaving over two hundred bodies of dead and near-dead piled up ready for the dustbins. All that came flooding up in my mind, and plenty more. I remembered the way Legs Diamond wrecked the Castilian Gardens just for kicks one night, and the nightmares I had after that other party of his. I remembered Frank Hitchcock piled in a ditch, and Capone's wife masquerading out at the Martinique, and Bow Gistensohn on a cold marble slab and Emil Burbacher in Joliet, the frightened girls trying to run away from the syndicate whorehouses and their pimps coming after them, the opium-smoking bigshots of the Purple Gang whose pictures were beginning to pop up in the papers because, one by one, they were being wheeled into the morgue icebox. Ten solid years of murder and riot. Ten years of a bloody showerbath. They kept unwinding in my head.

It looked to me like the whole continent was being drowned in a bath of blood, from coast to coast. The nation was committing mass suicide—it was like a slimy snake blowing its top, writhing and wriggling with the fits, beginning to chew up its own tail. Sure, I was surrounded by a race of gangsters running amuck, a hundred million blowtops, born with icecubes for hearts and the appetites of a cannibal. "They devour one another, and cannot even digest themselves." Nietzsche said that. "See them clamber, these nimble apes! They clamber over one another, and thus scuffle into the mud and the abyss." They were sure clambering some in the U.S. of A. Nobody was safe in this funky jungle. It was all one great big underworld, and they'd put their dirty grabbers on the one good thing left on earth, our music, and sucked it down into the mud with them.

I found I was getting so sensitive to odors, any strong smell was a torture. Almost any kind of heavy odor would make me dizzy and send me reeling down the street, my stomach quaking in shuffle rhythm. The worst ordeal of all, one I really dreaded, was to take the Seventh Avenue subway uptown, to get to where I was living with my family just then, on Park Avenue just below Fordham Road. There's a long stretch from 96th Street to 110th, where the train passes under

Central Park, heading into Harlem, and I used to go out of my mind there because of the extra strong odor of scorched steel. It reminded me of the burnt-rags stench of the ether they doused me with back in The Band House when they took my appendix out, and I couldn't stand it. I used to sit huddled up on my seat, shrinking into a corner, my head shoved down between my knees and my arms wrapped tight around it, to keep from screaming.

One day, just as the train pulled into 110th Street, I felt a gentle tap on my shoulder, and when I worked up enough courage to raise my head, there was a nice-looking old colored man with a thick crop of snow-white hair, looking down at me with the kindest, most sympathetic expression I ever saw. "Son," he said to me real soft, "if you can't make money, make friends," and with that he stepped out on the platform and drifted away. He saved my life that day. Of course, it wasn't money I was worrying about, it was that metallic odor that reminded me of jail and burnt powder and all the scowling evil in the gangster world I knew. But that old man had the answer anyway: fall in with some regular guys and you're saved. I had such a tender feeling for that man that when I was on a record date a little later I remembered his words, and that's how we got the title for those blues Jack Teagarden sang, *Makin' Friends*.

"Ten times must thou laugh during the day, and be cheerful; otherwise thy stomach, the father of affliction, will disturb thee in the night." That's what the wise man said to Zarathustra. I thought about those lines a lot—I sure had forgotten how to laugh, and my stomach was on the blink too, and maybe there was some connection. Well, the doctors couldn't give me any prescription for breaking out in smiles, but they at least might be able to set my stomach straight.

Tommy Dorsey sent me around to see his physician, Dr. Irving Grad, and he wanted to pump my stomach, but I couldn't see that at all. "Well," he told me, "you've got to get your system cleaned out somehow, so if you don't want to use a pump why don't you take an ocean trip? In your condition you're bound to get seasick, and Nature will do the job for you." I couldn't think of anywhere to go, that was the trouble. I didn't feel like taking one of them ocean jaunts; I just wanted to dig a hole in the ground and crawl way down into it and pull it in after me. I told him I would think it over.

The doc told me to take long walks and get as much fresh air as I could, so every day I would totter over to the Bronx Zoo, which was a little ways down Fordham Road from where I lived. Once I stopped by the seal pond and stood there for a long time, watching a big black glistening seal go jack-knifing through his tricks. It got me in a trance. All of a sudden it hit me that this high-spirited animal, that was so graceful it made me want to cry, really had the secret, and nobody suspected it. "And to me also, who appreciate life," said Nietzsche, "the butterflies, and soapbubbles, and whatever is like them amongst us, seem most to enjoy happiness." With those moustaches and that bright, clear-eyed look of his, this seal struck me as being a gentle and wise old man, digging the whole world and at peace with it. He belonged to the world of butterflies and soapbubbles. While all us two-legged ounce-brains jittered around real frantic outside his bars, cutting our throats and bumping each other off, he just kept diving and leapfrogging through the water with that heartbreaking ease and sureness, one tight beautiful unit from head to tail—sunning himself, knowing his natural strength and ability to use it, taking a gang of delight in his sleek supple body, just coasting along without tension or nerve-knotting worry. That fine animal never suffered from nervous indigestion a day in his life; thy stomach, the father of affliction, never broke up his solid sleep. He laughed ten times a day every day at us strutting simps. It became very important to me to study every flick and ripple of his body, to try and dig his marvelous control, the secret of his ease.

Goddamn if that animal wasn't so anxious to help me out, he started romping around just for my benefit. He would dive and then go through his wriggles slow-motion, right at the surface of the pond so I could follow him. Then he would climb right up in front of me and look straight in my eyes and I knew he was saying to me, Well brother, you see how it's done, watch close now—all you got to do is relax and take it easy and use yourself the way Nature intended you to, and then you'll be happy just like all us seals, you'll live forever and you'll never need a Seidlitz powder. He was pointing his wise old snout straight at the millennium, and wanted me to follow him there. We understood each other so perfectly, I got self-conscious. Pretty soon I hurried away because other people were drifting near and I didn't want any square outsiders standing around while that seal and I spoke to each other. They wouldn't have understood.

WELL, ON January 23rd, 1929, I got a cablegram from Dave Tough in Paris saying, HAVE GOOD JOB COME AT ONCE BRING RECORDS AND MUSIC WIRE IMMEDIATELY. Right away I thought of Doc Grad's advice about a sea voyage. Here was the answer, dropped right in my lap.

Now all I had to do was raise money for my passage. As luck would have it, Gil Rodin, who was playing with Ben Pollack's band just then at the Park Central Grille, was going to have his tonsils out and asked would I take his place for a couple of weeks. So I played there, alongside Benny Goodman and his brother Harry, Jimmy MacPartland, Glenn Miller, Jack Teagarden and Ray Bauduc. Even though we played all show tunes and dreamy dance music, things sometimes began to happen when Jack Teagarden, taking his trombone apart and playing with just the slide and a water glass like the colored boys sometimes did, would start off the blues in a major key, then change to the minor, same as he does on *Makin' Friends*. Jack could really get in the jazz idiom, and he did a lot to make this job bearable to me.

During this period I sat in on a recording date with the Pollack band, just a couple hours after I'd had a gang of teeth yanked, because my biters were going bad along with all my other parts. It turned out that the piano player had had a tooth pulled that morning too, so we sat with a spittoon between us and took turns spitting blood between choruses. Then there was another date, under the title of "Eddie Condon And His Foot Warmers," where a band made up mostly of Chicagoans recorded *Makin' Friends* and *I'm Sorry I Made You Cry* for Okeh. Then we got together for Victor, under the title of

"Eddie Condon's Hot Shots," and made two more sides, *I'm Gonna Stomp Mr. Henry Lee* and *That's a Mighty Serious Thing*. (On this date we had one of the first mixed groups that ever recorded—besides three colored boys from Harlem, there were Teagarden, Sullivan, Condon, and me.) Jimmy Dorsey asked me to substitute for him for a couple of weeks in the pit orchestra at the "Rain and Shine" show. Finally I had enough loot for the trip.

I wrote home for a birth certificate, which I needed to get my passport, and my dad sent it to me along with a note. "Go anywhere you wish son," he wrote, "but always remember, *sei a mensch*." That's the Yiddish for "be a human being." Then I booked passage for a second-class stateroom on the *Île de France*. Nobody knew I was leaving except my wife. Close to midnight on March the 2nd, 1929, I drove down to Pier 54, Bonnie coming along with me because I was so hopped-up she didn't dare let me go alone. All the taxis honking and the porters yelling drove me near crazy; I had to chew on my tongue to keep from screaming. Until the whistle tooted its last phlegmy good-bye and the boat started to creep down the Hudson I was in steady fear. I couldn't stop shaking.

Weaving from side to side like a lushhead, I groped my way to my stateroom. My stomach was churning worse than a volcano. I felt like I wouldn't live through the night. I crawled into my cubby and found I had a roommate, no butterfly or soapbubble exactly, but a suave and oily continental guy, who was counting a tremendous roll of hundred-dollar bills. He informed me cheerfully that he had strangled one man in Europe for raping his sister, stabbed another to death in a gambling fracas, and was now beating it from the States because of a third murder rap.

Really the Blues, 1946

Miles Davis
(1926–1991)

Bop was the font of postwar hipness and Charles "Yardbird" Parker was its prophet. Miles Davis began playing with Bird around 1945 when he was nineteen, and from there he went on to transform jazz with genre-making innovations, transitioning from bop to the cool school he founded, from modality to fusion (its best exemplar). Miles's style extended to everything he did—from his clothes to his paintings to his speech. When poet Quincy Troupe collaborated with Miles on his life story they set it down the way Miles told it—in language as close to the bone as his horn. Here's Miles on Bird, close-up and personal.

from *Miles: The Autobiography*

I KEPT LOOKING for Bird. One night I found myself just sort of standing around in the doorway at the Three Deuces when the owner came up and asked me what I was doing there. I guess I looked young and innocent; I couldn't even grow a moustache back then. Anyway, I told him I was looking for Bird and he told me he wasn't there and that I had to be eighteen to come in the club. I told him I *was* eighteen and all I wanted to do was to find Bird. Then the dude start telling me what a fucked-up motherfucker Bird was, about him being a dope addict and all that kind of shit. He asked me where I was from and when I told him, he come telling me that I ought to go on back home. Then he called me "son," a name I never liked, especially from some white motherfucker who I didn't know. So I told him to go fuck himself and turned around and left. I already *knew* Bird had a bad heroin habit; he wasn't telling me nothing new.

After I left the Three Deuces, I walked up the street to the Onyx Club and caught Coleman Hawkins. Man, the Onyx was jam-packed with people there to see Hawk, who played there regularly. So, because

Miles Davis ... **17**

I still didn't know anybody I just hung around the doorway like I had done at the Three Deuces, looking for a face I might recognize, you know, maybe somebody from B's band. But I didn't see anyone.

When Bean—that's what we called Coleman Hawkins—took a break, he came over to where I was, and until this day I don't know why he did this. I guess it was a lucky break. Anyway, I knew who he was and so I spoke to him and introduced myself and told him that I had played with B's band back in St. Louis and that I was in New York going to Juilliard but really trying to find Bird. I told him that I wanted to play with Bird and that he had told me when I got to New York to look him up. Bean kind of laughed and told me that I was too young to get mixed up with somebody like Bird. Man, he was making me mad with all this shit. This was the second time I had heard this that night. I didn't want to hear it no more, even if it came from somebody that I loved and respected as much as Coleman Hawkins. I got a real bad temper, so the next thing I know I'm saying to *Coleman Hawkins* something like, "Well, you know where he is or not?"

Man, I think Hawk was shocked by a young little black motherfucker like me talking to him like that. He just looked at me and shook his head and told me the best place to find Bird was up in Harlem, at Minton's or Small's Paradise. Bean said, "Bird loves to jam in those places." He turned to walk away, then added, "My best advice to you is just finish your studies at Juilliard and forget Bird."

Man, those first weeks in New York were a motherfucker—looking for Bird, and trying to keep up with my studies. Then somebody told me that Bird had friends in Greenwich Village. I went down there to see if I could find him. I went to coffeehouses on Bleecker Street. Met artists, writers, and all these long-haired, bearded beatnik poets. I had never met no people like them in all my life. Going to the Village was an education for me.

I began to meet people like Jimmy Cobb and Dexter Gordon as I moved around Harlem, the Village, and 52nd Street. Dexter called me "Sweetcakes" because I was drinking malted milks and eating cakes, pies, and jelly beans all the time. I was even getting friendly with Coleman Hawkins. He took a liking to me, watched out for me, and helped me all he could to find Bird. By now Bean thought I was really serious about the music and he respected that. But, still no Bird. And not even Diz knew where he was at.

One day I saw in the paper where Bird was scheduled to play in a jam session at a club called the Heatwave, on 145th Street in Harlem. I remember asking Bean if he thought Bird would show up there, and Bean just kind of smiled that slick, sly smile of his and said, "I'll bet *Bird* doesn't even know if he'll really be there or not."

That night I went up to the Heatwave, a funky little club in a funky neighborhood. I had brought my horn just in case I did run into Bird—if he remembered me, he might let me sit in with him. Bird wasn't there, but I met some other musicians, like Allen Eager, a white tenor player; Joe Guy, who played a great trumpet; and Tommy Potter, a bass player. I wasn't looking for them so I didn't pay them hardly no attention. I just found a seat and kept my eye fixed on the door, watching out for Bird. Man, I had been there almost all night waiting for Bird and he hadn't shown up. So I decided to go outside and catch a breath of fresh air. I was standing outside the club on the corner when I heard this voice from behind me say, "Hey, Miles! I heard you been looking for me!"

I turned around and there was Bird, looking badder than a motherfucker. He was dressed in these baggy clothes that looked like he had been sleeping in them for days. His face was all puffed up and his eyes were swollen and red. But he was cool, with that hipness he could have about him even when he was drunk or fucked up. Plus, he had that confidence that all people have when they *know* their shit is bad. But no matter *how* he looked, bad or near death, he still looked good to me that night after spending all that time trying to find him; I was just glad to see him standing there. And when he remembered where he had met me, I was the happiest motherfucker on earth.

I told him how hard it had been to find him and he just smiled and said that he moved around a lot. He took me into the Heatwave, where everybody greeted him like he was the king, which he was.

And since I was with him and he had his arm around my shoulder, they treated me with a lot of respect, too. I didn't play that first night. I just listened. And, man, I was amazed at how Bird changed the minute he put his horn in his mouth. Shit, he went from looking real down and out to having all this power and beauty just bursting out of him. It was amazing the transformation that took place once he started playing. He was twenty-four at the time, but when he wasn't playing he looked older, especially off stage. But his whole appearance changed as soon as he put that horn in his mouth. He could play like a motherfucker even when he was almost falling-down drunk and nodding off behind heroin. Bird was something else.

Anyway, after I hooked up with him that night, I was around Bird all the time for the next several years. He and Dizzy became my main influences and teachers. Bird even moved in with me for a while, until Irene came. She came to New York in December 1944. All of a sudden, there she was, knocking on my motherfucking door; my mother had told her to come. So I found Bird a room in the same rooming house, up on 147th and Broadway.

But I couldn't handle Bird's lifestyle then—all the drinking and eating and using dope. I had to go to school in the daytime and he'd be laying up there fucked up. But he was teaching me a lot about music—chords and shit—that I would go and play on the piano when I got to school.

WHEN DIZZY left their band at the Three Deuces, I thought Bird was going to take a band uptown, but he didn't, at least not right away. A lot of club owners on 52nd began asking Bird who his trumpet player was going to be since Dizzy quit. I remember being with Bird one time in a club when the owner asked that, and Bird turned to me and said, "Here's my trumpet player right here, Miles Davis." I used to kid Bird by saying, "If I hadn't joined your band, *you* wouldn't even have a job, man." He would just smile, because Bird enjoyed a good joke and one-upmanship. Sometimes it didn't work—me being in the band—because the owners liked Bird and Dizzy together. But the owner of the Three Deuces hired us in October of 1945. The group had Bird, Al Haig on piano, Curly Russell on bass, Max Roach and Stan Levey on drums, and me. It was the same rhythm section that Bird and Dizzy had right before Dizzy quit. I remember the gig at the Three Deuces being for about two weeks. Baby Laurence, the tap dancer, was the floor show. He took four and eights with the band and was a motherfucker. Baby was the greatest tap dancer that I have ever seen, or heard, because his tap dancing sounded just like a jazz drummer. He was something else.

I was so nervous on that first real gig with Bird that I used to ask if I could quit every night. I had sat in with him, but this was my first real paying gig with him. I would ask, "What do you need me for?" because that motherfucker was playing so much shit. When Bird played a melody I would just play under him and let him lead the fucking note, let him sing the melody and take the lead on everything. Because what would it look like, me trying to lead the leader of all the music? Me playing lead for Bird—are you kidding? Man, I was scared to death that I was going to fuck up. Sometimes I would act like I was quitting, because I thought he might fire me. So I was going to quit before he did, but he would always encourage me to stay by saying that he needed me and that he loved the way I played. I hung in there and learned. I knew everything Dizzy was playing. I think that's why Bird hired me—also because he wanted a different kind of trumpet sound. Some things Dizzy played I could play, and other things he played, I couldn't. So, I just didn't play those licks that I knew I couldn't play, because I realized early on that I had to have my own voice—whatever that voice was—on the instrument.

That first two weeks with Bird was a motherfucker, but it helped me grow up real fast. I was nineteen years old and playing with the baddest alto saxophone player in the history of music. This made me feel real good inside. I might have been scared as a motherfucker, but I was getting more confident too, even though I didn't know it at the time.

But Bird didn't teach me much as far as music goes. I loved playing with him, but you couldn't copy the shit he did because it was so original. Everything I learned about jazz back then I learned from Dizzy and Monk, maybe a little from Bean, but not from Bird. See, Bird was a soloist. He had his own thing. He was, like, isolated. And there was nothing you could learn from him unless you copied him. Only saxophone players could copy him, but even they didn't. All they could do was try to get Bird's approach, his concept. But you couldn't play that shit he played on saxophone with the same feeling on trumpet. You could learn the notes but it won't sound the same. Even great saxophonists couldn't copy him. Sonny Stitt tried, and Lou Donaldson a little later, and Jackie McLean a little later than both of them. But Sonny had more of Lester Young's style. And Bud Freeman used to play a lot like Sonny Stitt played. I guess Jackie and Lou came the closest to Bird, but only in their sound, not in *what* they played. Nobody could play like Bird, then or now.

BUT AS good as my relationship with Bird was getting in music, our private relationship was getting worse. Like I said, Bird lived with me for a minute, but it wasn't as long as a lot of writers say it was. I mean, I got him a room in the same apartment building where me and my family lived. But he would be down to our apartment all the time, borrowing money and shit, eating Irene's cooking, passing out drunk on the couch or the floor. Plus, when he would come by, he was constantly bringing all kinds of women and hustlers, dope dealers and all kinds of dope-fiend musicians.

One of the things I never understood about Bird was why he did all the destructive shit he used to do. Man, Bird knew better. He was an intellectual. He used to read novels, poetry, history, stuff like that. And he could hold a conversation with almost anybody on all kinds of things. So the motherfucker wasn't dumb or ignorant or illiterate or anything like that. He was real sensitive. But he had this destructive streak in him that was something else. He was a genius and most geniuses are greedy. But he used to talk a lot about political shit and he loved to put a motherfucker on, play dumb to what was happening and then zap the sucker. He used to especially like to do this to white people. And then he would laugh at them when they found out they had been had. He was something—a very complex person.

But the worst thing that Bird did back then was to take advantage of my love and respect for him as a great musician. He would tell dope dealers that I was going to be paying the money *he* owed them. So them dudes would be coming by looking like they wanted to kill me sometimes. That shit was dangerous. Finally I just told him and all the rest of them motherfuckers not to come by my house no more. That shit got so bad that Irene went back to East St. Louis, but she came back to New York as soon as Bird stopped coming around so much. Bird met Doris Sydnor about this time and he moved into her apartment, somewhere on Manhattan Avenue. But when Bird moved out of my place and before Irene came back from East St. Louis, Freddie Webster moved in and we would talk all night. He was a whole lot better to get along with than Bird was.

———

Early in the spring of 1946, I think it might have been March, Ross Russell set up a recording session with Dial Records for Bird. Ross made sure that Bird was sober, and hired me and Lucky Thompson on tenor, a guy named Arv Garrison on guitar, Vic McMillan on bass, Roy Porter on drums, and Dodo Marmarosa on piano.

At this time, Bird was drinking cheap wine and shooting heroin. People on the West Coast weren't into bebop like people in New York were and they thought some of the shit we were playing and doing was weird. Especially with Bird. He didn't have no money, was looking bad and raggedy, and everybody *knew* who he was, *knew* he was a bad motherfucker who didn't care. But the rest of the people who were being told that Bird was a star could only see this broke, drunken dude playing this weird shit up on stage. A lot of them didn't buy all that shit about Bird being this genius, they just ignored him, and I think this hurt his confidence in himself and what he was doing. When Bird left New York he was a king, but out in Los Angeles he was just another broke, weird, drunken nigger playing some strange music. Los Angeles is a city built on celebrating stars and Bird didn't look like no star.

But at this recording session that Ross set up for Dial, Bird pulled himself together and played his ass off. I remember we rehearsed at the Finale Club the night before we recorded. We argued half the night about what we were going to play and who was going to play what. There had been no rehearsal for the recording date, and the musicians were pissed because they were going to be playing tunes they were unfamiliar with. Bird was never organized about telling people what he wanted them to do. He just got who he thought could play the shit he wanted and left it at that. Nothing was written down, maybe a sketch of a melody. All he wanted to do was play, get paid, and go out and buy himself some heroin.

Bird would play the melody he wanted. The other musicians had to remember what he had played. He was real spontaneous, went on his instinct. He didn't conform to Western ways of musical group interplay by organizing everything. Bird was a great improviser and that's where he thought great music came from and what great musicians were about. His concept was "fuck what's written down." Play what you know and play that well and everything will come together—just the opposite of the Western concept of notated music.

I loved the way Bird did that. I learned a lot from him that way. It would later help me with my own music concepts. When that shit works, man, it's a motherfucker. But if you get a group of guys who don't understand what's happening, or they can't handle all that freedom you're laying on them, and they play what *they* want, then it's no good. Bird would get guys in who couldn't handle the concept. He did it in the recording studio and when they were playing a live performance. That's what a lot of that argument was about at the Finale the night before we recorded.

MEANWHILE, BIRD was forming a new band and asked me to come with him, and I did. The two records Bird had recorded for Dial out in Los Angeles had been released. I was on one and Howard McGhee was on the other, I think. They had been released in late 1946 and were now big jazz hits. So, with 52nd Street open again and Bird back in town, the club owners wanted Bird. Everybody was after him. They wanted small bands again and they felt that Bird would pack them in. They offered him $800 a week for four weeks at the Three Deuces. He hired me, Max Roach, Tommy Potter, and Duke Jordan on piano. He paid me and Max $135 a week and Tommy and Duke $125. Bird made the most he had ever made in his life, $280 a week. It didn't matter to me that I was making $65 a week less than what I had made in B's band; all I wanted to do was play with Bird and Max and make some good music.

I felt good about it, and Bird was clear-eyed, not like the crazed look he had in California. He was slimmer and seemed happy with Doris. She had gone out to California to get him when he got out of Camarillo, and accompanied him east on the train. Man, Doris loved her Charlie Parker. She would do anything for him. Bird seemed happy and ready to go. We opened in April 1947, opposite Lennie Tristano's trio.

I was really happy to be playing with Bird again, because playing with him brought out the best in me at the time. He could play so many different styles and never repeat the same musical idea. His creativity and musical ideas were endless. He used to turn the rhythm section around every night. Say we would be playing a blues. Bird would start on the eleventh bar. As the rhythm section stayed where they were, then Bird would play in such a way that it made the rhythm section sound like it was on 1 and 3 instead of 2 and 4. Nobody could keep up with Bird back in those days except maybe Dizzy. Every time he would do this, Max would scream at Duke not to try to follow Bird. He wanted Duke to stay where he was, because he wouldn't have been able to keep up with Bird and he would have fucked up the rhythm. Duke did this a lot when he didn't listen. See, when Bird went off like that on one of his incredible solos all the rhythm section had to do was to stay where they were and play some straight shit. Eventually Bird would come back to where the rhythm was, right on time. It was like he had planned it in his mind. The only thing about this is that he couldn't explain it to nobody. You just had to ride the music out. Because anything might happen musically when you were playing with Bird. So I learned to play what I knew and extend it upwards— a little *above* what I knew. You had to be ready for anything.

A week or so before opening night, Bird called for rehearsals at a studio called Nola. A lot of musicians rehearsed there during those days. When he called the rehearsals, nobody believed him. He never had done this in the past. On the first day of rehearsal, everybody showed up but Bird. We waited for a couple of hours and I ended up rehearsing the band.

Now, opening night, the Three Deuces is packed. We ain't seen Bird in a week, but we'd been rehearsing our asses off. So here this nigger comes in smiling and shit, asking is everybody ready to play in that fake British accent of his. When it's time for the band to hit he asks, "What are we playing?" I tell him. He nods, counts off the beat and plays every motherfucking tune in the exact key we had rehearsed it in. He played like a motherfucker. Didn't miss one beat, one note, didn't play out of key all night. It was something. We were fucking amazed. And every time he'd look at us looking at him all shocked and shit, he'd just smile that "Did you ever doubt this?" kind of smile.

After we got through with that first set, Bird came up and said— again in that fake British accent—"You boys played pretty good tonight, except in a couple of places where you fell off the rhythm and missed a couple of notes." We just looked at the motherfucker and laughed. That's the kind of amazing shit that Bird did on the bandstand. You came to expect it. And if he didn't do something incredible, *that's* when you were surprised.

Bird often used to play in short, hard bursts of breath. Hard as a mad man. Later on Coltrane would play like that. Anyway, so then, sometimes Max Roach would find himself in between the beat. And I wouldn't know what the fuck Bird was doing because I wouldn't have never heard it before. Poor Duke Jordan and Tommy Potter, they'd just be there lost as motherfuckers—like everybody else, only more lost. When Bird played like that, it was like hearing music for the first time. I'd never heard anybody play like that. Later, Sonny Rollins and I would try to do things like that, and me and Trane, playing those short, hard bursts of musical phrases. But when Bird played like that, he was outrageous. I hate to use a word like "outrageous," but that's what he was. He was notorious in the way he played combinations of notes and musical phrases. The average musician would try to develop something more logically, but not Bird. Everything he played—when he was on and *really* playing—was terrifying, and I was there every night! And so we couldn't just keep saying, "What? Did you hear *that!*" all night long. Because then *we* couldn't play nothing. So we got to the point where, when he played something that was just so outrageous, we blinked our eyes. They would just get wider than they were, and they already were *real* wide. But after a while it was just another day at the office playing with this bad motherfucker. It was unreal.

I was the one who rehearsed the band and kept it tight. Running that band made me understand what you had to do to have a great band. People said it was the best bebop band around. So I was proud of being the band's musical director. I wasn't twenty-one years old yet in 1947, and I was learning real quick about what music was all about.

Bird never talked about music, except one time I heard him arguing with a classical musician friend of mine. He told the cat that you can do anything with chords. I disagreed, told him that you couldn't play D natural in the fifth bar of a B flat blues. He said you could. One night later on at Birdland, I heard Lester Young do it, but he bent the note. Bird was there when it happened and he just looked over at me with that "I told you so" look that he would lay on you when he had proved you wrong. But that's all he ever said about it. He knew you could do it because he had done it before. But he didn't get up and show nobody *how* to do it or nothing. He just let you pick it up for yourself, and if you didn't, then you just didn't.

I learned a lot from Bird in this way, picking up from the way he played or didn't play a musical phrase or idea. But like I said, I never did talk to Bird much, never talked to him over fifteen minutes at a time, unless we were arguing about money. I'd tell him right up front, "Bird, don't fuck with me about money." But he always did.

Miles: The Autobiography (with Quincy Troupe), 1989

Henry Miller
(1891–1980)

*Henry Miller was the archetypal drop-out before there were drop-outs, quitting family, job, and the U.S. to lead a bohemian existence in Paris while writing books—*Tropic of Cancer, Tropic of Capricorn, Black Spring—*whose sexual frankness made them unpublishable for decades in his native land. Returning to America in the 1940s, he found himself still at odds with the mainstream culture, as evidenced by the following account of a drunken Hollywood dinner party. Settling at Big Sur, Miller was a liberating father figure to succeeding generations of writers and artists.*

Soirée in Hollywood

M Y FIRST evening in Hollywood. It was so typical that I almost thought it had been arranged for me. It was by sheer chance, however, that I found myself rolling up to the home of a millionaire in a handsome black Packard. I had been invited to dinner by a perfect stranger. I didn't even know my host's name. Nor do I know it now.

The first thing which struck me, on being introduced all around, was that I was in the presence of wealthy people, people who were bored to death and who were all, including the octogenarians, already three sheets to the wind. The host and hostess seemed to take pleasure in acting as bartenders. It was hard to follow the conversation because everybody was talking at cross purposes. The important thing was to get an edge on before sitting down to the table. One old geezer who had recently recovered from a horrible automobile accident was having his fifth old-fashioned—he was proud of the fact, proud that he could swill it like a youngster even though he was still partially crippled. Every one thought he was a marvel.

There wasn't an attractive woman about, except the one who had brought me to the place. The men looked like business men, except for one or two who looked like aged strike-breakers. There was one fairly young couple, in their thirties, I should say. The husband was a typical go-getter, one of those ex-football players who go in for publicity or insurance or the stock market, some clean all-American pursuit in which you run no risk of soiling your hands. He was a graduate of some Eastern University and had the intelligence of a high-grade chimpanzee.

That was the set-up. When every one had been properly soused dinner was announced. We seated ourselves at a long table, elegantly decorated, with three or four glasses beside each plate. The ice was abundant, of course. The service began, a dozen flunkeys buzzing at your elbow like horse flies. There was a surfeit of everything; a poor man would have had sufficient with the hors-d'oeuvre alone. As they ate, they became more discursive, more argumentative. An elderly thug in a tuxedo who had the complexion of a boiled lobster was railing against labor agitators. He had a religious strain, much to my amazement, but it was more like Torquemada's than Christ's. President Roosevelt's name almost gave him an apoplectic fit. Roosevelt, Bridges, Stalin, Hitler—they were all in the same class to him. That is to say, they were anathema. He had an extraordinary appetite which served, it seemed, to stimulate his adrenal glands. By the time he had reached the meat course he was talking about hanging being too good for some people. The hostess, meanwhile, who was seated at his elbow, was carrying on one of those delightful inconsequential conversations with the person opposite her. She had left some beautiful dachshunds in Biarritz, or was it Sierra Leone, and to believe her, she was greatly worried about them. In times like these, she was saying, people forget about animals. People can be so cruel, especially in time of war. Why, in Peking the servants had run away and left her with forty trunks to pack—it was outrageous. It was so good to be back in California. God's own country, she called it. She hoped the war wouldn't spread to America. Dear me, where was one to go now? You couldn't feel safe anywhere, except in the desert perhaps.

The ex-football player was talking to some one at the far end of
the table in a loud voice. It happened to be an Englishwoman and he
was insulting her roundly and openly for daring to arouse sympathy
for the English in this country. "Why don't you go back to England?"
he shouted at the top of his voice. "What are you doing here? You're a
menace. We're not fighting to hold the British Empire together. You're
a menace. You ought to be expelled from the country."

The woman was trying to say that she was not English but Cana-
dian, but she couldn't make herself heard above the din. The octo-
genarian, who was now sampling the champagne, was talking about
the automobile accident. Nobody was paying any attention to him.
Automobile accidents were too common—every one at the table had
been in a smash-up at one time or another. One doesn't make a point
about such things unless one is feeble-minded.

The hostess was clapping her hands frantically—she wanted to
tell us a little story about an experience she had had in Africa once,
on one of her safaris.

"Oh, can that!" shouted the football player. "I want to find out why
this great country of ours, in the most crucial moment . . ."

"Shut up!" screamed the hostess. "You're drunk."

"That makes no difference," came his booming voice. "I want
to know if we're all hundred percent Americans—and if not why
not. I suspect that we have some traitors in our midst," and because
I hadn't been taking part in any of the conversation he gave me a
fixed, drunken look which was intended to make me declare myself.
All I could do was smile. That seemed to infuriate him. His eyes
roved about the table challengingly and finally, sensing an antagonist
worthy of his mettle, rested on the aged, Florida-baked strike-breaker.
The latter was at that moment quietly talking to the person beside
him about his good friend, Cardinal So-and-so. He, the Cardinal, was
always very good to the poor, I heard him say. A very gentle hard-
working man, but he would tolerate no nonsense from the dirty labor
agitators who were stirring up revolution, fomenting class hatred,
preaching anarchy. The more he talked about his holy eminence,

the Cardinal, the more he foamed at the mouth. But his rage in no way affected his appetite. He was carnivorous, bibulous, querulous, cantankerous and poisonous as a snake. One could almost see the bile spreading through his varicose veins. He was a man who had spent millions of dollars of the public's money to help the needy, as he put it. What he meant was to prevent the poor from organizing and fighting for their rights. Had he not been dressed like a banker he would have passed for a hod carrier. When he grew angry he not only became flushed but his whole body quivered like guava. He became so intoxicated by his own venom that finally he overstepped the bounds and began denouncing President Roosevelt as a crook and a traitor, among other things. One of the guests, a woman, protested. That brought the football hero to his feet. He said that no man could insult the President of the United States in his presence. The whole table was soon in an uproar. The flunkey at my elbow had just filled the huge liquor glass with some marvelous cognac. I took a sip and sat back with a grin, wondering how it would all end. The louder the altercation the more peaceful I became. *"How do you like your new boarding house, Mr. Smith?"* I heard President McKinley saying to his secretary. Every night Mr. Smith, the president's private secretary, used to visit Mr. McKinley at his home and read aloud to him the amusing letters which he had selected from the daily correspondence. The president, who was overburdened with affairs of state, used to listen silently from his big armchair by the fire: it was his sole recreation. At the end he would always ask *"How do you like your new boarding house, Mr. Smith?"* So worn out by his duties he was that he couldn't think of anything else to say at the close of these séances. Even after Mr. Smith had left his boarding house and taken a room at a hotel President McKinley continued to say *"How do you like your new boarding house, Mr. Smith?"* Then came the Exposition and Csolgosz, who had no idea what a simpleton the president was, assassinated him. There was something wretched and incongruous about murdering a man like McKinley. I remember the incident only because that same day the horse that my aunt was using for a buggy

ride got the blind staggers and ran into a lamp post and when I was
going to the hospital to see my aunt the extras were out already and
young as I was I understood that a great tragedy had befallen the
nation. At the same time I felt sorry for Csolgosz—that's the strange
thing about the incident. I don't know why I felt sorry for him, except
that in some vague way I realized that the punishment meted out to
him would be greater than the crime merited. Even at that tender
age I felt that punishment was criminal. I couldn't understand why
people should be punished—I don't yet. I couldn't even understand
why God had the right to punish us for our sins. And of course, as I
later realized, God doesn't punish us—we punish ourselves.

Thoughts like these were floating through my head when suddenly
I became aware that people were leaving the table. The meal wasn't
over yet, but the guests were departing. Something had happened
while I was reminiscing. Pre-civil war days, I thought to myself.
Infantilism rampant again. And if Roosevelt is assassinated they
will make another Lincoln of him. Only this time the slaves will still
be slaves. Meanwhile I overhear some one saying what a wonderful
president Melvyn Douglas would make. I prick up my ears. I wonder
do they mean Melvyn Douglas, the movie star? Yes, that's who they
mean. He has a great mind, the woman is saying. And character. And
savoir faire. Thinks I to myself "and who will the vice-president be,
may I ask? Shure and it's not Jimmy Cagney you're thinkin' of?" But
the woman is not worried about the vice-presidency. She had been
to a palmist the other day and learned some interesting things about
herself. Her life line was broken. "Think of it," she said, "all these years
and I never knew it was broken. What do you suppose is going to
happen? Does it mean war? Or do you think it means an accident?"

The hostess was running about like a wet hen. Trying to rustle up
enough hands for a game of bridge. A desperate soul, surrounded by
the booty of a thousand battles. "I understand you're a writer," she
said, as she tried to carom from my corner of the room to the bar.
"Won't you have something to drink—a highball or something? Dear
me, I don't know what's come over everbody this evening. I do hate to

hear these political discussions. That young man is positively rude. Of course I don't approve of insulting the President of the United States in public but just the same he might have used a little more tact. After all, Mr. So-and-so is an elderly man. He's entitled to some respect, don't you think? Oh, there's So-and-so!" and she dashed off to greet a cinema star who had just dropped in.

The old geezer who was still tottering about handed me a highball. I tried to tell him that I didn't want any but he insisted that I take it anyway. He wanted to have a word with me, he said, winking at me as though he had something very confidential to impart.

"My name is Harrison," he said. "H-a-r-r-i-s-o-n," spelling it out as if it were a difficult name to remember.

"Now what is your name, may I ask?"

"My name is Miller—M-i-l-l-e-r," I answered, spelling it out in Morse for him.

"Miller! Why, that's a very easy name to remember. We had a druggist on our block by that name. Of course. *Miller.* Yes, a very common name."

"So it is," I said.

"And what are you doing out here, Mr. Miller? You're a stranger, I take it?"

"Yes," I said, "I'm just a visitor."

"You're in business, are you?"

"No, hardly. I'm just visiting California."

"I see. Well, where do you come from—the Middle West?"

"No, from New York."

"From New York City? Or from up State?"

"From the city."

"And have you been here very long?"

"No, just a few hours."

"A few hours? My, my . . . well, that's interesting. Very interesting. And will you be staying long, Mr. Miller?"

"I don't know. It depends."

"I see. Depends on how you like it here, is that it?"

"Yes, exactly."

"Well, it's a grand part of the world, I can tell you that. No place like California, I always say. Of course I'm not a native. But I've been out here almost thirty years now. Wonderful climate. And wonderful people, too."

"I suppose so," I said, just to string him along. I was curious to see how long the idiot would keep up his infernal nonsense.

"You're not in business you say?"

"No, I'm not."

"On a vacation, is that it?"

"No, not precisely. I'm an ornithologist, you see."

"A what? Well, that's interesting."

"*Very*," I said, with great solemnity.

"Then you may be staying with us for a while, is that it?"

"That's hard to say. I may stay a week and I may stay a year. It all depends. Depends on what specimens I find."

"I see. Interesting work, no doubt."

"*Very!*"

"Have you ever been to California before, Mr. Miller?"

"Yes, twenty-five years ago."

"Well, well, is that so? *Twenty-five years ago!* And now you're back again."

"Yes, back again."

"Were you doing the same thing when you were here before?"

"You mean ornithology?"

"Yes, that's it."

"No, I was digging ditches then."

"Digging ditches? You mean you were—*digging ditches*?"

"Yes, that's it, Mr. Harrison. It was either dig ditches or starve to death."

"Well, I'm glad you don't have to dig ditches any more. It's not much fun—*digging ditches*, is it?"

"No, especially if the ground is hard. Or if your back is weak. Or vice versa. Or let's say your mother has just been put in the mad house and the alarm goes off too soon."

"I beg your pardon! *What did you say?*"

"If things are not just right, I said. You know what I mean—bunions, lumbago, scrofula. It's different now, of course. I have my birds and other pets. Mornings I used to watch the sun rise. Then I would saddle the jackasses—I had two and the other fellow had three. . . ."

"This was in California, Mr. Miller?"

"Yes, twenty-five years ago. I had just done a stretch in San Quentin. . . ."

"*San Quentin?*"

"Yes, attempted suicide. I was really gaga but that didn't make any difference to them. You see, when my father set the house afire one of the horses kicked me in the temple. I used to get fainting fits and then after a time I got homicidal spells and finally I became suicidal. Of course I didn't know that the revolver was loaded. I took a pot shot at my sister, just for fun, and luckily I missed her. I tried to explain it to the judge but he wouldn't listen to me. I never carry a revolver any more. If I have to defend myself I use a jack-knife. The best thing, of course, is to use your knee. . . ."

"Excuse me, Mr. Miller, I have to speak to Mrs. So-and-so a moment. Very interesting what you say. *Very interesting indeed.* We must talk some more. Excuse me just a moment. . . ."

I slipped out of the house unnoticed and started to walk towards the foot of the hill. The highballs, the red and the white wines, the champagne, the cognac were gurgling inside me like a sewer. I had no idea where I was, whose house I had been in or whom I had been introduced to. Perhaps the boiled thug was an ex-Governor of the State. Perhaps the hostess was an ex-movie star, a light that had gone out forever. I remembered that some one had whispered in my ear that So-and-so had made a fortune in the opium traffic in China. Lord Haw-Haw probably. The Englishwoman with the horse face may have been a prominent novelist—or just a charity worker. I thought of my friend Fred, now Private Alfred Perlès, No. 13802023 in the 137th Pioneer Corps or something like that. Fred would have sung the Lorelei at the dinner table or asked for a better brand of cognac or made grimaces at the hostess. Or he might have gone to the telephone and called up Gloria Swanson, pretending to be Aldous Huxley or Chatto & Windus of Wimbledon. Fred would never have permitted the dinner to become a fiasco. Everything else failing he would have slipped his silky paw in some one's bosom, saying as he always did— "The left one is better. Fish it out, won't you please?"

I think frequently of Fred in moving about the country. He was always so damned eager to see America. His picture of America was something like Kafka's. It would be a pity to disillusion him. And yet who can say? He might enjoy it hugely. He might not see anything but what he chose to see. I remember my visit to his own Vienna. Certainly it was not the Vienna I had dreamed of. And yet today, when I think of Vienna, I see the Vienna of my dreams and not the one with bed bugs and broken zithers and stinking drains.

I wobble down the canyon road. It's very Californian somehow. I like the scrubby hills, the weeping trees, the desert coolness. I had expected more fragrance in the air.

The stars are out in full strength. Turning a bend in the road I catch a glimpse of the city below. The illumination is more faërique than in other American cities. The red seems to predominate. A few hours ago, towards dusk, I had a glimpse of it from the bedroom window of the woman on the hill. Looking at it through the mirror on her dressing table it seemed even more magical. It was like looking into the future from the narrow window of an oubliette. Imagine the Marquis de Sade looking at the city of Paris through the bars of his cell in the Bastille. Los Angeles gives one the feeling of the future more strongly than any city I know of. A bad future, too, like something out of Fritz Lang's feeble imagination. *Good-bye, Mr. Chips!*

Walking along one of the Neon-lit streets. A shop window with Nylon stockings. Nothing in the window but a glass leg filled with water and a sea horse rising and falling like a feather sailing through heavy air. Thus we see how Surrealism penetrates to every nook and corner of the world. Dali meanwhile is in Bowling Green, Va., thinking up a loaf of bread 30 feet high by 125 feet long, to be removed from the oven stealthily while every one sleeps and placed very circumspectly in the main square of a big city, say Chicago or San Francisco. Just a loaf of bread, enormous of course. No raison d'être. No propaganda. And tomorrow night two loaves of bread, placed simultaneously in two big cities, say New York and New Orleans. Nobody knows who brought them or why they are there. And the next night three loaves of bread—one in Berlin or Bucharest this time. And so on, ad infinitum. Tremendous, no? Would push the war news off the front page. That's what Dali thinks, at any rate. Very interesting. *Very interesting, indeed.* Excuse me now, I have to talk to a lady over in the corner. . . .

Tomorrow I will discover Sunset Boulevard. Eurythmic dancing, ball room dancing, tap dancing, artistic photography, ordinary photography, lousy photography, electro-fever treatment, internal douche treatment, ultra-violet ray treatment, elocution lessons, psychic readings, institutes of religion, astrological demonstrations, hands read, feet manicured, elbows massaged, faces lifted, warts removed, fat reduced, insteps raised, corsets fitted, busts vibrated, corns removed, hair dyed, glasses fitted, soda jerked, hangovers cured, headaches driven away, flatulence dissipated, business improved, limousines rented, the future made clear, the war made comprehensible, octane made higher and butane lower, drive in and get indigestion, flush the kidneys, get a cheap car wash, stay awake pills and go to sleep pills, Chinese herbs are very good for you and without a Coca-cola life is unthinkable. From the car window it's like a strip teaser doing the St. Vitus dance—a corny one.

The Air-Conditioned Nightmare, 1945

Babs Gonzales
(1919–1980)

The self-styled "creator of the bebop language" was a grandmaster of jive talk and an inventor of vocalese or bop scat singing. Born Lee Brown, he took the name Gonzales to penetrate segregated hotels and once worked as Errol Flynn's chauffeur. Babs Gonzales hustled his way around the world as a musician, manager, and DJ. Here are two chapters from his self-published autobiography, I Paid My Dues, *celebrating the improv nature of life as well as music in the early days of bop, and explaining how he became a singer to seduce girls. His idiosyncratic punctuation is preserved from the original edition.*

from *I Paid My Dues*

JANUARY OF 1945 I was out of bread and I hadn't scored musically so I had to find me another day gig. I talked to two clothiers (F&F) and they gave me a salesman's job. This was really sweet. I started at ten and worked until five with an hour for lunch.

As part of my job, I had to stay sharp, so I got seven vines (suits) right away. In three months I had twenty bands buying their uniforms there. Whenever I wanted to hang out on Fifty-Second Street, I would tell the bosses I was courting a new account and they'd give me expense money. I'd been working four months before I noticed there were no Negro tailors, cutters, etc. I asked the bosses and they said it was because none had ever asked for jobs. I spoke to a friend and he came down one day and applied. When the ten "Jewish" employees found out this "Negro" tailor was even "LOOKING" for a job, they threatened to walk out. Finally the bosses broke down and told me. "Look, Babsie, It's not us, we're not prejudice but if we hired one we wouldn't be able to get any linings, buttons, or anything, plus the help would all leave." They also said they had a lot of pressure on them for having "ME" as a salesman.

By this time, the happenings had all moved to Fifty-Second Street. "Coleman Hawkins" and "Lady Day" were the king and queen. Dizzy and Oscar Pettiford had a band in the "Deuces", and "Clark Monroe" the only colored owner had his joint and was featuring "Bud Powell" and "Max Roach". "Miles Davis" had just come to study at "Juilliard" and was the envy of everyone because his father sent him seventy-five ($75) dollars a week which was as much as the guys working were getting. The new sound got to me so I found myself there every night. I began to get gigs on weekends going up to "Bridgeport" and "New Haven".

The street was really something in those days. The war was on and there were always loads of sailors and soldiers who wanted to and did fight every time they saw a Negro musician with a white girl. I'd seen a whore uptown beating her man with her shoe heel and him just holding his eyes screaming. When it was all over I asked her why the guy didn't fight back? She answered, "Just get a box of "red pepper" for a dime and throw it in his eyes and you'll win."

I took her advice and until today, I've never been without it.

The guys all laughed at me at first but after I saved "Oscar" and "Bird's" life with it, quite a few more colleagues copped some. There was one "Irish" bar on the corner of Sixth Avenue and Fifty-Second Street that wouldn't serve colored even though the law said so. One night four of us went in with our white girls. After refusing us, the girls ordered. The owner called them all kinds of tramps, bitches, for being with niggers, etc. There were about thirty ofays there so we left. At 4:30 that morning, we took trash cans and broke out all his windows. We did this five times in a year before he finally got the message.

Another incident involved "Ben Webster". At that time "Ben" weighed two hundred and forty pounds (240 lbs.) and was always ready to fight. "Baby Lawrence", the greatest jazz tap dancer that ever lived ran into the "Downbeat " and yelled "the sailors are beating up "Bud Powell". We all rushed around the corner to the "White Rose" bar and there was "Bud" in the street unconscious and bleeding. Ben grabbed two sailors, one in each hand by the backs of their necks. He ran them both from the curb straight through the plate glass windows and the rest took off like track stars.

I stayed on the job at the clothing store until November. "Nat Cole" had made it and was playing the "Apollo". I went by to see him and when he dug my clothes, I had to take the whole trio down to get wardrobes. To show his appreciation, he found an open date in his schedule and told me to hire a hall and do the publicity and we'd split after expenses.

I went to Mr. Buchanon and rented his other ballroom "The Golden Gate". He laughed and said I'd lose my shirt using a Wednesday night. The place could hold seven thousand people. When I arrived at eight o'clock to open the box office, the complete block was filled. Traffic had to be re-routed. By eleven o'clock I had sold five thousand tickets, when a police captain told me to shut down. I explained the fire marshall had okayed seven thousand, but they made me close anyway. The other two thousand people had come out to go to a dance so they just walked down one block and by midnight, the "Savoy" was full (dig it)?

"Nat and Nadine" were staying with "Andy Kirk" and that morning over breakfast we split twenty-eight hundred dollars. With all this bread I'm now really "Mr. New York". I moved to "Sugar Hill" took a kitchenette on "Hamilton Terrace". All the professional and good doing people were in that block. I invited "Dizzy" and "Web" by and reached under my bed and shocked them with a suitcase full of money.

———

MY NAME was going around. All the high powered broads were "shooting" on me. I'd let them think they were going to con me out of my bread until I had made it with them. I'd ran through about "ten" before the word got out that "Babs ain't gonna spend nothing, but the evening". "Lucky Thompson" left "Lionel Hampton" and moved in with me and two weeks later "Trummy Young" who was ducking the cops for non-support moved in. The old "West Indian" landlady tried to give me trouble for having two extra people, but with my money I just gave her an extra "ten". Trummy got out to "Hawaii" in a couple of weeks and "Lucky" got a gig in "New Haven" and took me on it.

We had a ball in "New Haven". There were a lot of "Portugese" chicks and beautiful little untouched "colored" orchids. I had been watching "Billy Eckstine", and I began to realize that to make long bread one needed to be a singer and look pretty for the girls. I started my singing career up there with "Lucky" and when we came back after three months, I was cool with about twenty tunes.

In May of "46" I started rehearsing my first group. It was "Babs Three Bips and A Bop". I had "Tad Dameron", who'd already made a name as a great arranger for "Basie" on piano and vocal. "Pee Wee Tinney" guitarist and vocal and "Art Phipps" bass and vocal. I had me a set of drums made so I could stand up and play them out front. We rehearsed at "Helen Humes" pad in the basement of the "Douglas Hotel" everyday for a month. I copped a gig at "Minton's" and one night "Alfred Lions" came in to dig us. He said we gassed him, but we were too far out for the people. We closed at "Minton's" and went back to rehearsing. Tad had to cut out and travel with "Basie" so I replaced him with "Bobby Tucker", who was idle because "Lady Day" had gotten busted.

"Nat" came in town and this time he gave me two open dates. I told my guys not to worry that I would send them fifteen dollars a week while I made this money with "Nat". I booked two places. "The Convention Hall" in "Atlantic City" and the "Newark Armory". Nat gave me three thousand for expense bread so for six weeks I was shuttling between "Newark" and "Atlantic City". I was a big man. Chicks in both towns were mine for the asking if I promised to introduce them to "Nat".

"Convention Hall" could hold fifteen thousand people and at six o'clock the night of the dance, I got a call from "Nat" that they were "stormed in" in "Milwaukee" and no planes were leaving. I kept my hopes up until eight o'clock then decided to go to the hall and watch all the money we could have had. It was a beautiful August night and since it was going to be his first appearance, I watched eight thousand people come and then turn around.

The hall and expenses were a two thousand dollar ($2,000) loss and the next night in "Newark" we only made three thousand ($3,000) profit so it was six weeks of running practically for nothing. "Nat" took two thousand to get even and gave me all the other grand so I could get me some uniforms for the guys and chalked it up to "Cest La Vie"...

Nothing exciting happened for the next seven months—just rehearsing and hoping. I had one thing in my favor. All the guys in the group, except me, were living at home with their folks and didn't need nothing more than cigarette money and carfare. Early in 1947, I persuaded "Al Lions" to give me a record date. I added "Rudy Williams" on alto for soloing and we cut our first date.

The tunes were "OOP-POP-A-DA". "PAY DEM DUES" "LOP POW" and "WEIRD LULLABY". "OOP-POP" was an instant hit around New York and the metropolitan area. "Freddie Robbins" a disc-jockey, of note at the time, played it every night for a couple of months.

At that time "Bluenote" was a very small record company and had been doing a mail order business in dixieland jazz. The result was our record wasn't heard outside the radius of "Freddie's" station unless they ordered it. Our jobs picked up around New York and we were booked into the "Onyx" club with "Billie Eckstine". "Metronome" picked us the number one vocal group in the country.

We worked all the clubs along the street during the next few months and it was during a rehearsal at the "Onyx" one afternoon when "Dizzy" came in and said his big band was auditioning for "Victor". He said he'd played a lot of tunes but hadn't moved the big brass. I told him to do "OOP-POP". Dizzy went back and did it for the big brass and they signed him immediately.

We left town to play an engagement at a lounge on the north side of "Chicago". When we arrived at the club, the manager counted us and said we had one too many.

I showed my contract which read "Babs and His Three Bips and Bop" which came to five people. He told us to go straight to the dressing room in the rear. The dressing room turned out to be a storage room for empty bottles and we had no mirrors, chairs, or anything to hang our clothes on. While we were changing, we could hear the solo colored pianist playing "The Nigger" and the white man played five up, "The Nigger" won the money and was scared to pick it up. We all looked at each other knowing this was going to be a drag. As we were going to the bandstand, the customers were yelling "Alright niggers get hot."

During our first set behind their long bar, we could see gangsters and police officers trading money and were called twenty-five "black bastards". All the big name jazz groups were playing this room and I wondered had they received this sort of treatment or had they been just waiting for us. Back in the "storage" room I asked all the guys did they want to quit and since nobody had any dependents, everybody agreed to split. I went up to the boss's office and asked for my transportation.

My contract read I was to receive it upon arrival. He told me "Nigger, can't you see I'm playing cards? I'll give it to you tomorrow." I went back and told the fellows what was happening, and that we were in trouble. I had a thirty-two pistol and my bass man had a thirty-eight. We knew we couldn't carry the instruments and protect ourselves too, so we decided to leave them. We'd only gotten about ten feet when the boss and two of his cronies confronted us. I told him we were leaving. He said "look you black bastards, all the big names play here and they don't mind being called a few Niggers". I told him they were getting two and three grand a week, but for seven fifty we wasn't going to take it. We both reached for our heat at the same time and I told him even if he got me, I'd get him. You'd be surprised to know that even a big gangster is humble looking down a thirty-two. I led my men out while the bass player covered us from the rear and made it back to the south side.

We were stranded in Chicago, so the next morning I went to see the president of the "Colored" local. He was the first of several "Uncle Tom" officials I was to encounter later in life. The white boss had already called him and gave him his orders. He berated me about being late and flirting with white women, etc. I knew I wasn't going to get any cooperation from him so I called the New York office of my local.

When I recorded "PAY DEM DUES" the union officials thought I meant "union dues" so I was held in regard at that time. I spoke to the president and told him of our plight. They wired us three hundred to pay hotel bills and get back. We were almost finished packing when the "spade" delegate showed up at our hotel. He said "why would you call the national office, I told you I would look into the matter." I told him "Look my man," my Men are out here stranded and we can't wait while letters take two or three months to be argued before the boards. We'll do our talking from New York." (Bye!)

As we were waiting for a cab, "Dinah Washington" rolled up with her entourage. After conversing with her, she explained she wouldn't be needing her station wagon for a while and if I drove it back to New York, we could save our train fare. I accepted her offer and we cut out in style with wheels.

I Paid My Dues: Good Times, No Bread, A Story of Jazz, 1967

Art Pepper
(1925–1982)

Many jazz musicians wrote autobiographies, but there is none quite like Art Pepper's brutally truthful Straight Life. *I can't think of anyone, musician or not, who has written a better description of the experience of heroin use, its veiled allure and rigorous dues. Here Pepper describes his eureka moment with the catalyst of his highest highs and lowest lows. Pepper's music was beautiful, bright and lyrical, breezy, almost the opposite of his life. It's fascinating to complete the picture with the hard downside of his history.*

Heroin

1946–1950

W HEN I came home Patti was staying with my dad and my step-mother, Thelma. And when I came to the door my daughter, Patricia, was there; she was walking and talking. She didn't respond to me: she was afraid of me. I resented her and I was jealous of her feelings for my dad. Naturally, she'd been with them so she didn't feel about me the way I wanted her to, and that started the whole thing off on the wrong foot.

I was bitter about the army and bitter about them making me have a kid I didn't want, bitter about being taken away when everything was going so good. I was drinking heavily and started using more pot and more pills, and I scuffled around and did a casual here and there or a couple of nights in some club, but nothing happened and I was getting more and more despondent when finally, by some miracle, Stan Kenton gave me a call.

STAN KENTON was incredible. He reminded me a lot of my dad, Germanic, with the blonde, straight hair. He was taller than my dad;

I think Stan was about six, three, slender, clothes hung on him beautifully. He had long fingers, a long, hawklike nose, and a very penetrating gaze. He seemed to look through you. It was hard to look him in the eye, and most people would look away and become uncomfortable in his presence. And, just like my dad, he had a presence. When he spoke people listened. He was a beautiful speaker and he had the capacity to communicate with any audience and to adapt to any group of people. We would play in some little town in Kansas and he'd talk to the people and capture them completely. We'd be in Carnegie Hall and he'd capture that crowd with another approach. We'd be at the Kavakos in Washington, D.C., a jazz club filled with the black pimp type cats and the hustling broads and the dope fiends—and he'd capture them. He would observe, study the people, and win them.

One time we did "City of Glass" at the Civic Opera House in Chicago. It was written by Bob Graettinger, a revolutionary composition, an incredibly hard musical exercise; it was a miracle we got through it. Bob conducted it, a tall, thin guy, about six, four: he looked like a living skeleton conducting, like a dead man with sunken eyes, a musical zombie. He took us through it, and he finished, and he turned around to the people, and he nodded, and the people didn't do *nothin'*. The place was packed; we'd played the shit out of this thing and now there wasn't a sound. They didn't know what to do. We didn't know what to do. I'm looking at Stan and I'm thinking, "Well, what's going to happen now? What's he going to do *now*?" Stan looked at the audience. I saw his mind, you could see it turning, and all of a sudden he *leaped* out onto the middle of the stage, gestured at us to rise, swung his body around again to the audience, and bam! They started clapping, and they clapped and clapped and clapped, and then they stood up with an ovation that lasted for maybe five minutes. He did it all himself. Stan did it with his little maneuver.

Once when I was interviewed for *down beat* they asked me about Stan, and I told the interviewer, "If Stan had entered the field of religion he would have been greater than Billy Graham." And Stan didn't like it. But he didn't understand it. Maybe he thought I was putting him down; maybe he thought I was belittling religion and ranking him for being a phony, but that wasn't my intention. I was talking about his strength. He was the strongest man I ever met.

I traveled with the band: Shelly Manne was playing drums; Conte Candoli was playing trumpet; Bud Shank was in the sax section; June Christy was singing; Laurindo Almeida was playing guitar; and I was featured with the band. We played a lot of different places, and I was getting a name, a following. At first Patti came along with me, so it was fun, but one day in New York, while we were working at the Paramount Theater, Patti got a telegram from my father saying that Patricia was sick. I don't remember what she had. I didn't even pay attention to it, I was so angry. To me it was as if Patricia had gotten sick purposely to rank things for me. So Patti left, and that was it. For all intents and purposes that was the end of our marriage. Patti started feeling it was her duty to stay with Patricia.

It was impossible to take Patricia with us. We tried to take her once to Salt Lake City. We drove instead of traveling on the bus. I bought a car, but all the oil ran out of the car, and we got stranded, and then Patricia got sick. It was impossible. It was too impossible. The mileage we had to cover was too demanding. They both went home, and I sold the car, and that was the last time Patti was on the road with me.

I really became bitter then because I was so lonely and I couldn't stand not having a woman. There were chicks following the band that were very groovy, that really dug me; they'd send notes and hit on me and wait for me after the job, but I'd rarely have anything to do with them because I felt so guilty when I did.

IN 1948 we were playing the Paramount Theater again in New York. Vic Damone was the single attraction. Sometimes we'd play seven shows a day, and there were a bunch of young girls who used to come around to all the performances. One day after a show, four of these girls came backstage and left a note. They wanted to meet me. I went to the stage door and said hello to them. I brought them into the dressing room and talked to them; they were sixteen, seventeen.

They said they wanted to form an Art Pepper Fan Club. Would I mind? I thought they were joking at first, but they were serious, so I told them no, I wouldn't mind, that I'd be flattered. But I couldn't understand what a fan club would entail.

We had just started at the Paramount. I think we played for thirteen weeks, and it was jam-packed. I was living at a hotel on Forty-seventh and Broadway, and these girls kept coming around so I'd take them out. We'd go to the drugstore. I'd buy them sandwiches, and they took pictures of me. They were fairly nice looking, and they must have been from the Bronx because they all had that accent. Finally they told me that they really cared for me, that they had a crush on me, and they would like to, you know—they'd work it out among themselves and come and visit me one at a time. I said okay, but I was thinking, "They're pretty young." And I didn't know for sure if *that* was what they wanted. The next day, the one they had elected president of the club was at the Paramount after the first show. This was in the morning, and we had two, two and a half hours between shows. She said, "Shall we go to your place?"

The president was about seventeen. She looked Jewish, and she had a slender body but nicely shaped. She had pretty eyes. She was the most attractive of the four, with lovely skin, dark coloring. We left for the hotel. The guys in the band were watching, giving me those looks. The president was really enthused. She had a pretty dress on, and her eyes were all lit up. Her whole manner had changed. She'd suddenly become sexy and sure of herself and very womanly.

We got out of the theater and it was chilly so I helped her on with her coat. And that was the part I felt bad about. Because when I'm with a woman and I'm very polite and mannerly it becomes like a love situation. I felt guilty when I put her coat on. And then she clutched my arm and it was as if we were lovers. I was hoping we could have got where we were going without all these formalities, walking on her right on the sidewalk, helping her across the street.

It was too cold to walk to the hotel. Ordinarily, it was a nice walk, and I had hoped it would relax us, although she seemed completely relaxed. I was the one who was nervous. I hailed a cab and opened the door for her, and there was another little pang. We walked into the hotel and I really felt strange. I started feeling that the house detective was watching or the guy at the desk. Walking from the elevator to the room I thought, "What am I letting myself in for? Maybe this is some sort of weird plan to blackmail me or take pictures. Maybe somebody is going to break in and beat me up." I remembered all these stories I'd heard about people being in the big city and getting taken; there were a lot of young people mixed up in terrible crimes. We got to the room. I closed the door. Locked it. My heart was pounding and I was almost to the point of telling her, "Let's forget it." But I had gone too far to stop, and I had been away from Patti for a long time, and I was going to be away from her for five months more, and the girl seemed so clean and nice.

I had a bottle in my room, a bottle of vodka. I poured some in a glass and some orange juice. I asked her if she wanted a drink. She said, "Just a little one." I drank mine down and then took a great big, straight shot of the vodka. She's just standing there waiting for me. She's still got her coat on. I took her coat and hung it in the closet. She's still standing there, looking at me with this adoring look, and at last the feeling that was coming from her, this admiration, started getting to my ego, and I began to relax, but I didn't know exactly what to do yet. I didn't want to do anything that would spoil it—make a mistake or seem foolish. I sat down on the bed and started making small talk, "It's a shame this isn't a nicer place but being on the road we just have to take a little place like this because all we do is sleep in it." She just kept gazing at me. I rattled on and on, nonsense, talking and talking. All of a sudden she sat down next to me, put her hand on my arm, and she said, "You're the most beautiful man I've ever seen."

She had her hand on my arm and her head on my shoulder. I put my arm around her and she shuddered. I could feel her whole body vibrating. She had short sleeves on her little dress; it was a jersey dress, and you could feel her body through it. I rubbed her arm with my hand and she shuddered and pushed herself up against me.

She put her hand on my leg, and I immediately got an erection. She smelled good. A lot of times I've been out with a woman that looked good, but when I got close her hair didn't smell nice or her breath, and it would turn me off because it would seem like she wasn't clean. This girl smelled good; her hair had just been washed; and she was so soft. There was no mistaking at that point what was going to happen. I bent down and turned her chin up so I could kiss her, and she started to squirm and tremble. I probed gently in her mouth with my tongue, and I could tell she was really inexperienced, but little by little she relaxed her mouth till I could feel the tip of her tongue touching mine. We kissed for a long time. I started kissing her eyes and everything, and she just flipped out and lay back on the bed. I put my hand on her leg and started rubbing really easy. She had stockings on, but she had them rolled, which has always turned me on. I pulled her dress up. Her skin was beautiful. I bent down and kissed her leg just above her stocking, and I ran my tongue around her leg. She started moving and grabbed my hair. I looked at the crotch of her panties. They were soaking wet. She had a great smell. I started kissing the outside of her panties. I don't know if she'd ever had anybody do that before because she really wigged out: she started murmuring things, "I love you." I stuck my tongue inside her panties where her lips were, and it was so moist. I rubbed my tongue up all around her, and then I pulled back her panties so I could get at her. I licked her really slowly, and she started quivering, and she grabbed hold of me, and she came immediately; almost as soon as I put my mouth on her she came. Then she said, "Wait a second!" She said, "My mother will see my dress." She got her dress off and her bra, and she was really beautiful. She had small breasts, but the nipples were hard. And she was very cute. I started to take my clothes off and got everything off but my shorts, and they were just standing out, and she said, "Come here." She sat on the edge of the bed and pulled me over to her and started caressing me through my shorts, and then she pulled them down real slow until my joint popped out, and she put her head against it and hugged me and put her arms around me and rubbed her face and her hair against me, and she started licking me. I could tell she didn't know how to suck on me; she just kissed it and licked it. I didn't want her to give me head because I was afraid I would come immediately, and she was so passionate I wanted to put it in her.

I put her on the bed and got over her and gradually put it in, and it felt wonderful. She was tight and moist. I finally got all the way in, which was hard to do at first because she was small, but she was completely turned on. I kissed her breasts, and she kept hollering, "I love you! You're the most beautiful man in the world! This is the greatest thing that ever happened to me! I'll never forget this moment as long as I live!" And I thought, "Wow! This is my fan club, and there's *four* of them!"

Usually when I'd ball the chicks that hung around the band, the minute it was over I'd have to leave. I'd have to get away from the girl because after my need for sex was satisfied I couldn't stand her. Her smell on my body was like a curse on me, and I'd have to wash myself and scrub because I felt so dirty. But this girl was so sweet that I felt some love and warmth for her, so later I *really* felt guilty, a million times more guilty. Because I felt like cuddling this girl, because I cared for this girl, I'd really betrayed Patti.

SEX WAS in my thoughts all the time, and because of my upbringing I felt it was evil. That made it even more attractive to me, and the alcohol and the pills I took made my sex drive even stronger. I was obsessed.

I used to room with different guys in the band, but if I had the money I'd room alone so I could fool around with the maids. The maid didn't exist for me as a person, so there was nothing Patti could be jealous of. Sometimes they would suck on me or something like that, but what I really wanted wasn't the consummation. I was away from Patti and, so that I wouldn't go out and goof, I wanted to have these experiences which would provide me with vivid mental pictures I could conjure up at will whenever I set about relieving myself by playing with myself.

If I was rooming alone I would wait for the maid to come; I'd peek out the door to see if she was there. I'd leave the door locked, but not from the inside, then she'd think I wasn't in the room. I would lie on the bed and expose myself. I'd fix the covers so the maid could see my joint. I'd pretend I was asleep and put my fingers over my eyes so I could peek out at her, and she'd come in and turn on the light and look and see me, and I used to wig out with their reactions. Some of them would go, "Oooohh!" and practically run out. Some would act nonchalant and just walk out. Others would stand and stare. Some would get nervous and uptight, but they'd be aroused. And then, after they'd leave, I'd throw a robe on and run out and say, "Do you want to get the room now?"

Down south the maids were great. They went along with whatever you wanted because they were afraid for their jobs and they were kind of naive. I'd say, "Well, come on. If you want to get the room, get it now." Or I'd make up an excuse, saying that I had to do this or that, or somebody was coming—anything to get them in there. Then I'd sit down on a chair and fix it so my robe was open just enough so they could see me, and I would offer them a drink and talk to them. I'd peek at them while they cleaned the bathtub. Usually in New York the chicks were too hep. I didn't even bother with them. If you came on they'd say, "Yeah, sure, if you want something give me five dollars," and I'd never do *that*.

But one morning at the Forrest Hotel a maid knocked on the door, and she said, "It's late, and I'd like to get the room. It's the last on the floor. I'll be able to go home after . . ." She was beautiful. She was some Latin type with light olive skin. She was about thirty years old and voluptuous. That word really describes this maid. She had on a black uniform with buttons down the front. It was made out of some light, silky stuff, and I noticed that the button at the bottom was open, and the button at the top was open. I said, "Go ahead."

She had green eyes. I'll never forget that, black hair and green eyes. I sat in a chair opposite the bathroom door. The door had a full-length mirror on it, and it was opened in such a way that I could see her in the mirror, but I was half in a daze. I really wasn't paying much attention because I had a heavy hangover. When I woke up I always had a hangover, and if I could get to a bar, I'd have a Bloody Mary. If not, I'd have a few shots in my room. So I was having a drink when I looked up and looked into this mirror, and I couldn't believe my eyes. She was cleaning the toilet bowl. She was standing, bent over but with her knees straight, which caused her dress to come up almost over her rear end, and she had black lace panties on. They usually wear white pants, something durable. She had these sexy panties on, and I could see the beginning of this little mound and some wispy black hairs sticking out the sides of these little panties. She had gorgeous legs. It was a beautiful sight, and I thought, "This is too good to be true!" When she came in, she'd closed the door behind her. Some of them leave the door open a little bit. When they leave it open you've got to sneak over and try to push it closed and catch their reaction if there is one. You hope there's no reaction.

I went and stood in the bathroom door, just looking at her. She's cleaning away. After she finishes the toilet she bends over to get the floor. She's wearing one of those half-brassieres, and with that button loose, I can see her breasts. I can see everything but the nipple. I can see down her dress to her navel. Needless to say I've got an erection. I move a little closer to her and she bends over the bathtub, and her uniform is all the way up over her ass. It was too much for me. I had my drink in my left hand; I put my right hand inside my robe and started playing with myself. If you can picture this . . . I'm standing in the bathroom right behind this beautiful creature who's bent over so her ass is practically in my face, with those lace panties, with hair sticking out of the panties, and I'm jerking myself off, and I came that way, and as soon as I came I looked down, and she was looking at me through her legs. Her hand was on her cunt, and she was rubbing her cunt.

I went to the closet, got an old shirt and wiped myself off. I went back and sat in my chair. I poured another drink. She kept rubbing her cunt, and I guess she came because she stopped, pulled her dress down, and finished cleaning the bathroom. She came out. She made the bed. Never a word passed between us. Then, as she started to leave, she turned and said, "Is there anything else?" I said, "No, that was great." She gave me a smile, walked out and closed the door. I checked out the next day.

I felt as long as I didn't know a chick and nothing was said, then there was no love involved, and I wouldn't feel as guilty. I used to go to all-night movie houses and sit next to some chick and rub my leg against her leg, and I've had chicks jerk me off, and I've played with them, and then I'd just get up and walk out. A lot of times the girl would say, "Let's go to my place" or something like that. I'd say, "Just a minute. I have to go to the bathroom." And I'd sneak away and go to another theater to try to find another chick to sit next to. Because I didn't want to ball them.

I spent hours and hours fooling with the maids and fantasizing and playing with myself and going to all-night movies. I was going insane. I had a little drill I carried with me. I'd bore holes in the doors in the hotels and then peep into the next room at night and watch the people make love.

I WAS playing with Kenton's band in L.A. on West Broadway at a nightclub. We did an afternoon job and then we had a few hours off before our night job at the same club. Everybody was eating or fucking around, so I went for a walk. I was in my band uniform. I walked down the residential streets near the club and it was just dusk, right before the street lights go on. When I walked I always watched the windows. When lights went on I'd go over to see if anything was happening.

So I was walking and I saw a light go on in a bathroom window. There was a driveway next to the window. I'd hardly ever walk into a driveway, but I noticed there was a house in the back so I'd have an excuse for being there. I walked back by this window. It was open, and I heard water running so I knew it was a bathing scene. I didn't know if it was a man or a woman, and I tried to peek in, but the window was too high to stand and see. Down at the bottom level, near the ground, there was a kind of vent. It had little slats where I could put my foot so I stood on it and reached up to the sill.

I peered in. It was a woman. She was in a brassiere and panties, and she was evidently going to take a bath. The tub was right under the window; the toilet was to the left; the washbasin was to the right; and there was a little scale. She got off the scale and then she stood looking in the mirror over the washbasin. This chick was very pretty. She had blonde hair and white skin, and when she took off her bra and panties I saw she had blonde hair on her cunt and her nipples were hard. I thought, "What am I *doing*, man? What if somebody sees me or the slats break and I fall?" But I was all fired up. I held on to the sill and peeked in.

She's standing in front of the mirror. She takes her breasts and hefts them in her hands, and then she rubs them around in a circular motion, looking at herself in the mirror, and she starts to get a glazed expression, and she rubs and tweaks at her nipples with her fingers. She does this for a little while and then she runs to turn off the bathwater. She stands and looks at herself. She starts rubbing her cunt, rubbing down her legs and rubbing her cunt. She sits on the toilet and spreads her legs and takes the first two fingers of her left hand and rubs up and down on her cunt, and she closes her eyes and she's got her head back and with her other hand she's tweaking her nipple, and she starts quivering and shaking and then she holds her hand real hard on her cunt, and I guess she had come, and then she got up and looked at herself again and she kissed those two fingers, which really turned me on. I just couldn't help myself. I had unzipped my fly and reached in and grabbed my joint and started rubbing across the bottom of my joint, and I came right about the same time she did. And then I really panicked. She got up and got into the tub, and I jumped down to the ground. I was scared to death. I thought, "What if somebody's seen me? What if somebody looked out a window and called the police?" I got back to the club and sneaked into the bathroom. I had come all over my shorts and the top of my pants. I wiped myself off, and when I buttoned my coat it covered the area. I felt awful and I thought, "What's happening to me? What would Stan think and the guys in the band?" I thought, "I've got to stop this!" Heroin stopped it for me.

In 1950 I was in Chicago at the Croyden Hotel. That was the hotel all the musicians stayed at. I was rooming with Sammy Curtis. He was a tall guy with a roundish face, rosy cheeks, blonde, curly hair, and he had this lopsided grin; he played the little boy bit. He thought it was charming. He was very talented.

I think we played the Civic Opera House that night. I was featured. I got all the praise and applause, and it was great while it was happening, but after everybody left, there I was alone. I wandered around the town. I went to all the bars. I ended up back at the hotel and went into the bar there. I just had to continue getting loaded; it was a compulsion; I had demons chasing me. The only way I ever got loaded enough, so I could be cool, was when I passed out, fell out someplace, which is what I used to do almost every night. They kicked me out of the bar at about four o'clock in the morning, and I didn't know what to do. There was no place I could get a drink. It was getting daylight, and I couldn't peep in any windows. There was no one on the streets.

I went back up to the room. Sammy was there and Roy King, a tenor player, and Sheila Harris, who's a singer, and some piano player. They were all using heroin. Sammy had been using stuff for a long time, and I knew it, but I never would try it because I knew that the minute I did it would be all over for me. I asked them if they had anything other than stuff, and they didn't. I was so unhappy, and Patti was two thousand miles away, and there was nothing I could do. I had to have something.

Sheila came over to me. She was a good singer who worked with another band. She was about five foot, two, and a little on the chubby side—what they call pleasingly plump. She had nice breasts, large, but nice, and although I've never liked chubby women she was one of the few that turned me on. She had long eyelashes and large eyes, bluish-green. Her face was oval and full, and she had full lips, and her eyebrows were full. Most women in those days plucked their eyebrows, but she had let hers grow, and I liked that. She had long fingers and nice nails. And she was a nymphomaniac. When she looked at a man she was thinking of sucking his cock; that was her thought and she turned you on because you could feel that; everyone could. And you were turned on by the stories. She was a legend among musicians. Whether they had ever made it with her or not they'd all tell stories about balling her. She was purely sensual, but only in a sexual way, no other. No warmth, no love, no beauty. When you looked at her you just saw your cock in her mouth.

She came over to me and offered me some stuff, just to horn it, sniff it. She said, "Why don't you hang up that jive and get in a different groove? Why don't you come in the bathroom with me? I'll show you a new way to go." I was at my wit's end. The only thing I could have done other than what I did was to jump out of the window of the hotel. I think we were on the fourteenth floor. I started to go into the bathroom with her, and Sammy saw what was happening and flipped out. He caused a big scene. He said, "I won't be responsible for you starting to use stuff!" But Roy said, "Man, anything would be better than that jive booze scene he's into now. What could be worse? That's really a bringdown." We cooled Sammy out, and me and Sheila walked into the bathroom and locked the door.

When we got in there she started playing with my joint. She said, "Do you want me to say hello to him?" She was marvelous, and she really turned me on, but I said, "Wait a minute. Let's get into this other thing and then we'll get back to that." I was all excited about something new, the heroin. I had made up my mind.

She had a little glass vial filled with white powder, and she poured some out onto the porcelain top of the toilet, chopped it up with a razor blade, and separated it into little piles, little lines. She asked me if I had a dollar bill. She told me to get the newest one I had. I had one, very clean and very stiff. I took it out of my pocket and she said,

"Roll it up." I started to roll it but she said, "No, not that way." She made a tube with a small opening at the bottom and a larger opening at the top. Then she went over to the heroin and she said, "Now watch what I do and do this." She put one finger on her left nostril and she stuck the larger end of the dollar bill into her right nostril. She put the tube at the beginning of one pile, made a little noise, and the pile disappeared. She said, "Now you do that." I closed my nostril. I even remember it was my left nostril. I sniffed it, and a long, thin pile of heroin disappeared. She told me to do the same with the other nostril. I did six little lines and then she said "Okay, wait a few minutes." While I'm waiting she's rubbing my joint and playing with me. I felt a tingly, burning sensation up in my sinuses, and I tasted a bitter taste in my throat, and all of a sudden, all of a sudden, all that feeling—wanting something but having no idea what it was, thinking it was sex and then when I had a chance to ball a chick not wanting to ball her because I was afraid of some disease and because of the guilt; that wandering and wandering like some derelict; that agony of drinking and drinking and nothing ever being resolved; and . . . no peace at all except when I was playing, and then the minute that I stopped playing there was nothing; that continual, insane search just to pass out somewhere and then to wake up in the morning and think, "Oh, my God," to wake up and think, "Oh God, here we go again," to drink a bottle of warm beer so I could vomit, so I could start all over again, so I could start that ridiculous, sickening, horrible, horrible life again—all of a sudden, all of a sudden, the demons and the devils and the wandering and wondering and all the frustrations just vanished and they didn't exist at all anymore because I'd finally found peace.

I felt this peace like a kind of warmth. I could feel it start in my stomach. From the whole inside of my body I felt the tranquility. It was so relaxing. It was so gorgeous. Sheila said, "Look at yourself in the mirror! Look in the mirror!" And that's what I'd always done: I'd stood and looked at myself in the mirror and I'd talk to myself and say how rotten I was—"Why do people hate you? Why are you alone?

Why are you so miserable?" I thought, "Oh, no! I don't want to do that! I don't want to spoil this feeling that's coming up in me!" I was afraid that if I looked in the mirror I would see it, my whole past life, and this wonderful feeling would end, but she kept saying, "Look at yourself! Look how beautiful you are! Look at your eyes! Look at your pupils!" I looked in the mirror and I looked like an angel. I looked at my pupils and they were pinpoints; they were tiny, little dots. It was like looking into a whole universe of joy and happiness and contentment.

I thought of my grandmother always talking about God and inner happiness and peace of mind, being content within yourself not needing anybody else, not worrying about whether anybody loves you, if your father doesn't love you, if your mother took a coathanger and stuck it up her cunt to try to destroy you because she didn't want you, because you were an unclean, filthy, dirty, rotten, slimy being that no one wanted, that no one ever wanted, that no one has still ever wanted. I looked at myself and I said, "God, no, I am not that. I'm beautiful. I am the whole, complete thing. There's nothing more, nothing more that I care about. I don't care about anybody. I don't care about Patti. I don't need to worry about anything at all." I'd found God.

I loved myself, everything about myself. I loved my talent. I had lost the sour taste of the filthy alcohol that made me vomit and the feeling of the bennies and the strips that put chills up and down my spine. I looked at myself in the mirror and I looked at Sheila and I looked at the few remaining lines of heroin and I took the dollar bill and horned the rest of them down. I said, "This is it. This is the only answer for me. If this is what it takes, then this is what I'm going to do, whatever dues I have to pay . . ." And I *knew* that I would get busted and I *knew* that I would go to prison and that I wouldn't be weak; I wouldn't be an informer like all the phonies, the no-account, the non-real, the zero people that roam around, the scum that slither out from under rocks, the people that destroyed music, that destroyed this country, that destroyed the world, the rotten, fucking, lousy people that for their own little ends—the black power people, the sickening, stinking motherfuckers that play on the fact that they're black, and all this fucking shit that happened later on—the rotten, no-account, filthy women that have no feeling for anything; they have no love for anyone; they don't know what love is; they are shallow hulls of nothingness—the whole group of rotten people that have nothing to offer, that are nothing, never will be anything, were never intended to be anything.

All I can say is, at that moment I saw that I'd found peace of mind. Synthetically produced, but after what I'd been through and all the things I'd done, to trade that misery for total happiness—that was it, you know, that was it. I realized it. I realized that from that moment on I would be, if you want to use the word, a junkie. That's the word they used. That's the word they still use. That is what I became at that moment. That's what I practiced; and that's what I still am. And that's what I will die as—a junkie.

Straight Life: The Story of Art Pepper (with Laurie Pepper), 1979

Herbert Huncke
(1915–1996)

Herbert Huncke's life was a relentless adventure: hobo wanderings in the Depression, pre-war junkie hustling, wartime Merchant Marine service, and serving as tribal elder to Burroughs, Ginsberg, and Kerouac, in whose books he appears as a character. A peerless raconteur, Huncke published his journals in 1965, followed in 1980 by the collection The Evening Sun Turned Crimson. *This selection from that volume evokes a Times Square bop age version of a salon.*

Spencer's Pad

SPENCER HAD a pad on 47th Street. It was one of the coziest pads in New York and one which it was an experience to visit for the first time and to always relax in. It existed in a period when the world was particularly chaotic and New York exceptionally so. For me it represented the one spot at the time where I could seek surcease from tension and invariably find a sense of peace.

Spencer had gone to some pains to make it attractive. He painted the walls a Persian blue and the woodwork a bone white. He kept the lighting soft and had placed big comfortable chairs around his main room. Along one wall he placed his Capehart with records stacked to one side. Long soft rose drapes hung across his windows. A chest sat between the two windows and opposite a fireplace was a studio couch (the same shade as the drapes) faced with a long coffee table.

Spencer presided over all this with great benevolence and good will, making each of his guests welcome and concerning himself with their wants.

Spencer never used drugs—although I have seen him try pot and recently he told me he had sniffed heroin. But anyone was quite free to use whatever he chose and Spencer always managed to maintain environmental conditions conducive to the fullest realization of whatever one happened to be using.

The Capehart was exceptionally fine and acted as a sort of focal point in the pad. Great sounds issued forth from its speaker and filled the whole place with awe inspiring visions. I can recall one incident clearly when the people on 47th Street stood along the curb listening and some were dancing and they were laughing and we were in the window watching while music flowed out on all sides.

At the time the streets of New York teemed with soldiers and sailors—lonely and bewildered—and many found their way to the pad—where for a little while at least life took on some meaning. Often they gave love and always found it. Some discovered God and hardly knew of their discovery. There many heard the great Bird and felt sadness as Lady Day cried out her anguished heart.

Others came also—42nd Street hustlers—poets—simple dreamers, thieves, prostitutes (both male and female), and pimps and wise guys and junkies and pot heads and just people—seeking sanctuary in a Blue Glade away from the merciless neon glare.

There were young boys who came and swaggered and talked wise and then spoke of their dreams and plans and went away refreshed and aware of themselves as having an identity.

Spencer accepted them all and gave of himself freely to each. The pad was his home and in it he could accept any confession, any seemingly strange behavior, idea, thought, belief and mannerism as part of one, without outward show of censure. Within the confines of his home one could be oneself.

Spencer lost his pad partly because the people in the building in which it was located resented his show of freedom and partly through a situation which developed out of a relationship with a young man.

Vernon was a young man who came to New York in search of a meaning to life. He wanted to write, he wanted to act, he wanted to be loved, he wanted to love, he wanted anything and everything. His background was somewhat more interesting because of having been raised by a father who was a minister of the Baptist church in his home town but who apparently was too busy preaching the gospel to give his own son other than scant attention. His mother had made an effort to make up the difference but her main interest remained with her husband.

Vernon had been in the war and had accomplished nothing except the nickname Angel among his friends because he was always talking about God and because he would listen to anyone's problems. Also he learned to smoke pot.

His appearance was rather striking and upon reaching New York he had no trouble making contacts. Just how he eventually met Spencer I don't know but meet they did and became good friends.

One night they had both been out drinking—Vernon smoking pot and both taking nembutals—and had returned to the pad to get some sleep. Both stripped naked and fell on to the bed and into a deep sleep. When they awakened they were in Bellevue.

It seems one or the other must have accidentally brushed against the gas plate opening a valve and that the neighbors, smelling gas in the hallway, upon investigating traced it to Spencer's and being unable to arouse anyone called the police who broke in and finding them both out cold had them rushed to Bellevue, where after reviving them decided they be held for observation. Spencer has since told me, it was a harrowing experience.

Meanwhile the people in the building all got together and signed a petition requesting that Spencer be evicted. As one old queen—who had the apartment next to Spencer's—told me—"My dear—it was really too much. It was a regular black and tan fantasy. Both stark naked—and who knows what they had been doing—Spencer so dark and Vernon pale white. It would have been bad enough if both were the same color. Really, if Spencer wants to end it all he shouldn't try and take one of his lovers with him."

I saw Spencer not long ago and once again he has a charming little place of his own but it isn't quite the 47th Street pad.

The Evening Sun Turned Crimson, 1980

Carl Solomon
(1928–1993)

Some hip cats were so fractured by intellect, temperament, and experience that they could never fit into straight society. Carl Solomon was a Marine at sixteen and after his service he traveled in Europe encountering the Surrealists, especially the visionary Antonin Artaud, who seemed to propose madness as a viable pursuit. Returning to the U.S., Solomon promptly committed himself in 1949 to the New York State Psychiatric Institute, where he met Allen Ginsberg (who would dedicate Howl *to him). Solomon described his institutionalization and shock treatments in* Mishaps, Perhaps *from which the following piece is taken.*

A Diabolist

PERVERSITY IN all forms appeals to those who desire a new reality. The quintessence of evil suddenly seems desirable because you are bored with "What's new?" and "How do you do?" Of all poets, the perverts seem most interesting.

Turn off the ball game. Do something odd. Run a bath and stay in for three hours, or talk to an odd-looking man you meet on the street. Then you are on the path of what certain writers call the marvelous. The end is dementia praecox. What you have been seeking is absolutely dementia, a seclusion room by yourself or a straitjacket all your own. This because you desired to turn things around to make the ugly beautiful. Such alchemy is not a pretense and is not limited to one writer. It is domain on which any daring individual may trespass. It has existed for many centuries. And the unusual says Lautréamont is to be found in the banal. The extraordinary is to be found where you sit. I cannot break the fascination with this view of life, call it the bright orange view as opposed to the gray view.

This is better than a hobby; it is almost the equivalent of a religion. I shall make up a dream I never dreamed and you may explore it for significance. I was sitting on a beach; a dog came up to me and licked my leg; a fat boy came by; he wanted to play ball. It seems that we played ball for years. Then the dream ended. What a silly dream! Sometimes the diabolist regrets his sins against nature and dreams of gods or reality. But reality persists in being boring.

Who can understand my odd nature. My passion for the absurd or the prank. I live for these things. I have traveled and travel is a flop so far as I am concerned. Wherever you go you are a tourist, that is to say some sucker to the odd denizens of the place. Give me my home, my imagination and my dreams.

It is almost as though the "real" world were an asylum and the unreal world is a super-asylum . . . for those who have gone insane in the outer madhouse and been placed in this outer void. It is a place where those who don't know they are insane are placed. Those who know they are ill are outside consulting psychiatrists. Pilgrim is the sort of place you leave by asserting that the correct date is actually the date and the correct man is actually the president. There is a definite letdown in being released . . . you feel upon leaving the Insane Asylum as though you are entering the Sane Asylum.

This all is a task too difficult to describe once you have attained this dimension. It is like hearing the inaudible . . . seeing the invisible.

Mishaps, Perhaps, 1966

Neal Cassady
(1926–1968)

A juvenile car thief and reform-school graduate, a con man, and bigamist, Neal Cassady inhabited the road that Kerouac celebrated. He served time, lived with Ginsberg, and drove Ken Kesey's magic Merry Pranksters bus through Tom Wolfe's The Electric Kool-Aid Acid Test *and into legend. Cassady was Dean Moriarty in* On the Road, *and Cody Pomeray in other Kerouac novels. His hundreds of letters to Kerouac inspired and fed the fire of what Ginsberg called "spontaneous bop prosody." Cassady died at forty-two under mysterious circumstances and his own autobiographical novel* The First Third *was published posthumously.*

Letter to Jack Kerouac, March 7, 1947 (Kansas City, Mo.)

D EAR JACK:
   I am sitting in a bar on Market St. I'm drunk, well, not quite, but I soon will be. I am here for 2 reasons; I must wait 5 hours for the bus to Denver & lastly but, most importantly, I'm here (drinking) because, of course, because of a woman & *what* a *woman*! To be chronological about it:

I was sitting on the bus when it took on more passengers at Indianapolis, Indiana—a perfectly proportioned beautiful, intellectual, passionate, personification of Venus De Milo asked me if the seat beside me was taken!!! I gulped, (I'm drunk) gargled & stammered NO! (Paradox of expression, after all, how can one stammer No!!?) She sat—I sweated—She started to speak, I knew it would be generalities, so to tempt her I remained silent.

She (her name Patricia) got on the bus at 8 PM (Dark!) I didn't speak until 10 PM—in the intervening 2 hours I not only of course, determined to make her, but, how to *DO IT.*

I naturally can't quote the conversation verbally, however, I shall attempt to give you the gist of it from 10 PM to 2 AM. Without the slightest preliminaries of objective remarks (what's your name? where are you going? etc.) I plunged into a completely knowing, completely subjective, personal & so to speak "penetrating her core" way of speech; to be shorter, (since I'm getting unable to write) by 2 AM I had her swearing eternal love, complete subjectivity to me & immediate satisfaction. I, anticipating even more pleasure, wouldn't allow her to blow me on the bus, instead we played, as they say, with each other.

Knowing her supremely perfect being was completely mine (when I'm more coherent, I'll tell you her complete history & psychological reason for loving me) I could conceive of no obstacle to my satisfaction, well, "the best laid plans of mice & men go astray" and my nemesis was her sister, the bitch.

Pat had told me her reason for going to St. Louis was to see her sister; she had wired her to meet her at the depot. So, to get rid of the sister, we peeked around the depot when we arrived at St. Louis at 4 AM to see if she (her sister) was present. If not, Pat would claim her suitcase, change clothes in the rest room & she and I proceed to a hotel room for a night (years?) of perfect bliss. The sister was not in sight, so She (note the capital) claimed her bag & retired to the toilet to change————long dash————

This next paragraph must, of necessity, be written completely objectively————

Edith (her sister) & Patricia (my love) walked out of the pisshouse hand in hand (I shan't describe my emotions). It seems Edith (bah) arrived at the bus depot early & while waiting for Patricia, feeling sleepy, retired to the head to sleep on a sofa. That's why Pat & I didn't see her.

My desperate efforts to free Pat from Edith failed, even Pat's terror & slave-like feeling toward her rebelled enough to state she must see "someone" & would meet Edith later, *all* failed. Edith was wise; she saw what was happening between Pat & I.

Well, to summarize: Pat & I stood in the depot (in plain sight of the sister) & pushing up to one another, vowed to never love again & then I took the bus for Kansas City & Pat went home, meekly, with her dominating sister. Alas, alas————

In complete (try & share my feeling) dejection, I sat, as the bus progressed toward Kansas City. At Columbia, Mo. a young (19) completely passive (my meat) *virgin* got on & shared my seat . . . In my dejection over losing Pat, the perfect, I decided to sit on the bus (behind the driver) in broad daylight & seduce her, from 10:30 AM to 2:30 PM I talked. When I was done, she (confused, her entire life upset, metaphysically amazed at me, passionate in her immaturity) called her folks in Kansas City, & went with me to a park (it was just getting dark) & I banged her; I screwed as never before; all my pent up emotion finding release in this young virgin (& she was) who is, by the by, a *school teacher*! Imagine, she's had 2 years of Mo. St. Teacher's College & now teaches Jr. High School. (I'm beyond thinking straightly).

I'm going to stop writing. Oh, yes, to free myself for a moment from my emotions, you must read "Dead Souls" parts of it (in which Gogol shows his insight) are quite like you.

I'll elaborate further later (probably?) but at the moment I'm drunk & happy (after all, I'm free of Patricia already, due to the young virgin. I have no name for her. At the happy note of Les Young's "jumping at Mesners" (which I'm hearing) I close till later.

To my Brother

Carry On!

N. L. Cassady

1947; *The First Third and Other Writings*, revised edition, 1981

Anatole Broyard
(1920–1990)

Norman Mailer defined the hipster as white Negro. Anatole Broyard was the flip side, the Negro white. He served as a white in the segregated U.S. Army in World War II and continued to pass thereafter. After studying at the New School Broyard became dean of postwar Greenwich Village intellectuals, as recounted in his posthumous memoir Kafka Was the Rage, *serving as regular book critic of* The New York Times *and informal arbiter of what was hip. Here he coolly dissects the hip prototype as perceived in 1948.*

A Portrait of the Hipster

As HE was the illegitimate son of the Lost Generation, the hipster was really *nowhere.* And, just as amputees often seem to localize their strongest sensations in the *missing* limb, so the hipster longed, from the very beginning, to be *somewhere.* He was like a beetle on its back; his life was a struggle to get *straight.* But the law of human gravity kept him overthrown, because he was always of the minority—opposed in race or feeling to those who owned the machinery of recognition.

The hipster began his inevitable quest for self-definition by sulking in a kind of inchoate delinquency. But this delinquency was merely a negative expression of his needs, and, since it led only into the waiting arms of the ubiquitous law, he was finally forced to *formalize* his resentment and express it *symbolically.* This was the birth of a philosophy—a philosophy of *somewhereness* called *jive,* from *jibe:* to agree, or harmonize. By discharging his would-be aggressions *symbolically,* the hipster harmonized or reconciled himself with his society.

At the natural stage in its growth, jive began to talk. It had been content at first with merely making sounds—physiognomic talk—but then it developed language. And, appropriately enough, this language described the world as seen through the hipster's eyes. In fact, that was its function: to re-edit the world with new definitions . . . jive definitions.

Since articulateness is a condition for, if not actually a cause of, anxiety, the hipster relieved his anxiety by disarticulating himself. He cut the world down to size—reduced it to a small stage with a few props and a curtain of jive. In a vocabulary of a dozen verbs, adjectives, and nouns he could describe everything that happened in it. It was poker with no joker, nothing wild.

There were no neutral words in this vocabulary; it was put up or shut up, a purely polemical language in which every word had a job of *evaluation* as well as designation. These evaluations were absolute; the hipster banished all comparatives, qualifiers, and other syntactical uncertainties. Everything was dichotomously *solid, gone, out of this world,* or *nowhere, sad, beat,* a *drag.*

In there was, of course, somewhereness. *Nowhere,* the hipster's favorite pejorative, was an *abracadabra* to make things disappear. *Solid* connoted the stuff, the reality, of existence; it meant concreteness in a bewilderingly abstract world. A *drag* was something which "dragged" implications along with it, something which was embedded in an inseparable, complex, ambiguous—and thus, possibly threatening—context.

Because of its polemical character, the language of jive was rich in aggressiveness, much of it couched in sexual metaphors. Since the hipster never did anything as an end in itself, and since he only gave of himself in aggression of one kind or another, sex was subsumed under aggression, and it supplied a vocabulary for the mechanics of aggression. The use of the sexual metaphor was also a form of irony, like certain primitive peoples' habit of parodying civilized modes of intercourse. The person on the tail end of a sexual metaphor was conceived of as lugubriously victimized; i.e., expecting but not receiving.

One of the basic ingredients of jive language was a priorism. The a priori assumption was a short cut to somewhereness. It arose out of a desperate, unquenchable need to know the score; it was a great projection, a primary, self-preserving postulate. It meant "it is given to us to understand." The indefinable authority it provided was like a powerful primordial or instinctual orientation in a threatening chaos of complex interrelations. The hipster's frequent use of metonymy and metonymous gestures (e.g., brushing palms for handshaking, extending an index finger, without raising the arm, as a form of greeting, etc.) also connoted prior understanding, there is no need to elaborate, I dig you, man, etc.

CARRYING HIS language and his new philosophy like concealed weapons, the hipster set out to conquer the world. He took his stand on the corner and began to direct human traffic. His significance was unmistakable. His face—"the cross-section of a motion"—was frozen in the "physiognomy of astuteness." Eyes shrewdly narrowed, mouth slackened in the extremity of perspicuous sentience, he kept tabs, like a suspicious proprietor, on his environment. He stood always a little apart from the group. His feet solidly planted, his shoulders drawn up, his elbows in, hands pressed to sides, he was a pylon around whose implacability the world obsequiously careered.

Occasionally he brandished his padded shoulders, warning humanity to clear him a space. He flourished his thirty-one inch pegs like banners. His two and seven-eighths inch brim was snapped with absolute symmetry. Its exactness was a symbol of his control, his domination of contingency. From time to time he turned to the candy store window, and with an esoteric gesture, reshaped his roll collar, which came up very high on his neck. He was, indeed, up to the neck in somewhereness.

He affected a white streak, made with powder, in his hair. This was the outer sign of a significant, prophetic mutation. And he always wore dark glasses, because normal light offended his eyes. He was an underground man, requiring especial adjustment to ordinary conditions; he was a lucifugous creature of the darkness, where sex, gambling, crime, and other bold acts of consequence occurred.

At intervals he made an inspection tour of the neighborhood to see that everything was in order. The importance of this round was implicit in the portentous trochees of his stride, which, being unnaturally accentual, or discontinuous, expressed his particularity, lifted him, so to speak, out of the ordinary rhythm of normal cosmic pulsation. He was a discrete entity—separate, critical, and defining.

JIVE MUSIC and tea were the two most important components of the hipster's life. Music was not, as has often been supposed, a stimulus to dancing. For the hipster rarely danced; he was beyond the reach of stimuli. If he did dance, it was half parody—"second removism"—and he danced only to the off-beat, in a morganatic one to two ratio with the music.

Actually, jive music was the hipster's autobiography, a score to which his life was the text. The first intimations of jive could be heard in the Blues. Jive's Blue Period was very much like Picasso's: it dealt with lives that were sad, stark, and isolated. It represented a relatively realistic or naturalistic stage of development.

Blues turned to jazz. In jazz, as in early, analytical cubism, things were sharpened and accentuated, thrown into bolder relief. Words were used somewhat less frequently than in Blues; the instruments talked instead. The solo instrument became the narrator. Sometimes (e.g., Cootie Williams) it came very close to literally talking. Usually it spoke passionately, violently, complainingly, against a background of excitedly pulsating drums and guitar, ruminating bass, and assenting orchestration. But, in spite of its passion, jazz was almost always coherent and its intent clear and unequivocal.

Bebop, the third stage in jive music, was analogous in some respects to synthetic cubism. Specific situations, or referents, had largely disappeared; only their "essences" remained. By this time the hipster was no longer willing to be regarded as a primitive; bebop, therefore, was "cerebral" music, expressing the hipster's pretensions, his desire for an imposing, fulldress body of doctrine.

Surprise, "second-removism" and extended virtuosity were the chief characteristics of the bebopper's style. He often achieved surprise by using a tried and true tactic of his favorite comic strip heroes:

> The "enemy" is waiting in a room with drawn gun. The hero kicks open the door and bursts in—*not upright, in the line of fire*—but cleverly lying on the floor, from which position he triumphantly blasts away, while the enemy still aims, ineffectually, at his own expectations.

Borrowing this stratagem, the bebop soloist often entered at an unexpected altitude, came in on an unexpected note, thereby catching the listener off guard and conquering him before he recovered from his surprise.

"Second-removism"— *capping* the *squares*—was the dogma of initiation. It established the hipster as keeper of enigmas, ironical pedagogue, a self-appointed exegete. Using his *shrewd* Socratic method, he discovered the world to the naive, who still tilted with the windmills of one-level meaning. That which you heard in bebop was always *something else, not* the thing you expected; it was always negatively derived, abstraction *from*, not *to*.

The virtuosity of the bebopper resembled that of the street-corner evangelist who revels in his unbroken delivery. The remarkable run-on quality of bebop solos suggested the infinite resources of the hipster, who could improvise indefinitely, whose invention knew no end, who was, in fact, omniscient.

All the best qualities of jazz—tension, élan, sincerity, violence, immediacy—were toned down in bebop. Bebop's style seemed to consist, to a great extent, in *evading* tension, in connecting, by extreme dexterity, each phrase with another, so that nothing remained, everything was lost in a shuffle of decapitated cadences. This corresponded to the hipster's social behavior as jester, jongleur, or prestidigitator.

But it was his own fate he had caused to disappear for the audience, and now the only trick he had left was the monotonous gag of pulling himself—by his own ears, grinning and gratuitous—up out of the hat. The élan of jazz was weeding out of bebop because all enthusiasm was naive, nowhere, too simple. Bebop was the hipster's seven types of ambiguity, his Laocoön, illustrating his struggle with his own defensive deviousness. It was the disintegrated symbol, the shards, of his attitude toward himself and the world. It presented the hipster as performer, retreated to an abstract stage of *tea* and pretension, losing himself in the multiple mirrors of his fugitive chords. This conception was borne out by the surprising mediocrity of bebop orchestrations, which often had the perfunctory quality of vaudeville music, played only to announce the coming spectacle, the soloist, the great Houdini.

Bebop rarely used words, and, when it did, they were only nonsense syllables, significantly paralleling a contemporaneous loss of vitality in jive language itself. Blues and jazz were documentary in a social sense; bebop was the hipster's Emancipation Proclamation in double talk. It showed the hipster as the victim of his own system, volubly tongue-tied, spitting out his own teeth, running between the raindrops of his spattering chords, never getting wet, washed clean, baptized, or quenching his thirst. He no longer had anything relevant to himself to say—in both his musical and linguistic expression he had finally abstracted himself from his real position in society.

His next step was to abstract himself in action. *Tea* made this possible. Tea (marihuana) and other drugs supplied the hipster with an indispensable outlet. His situation was too extreme, too tense, to be satisfied with mere fantasy or animistic domination of the environment. Tea provided him with a free world to expatiate in. It had the same function as trance in Bali, where the unbearable flatness and de-emotionalization of "waking" life is compensated for by trance ecstasy. The hipster's life, like the Balinese's, became schizoid; whenever possible, he escaped into the richer world of tea, where, for the helpless and humiliating image of a beetle on its back, he could substitute one of himself floating or flying, "high" in spirits, dreamily dissociated, in contrast to the ceaseless pressure exerted on him in real life. Getting high was a form of artificially induced dream catharsis. It differed from *lush* (whisky) in that it didn't encourage aggression. It fostered, rather, the sentimental values so deeply lacking in the hipster's life. It became a *raison d'être*, a calling, an experience shared with fellow believers, a respite, a heaven or haven.

UNDER JIVE the external world was greatly simplified for the hipster, but his own role in it grew considerably more complicated. The function of his simplification had been to reduce the world to schematic proportions which could easily be manipulated in actual, symbolical, or ritual relationships; to provide him with a manageable mythology. Now, moving in this mythology, this tense fantasy of somewhereness, the hipster supported a completely solipsistic system. His every word and gesture now had a history and a burden of implication.

Sometimes he took his own solipsism too seriously and slipped into criminal assertions of his will. Unconsciously, he still wanted terribly to take part in the cause and effect that determined the real world. Because he had not been allowed to conceive of himself functionally or socially, he had conceived of himself *dramatically*, and, taken in by his own art, he often enacted it in actual defiance, self-assertion, impulse, or crime.

That he was a direct expression of his culture was immediately apparent in its reaction to him. The less sensitive elements dismissed him as they dismissed everything. The intellectuals *manqués*, however, the desperate barometers of society, took him into their bosom. Ransacking everything for meaning, admiring insurgence, they attributed every heroism to the hipster. He became their "there but for the grip of my superego go I." He was received in the Village as an oracle; his language was *the revolution of the word, the personal idiom*. He was the great instinctual man, an ambassador from the Id. He was asked to read things, look at things, feel things, taste things, and report. What was it? Was it *in there*? Was it *gone*? Was it *fine*? He was an interpreter for the blind, the deaf, the dumb, the insensible, the impotent.

With such an audience, nothing was too much. The hipster promptly became, in his own eyes, a poet, a seer, a hero. He laid claims to apocalyptic visions and heuristic discoveries when he *picked up*; he was Lazarus, come back from the dead, come back to tell them all, he would tell them all. He conspicuously consumed himself in a high flame. He cared nothing for catabolic consequences; he was so prodigal as to be invulnerable.

And here he was ruined. The frantic praise of the impotent meant recognition—*actual somewhereness*—to the hipster. He got what he wanted; he stopped protesting, reacting. He began to bureaucratize jive as a machinery for securing the actual—really the *false*—somewhereness. Jive, which had originally been a critical system, a kind of Surrealism, a personal revision of existing disparities, now grew moribundly self-conscious, smug, encapsulated, isolated from its source, from the sickness which spawned it. It grew more rigid than the institutions it had set out to defy. It became a boring routine. The hipster—once an unregenerate individualist, an underground poet, a guerrilla—had become a pretentious poet laureate. His old subversiveness, his ferocity, was now so manifestly rhetorical as to be obviously harmless. He was bought and placed in the zoo. He was *somewhere* at last—comfortably ensconced in the 52nd Street clip joints, in Carnegie Hall, and *Life*. He was *in-there* . . . he was back in the American womb. And it was just as unhygienic as ever.

Partisan Review, June 1948

Delmore Schwartz
(1913–1966)

Heroic waste is a perennial hipster theme, and few men have rivaled Delmore Schwartz as an avatar of underachievement. A brilliant student, defrauded of his inheritance after his father's early death, he turned his youthful trials into a famous story and book, In Dreams Begin Responsibilities. *Once the wunderkind of the New York literary world—poet, fiction writer, dramatist, essayist, professor, and legendary conversationalist—Schwartz spiraled into drink, drugs, and paranoia. He died at fifty-two in the lobby of a Times Square hotel where he had lived reclusively. Today he's perhaps best known by the musical tributes written by his student Lou Reed. Here, in what seems an oblique self-portrait, Schwartz sees Hamlet as a victim of bipolar disorder.*

Hamlet, or There Is Something Wrong With Everyone

H AMLET CAME from an old upper-class family. He was the only son of a king. He was very intelligent, though somewhat of an intellectual, and he was quite handsome too, except for a tendency to get fat in the face and thicken. The Prime Minister Polonius itched with an eagerness to get Hamlet to marry his beautiful, charming and sweet-tempered daughter Ophelia. Not only that, but more important by far, Ophelia was very much in love with Hamlet, and when Hamlet went to Germany to study metaphysics and lager beer, she thought about him all the time. "That's what love or infatuation seems to me," said Ophelia, "it's when you think of someone all the time, wondering what the loved one is thinking, what he is doing, and if he will ever love you the way you love him," which is not very likely, most things tending to be one-sided affairs.

Hamlet's father, the king, died suddenly, and right after the funeral,

Hamlet's mother remarried, her new husband being Claudius, the king's brother who now became king himself. The marriage took place very soon after the funeral and Hamlet was enraged and it was then that Hamlet began to behave in a most peculiar manner much to everyone's surprise and perplexity. He had always been very careful about his appearance, even somewhat of a dandy: now he looked like someone who has slept for three nights in a railroad coach, and slept very poorly at that. He had always been consistently sensible, polite and full of tact. Now he made all kinds of remarks which no one could understand, and he went about looking very glum, but it was better when he was glum because when he opened his mouth, he said something which seemed, at best, mysterious, and often enough, maniacal. For example, when his mother said that he ought not to be so sad about his father's death, because the show must go on, life is full of inevitable losses, everyone is bound to die, sooner or later, what did Hamlet say in answer? He requested his mother to sing for him as she had when he was a child, the old songs "My Old Kentucky Womb," and "Carry Me Back To Old Virginity." Naturally she did not know what to make of this.

Some people thought that he was behaving like that because he was very much in love with Ophelia. But that's ridiculous. Ophelia would have married him without hesitation. And even those who thought that he was just a lovesick young man were not sure of this explanation and went about eavesdropping and looking through transoms each time Hamlet and Ophelia were alone with each other.

Other people, particularly Claudius his uncle the new king thought that Hamlet was very angry because he wanted to be king himself. Claudius thought that everyone was just like he was, for he had wanted to be king very much.

The truth is that Hamlet did not care about being king because he was very depressed about everything. He just felt rotten, no matter what he did. And when he talked to his best friend Horatio, or visited with his old friend the local undertaker, what he talked about in the main was how depressed he was, how meaningless life seemed to him, and how he would like to commit suicide.

"There's an eternity that mocks our hopes," he said one day to Horatio, "no matter what we try." This was supposed to explain why he did not commit suicide, even though he felt like it. Horatio was polite, so he did not tell Hamlet that he did not understand a word of what he was saying.

Some people supposed that his mother's second marriage, and right after the funeral of his father, was what upset Hamlet so much. It is certainly true that Hamlet did behave in an extraordinary and offensive way with his mother, telling her that she had married too soon, that her new husband and his uncle was far from being as fine a man as his father had been, and that she ought not to let her new husband make love to her, among other ridiculous suggestions. According to this view of his conduct, he was jealous of his uncle and in love with his mother, who was still a very attractive woman.

There may be a great deal of truth in this view of Hamlet's behavior, for all we know, but then again how about his father? He never behaved like that when his father was alive, nor did he carry on in a sullen and disgruntled manner, not even as an infant. Still and all, this may be a superficial difficulty in observing Hamlet's true state of mind, for he was certainly horrified by the very idea of his uncle just touching his mother.

He said to her in fury one night in her bedroom,—*to live,*
> *In the rank sweat of an enseaméd bed,*
> *Stewed in corruption, honeying, and making love*
> *Over the nasty sty.*

And many more remarks of the same kind, just as adolescent and irritating, indicating that he had a distinct aversion, to say the least, to the idea of people making love. Love seems to have been something dirty to him, in fact, a four letter word: L-O-V-E.

But something more than this incestuous jealousy was wrong with Hamlet, as you can see when you know that he told the sweet and likable Ophelia to become a nun. It's one thing to turn a girl down, but to make these proposals about her future, a future with which you refused to have anything to do, is quite insulting and shows how disgusted Hamlet was with the idea of anyone making love to anyone else. Probably he wanted Ophelia to become a nun so that no one would ever make love to her. And Horatio, who was a kind and well-meaning fellow, as well as a good friend, said to Hamlet that he had been very cruel to Ophelia and that he ought not to mistreat a girl just because she was very much in love with him.

"A pretty girl is like a canteloupe," replied Hamlet, "once opened, begins to get rotten." What kind of remark was that for a well-bred young man to make?

Horatio just sighed when he heard such things, for he realized that his friend was under a severe emotional strain.

"You never step twice into the same girl, as Heraclitus should have said," Hamlet continued, now that he was on the subject of girls. "I would like something more permanent."

"You did not always feel like this," Horatio remarked, "perhaps this is just a passing phase?"

Hamlet shrugged his shoulders and expressed contempt for his uncle the king on the ground that he drank too much.

"Those whom the gods would destroy, they first make success-ful," said Hamlet, apropos of nothing at all and at the same time everything, including his uncle's success and alcoholism for he had become more and more given to statements of a quasi-philosophical and invariably cynical character.

"You better watch those human relationships," said Horatio, think-ing again of how cruel Hamlet had been to Ophelia.

"That's what upset me so much," Hamlet fatuously replied, "I've been watching those human relationships, and I do not like them very much."

You can see how sick a young man he was also when you remem-ber how beautiful, lovable, and delightful a creature Ophelia was. She would have done anything to make Hamlet happy. The fact that she was in love with him made absolutely no impact on him, except perhaps to irritate him because it was a distraction from what really preoccupied him.

"I had not thought life has undone so many," said Hamlet to Horatio and to Ophelia, in passing.

Some people also thought that Hamlet suspected his uncle of killing his father in order to get his throne and his wife, and consequently the reason that he felt badly and behaved strangely was that he felt that he ought to avenge his father's murder but suffered from a lack of will-power. But he did not suffer from lack of will-power, nor was he a coward, as some have supposed. This should be obvious because when he was sent to England by his uncle, ostensibly for a change of scene to improve his health and emotions, and when he found out that this trip was really a plot to get him killed in England, he acted swiftly, bravely, and with resolution, stealing the secret papers which contained orders to have him killed and fixing it so that his accompanists, who were in the pay of his uncle, would be wiped out instead of him: *hardly* the behavior of a coward with no will-power!

It's true that he was disturbed by his father's death and detested his uncle but this hardly explains his state of mind, and he killed a man suddenly because he was eavesdropping behind the curtain when he was talking to his mother. He thought the spy was his uncle, but it was Ophelia's father, poor Polonius. Ophelia went insane quite reasonably because the man she loved had killed her father and she was in an inexorable emotional trap, from which she fled by means of drowning herself, an event which brought her brother back from his studies in France to challenge Hamlet to a duel. But as a result of tricky and despicable Claudius' machinations, this duel resulted in a virtual holocaust: everyone was stabbed or poisoned to death, except Horatio.

People have been arguing for hundreds of years about what was really wrong with Hamlet. Some say that he must have been a woman, some say that he was homosexual, in love with his uncle or with Horatio, and unable to bear the fact that his uncle slept with a woman, and there is one fascinating view which maintains that all the mystery is utterly clarified if we suppose that everyone is roaring drunk from the beginning to the end of the play. This view is very fine except that I don't see how it clarifies anything, for drunk or sober, not everyone behaves the same, and the real question is why Hamlet behaved as he did: certainly just hitting the bottle does not account for all his emotions and opinions, and *in vino veritas*, anyway.

Needless to say, I have a theory too; in fact, several. But I don't know if it is correct or not? For if after all these years no one has explained why Hamlet felt as he did, it does not seem very likely that I can. However, for what it is worth, and to use clinical terms, I will say in brief that I think Hamlet suffered from a well-known pathological disorder. He was manic; and he was depressive. No one knows what the real causes of the manic-depressive disorder are, whether physical or mental or both, and that is why no one understands Hamlet.

Now that is my point, the fact that you can have this gift or that disease, and no one understands why, no one is responsible, and no one can really alter matters, and yet no one can stop thinking that someone is to blame. To be manic-depressive is just like being small or tall, strong, blond, fat,—there is no clear reason for it, it is quite arbitrary, no one seems to have had any choice in the matter, and it is very important, certainly it is very important. This is the reason that the story of Hamlet is very sad, bad and immoral. It has all these traits because Hamlet's diseased emotions caused the deaths of the beautiful Ophelia, her pompous but well-meaning father, her hot-headed brother Laertes, and his own talented self. In this way we must recognize the fact that there is something wrong with everyone and everything.

Vaudeville for a Princess and Other Poems, 1950

Chandler Brossard
(1922–1993)

New Directions published Chandler Brossard's Who Walk in Darkness *in 1952, billing it as "the first time the new generation of American bohemians are presented in fiction." Brossard did not identify with the hipsters he portrayed—"they measure their cool by the length of time they refuse to say anything to each other," he told a friend—but as an editor and writer, he knew them well. This chapter depicts a well-heeled ad exec who goes in search of the authentic underground in a Village bar: the archetypal encounter of hip and square that is fodder for* Mad Men *today.*

from *Who Walk in Darkness*

WE STOPPED in at the Sporting Club Bar to see what was going on there. Harry Lees was standing at the bar with a girl named Julia and a man I had never seen before. The man was expensively dressed in sport clothes and he had a crew haircut. The place was jumping. It was jammed. You could barely move it was so crowded.

"Come on over here," Lees shouted across the bar.

"I'm going to case the place first," Max said. "I'll be over later."

He walked through the crowd examining everybody.

Porter and I went over to the bar. We said hello to Harry and Julia. Porter called her Slim.

"I want you to meet Russell Goodwin," Julia said. "He is an account executive and he makes four hundred dollars a week."

"That's quite an introduction," Goodwin said, smiling. "I'm very glad to meet you. Won't you have a drink with us?"

We said all right. I said it was nice of him to do this.

"Don't mention it," he said. "It gives me a great deal of pleasure."

"It does too," Julia said.

"Four hundred dollars a week," said Harry.

Goodwin laughed. "Don't keep saying that. You'll make me feel self-conscious."

"Not a bad way to be self-conscious," I said.

The bartender put our drinks on the bar and Goodwin paid for them from a long pigskin wallet he kept inside his jacket, and handed the drinks to us.

"Here's mud," he said. We drank. "Harry," he said, "I think you and Julia need yours freshened up a bit."

He called for two more Scotch and sodas. He looked at the crowd around us. "I'm crazy about this place," he said. "I just stumbled on it tonight."

Porter and I looked at each other, and Porter made a questioning gesture with his eyebrows. Then he slapped Harry on the shoulder. "Hey, old sport. What have you been up to?"

Goodwin was watching and listening and smiling. I could not help noticing again how well-dressed and set up he was.

"That is an ambiguous question, old sport," Harry said to Porter.

I felt Harry was doing this just for fun, not for any other reason. Goodwin had handed Harry his new drink and was watching him and Porter.

"I don't know exactly how to answer you," said Harry. "When you say what am I up to do you mean what am I capable of doing? Or do you mean to what point have I risen? The assumption being I am low and going up. You see, old sport, it's very ambiguous."

Goodwin laughed. "That's very clever, Harry. I had never thought of it that way."

"Take it any way you like," Porter said.

"All right. To be honest, Porter, I haven't been up to anything. I've been pretty low."

"Won't you have another drink?" Goodwin asked me, looking at Porter too.

"No thanks," Porter said.

"Are you sure? Come on. Have another."

"Don't be dull," Julia said. "Have another drink, Porter."

"I'm not a drinking man," Porter said. "It makes me dizzy and confused."

"Are you afraid somebody is going to put something over on you when you are tight?" Harry asked him.

"No. I just don't like feeling confused."

"I'm not afraid of feeling confused," said Harry.

"But you will have one, won't you, Blake," Goodwin said to me.

"Sure. Blake will have one. He's not afraid of getting dizzy."

"Thanks," I said.

"That's the boy, Blake. Stay with us," Julia said. "Don't let us down."

"Or bring us down."

"Oh. I get it," Goodwin said. "I get that one. It's a jive expression. Right?"

"You're in," Porter said.

"He's a very solid citizen," Harry said. "He makes four hundred a week."

"What do you do?" Goodwin asked Porter.

"I write fiction."

"Really? I used to write fiction, when I was in college."

"And?"

"It was pretty good. I gave up writing because nobody bought my stories. But it was good. Now I wish I had kept at it."

"You're doing all right," Julia said.

"Oh yes. I do all right. Harry, when do you expect to finish your book?"

"Are you writing a book, Harry?" I asked.

Goodwin answered me. "Didn't he tell you? He told me he's doing a book on the end of the Renaissance. Aren't you, Harry?"

"I'm not only doing it, I'm living it. Which reminds me. What happened to that underground man you came in with?"

"He's casing the joint," Porter said. "He'll be back."

"What do you mean by the underground man?" Goodwin asked.

"The man who will do anything. He's a spiritual desperado."

"He means Max Glazer," Porter said. "He's a very smart guy. Really very hip."

"I didn't say he wasn't. He is a desperado, though. Do you know what his ideal is? His ideal is to look like a street corner hoodlum and be the finest lyric poet in America at the same time."

"He sounds remarkable," Goodwin said. "I would enjoy meeting him."

"Don't say it that way," Julia said. "You'll meet him."

"There's a booth. Let's get it."

We pushed through the crowd on our left and got to the empty booth just ahead of some other people. "Very sorry," Goodwin said to them, smiling nicely. They did not say anything and went away.

"Tell me some more about the underground man, Harry," Goodwin said.

"I'm writing a book about him too."

"It seems that you are writing these books with your mouth, Harry," said Porter.

"It is a new literary form,'" Harry said. "Anyway, about the underground man. Max. His favorite reading is Andrew Marvell and the *Daily Mirror* comics. You might say he is the Neanderthal man of the new world."

"Here he is," Julia said.

Goodwin stood up. We all looked at him as he did this. He held out his hand to Max. "You're Max Glazer, aren't you? My name is Goodwin, Russell Goodwin. We've been talking about you."

Max did not return Goodwin's greeting, though he did shake his hand gently. He made a surprised expression and smiled at us.

"Sit down, Max," Goodwin said, and gave Max his seat in the booth. "I'll get a chair from the dining room." He shouldered through the crowd and went back to the dining room.

"I don't dig this guy," Max said. "What's his story? Is he a fruit or something?"

"He's not a fruit," said Julia. "He's just lonely."

"Julia and I met him at the bar," Harry explained. "He was alone and he asked us if he could buy us a drink. Just like that. He makes four hundred dollars a week."

"He is an uptown operator, Max," Porter said. "But he might be good for laughs."

"You're a cool son of a bitch, Porter," Julia said.

"Are you so hot?"

"Oh nuts to you."

"Even though the guy is uptown, he's an interesting sociological study," Porter said to Max.

"You don't say."

"What are you drinking?" Max asked me.

"Scotch. He's been standing everybody liquor. You can't stop him."

"Who would want to? Give me a drink, will you?"

I let Max take a drink from my glass. Goodwin came back with a chair. He sat down on the outside. "You will have a drink, won't you, Max?" he asked.

Max said he would. Goodwin ordered from a waiter passing us with his hands full of empty beer glasses. He was one of the good waiters.

"Subito, subito," he said. He liked to speak Italian every now and then. He thought it was amusing. He spoke it with a sharp northern accent. Everyone liked him. He was never sullen. The place was very noisy now. The bartenders were shouting for the dining room waiters to pick up their drinks. People were standing in both doorways talking and drinking and looking all around. You could not tell whether they were on their way in or on their way out.

A headache was beginning to work up the back of my neck and head and I was feeling the drinks. I was thinking about Grace's abortion and about the big fight and about going away for a few days to Harry Lees's father's place up on the Cape. And about a job. Goodwin's being there made me think about the job. An uptown job. There were no other jobs. They were all uptown. And you had to go uptown to keep them too. I did not want to do that.

"You'll have another drink, won't you, Blake?" Goodwin asked me.

"No thanks, Goodwin. I'll nurse this one."

"You're sure?"

"Yes. Thanks anyway."

Max smiled at me. "Why do you play tag this way with corruption, Blake?"

"I'm not playing tag. I just don't want another drink."

He kept on smiling. The others were watching him. "That isn't what I'm talking about. You know that."

"What are you talking about, Max?" Goodwin asked.

"I'm talking about your buying Blake a drink. Blake feels it's corrupt to let people buy for him. And he feels nervous because you're buying it the way you are."

He was right. And he was not stopping there.

"How am I buying it, Max?" Goodwin asked him.

Max laughed softly. "You're buying in," he said.

"Oh nuts, Max," Julia said. "Why do you have to get so salty when people want to have fun?"

Goodwin's smile had gone now. He was looking in his drink. Harry was looking at me. We were both thinking the same thing. I guess Goodwin had it coming to him. Here or someplace else.

"You're right, Max," Goodwin said, looking up. "You're quite right. That's what I've been doing."

"I didn't say there was anything wrong with it," Max said. "I just said that's what you're doing and that's what Blake was feeling bad about. Blake thinks things like that are bad."

"How long have you known everything?" I said.

"Let's forget it," Lees said. "I'll tell a dirty joke."

"Why should you feel bad about this?" Max asked Goodwin. "You get in however you can. In this case you buy in. One way is as good as another."

"You really think you have everybody taped, don't you, Max?" I said.

He smiled and shook his head and patted my arm. "Slow down, man. Slow down. Don't take everything so personally."

"Do you dislike me for doing this?" Goodwin asked, looking at Porter now.

Porter shrugged. "I don't know you well enough to either like you or dislike you, old man."

"Come on. Let's drop it," Julia said. "Tell the dirty joke, Harry. Or whistle 'Dixie.' Do something."

Harry told the dirty joke. It was not so dirty. But it was funny. It involved a Jewish man catching something from a hustler in Atlantic City. Porter laughed very loud when it was over, laughing that ha-ha-ha, loud laugh. Goodwin laughed too. The joke seemed to have relaxed him.

"How do you make four hundred a week?" Max asked Goodwin.

"I am an account executive at an advertising agency."

"You must live pretty well."

"Well, I guess I do."

"Let me guess. You live on the upper East side and you probably have a charge account at Abercrombie & Fitch."

"You're doing very well."

"And you read the New Yorker regularly and think it is really terrific. And you often tell your friends you heard something funny the other day which you think you will send to the New Yorker."

"Go on."

"Your idea of a vacation is to go to Fire Island and you probably listen to WQXR very often. You see all the shows at the Museum of Modern Art."

"You are batting a thousand. Go on."

"You see all the French movies and you think they are much better than the American movies."

"You're doing great."

"You still think you would like to live in Paris for a year. Because that is where things happen."

"I do, too."

"What are you doing down here?"

"Oh, looking around."

"Pretty expensive looking, isn't it? One way or another."

"That is what the four hundred is for, Max."

Max smiled and finished his drink. "You're O.K., Goodwin, you're O.K."

"Thanks, Max."

"Underground Max," I said. "Working overtime."

"You're underground too, Blake, old boy. You're the Arrow Collar man of the underground."

"Would anyone like to hear another joke?" Harry asked. "This is getting too serious for me."

"By all means another joke, Harry," Julia said.

"Jokes drag me," Porter said. "One joke was enough. Tell something else, but not a joke."

"That is your trouble, Porter," said Harry. "You are a one joke man. Spread out. Be a two joke man."

"Don't let it worry you, old sport," Porter said, laughing and slapping him on the back. "I leave the clowning to the clowns."

"I'll tell you about the time I got drunk in Boston and a couple of jokers put me in the dumb-waiter. I fell asleep. The next morning a lady tenant in the building pulled the dumb-waiter down to put her garbage on. She saw me and screamed and fainted. She thought I was a dead body."

"Wonderful, wonderful," Julia said, shrieking.

"What was it like? Back in the womb?" Porter asked.

"Yes, and I liked it."

"It is amazing," Goodwin said. "Did it really happen, Harry?"

"No. I made it up."

"Well I'll be damned."

"Are you disappointed?" Porter asked him. "Do you want everything to be true?"

"Perhaps I'm naïve."

Goodwin signaled to the waiter as he passed and asked for another round. "Just this last one," he said, smiling at us.

"Don't apologize," Julia said.

"Let's make it quick, though," Porter said, "because I have to be leaving. I have to finish some work."

"All right, man, all right," Max said. "Take it easy."

The waiter brought the drinks. None for me or Porter. I wanted to go home. They drank up. Porter was looking nervously around the bar. Afraid he would miss something or somebody. Max was looking at Julia. Examining her nearsightedly. Goodwin and Harry were talking about clubs. I was the first to get up.

"You may not believe me," Goodwin said, getting up with the others, "but I've really enjoyed this. I want to get together with you again. How about coming up to my place next week for dinner? Will you?"

"We would love to, Goodwin," Max said.

Goodwin wrote his name and address down on the back of a card he took from his wallet. "Next Tuesday, say at eight," he said. Then he left a big tip for the waiter. I knew none of us would go to Goodwin's house.

"They'll think you're crazy," Julia said about the tip.

"I don't care," Goodwin said, smiling. "I'm driving uptown. Can I give anybody a lift?"

We all said we were walking. All except Julia. She said he could give her a lift. Harry looked at her, surprised.

"But I thought I was going to walk you home," he said.

"Forgive me, darling," she said. "But I'm tired, really beat. Honestly."

Lees cocked his head and looked that way at Julia. "O.K.," he said.

"Some other time, Harry," she said.

We left. Outside Goodwin and Julia got into his Buick convertible.

"Next Tuesday then," Goodwin said. "Don't forget."

We said we wouldn't. Julia waved good-bye and they drove off. Lees just watched them, not waving.

"She can drop dead," he said.

"Don't take it so hard," Porter said. "She's just a tramp."

Max said he was going to a movie, a double feature on Forty-Second Street. There was nothing else to do. Porter said that must be the fourth movie he had gone to in the last week. Max said so what. He liked movies.

Porter and Max were going in the same direction. We said so long and they walked off.

"I'll walk home with you, O.K.?" Harry said to me. "I have a lot of time to kill."

"Sure. Come on."

I did not feel like passing by the Mills Hotel and the bruise-faced drunks there so instead of going up Bleecker as I usually did we went south toward Houston Street. We walked for a while without talking.

Harry said, finally, "I don't blame her. She played it smart and went with the better man."

"Don't say that. You'll begin to believe those things about yourself after a while."

"I do already, Blake. That's the crumby part of it."

"No you don't, Harry. You're talking yourself into it. Don't do that. You've got to keep up some sort of a front, even for yourself."

"Do you believe that?"

"That's the only way you can make it. That's the truth."

"I wish I could do it."

"If I were Porter I would call it a 'personal myth.' But whatever you call it, you have to have it."

Now the street darkened. I felt the darkness suddenly. I had not remembered this street being so dark. As Harry talked I kept feeling the darkness of the street. Then I saw why. The two street lamps were out. I thought somebody had stoned them out. But this was not so. The glass was not broken. The lamps had just gone out. I could see a bunch of the local hoods standing together way down at the corner we were approaching.

"Maybe I should get analyzed," Harry said. "I've often thought of that."

"It's tough. A lot of strange things happen to you."

"I know it's tough. You know something? I'm afraid of it."

"So are a lot of people."

"I'm afraid it will make me just like everybody else. That it will take some special juice out of me. Then I'll be a mediocrity. Maybe I am one already and don't know it."

"That would sound like a symptom."

"I guess it does, Blake. And then I'm afraid of a lot of things it might bring up."

I knew that even before he told me. He had always given me that feeling, as long as I had known him. He was keeping the lid on. Sometimes I thought it was better he did keep it on. It was safer for him that way.

"That's what makes it tough," I said. "But you are supposed to feel better after you bring it up."

"Like puking."

"Something like that."

"Blake, do you have bad dreams?"

"Doesn't everybody?"

"I mean really bad ones."

"Sometimes. Why?"

"I wondered if you had them like mine. Do you mind if I tell you about a dream?"

"Go ahead."

"Well, I have this one a lot of times. Someone is after me. I think I know who it is, then I am not sure. He is close behind me. I am scared. Scared stupid. So scared I want to scream. Then I run into a building. A building just going up. This person is getting closer. He is dressed in black. Now I run up a flight of stairs. I hear him jumping up the stairs. I think I might get away up the stairs. Suddenly the stairs end in a blank wall. I could scream. I hear him after me. He is almost on me. Then I find myself running in another part of the building. He's still after me. I run up another flight of stairs. Just then the stairs end in a blank wall again. And he's almost on me."

"Jesus Christ. Then what happens?"

"I keep running up these dead-end stairways. Then I wake up."

I wanted to say something enlightening about the dream that

would make Harry feel better. But I could not think of anything that would not sound dumb. So I just said the dream sounded horrible. We were getting closer to the group of hoods.

"I wish I knew what the goddamn thing meant," he said. "Do you have any idea?"

"Nothing that would help."

Harry had been talking with his head turned toward me or looking down at the ground and apparently he had not seen the hoods at the corner. But now he saw them. I could feel him tighten as he looked at them. They were standing all over the sidewalk. Blocking the way. They were looking our way now. Harry was staring at them. There were eight of them.

I could feel the way Harry was holding himself tight as we came toward the hoods standing there on the sidewalk blocking it. Harry was staring straight ahead at them. I heard them talking now. I could feel Harry's fear.

They were standing in our way unmoving. Then we walked through them. Brushing against them. They moved slightly. We passed through them and on. We did not say anything.

We crossed Houston Street and walked east on it toward Greene Street. There were no cars in the big cobbled street.

"Those sons of bitches give me the creeps," Harry said.

I could feel his fear relaxing now.

"There are too many of them for us to start anything," I said. There were many stories around about the hoods ganging up on people.

"It makes you sick to be so outnumbered," he said.

"I know it. But what can you do?"

"Nothing, I guess. They don't have any rules to keep them back. You can't do anything with people who don't have any rules."

"To hell with them, Harry. Forget it."

"I guess so. I'll have to."

I slapped him on the back. "Old Renaissance Man."

No people were in the streets but us. Harry was walking with his hands in his pockets and his head down looking at the sidewalk. I watched the street lights blinking red and green in the deserted street, no cars to obey them. They were blinking for blocks down the street. We turned into Greene Street and walked south on it.

"Speaking of Renaissance men, Blake," Harry said, "what was this Max said about you being the Arrow Collar underground man?"

"That's what I am," I said, laughing a little. "Partly underground."

"Do you think you will ever go all the way?"

"I wish I could tell."

"It is like a joke become serious," Harry said. "I don't know when to take this underground business as a laugh or when to take it as a real thing."

"Neither do I."

We came to my building. "Want to come up?" I asked him. I really wanted to go to sleep.

"Thanks, Blake, but I had better be going along. I might start in on some more dreams."

"Don't let them get you, Harry."

"I have one of the best collections in the country. Like a jewel collection. Maybe I could sell it to the American Association of Head Doctors."

"You might try."

"Are the busses still running down here? I don't want to walk back."

"Yes."

"Good. Adios, kid."

"So long."

I went upstairs. When I got into bed I did not feel so sleepy any more. I lay awake thinking.

Who Walk in Darkness, 1952

Terry Southern
(1924–1995)

Terry Southern was the most successful of hipster writers, authoring best-selling novels, hit movies, and journalism that paved the way for the new and the gonzo—he even wrote for Saturday Night Live. *A Texan, Southern moved to Paris in 1948 to study at the Sorbonne, but in the cafés and jazz caves discovered what was really going on. He wrote the hilarious porn parody* Candy *with Mason Hoffenberg, and the novels* Flash and Filigree *and* The Magic Christian. *Peter Sellers, a fan of the latter, gave a copy to Stanley Kubrick who was embarking on a film project about The Bomb. Kubrick decided to make the film a black comedy, hired Southern, and Dr.* Strangelove *was born. In "You're Too Hip, Baby," written in the 1950s and collected in* Red-Dirt Marijuana and Other Tastes *(1967), the bohemian Paris of Southern's wild youth provides the setting for a witty take on hip wannabes and a survey of the fault-lines of race.*

You're Too Hip, Baby

THE SORBONNE, where Murray was enrolled for a doctorate, required little of his time; class attendance was not compulsory and there were no scheduled examinations. Having received faculty approval on the subject of his thesis—"The Influence of Mallarmé on the English Novel Since 1940"—Murray was now engaged in research in the libraries, developing his thesis, writing it, and preparing himself to defend it at some future date of his own convenience. Naturally he could attend any lectures at the University which he considered pertinent to his work, and he did attend them from time to time—usually those of illustrious guest speakers, like Cocteau, Camus, and Sartre, or Marcel Raymond, author of *From Baudelaire to Surrealism*.

But for the most part, Murray devoted himself to less formal pursuits; he knew every Negro jazz musician in every club in Paris. At night he made the rounds. If there was someone really great in town he would sit at the same bar all evening and listen to him; otherwise he made the rounds, one club after another, not drinking much, just listening to the music and talking to the musicians. Then, toward morning, he would go with them to eat—down the street to the Brasserie Civet or halfway across Paris to a place in Montmartre that served spareribs and barbecued chicken.

What was best though was to hang around the bar of his own hotel, the Noir et Blanc, in the late afternoon during a rehearsal or a closed session. At these times everyone was very relaxed, telling funny stories, drinking Pernod, and even turning on a bit of hashish or marijuana, passing it around quite openly, commenting on its quality. Murray derived a security from these scenes—the hushed camaraderie and the inside jokes. Later, in the evening, when the place was jumping, Murray kept himself slightly apart from the rest of the crowd—the tourists, the students, the professional beats, and the French *de bonne famille*—who all came to listen to the great new music. And always during the evening there would be at least one incident, like the famous tenor-man's casually bumming a cigarette from him, which would prove Murray's intimacy with the group to those who observed. Old acquaintances from Yale, who happened in, found Murray changed; they detected in his attitude toward them, their plans, and their expressed or implied values a sort of bemused tolerance—as though he were in possession of a secret knowledge. And then there would be the inevitable occasion when he was required to introduce them to one of the musicians, and that obvious moment when the musician would look to Murray for his judgment of the stranger as in the question: "Well, man, who *is* this cat? Is he *with* it?" None of this lessened Murray's attractiveness, nor his mystery, no less to others, presumably, than to himself; but he was never too hard on his old friends—because he was swinging.

WHEN THE Negro pianist Buddy Talbott was hired, along with a French drummer and bass, to play the Noir et Blanc, he and his wife had been in Paris for only three days. It was their first time out of the States, and except for a few band jobs upstate, it was their first time out of New York City.

Toward the end of the evening, during a break, Murray went into the men's room. Buddy Talbott was there alone, in front of the mirror, straightening his tie. Their eyes fixed for an instant in the glass as Murray entered and walked over to the urinal; the disinfectant did not obscure a thin smell of hashish recently smoked in the room. Murray nodded his head in the direction of the bandstand beyond the wall. "Great sound you got there, man," he said, his voice flat, almost weary in its objectiveness. Buddy Talbott had a dark and delicate face which turned slowly, reluctantly it seemed, from the glass to Murray, smiling, and he spoke now in soft and precisely measured tones: "Glad you like it."

And, for the moment, no more was said, Murray knowing better than that.

Although Murray smoked hashish whenever it was offered, he seldom took the trouble to go over to the Arab quarter and buy any himself; but he always knew where to get the best. And the next evening, when Buddy Talbott came into the men's room, Murray was already there.

They exchanged nods, and Murray wordlessly handed him the smoking stick, scarcely looking at him as he did, walking past to the basin—as though to spare him witness to even the merest glimpse of hesitancy, of apprehension, calculation, and finally, of course, of perfect trust.

"I've got a box, man," Murray said after a minute, by which he meant record player, "and some new Monk—you know, if you ever want to fall by. . . ." He dried his hands carefully, looking at the towel. "Upstairs here," he said, "in number eight. My name is on the door— 'Murray.'"

The other nodded, savoring the taste, holding it. "I'd like to very much," he said finally, and added with an unguarded smile, "*Murray.*" At which Murray smiled too, and touching his arm lightly said: "Later, man." And left.

THE HASH seemed to have a nice effect on Buddy's playing. Certainly it did on Murray's listening—every note and nuance came straight to him, through the clatter of service at the bar and the muttered talk nearby, as though he were wearing earphones wired to the piano. He heard subtleties he had missed before, intricate structures of sound, each supporting the next, first from one side, then from another, and all being skillfully laced together with a dreamlike fabric of comment and insinuation; the runs did not sound either vertical or horizontal, but circular ascensions, darting arabesques and figurines; and it was clear to Murray that the player was constructing something there on the stand . . . something splendid and grandiose, but perfectly scaled to fit inside this room, to sit, in fact, alongside the piano itself. It seemed, in the beginning, that what was being erected before him was a castle, a marvelous castle of sound . . . but then, with one dramatic minor—just as the master builder might at last reveal the nature of his edifice in adding a single stone—Murray saw it was not a castle being built, but a cathedral. "*Yeah, man,*" he said, nodding and smiling. A cathedral—and, at the same time, around it the builder was weaving a strange and beautiful tapestry, covering the entire structure. At first the image was too bizarre, but then Murray smiled again as he saw that the tapestry was, of course, being woven *inside* the cathedral, over its interior surface, only it was so rich and strong that it sometimes seemed to come right through the walls. And then Murray suddenly realized—and this was the greatest of all, because he was absolutely certain that only he and Buddy knew—that the fantastic tapestry was being woven, quite deliberately, face against the wall. And he laughed aloud at this, shaking his head, "*Yeah, man,*" the last magnificent irony, and Buddy looked up at the sound, and laughed too.

AFTER THE set, Buddy came over and asked Murray if he wanted a drink. "Let's take a table," he said. "My old lady's coming to catch the last set."

"Solid," said Murray, so soft and without effort that none would have heard.

They sat down at a table in the corner.

"Man, that sure is fine gage," Buddy said.

Murray shrugged.

"Glad you like it," he said then, a tone with an edge of mock haughtiness, just faintly mimicking that used by Buddy when they had met; and they both laughed, and Buddy signaled the waiter.

"I was wondering," said Buddy after the waiter had left, "if you could put me onto some of that."

Murray yawned. "Why don't you meet me tomorrow," he said quietly. "I could take you over to the café and, you know, introduce you to the guy."

Buddy nodded, and smiled. "Solid," he said.

BUDDY'S WIFE, Jackie, was a tall Negro girl, sort of lank, with great eyes, legs, and a lovely smile.

"What we'd like to do," she said, "is to make it here—you know, like *live* here—at least for a couple of years anyway."

"It's the place for living all right," said Murray.

MURRAY WAS helpful in much more than introducing them to a good hash connection. Right away he found them a better and cheaper room, and nearer the Noir et Blanc. He showed Jackie how to shop in the quarter, where to get the best croissants, and what was the cheap wine to buy. He taught them some French and introduced them to the good inexpensive restaurants. He took them to see *L'Âge d'Or* at the Cinémathèque, to the catacombs, to the rib joint in Montmartre, to hear Marcel Raymond speak at the Sorbonne, to the Flea Market, to the Musée Guimet, Musée de l'Homme, to the evening exhibitions at the Louvre. . . . Sometimes Murray would have a girl with him, sometimes not; or on some Sundays when the weather was fine he would get someone with a car, or borrow it himself, and they would all drive out to the Bois de Boulogne and have a picnic, or to Versailles at night. Then again, on certain nights early, or when Buddy wasn't playing, they might have dinner in Buddy and Jackie's room, listening to records, smoking a piece of hash now and then, eating the red beans and rice, the fish, ribs, and chicken that Jackie cooked. The most comfortable place in the small room was the bed, and after a while the three of them were usually lying or half reclining across it, except when one of them would get up to put on more records, get a drink, or go to the bathroom, everything very relaxed, not much talk, occasionally someone saying something funny or relating a strange thing they had seen or heard, and frequently, too, just dozing off.

Once Murray bought a pheasant, had it cooked, and brought it up to their room, along with a couple of bottles of chilled Liebfraumilch, some wild rice, asparagus, and strawberries and cream.

Jackie was quite excited, opening the packages. "You're too much, baby," she said, giving Murray a kiss on the cheek.

"What's the grand occasion, man?" asked Buddy, beaming at him.

Murray shrugged. "I guess we'll have to dream one up," he said.

"I guess we will," said Buddy smiling, and he started slicing up a piece of hash.

Afterward they lay across the bed, smoking and listening to music.

"It's funny, isn't it," said Murray, while they were listening to Billie, "that there aren't any great ofay singers."

The others seemed to consider it.

"Anita O'Day is all right," said Jackie.

"Yeah, but I mean you wouldn't compare her with Billie, would you," said Murray.

"Some of the French chicks swing," said Buddy absently, ". . . Piaf . . . and what's that other chick's name. . . ."

"Yeah, but I mean like that's something else, isn't it," said Murray.

Buddy shrugged, passing the cigarette, "Yeah, I guess so," he said, sounding half asleep; but his eyes were open, and for several minutes he lay simply staring at Murray with an expression of mild curiosity on his face.

"Murray," he asked finally, "did you want to learn piano . . . or what?" Then he laughed, as though he might not have meant it to sound exactly like that, and he got up to get some wine.

Jackie laughed too. "Maybe he just *likes* you, baby—ever think of that?"

"Yeah, that's right," said Buddy, making a joke of it now, pouring the wine, "that ought to be considered." He was still smiling, almost sheepishly. "Well, here's to friendship then," he said, taking a sip.

"You're making me cry," said Murray in his flat, weary voice, and they all laughed.

Then it was time for Buddy to go to the club.

"I'll make it over with you, man," said Murray, slowly raising himself up on the bed.

"Stick around," said Buddy, putting on his tie. "Nothing's happening there yet—you can come over later with Jackie."

"That seems like a good idea," said Jackie.

Murray sat there, staring at nothing.

"It's cool, man," said Buddy smiling and giving Murray an elaborate wink of conspiracy, "it's cool. I mean, you know—make it."

"Solid," said Murray, after a minute, and he lay back across the bed again.

"See you cats," said Buddy, opening the door to leave.

"Later," said Murray.

"Later, baby," said Jackie, getting up and going to the door and locking it. Then she went over to the basin and began brushing her teeth.

"That was a funny thing for him to say, wasn't it," said Murray after a minute, "I mean about did I want 'to learn piano, or *what*?'"

Jackie moved the brush in a slow, languorous motion, looking at Murray in the mirror. "Well, it's very simple really. . . . I mean, he *digs* you, you know—and I guess he would like to do something for you, that sort of thing." She rinsed her mouth and held the brush under the water. "I thought he made that part of it pretty clear," she said, then looking directly at him. She crossed over to the dressing table and stood in front of it, straightening her dress; it was a cream-colored jersey which clung without tightness to all of her. She stood in front of the glass, her feet slightly apart, and touched at her hair. He watched the back of her brown legs, the softly rounded calves, tracing them up past the cream-colored hem behind her knees into their full lean contours above—lines which were not merely suggested, but, because of the clinging jersey and the way she stood, convincingly apparent.

"That's a groovy thread," said Murray, sitting up and taking the glass of wine Buddy had left on the night table.

"Oh?" She looked down at the dress reflexively and again at the mirror. "Madame what's-her-name made it—you know, that seamstress you put me onto." She sat down on a chair by the mirror and carefully wiped the lipstick from her mouth with a Kleenex.

"Yeah, it's crazy," said Murray.

"Glad you like it, Murray." The phrase had become an occasional joke between the three of them.

"I was by the Soleil du Maroc this afternoon," he began then, taking a small packet out of his shirt pocket, unwrapping it as he leaned toward the light at the night table, "I just thought I would twist up a few to take to the club." He looked up at her and paused. "I mean, you know, if there's time."

Jackie's head was cocked to one side as she dabbed perfume behind an ear and watched Murray in the mirror. "Oh there's *time*, baby," she said with a smile, ". . . make no mistake about that."

When Murray had twisted one, he lit it and, after a couple of drags, sat it smoking on the tray, continuing to roll them carefully, placing them in a neat row on the night table.

Jackie finished at the mirror, put another record on, and came over to the bed. As she sat down, Murray passed the cigarette to her, and she lay back with it, head slightly raised on a pillow against the wall, listening to *Blue Monk*.

When Murray had rolled several, he put the packet of hash away and stashed the cigarettes in with his Gauloises. Then he leaned back, resting his head on Jackie's lap, or rather on what would have been her lap had she been sitting instead of half lying across the bed; she passed the cigarette to Murray.

"Has a good taste, hasn't it," said Murray.

Jackie smiled. "Yes, indeed," she said.

"Hadj says it's from the Middle Congo," said Murray with a laugh, "'C'est du vrai congolais!'" he went on, giving it the Arab's voice.

"That's just how it tastes," said Jackie.

With his face turned toward her, Murray's cheek pressed firmly against the softness of her stomach which just perceptibly rose and fell with breathing, and through the fine jersey he could feel the taut sheen of her pants beneath it, and the warmth. There was nothing lank about her now.

"Yeah," said Murray after a minute, "that's right, isn't it, that's just how it tastes."

They finished the cigarette, and for a while, even after the record had ended, they lay there in silence, Jackie idly curling a finger in Murray's hair. For a long time Murray didn't move.

"Well," he finally said instead, "I guess we'd better make it—over to the club, I mean."

Jackie looked at him for a minute, then gave a gentle tug on the lock of his hair, shrugged, and laughed softly.

"Anything you say, Murray."

THAT SUNDAY was a fine day, and Murray borrowed a car for them to go out to the Bois. Jackie had fried some chicken the night before and prepared a basket of food, but now she complained of a cold and decided not to go. She insisted though that Murray and Buddy go.

"It's a shame to waste the car and this great weather. You ought to make it."

So they went without her.

They drove up the Champs through a magnificent afternoon, the boulevard in full verdure and the great cafés sprawled in the sun like patches of huge flowers. Just past the Étoile they noticed a charcuterie which was open and they stopped and bought some more to put in the basket—céleri rémoulade, artichoke hearts, and cheese covered with grape seeds. At a café next door Murray was able to get a bottle of cognac.

At the Bois they drove around for a while, then parked the car and walked into the depth of the woods. They thought they might discover a new place—and they did, finally, a grove of poplars which led to the edge of a small pond; and there, where it met the pond and the wooded thicket to each side, it formed a picture-book alcove, all fern, pine and poplar. There was no one else to be seen on the pond, and they had passed no one in the grove. It was a pleasing discovery.

Together they carefully spread the checkered tablecloth the way Jackie always did, and then laid out the food. Buddy had brought along a portable phonograph, which he opened up now while Murray uncorked the wine.

"What'll it be," Buddy asked with a laugh, after looking at the records for several minutes, "Bird or Bartók?"

"Bartók, man," said Murray, and added dreamily, "where do you go after Bird?"

"Crazy," said Buddy, and he put on *The Miraculous Mandarin.*

Murray lay propped on his elbow, and Buddy sat opposite, cross-legged, as they ate and drank in silence, hungry but with deliberation, sampling each dish, occasionally grunting an appreciative comment.

"Dig that bridge, man," said Buddy once, turning to the phonograph and moving the needle back a couple of grooves, "like that's what you might call an 'augmented *oh-so-slightly.*'" He laughed. "Cat's too much," he said, as he leaned forward to touch a piece of chicken to the mayonnaise.

Murray nodded. "Swings," he said.

THEY LAY on the grass, smoking and drinking the cognac, closing their eyes or shading them against the slanting sun. They were closer together now, since only Buddy had gotten up to stretch and then, in giving Murray a cigarette, had sat down beside him to get a light.

After a while Buddy seemed to half doze off, and then he sleepily turned over on his stomach. As he did, his knee touched Murray's leg, and Murray moved lightly as if to break the contact—but then, as if wondering why he had reacted like that, let his leg ease back to where it had been, and almost at once dropped into a light sleep, his glass of cognac still in his hand, resting on his chest.

When Murray awoke, perhaps only seconds later, the pressure of Buddy's leg on his own was quite strong. Without looking at Buddy, he slowly sat up, raising his legs as he did, sitting now with knees under his folded arms. He looked at the glass of cognac still in his hand, and finished it off.

"That sort of thing," said Buddy quietly, "doesn't interest you either." It was not put as a question, but as a statement which required confirmation.

Murray turned, an expression of bland annoyance on his face, while Buddy lay there looking at him pretty much the same as always.

"No, man," said Murray, then almost apologetically: "I mean, like I don't put it down—but it's just not a scene I make. You know?"

Buddy dropped his eyes to a blade of grass he was toying with; he smiled. "Well, anyway," he said with a little laugh, "no offense."

Murray laughed, too. "None taken, man," he said seriously.

MURRAY HAD risen at his more or less usual hour, and the clock at Cluny was just striking eleven when he emerged from the hotel stairway, into the street and the summer morning. He blinked his eyes at the momentary brightness and paused to lean against the side of the building, gazing out into the pleasantly active boulevard.

When the clock finished striking he pushed himself out from the wall and started towards the Royale, where he often met Buddy and Jackie for breakfast. About halfway along Boulevard Saint-Germain he turned in at a small café to get some cigarettes. Three or four people were coming out the door as Murray reached it, and he had to wait momentarily to let them pass. As he did he was surprised to notice, at a table near the side, Buddy and Jackie, eating breakfast. Buddy was wearing dark glasses, and Murray instinctively reached for his own as he came through the door, but discovered he had left them in his room. He raised his hand in a laconic greeting to them and paused at the bar to get the cigarettes. Buddy nodded, but Jackie had already gotten up from the table and was walking toward the girls' room. Murray sauntered over, smiling, and sat down.

"What are you doing here, man?" he asked. "I didn't know you ever came here."

Buddy shrugged. "Thought we'd give it a try," he said seriously examining a dab of butter on the end of his knife. Then he looked up at Murray and added with a laugh, "You know—new places, new faces."

Murray laughed too, and picked at a piece of an unfinished croissant. "That's pretty good," he said. "What's that other one? You know, the one about—oh yeah, 'Old friends are the best friends.' Ever hear that one?"

"I have heard that one," said Buddy nodding, "yes, I have heard that one." His smile was no longer a real one. "Listen, Murray," he said, wiping his hands and sitting back, putting his head to one side, "let me ask you something. Just what is it you want?"

Murray frowned down at where is own hands slowly dissected the piece of croissant as though he were shredding a paper napkin.

"What are you talking about, man?"

"You *don't* want to play music," Buddy began as though he were taking an inventory, "and you *don't* want . . . I mean just what have we *got* that interests you?"

Murray looked at him briefly, and then looked away in exasperation. He noticed that Jackie was talking to the patron who was standing near the door. "Well, what do *you* think, man?" he demanded, turning back to Buddy. "I dig the *scene,* that's all. I dig the *scene* and the *sounds.*"

Buddy stood up, putting some money on the table. He looked down at Murray, who sat there glowering, and shook his head. "You're too hip, baby. That's right. You're a *hippy.*" He laughed. "In fact, you're what we might call a kind of professional *nigger lover.*" He touched

Murray's shoulder as he moved to leave. "And I'm not putting you down for it, understand, but, uh, like the man said, 'It's just not a scene I make.'" His dark face set for an instant beneath the smoky glasses and he spoke, urgent and imploring, in a flash of white teeth, almost a hiss, "I mean *not when I can help it*, Murray, *not when I can help it.*" And he left. And the waiter arrived, picking up the money.

"*Monsieur désire?*"

Still scowling, staring straight ahead, Murray half raised his hand as to dismiss the waiter, but then let it drop to the table. "*Café*," he muttered.

"*Noir, monsieur?*" asked the waiter in a suggestively rising inflection.

Murray looked up abruptly at the man, but the waiter was oblivious, counting the money in his hand.

Murray sighed. "*Oui*," he said softly, "*noir.*"

Esquire, 1952; *Red-Dirt Marijuana and Other Tales*, 1967

Annie Ross
(b. 1930)

Born Annabelle Short in London, Annie Ross appeared as a child singer and actor under the name Annabelle Logan. As a teenager she changed her name to Annie Ross and split for Europe to become a jazz singer. In 1952 Ross wrote lyrics to a composition by bebop saxophonist Wardell Gray and this novelty song was released on the album King Pleasure Sings / Annie Ross Sings *by Prestige Records. The vocalese trio Lambert, Hendricks & Ross, formed in 1957, was enormously successful until 1963, when she quit the group and moved to London. Ross opened a jazz club there and branched out into acting. Her lyrics for "Twisted," a send-up of psychoanalysis and neurosis, were a wry anthem for hipsters who spurned normality or healthy adjustment.*

Twisted

My analyst told me that I was right out of my head
The way he described it, he said I'd be better dead than live
I didn't listen to his jive
I knew all along he was all wrong
And I knew that he thought I was crazy but I'm not
Oh no

My analyst told me that I was right out of my head
He said I'd need treatment but I'm not that easily led
He said I was the type that was most inclined
When out of his sight to be out of my mind
And he thought I was nuts, no more ifs or ands or buts
Oh no

They say as I child I appeared a little bit wild
With all my crazy ideas

But I knew what was happenin', I knew I was a genius
What's so strange if you know that you're a wizard at three?
I knew that this was meant for me

I heard little children were supposed to sleep tight
That's why I drank a fifth of vodka one night
My parents got frantic, didn't know what to do
But I saw some crazy scenes before I came to
Now do you think I was crazy?
I may have been only three but I was swingin'

They all laughed at A. Graham Bell
They all laughed at Edison and also at Einstein
So why should I feel sorry if they just couldn't understand
The reasoning and the logic that went on in my head?
I had a brain, it was insane
So I just let them laugh at me
When I refused to ride on all the double decker buses
All because there was no driver on the top

My analyst told me that I was right out of my head
The way he described it, he said I'd be better dead than live
I didn't listen to his jive
I knew all along he was all wrong
And I knew that he thought I was crazy but I'm not
Oh no

My analyst told me that I was right out of my head
But I said, Dear doctor, I think that it's you instead
'Cause I have got a thing that's unique and new
It proves that I'll have the last laugh on you
'Cause instead of one head, I got two
And you know two heads are better than one

King Pleasure Sings/Annie Ross Sings, 1952

Lord Buckley
(1906–1960)

Richard Myrle Buckley had a long career as a comic before styling himself Lord, an "immaculately hip aristocrat" monologist. Mixing jive talk with grandiloquence, he seamlessly blended classical rhetoric, stand-up schtick, scat, and Surrealism into a language he called "hipsemantics." Lord Buckley looked the part with his waxed moustache, pith helmet, and proper evening clothes. His record albums and live performances won him a devoted following in the fifties —City Lights published a collection of his monologues as Hiparama of the Classics—*but Buckley's penchant for marijuana (sometimes smoked onstage) led to revocation of his cabaret card by New York's police commissioner in 1960. He died of a stroke shortly thereafter, but his monologues live on. "The Naz," from 1952, is one of the Lord's earliest recordings; its subject is another Lord, Jesus of Nazareth.*

The Naz

in modern reverence

LOOK AT all you Cats and Kitties out there! Whippin' and wailin' and jumpin' up and down and suckin' up all that fine juice and pattin' each other on the back and Hippin' each other who the greatest Cat in the world is! Mr. Melanencoff, Mr. Dalencoff and Mr. Zelencoff and all them Coffs, and Mr. Eisenhower, Mr. Woosenwiser, Mr. Weesenwooser and all them Woosers, Mr. Woodhill and Mr. Beachill and Mr. Churchill and all them Hills, Gonna' get you straight! If they can't get you straight, they know a Cat, that knows a Cat, that'll Straighten you!

But, I'm gonna' put a Cat on you, who was the Sweetest, Grooviest, Strongest, Wailinest, Swinginest, Jumpinest most far out Cat that ever Stomped on this Sweet Green Sphere, and they called this here Cat, THE NAZ, that was the Cat's name.

He was a carpenter kitty. Now the Naz, was the kind of a Cat that came on so cool and so wild and so groovy and so *WITH IT*, that when he laid it *down WHAM!* It stayed there! Naturally, all the rest of the Cats say:

"Dig what this Cat is puttin' down! Man! Look at that Cat Blow!"

"Let the Cat Go!"

"Hey, there, Get out of the way, don't bug me lad, Get off my back, I'm tryin' to dig what the Cat's sayin' Jack, Cool!"

They're Pushin' The Naz! 'Cause they wanted to dig his Lick, you see, Dig his Miracle Lick!

So the Naz say, "Wait a minute Babies, tell you what I'm gonna do, I ain't gonna take two, four, six or eight of you Cats, but I'm gonna take all twelve of you Studs and Straighten You All at the same time. You look like pretty Hip Cats, You buddy with me!"

So the Naz and his Buddies was goofin' off down the boulevard one day, and they run into a little Cat with a bent frame. So the Naz look at the little Cat with the bent frame and he say:

"What's de matter wid you baby?"

And the little Cat with the bent frame say, "My frame is bent, Naz. It's been bent, from in front!!!"

So the Naz looked at the little Cat wid the bent frame, and he put the golden eyes of love on this here little Kitty and he looked right down into the windows of the little Cat's soul, and he said to the little Cat, he say:

"*STRAIGHTEN!!*"

Up, Zoom-Boom! The Cat went up straighter than an arrow and everybody Jumpin' Up and Down and they say:

"Look What The Naz Put On That Boy. You Dug Him Before, *Dig Him Now!!*"

Now you see the Naz is comin' on so strong and so fine and so Great. They is talkin' about when he's gonna appear next. What did he do there? How he swung thru the land with great ribbons of love sounds. How he laid down the truth and made it live, just like a jumpin' garden of king size roses. How he stomped into the money changin' Court and kicked the short change all over the place. Knocked the corners off the Squares! How he put the truth down once for the Cat, he dug it, didn't dig it; put it down twice, the Cat dug it didn't dig it; Put it down the third time, *WHAM*, the Cat *DUG IT!* WALKED AWAY WITH HIS EYES, BULGING, Bumping into Everybody!

The Naz is comin' on so fine and so strong they is pullin' on his coat-tail. Wanting him to sign the autograph, they want him to do this gig here, they want him do that gig there, play the radio do the video and all the JAZZ, he can't make all that Jazz, Like I explained to you, 'cause he's a carpenter Kitty and he's got his own lick. But when he knows he should show to blow and cannot Go 'cause, he's got some strain on him, Straightenin' out the Squares, he sends a couple of these Cats that he's Hippin'!

So came a little sixty cent gig one day and the Naz was in a bind so he put it on a couple of his Buddy-Cats.

"Say Boys, will you straighten that out for me?"

"Take it off you wig Naz, we've got it covered!"

And they swung out to straighten this gig for The Naz when they run into a little olde twenty cent pool of water. And when they got in the middle of the pool in the boat, All of a Sudden, WHAM — BOOM!! The Storm is Stormin' and the Lightin' Flashin' and the Thunder Roarin' and the boat goin' up and down and these poo' cats figurin' every minute gonna be the *Last!* When all of a sudden! One Cat look up and *Here Comes The Naz, Stompin'!* anyone you ever seen, Right Across the Water—*Stompin'!*

There was a little Cat on board, I thank his name was Jude and he yelled:

"Hey Naz, Can I make it out there withcha?"

And the Naz say, "*MAKE IT JUDE!*"

And ole Jude went stompin' off that boat, took about four steps, dropped his hole card and ZOOT, Naz had to stash him back on board again. So The Naz look at these Kitties and he say:

"What's the matter with you Babies now? What's goin' on here boys? What's takin' place? You knockin' on that S.O.S. bell pretty hard! You're gonna bend that bell knockin' on it like that!"

One Cat say, "What seems to be the trouble? Can't you see the Storm Stormin' and the Lightin' Flashin' and the Thunder Roarin' and the waves flippin'?"

And The Naz say, "I told you to stay COOL, didn't I?" (To stay cool means to Believe in the Magic Power of Love.)

Now the fame of The Naz is jumpin'! How he lays it down the same way every day, how he Hipped the Cats to fo-give and fo-get and how he say:

"Dig, and Thou Shalt be Dug!"

"Drag Not, and Thou Shalt not be Drug!"

And many other Hip truths! The Beauty Sparks shootin' out the grapevine are sixty-five feet long till there is now Five Thousand Cats and Kitties in the Naz's little home town, where the Cat Live, Lookin' to get *STRAIGHT!* Well, The Naz know he kain't straighten them there, it's too small a place, don't want to hang everybody up, so nobody can make it!

So The Naz back away a little bit and he looked at the Cats and Kitties and a great Love Look came on his face and he say with the bird bell tones in his voice:

"Come on Babies, let's cut on out down the pike.'

And there went The Naz with his Five Thousand Cats and Kitties behind him stompin' up a great necklace of beauty. Flocks of Blue Birds were flyin' along his side riffin' up a high orchestration of Bird Love. And it's brother to brother, sister to sister, and a great river of love is chargin' and super chargin' thru these Cats and Kitties, and The Naz is a talkin' and a swingin' with:

"How pretty the hour, how pretty the flower, how pretty you, how pretty he, how pretty she, how pretty the tree!"

Naz had them Love Eyes, he wanted everybody to see thru his Eyes, to Pin the Golden Rosetta of Reality. And they is havin' such a Wailin', Swingin' Glorianna style stompin' hike that before you know it, it was Scoffin' Time and these poo' Cats is Forty miles out of town and ain't nobody got the first biscuit. Well, The Naz look at all the Cats and Kitties kickin' and sand and he say:

"You Hongry, Ain't Ya, Babies?"

And one tall Cat say, "Yea, Naz, we were so busy diggin' what you puttin' down, that we didn't *pre-pare*; Naz, we Goofed!"

The Naz say, "Well, We got to take it easy here, We wouldn't want to go ahead and order up sumpin' you might not like, would We?"

And the tall Cat, kickin' the sand say, Sweet Double Hippness, You put it Down, and we'll pick it Up!"

So The Naz backed away a little bit and his head turned slowly to one side and then to the other, diggin' all these Cats and Kitties and he laid down a Sound of Great Love:

"*Oh, Sweet Swingin' Flowers of the Field!*"

And they answered, "*Oh, Great Singular Non-Stop Singular Sound Of Beauty!*"

And he said, "*Stomp Upon the Terra!*" And they *HIT IT!!!!!*

And he said, "*Straighten your Miracle, The Body!*" And the Body *WENT UP!!*

"*Lift Your Glorious Arms to Heaven!*" and he said, "Higher!" And they went *Higher!!*

And he said, "*Lift Your Love Eyes To The Skies!*" And they *Did!!*

And he said, "*Widen Your Eyes and Look HARDER!*" And they *Did!!*

And the Naz say, "*DIG INFINITE!!!*" And they *DUG IT!!*

And When they did, WHAMMMMM!! Just then a Great flash of Lightin' and a Roll of Thunder *HIT* the Scene! And the Cats looked down and in one hand was a Great bit of swingin, juicy stuffed Smoked Fish, and in the other a big thick gone loaf of that honey tastin' ever-lovin', good, groovey Home-lovin' made Bread! Why, these poo' Cats *FLIPPED!!!*

The Naz Never Did Nothin' Simple.

When He Laid It, *HE LAID IT!!*

1952; *Hiparama of the Classics*, 1960

King Pleasure
(1922–1981)

Born Clarence Beeks in Oakdale, Tennessee, King Pleasure moved to New York City where he was a part of the bebop scene, first as a fan, then as a performer. He became popular for covering "Moody's Mood for Love," a vocalese performance by singer Eddie Jefferson based on James Moody's saxophone solo on "I'm in the Mood for Love." "Parker's Mood" followed in 1954, with lyrics to Charlie Parker's sax solo on his 1948 recording. The words seem prophetic, as Parker died the next year and the graffiti BIRD LIVES soon became prevalent in Greenwich Village and other hip enclaves.

Parker's Mood

Come with me
If you want to go to Kansas City.

I'm feeling lowdown and blue,
My heart's full of sorrow.
Don't hardly know what to do,
Where will I be tomorrow?

Going to Kansas City,
Wanna go too?
No, you can't make it with me.
Going to Kansas City,
Sorry that I can't take you.

When you see me coming
Raise your window high.
When you see me leaving, baby,
Hang your head and cry.

I'm afraid there's nothing in this cream, this dreamy town
A honky tonky monkey woman can do.
She'd only bring herself down.

So long everybody,
The time has come
And I must leave you
So if I don't ever see your smiling face again
Make a promise you'll remember
Like a Christmas day in December
That I told you all through thick and thin
On up until the end
Parker's been your friend.

Don't hang your head
When you see those six pretty horses pulling me.
Put a twenty dollar silver piece on my watch-chain
Look at the smile on my face
And sing a little song
To let the world know I'm really free.
Don't cry for me
'Cause I'm going to Kansas City.

Come with me
If you want to go to Kansas City.

1954

Diane di Prima
(b. 1934)

A Brooklynite and granddaughter of an Italian anarchist, Diane di Prima became a Beat poet as a teenager. Her first book, This Kind of Bird Flies Backward, *was published when she was twenty-four. She edited* The Floating Bear, *a newsletter of the new writing, with LeRoi Jones, and founded the Poets Press and the New York Poets Theatre. After an interval at Timothy Leary's psychedelic commune at Millbrook, New York, she relocated to San Francisco where she has been active ever since, working with the Diggers in the late sixties, studying Buddhism, helping found the San Francisco Institute of Magical and Healing Arts, publishing the poem-cycle* Loba *and the autobiography* Recollections of My Life as a Woman, *and working as a photographer and visual artist. This selection from di Prima's* Memoirs of a Beatnik *(1969) describes a time when there was a genuine underground and an alternative consciousness, and evokes an epiphany of generational shift—one of those turning points that often get lost in the shuffle of official history.*

from *Memoirs of a Beatnik*

MEANWHILE, in the outside world everything was changing faster and more than we realized. We thought we were doing the same things we'd always done because the changes happened in slow motion, but happen they did, and when we looked out the window again we were someplace else.

We had run through a variety of aesthetic games: little magazines for which we couldn't raise any bread, theatre projects in gigantic lofts which never materialized, a visit by me and Susan to Ezra Pound, who wanted us single-handed to change the nature of the programming on nationwide television. Leslie choreographed and produced his first dance recital; Pete's fantasy paintings became eight feet wide

118

and gloomier; I put together *This Kind of Bird Flies Backward*, my first book of poems, and Pete and Leslie solemnly assured me that it could not be published because no one would understand a word of the street slang. Don wasn't accepted at Actor's Studio and made a movie instead. Most of his friends *were* accepted and stopped coming to see us. Miles Davis moved away from Tenth Avenue; we no longer ran into him at three in the afternoon hailing a taxi in his dark glasses, looking as if he had just gotten up.

We lived through the horror of the 1956 election as we had lived through the horror of the Rosenberg executions and the Hungarian revolution: paranoid, glued to the radio, and talking endlessly of where we could possibly go into exile. Every inch of walls and floor in the apartment was covered with murals and wise sayings: "The unicorns shall inherit the earth." "Sacrifice everything to the clean line." "Think no twisty thoughts." Etc., etc. Wilhelm Reich was in federal prison.

The first fallout terror had finally struck, and a group of people were buying land in Montana to construct a city under a lead dome. In New York, the beginnings of neo-fascist city planning were stirring, and the entire area north of our pad was slated for destruction, to make way for what was to become Lincoln Center. The house next door to us, which had been empty for twenty-eight years, and had functioned as our own private garbage dump for as long as we lived there, was suddenly torn down, leaving a number of bums homeless and scattering thousands of rats—most of them into our walls.

Most of the more outrageous gay bars had been closed, and people cruised Central Park West more cautiously: there were many plain-clothes busts. There were more and more drugs available: cocaine and opium, as well as the ubiquitous heroin, but the hallucinogens hadn't hit the scene as yet. The affluent post-Korean-war society was settling down to a grimmer, more long-term ugliness. At that moment, there really seemed to be no way out.

As far as we knew, there was only a small handful of us—perhaps forty or fifty in the city—who knew what we knew: who raced about in Levis and work shirts, made art, smoked dope, dug the new jazz, and spoke a bastardization of the black argot. We surmised that there might be another fifty living in San Francisco, and perhaps a hundred more scattered throughout the country: Chicago, New Orleans, etc., but our isolation was total and impenetrable, and we did not try to communicate with even this small handful of our confreres. Our chief concern was to keep our integrity (much time and energy went into defining the concept of the "sellout") and to keep our cool: a hard, clean edge and definition in the midst of the terrifying indifference and sentimentality around us—"media mush." We looked to each other for comfort, for praise, for love, and shut out the rest of the world.

THEN ONE evening—it was an evening like many others, there were some twelve or fourteen people eating supper, including Pete and Don and some Studio people, Betty McPeters and her entourage, people were milling about, drinking wine, talking emphatically in small groups while Beatrice Harmon and I were getting the meal together—the priestly ex-book-thief arrived and thrust a small black and white book into my hand, saying, "I think this might interest you." I took it and flipped it open idly, still intent on dishing out beef stew, and found myself in the middle of *Howl* by Allen Ginsberg. Put down the ladle and turned to the beginning and was caught up immediately in that sad, powerful opening: "I saw the best minds of my generation destroyed by madness . . ."

I was too turned on to concern myself with the stew. I handed it over to Beatrice and, without even thanking Bradley, walked out the front door with his new book. Walked the few blocks to the pier on Sixtieth Street and sat down by the Hudson River to read and to come to terms with what was happening. The phrase "breaking ground" kept coming into my head. I knew that this Allen Ginsberg, whoever he was, had broken ground for all of us—all few hundreds of us—simply by getting this published. I had no idea yet what that meant, how far it would take us.

The poem put a certain heaviness in me, too. It followed that if there was one Allen there must be more, other people besides my few buddies writing what they spoke, what they heard, living, however obscurely and shamefully, what they knew, hiding out here and there as we were—and now, suddenly, about to speak out. For I sensed that Allen was only, could only be, the vanguard of a much larger thing. All the people who, like me, had hidden and skulked, writing down what they knew for a small handful of friends—and even those friends claiming it "couldn't be published"—waiting with only a slight bitterness for the thing to end, for man's era to draw to a close in a blaze of radiation—all these would now step forward and say their piece. Not many would hear them, but they would, finally, hear each other. I was about to meet my brothers and sisters.

We had come of age. I was frightened and a little sad. I already clung instinctively to the easy, unselfconscious Bohemianism we had maintained at the pad, our unspoken sense that we were alone in a strange world, a sense that kept us proud and bound to each other. But for the moment regret for what we might be losing was buried under a sweeping sense of exhilaration, of glee; someone was speaking for all of us, and the poem was good. I was high and delighted. I made my way back to the house and to supper, and we read *Howl* together, I read it aloud to everyone. A new era had begun.

MEANWHILE THE changes started going down around us thicker and heavier than ever—so that even we couldn't help noticing them. The first thing I noticed, and it gave me quite a jolt, was that the pad was going away, was quite used up. Nothing in particular happened, but it just began to have that air about it, that feeling when you unlocked the door and walked in, of a place that hadn't been lived in for some time, where the air had not been stirred. Places do that, I've noticed. They turn round without warning, turn in on themselves, and suddenly it's like living in a morgue, or a refrigerator; the vital impulse that made a hearth, a living center of some sort, has changed directions like an ocean current, and that particular island is no longer in its path. You can tell because even in the height of summer there's a chill in the air, a something that gets into your bones.

The rats were part of it. They had moved in, *en masse*, from the demolished building next door, and they scampered and played about the kitchen at night, making quite a racket. They came in through a hole under the kitchen sink, and we covered it again and again with pieces of tin, till finally there was nothing left to nail the tin to but more tin, and I gave up. But it did often give me a deep shudder as of awe to awaken in the morning and find that a whole loaf of bread in its plastic bag had been carried halfway across the room, or to find, half an inch long, the neat little claw prints of one of my furry roommates in the congealed fat of yesterday's roast.

O'Reilley had already split with our scene more or less completely. Occasionally she did stop down for a night or two, like gingerly putting one toe into some rather scummy water, and then withdrew to the safety and order of her new East Side flat. Don, having completed his movie, decided to take himself seriously and set out for Hollywood. And Pete fell ill, as I have since learned that he does every three or four years: fell seriously, heavily ill with pneumonia and had to be shipped home to Kew Garden Hills in a taxi at his father's expense while his fever raged. The disease itself abated rather quickly, but the weakness remained, and Pete stayed in the comparative luxury of his family's house, eating minute steaks and resting.

It may have been our large rat population that drove Leslie out into the world, but I think it was simply growing pains: he suddenly felt old enough to have a pad of his own, and he set out to get one. He found a loft on Prince Street in a part of the Village that had just opened up. The loft was the top floor of three. They were open to each other at staircase and hall, and they all shared one john. Previous tenants had installed a bathtub and hot water heater on the second floor and Leslie's present downstairs neighbor had just added a small washbasin which also served for everyone's dishes. Leslie had a two-burner hotplate on top of a small, rickety office frig, and a table with three wobbly chairs. All the water came from downstairs and was carted up in gallon wine jugs. It was dumped out the window when one didn't feel like making the trip down to the second-floor john. No one worried about sprinkler systems, exits, or other such regulations; living in lofts was illegal, and everyone who could afford it did it. The light and space in Leslie's place was lovely: huge front room like a big barn, green plants everywhere. White curtains that were probably just sheets let in the play of light. Almost equally large back room faced north on paved courtyard and endless possibilities of rooftops. And kitchen off to one side. It was the most luxurious (and most expensive) apartment that any of us had attempted yet. It cost eighty dollars a month and we all admired Leslie for braving such a rent.

With the pad, Leslie took on a roommate, a long, lanky, funny-looking boy named Benny Hudson. Benny's ears stuck out, and he had a herringbone coat. He smelled of soap and earnestness and other Midwestern virtues, but he had a job and could pay half of the rent—all of it in emergencies—so here he was. He and Leslie were lovers, of sorts. That is, they were making it, and Benny was in love.

As for me, I still clung, out of sentiment and attachment, to the uptown pad. It was my home base, though I slept there seldom now. I had stopped paying rent several months before, but hung on, muttering "Health Department" at the landlord, whenever he muttered "Eviction" at me. We were at an impasse.

Since I wasn't paying any more rent, the landlord wasn't making any more repairs, which meant that when the local gang broke the windows they stayed broken, and finally nearly all of them were. The place was breezy, but it was getting warm again, and so it didn't matter. Then the lights and gas went off; I took to eating out, eating and bathing in other people's houses, and reading by candlelight, which was scary because of the rats. I didn't relish the thought of meeting a rat as big as a cat by candlelight in my kitchen. I began to look for someplace else to live.

Memoirs of a Beatnik, 1969; second edition, 1988

Jack Kerouac
(1922–1969)

Movie-star handsome and con-man charming, Jack Kerouac was a romantic and contradictory literary pop star. He made a movement, or at least named it; he set out its ground rules and then broke them. Kerouac changed the novel forever, speed-typing madly on rolls of paper. He practiced poetry, fusing haikus with bop and blues. After On the Road *came out in 1957 and made him overnight into the emblem of a generation, there was no turning back. The underground had gone mainstream, and Kerouac lost his footing in the swirl of adulation, media attention, and self-indulgence. He would be dead at forty-seven, a burned-out hulk—but what a fire he left behind him. Here's one of several attempts he made to explain the Beat Generation and his role as its prime mover.*

The Origins of the Beat Generation

THIS ARTICLE necessarily'll have to be about myself. I'm going all out.

That nutty picture of me on the cover of *On the Road* results from the fact that I had just gotten down from a high mountain where I'd been for two months completely alone and usually I was in the habit of combing my hair of course because you have to get rides on the highway and all that and you usually want girls to look at you as though you were a man and not a wild beast but my poet friend Gregory Corso opened his shirt and took out a silver crucifix that was hanging from a chain and said "Wear this and wear it outside your shirt and don't comb your hair!" so I spent several days around San Francisco going around with him and others like that, to parties, arties, parts, jam sessions, bars, poetry readings, churches, walking talking poetry in the streets, walking talking God in the streets (and at one point a strange gang of hoodlums got mad and said "What right does he got to wear that?" and my own gang of musicians and poets told them to cool it) and finally on the third day *Mademoiselle* magazine wanted to take pictures of us all so I posed just like that, wild hair, crucifix, and all, with Gregory Corso, Allen Ginsberg and Phil Whalen, and the only publication which later did not erase the crucifix from my breast (from that plaid sleeveless cotton shirt-front) was *The New York Times*, therefore *The New York Times* is as beat as I am, and I'm glad I've got a friend. I mean it sincerely, God bless *The New York Times* for not erasing the crucifix from my picture as though it was something distasteful. As a matter of fact, who's *really* beat around here, I mean if you wanta talk of Beat as "beat down" the people who erased the crucifix are really the "beat down" ones and not *The New York Times*, myself, and Gregory Corso the poet. I am not ashamed to wear the crucifix of my Lord. It is because I am Beat, that is, I believe in beatitude and that God so loved the world that he gave his only begotten son to it. I am sure no priest would've condemned me for wearing the crucifix outside my shirt everywhere and *no matter where* I went, even to have my picture taken by *Mademoiselle*. So you people don't believe in God. So you're all big smart know-it-all Marxists and Freudians, hey? Why don't you come back in a million years and tell me all about it, angels?

Recently Ben Hecht said to me on TV "Why are you afraid to speak out your mind, what's wrong with this country, what is everybody afraid of?" Was he talking to me? And all he wanted me to do was speak out my mind *against* people, he sneeringly brought up Dulles, Eisenhower, the Pope, all kinds of people like that habitually he would sneer at with Drew Pearson, *against* the world he wanted, this is his idea of freedom, he calls it freedom. Who knows, my God, but that the universe is not one vast sea of compassion actually, the veritable holy honey, beneath all this show of personality and cruelty. In fact who knows but that it isn't the solitude of the oneness of the essence of everything, the solitude of the actual oneness of the unbornness of the unborn essence of everything, nay the true pure foreverhood, that big blank potential that can ray forth anything it wants from its pure store, that blazing bliss, *Mattivajrakaruna* the Transcendental Diamond Compassion! No, I want to speak *for* things, for the crucifix I speak out, for the Star of Israel I speak out, for the divinest man who ever lived who was a German (Bach) I speak out, for sweet Mohammed I speak out, for Buddha I speak out, for Lao-tse and Chuang-tse I speak out, for D. T. Suzuki I speak out . . . why should I attack what I love out of life. This is Beat. Live your lives out? Naw, *love* your lives out. When they come and stone you at least you won't have a glass house, just your glassy flesh.

That wild eager picture of me on the cover of *On the Road* where I look so Beat goes back much further than 1948 when John Clellon Holmes (author of *Go* and *The Horn*) and I were sitting around trying to think up the meaning of the Lost Generation and the subsequent Existentialism and I said "You know, this is really a beat generation" and he leapt up and said "That's it, that's right!" It goes back to the 1880s when my grandfather Jean-Baptiste Kerouac used to go out on the porch in big thunderstorms and swing his kerosene lamp at the lightning and yell "Go ahead, go, if you're more powerful than I am strike me and put the light out!" while the mother and the children cowered in the kitchen. And the light never went out. Maybe since I'm supposed to be the spokesman of the Beat Generation (I *am* the originator of the term, and around it the term and the generation have taken shape) it should be pointed out that all this "Beat" guts therefore goes back to my ancestors who were Bretons who were the most independent group of nobles in all old Europe and kept fighting Latin France to the last wall (although a big blond bosun on a merchant ship snorted when I told him my ancestors were Bretons in Cornwall, Brittany, "Why, we Wikings used to swoop down and steal your nets!") Breton, Wiking, Irishman, Indian, madboy, it doesn't make any difference, there is no doubt about the Beat Generation, at least the core of it, being a swinging group of new American men intent on joy . . . Irresponsibility? Who wouldn't help a dying man on an empty road? No and the Beat Generation goes back to the wild parties my father used to have at home in the 1920s and 1930s in New

England that were so fantastically loud nobody could sleep for blocks around and when the cops came they always had a drink. It goes back to the wild and raving childhood of playing the Shadow under windswept trees of New England's gleeful autumn, and the howl of the Moon Man on the sandbank until we caught him in a tree (he was an "older" guy of 15), the maniacal laugh of certain neighborhood madboys, the furious humor of whole gangs playing basketball till long after dark in the park, it goes back to those crazy days before World War II when teenagers drank beer on Friday nights at Lake ballrooms and worked off their hangovers playing baseball on Saturday afternoon followed by a dive in the brook—and our fathers wore straw hats like W. C. Fields. It goes back to the completely senseless babble of the Three Stooges, the ravings of the Marx Brothers (the tenderness of Angel Harpo at harp, too).

It goes back to the inky ditties of old cartoons (Krazy Kat with the irrational brick)—to Laurel and Hardy in the Foreign Legion—to Count Dracula and his *smile* to Count Dracula shivering and hissing back before the Cross—to the Golem horrifying the persecutors of the Ghetto–to the quiet sage in a movie about India, unconcerned about the plot—to the giggling old Tao Chinaman trotting down the sidewalk of old Clark Gable Shanghai—to the holy old Arab warning the hotbloods that Ramadan is near. To the Werewolf of London a distinguished doctor in his velour smoking jacket smoking his pipe over a lamplit tome on botany and suddenly hairs grown on his hands, his cat hisses, and he slips out into the night with a cape and a slanty cap like the caps of people in breadlines—to Lamont Cranston so cool and sure suddenly becoming the frantic Shadow going mwee hee hee ha ha in the alleys of New York imagination. To Popeye the sailor and the Sea Hag and the meaty gunwales of boats, to Cap'n Easy and Wash Tubbs screaming with ecstasy over canned peaches on a cannibal isle, to Wimpy looking X-eyed for a juicy hamburger such as they make no more. To Jiggs ducking before a household of furniture flying through the air, to Jiggs and the boys at the bar and the corned beef and cabbage of old woodfence noons—to King Kong his eyes looking into the hotel window with tender huge love for Fay Wray—

nay, to Bruce Cabot in mate's cap leaning over the rail of a fogbound ship saying "Come aboard." It goes back to when grapefruits were thrown at crooners and harvestworkers at bar-rails slapped burlesque queens on the rump. To when fathers took their sons to the Twi League game. To the days of Babe Callahan on the waterfront, Dick Barthelmess camping under a London streetlamp. To dear old Basil Rathbone looking for the Hound of the Baskervilles (a dog big as the Gray Wolf who will destroy Odin)—to dear old bleary Doctor Watson with a brandy in his hand. To Joan Crawford her raw shanks in the fog, in striped blouse smoking a cigarette at sticky lips in the door of the waterfront dive. To train whistles of steam engines out above the moony pines. To Maw and Paw in the Model A clanking on to get a job in California selling used cars making a whole lotta money. To the glee of America, the honesty of America, the honesty of oldtime grafters in straw hats as well as the honesty of old time waiters in line at the Brooklyn Bridge in *Winterset*, the funny spitelessness of old bigfisted America like Big Boy Williams saying "Hoo? Hee? Huh?" in a movie about Mack Trucks and slidingdoor lunchcarts. To Clark Gable, his certain smile, his confident leer. Like my grandfather this America was invested with wild selfbelieving individuality and this had begun to disappear around the end of World War II with so many great guys dead (I can think of half a dozen from my own boyhood groups) when suddenly it began to emerge again, the hipsters began to appear gliding around saying "Crazy, man."

When I first saw the hipsters creeping around Times Square in 1944 I didn't like them either. One of them, Huncke of Chicago, came up to me and said "Man, I'm beat." I knew right away what he meant somehow. At that time I still didn't like bop which was then being introduced by Bird Parker and Dizzy Gillespie and Bags Jackson (on vibes), the last of the great swing musicians was Don Byas who went to Spain right after, but then I began . . . but earlier I'd dug all my jazz in the old Minton Playhouse (Lester Young, Ben Webster, Joey Guy, Charlie Christian, others) and when I first heard Bird and Diz in the Three Deuces I knew they were serious musicians playing a goofy new sound and didn't care what I thought, or what my friend Seymour thought. In fact I was leaning against the bar with a beer when Dizzy came over for a glass of water from the bartender, put himself right against me and reached both arms around both sides of my head to get the glass and danced away, as though knowing I'd be singing about him someday, or that one of his arrangements would be named after me someday by some goofy circumstance. Charlie Parker was spoken of in Harlem as the greatest new musician since Chu Berry and Louis Armstrong.

Anyway, the hipsters, whose music was bop, they looked like criminals but they kept talking about the same things I liked, long outlines of personal experience and vision, nightlong confessions full of hope that had become illicit and repressed by War, stirrings, rumblings of a new soul (that same old human soul). And so Huncke appeared to us and said "I'm beat" with radiant light shining out of his despairing eyes . . . a word perhaps brought from some midwest carnival or junk cafeteria. It was a new language, actually spade (Negro) jargon but you soon learned it, like "hung up" couldn't be a more economical term to mean so many things. Some of these hipsters were raving mad and talked continually. It was jazzy. Symphony Sid's all-night modern jazz and bop show was always on. By 1948 it began to take shape. That was a wild vibrating year when a group of us would walk down the street and yell hello and even stop and talk to anybody that gave us a friendly look. The hipsters had eyes. That was the year I saw Montgomery Clift, unshaven, wearing a sloppy jacket, slouching down Madison Avenue with a companion. It was the year I saw Charley Bird Parker strolling down Eighth Avenue in a black turtleneck sweater with Babs Gonzales and a beautiful girl.

By 1948 the hipsters, or beatsters, were divided into cool and hot. Much of the misunderstanding about hipsters and the Beat Generation in general today derives from the fact that there are two distinct styles of hipsterism: the cool today is your bearded laconic sage, or schlerm, before a hardly touched beer in a beatnik dive, whose speech is low and unfriendly, whose girls say nothing and wear black: the "hot" today is the crazy talkative shining eyed (often innocent and openhearted) nut who runs from bar to bar, pad to pad looking for everybody, shouting, restless, lushy, trying to "make it" with the subterranean beatniks who ignore him. Most Beat Generation artists belong to the hot school, naturally since that hard gemlike flame needs a little heat. In many cases the mixture is 50–50. It was a hot hipster like myself who finally cooled it in Buddhist meditation, though when I go in a jazz joint I still feel like yelling "Blow baby blow!" to the musicians though nowadays I'd get 86d for this. In 1948 the "hot hipsters" were racing around in cars like in *On the Road* looking for wild bawling jazz like Willis Jackson or Lucky Thompson (the early) or Chubby Jackson's big band while the "cool hipsters" cooled it in dead silence before formal and excellent musical groups like Lennie Tristano or Miles Davis. It's still just about the same, except that it has begun to grow into a national generation and the name "Beat" has stuck (though all hipsters hate the word).

The word "beat" originally meant poor, down and out, deadbeat, on the bum, sad, sleeping in subways. Now that the word is belonging officially it is being made to stretch to include people who do not sleep in subways but have a certain new gesture, or attitude, which I can only describe as a new *more*. "Beat Generation" has simply become the slogan or label for a revolution in manners in America. Marlon Brando was not really first to portray it on the screen. Dane Clark with his pinched Dostoievskyan face and Brooklyn accent, and of course Garfield, were first. The private eyes were Beat, if you will recall. Bogart. Lorre was Beat. In *M*, Peter Lorre started a whole revival, I mean the slouchy street walk.

I wrote *On the Road* in three weeks in the beautiful month of May 1941 while living in the Chelsea district of lower West Side Manhattan, on a 100-foot roll and put the Beat Generation in words in there, saying at the point where I am taking part in a wild kind of collegiate party with a bunch of kinds in an abandoned miner's shack "These kids are great but where are Dean Moriarty and Carlo Marx? Oh well I guess they wouldn't belong in this gang, they're too *dark*, too strange, too subterranean and I am slowly beginning to join a new kind of *beat* generation." The manuscript of *Road* was turned down on the grounds that it would displease the sales manager of my publisher at that time, though the editor, a very intelligent man, said "Jack this is just like Dostoievsky, but what can I do at this time?" It was too early. So for the next six years I was a bum, a brakeman, a seaman, a panhandler, a pseudo-Indian in Mexico, anything and everything, and went on writing because my hero was Goethe and I believed in art and hoped some day to write the third part of *Faust*, which I have done in *Doctor Sax*. Then in 1952 an article was published in *The New York Times* Sunday magazine saying, the headline, "'This is a Beat Generation'" (in quotes like that) and in the article it said that I had come up with the term first "when the face was harder to recognize," the face of the generation. After that there was some talk of the Beat Generation but in 1955 I published an excerpt from *Road* (melling it with parts of *Visions of Neal*) under the pseudonym "Jean-Louis," it was entitled *Jazz of the Beat Generation* and was copyrighted as being an excerpt from a novel-in-progress entitled *Beat Generation* (which I later changed to *On the Road* at the insistence of my new editor) and so then the term moved a little faster. The term and the cats. Everywhere began to appear strange hepcats and even college kids went around hep and cool and using the terms I'd heard on Times Square in the early Forties, it was growing somehow. But when the publishers finally took a dare and published *On the Road* in 1957 it burst open, it mushroomed, everybody began yelling about a Beat Generation. I was being interviewed everywhere I went for "what I meant" by such a thing. People began to call themselves beatniks, beats, jazzniks, bopniks, bugniks and finally I was called the "avatar" of all this.

Yet it was as a Catholic, it was not at the insistence of any of these "niks" and certainly not with their approval either, that I went one afternoon to the church of my childhood (one of them), Ste. Jeanne d'Arc in Lowell, Mass., and suddenly with tears in my eyes and had a vision of what I must have really meant with "Beat" anyhow when I heard the holy silence in the church (I was the only one in there, it was five P.M., dogs were barking outside, children yelling, the fall leaves, the candles were flickering alone just for me), the vision of the word Beat as being to mean beatific . . . There's the priest preaching on Sunday morning, all of a sudden through a side door of the church comes a group of Beat Generation characters in strapped raincoats like the I.R.A. coming in silently to "dig" the religion . . . I knew it then.

But this was 1954, so then what horror I felt in 1957 and later in 1958 naturally to suddenly see "Beat" being taken up by everybody, press and TV and Hollywood borscht circuit to include the "juvenile delinquency" shot and the horrors of a mad teeming billyclub New York and L.A. and they began to call *that* Beat, *that* beatific . . . bunch of fools marching against the San Francisco Giants protesting baseball, as if (now) in my name and I, my childhood ambition to be a big league baseball star hitter like Ted Williams so that when Bobby Thomson hit that homerun in 1951 I trembled with joy and couldn't get over it for days and wrote poems about how it is possible for the human spirit to win after all! Or, when a murder, a routine murder took place in North Beach, they labeled it a Beat Generation slaying although in my childhood I'd been famous as an eccentric in my block for stopping the younger kids from throwing rocks at the squirrels, for stopping them from frying snakes in cans or trying to blow up frogs with straws. Because my brother had died at the age of nine, his name was Gerard Kerouac, and he'd told me "Ti Jean never hurt any living being, all living beings whether it's just a little cat or squirrel or whatever, all, are going to heaven straight into God's snowy arms so never hurt anything and if you see anybody hurt anything stop them as best you can" and when he died a file of gloomy nuns in black from St. Louis de France parish had filed (1926) to his deathbed to hear his last words about Heaven. And my father too, Leo, had never lifted a hand to punish me, or to punish the little pets in our house, and this teaching was delivered to me by the men in my house and I have never had anything to do with violence, hatred, cruelty, and all that horrible nonsense which, nevertheless, because God is gracious beyond all human imagining, he will forgive in the long end . . . that million years I'm asking about you, America.

And so now they have beatnik routines on TV, starting with satires about girls in black and fellows in jeans with snap-knives and sweatshirts and swastikas tattooed under their armpits, it will come to respectable m.c.s of spectaculars coming out nattily attired in Brooks Brothers jean-type tailoring and sweater-type pull-ons, in other words, it's a simple change in fashion and manners, just a history crust—like from the Age of Reason, from old Voltaire in a chair to romantic Chatterton in the moonlight—from Teddy Roosevelt to Scott Fitzgerald . . . So there's nothing to get excited about. Beat comes out, actually, of old American whoopee and it will only change a few dresses and pants and make chairs useless in the livingroom and pretty soon we'll have Beat Secretaries of State and there will be instituted new tinsels, in fact new reasons for malice and new reasons for virtue and new reasons for forgiveness . . .

But yet, but yet, woe, woe unto those who think that the Beat Generation means crime, delinquency, immorality, amorality . . . woe unto those who attack it on the grounds that they simply don't understand history and the yearnings of human souls . . . woe unto those who don't realize that America must, will, is, changing now, for the better I say. Woe unto those who believe in the atom bomb, who believe in hating mothers and fathers, who deny the most important of the Ten Commandments, woe unto those (though) who don't believe in the unbelievable sweetness of sex love, woe unto those who are the standard bearers of death, woe unto those who believe in conflict and horror and violence and fill our books and screens and livingrooms with all that crap, woe in fact unto those who make evil movies about the Beat Generation where innocent housewives are raped by beatniks! Woe unto those who are the real dreary sinners that even God finds room to forgive . . . woe unto those who spit on the Beat Generation, the wind'll blow it back.

Joyce Johnson
(b. 1935)

The Beats were not entirely a boys' club, but their scene could pass for one most of the time. Joyce Johnson's 1983 memoir Minor Characters *provides an alternate take. Johnson tells of her first encounters as a Barnard student with what would be (courtesy of a magazine article by novelist John Clellon Holmes) called the Beat Generation. Set up on a blind date with Jack Kerouac, she began a long, turbulent, and intermittent romance that kept her near the center of that crazy cultural experiment. Johnson eloquently and meticulously describes that world through a woman's eyes, providing a revealing perspective that cuts through the clichés and hype that accumulate around legends.*

from *Minor Characters*

H E CAME back not because of me but because he was profoundly homesick. He wanted America, a bowl of Wheaties by a kitchen window; he wanted Lowell, not New York.

Across the Atlantic he hadn't found the Old World but a new one he was inadvertently helping to create. Through a perpetual haze of marijuana he'd viewed the international scene like a dismayed elder, noting a cool that was colder and deader than any hipster's earned fatalism, a pose conveying nothing. He saw himself imitated, and hated what he saw. Was that bored indifference his? These new young people with their cultivated inertia, their laconic language (consisting mainly, he observed derisively, of the word *like*), seemed to have the uniformity of an army. They'd invaded Tangier, swarming around Burroughs; when Jack went to Paris, he found them there too. He left and went to London, but stayed less than a week. Just before he'd sailed, he'd found his family's genealogy in the British Museum and read for the first time the emblematic motto of the Kerouacs: *Aimer, travailler, souffrir.*

Five days after I sent the cable, he knocked on my door. He stood out in the hall, smiling rather shyly, the rucksack at his feet. Since early that morning I'd been waiting, calling the office to say I was sick, wanting to go down to the dock and actually see the ship come in, but what if I missed him there? Now he was here, and in that first moment I thought Who is he? But I kissed him in the doorway and he followed me inside. He left his rucksack on the floor and we lay down on the couch. The cat walked all over our bodies with utter disdain. "Ti Gris, Ti Gris," Jack called to it coaxingly, and then I knew he was back.

But it turned out he wasn't. He'd only be passing through for a few days—three or four at most—to pick up some money the publisher owed him. Then he'd be taking the bus down to Orlando, Florida, where his mother was now. Maybe he'd be back in the fall when Viking was publishing *On the Road*. He seemed a little embarrassed. "You have to let me go and be a hermit," he said, as if he was counting on me to understand.

I remember I went into the bathroom and cried and splashed a lot of cold water on my face before I came out. I got up my courage and said brightly, "How about staying a week?" But he shook his head and said he couldn't.

Hadn't I been the one, he reminded me, to say that what he needed was a home? Hadn't I said exactly that to him before he went off on this trip he never would have taken if he'd had any sense? Well, now he was going to have a home at last—in California. Ah, Berkeley was the place... A beautiful little wooden house with trees and flowering bushes in the yard, where he could lie on the grass and write haikus like Li Po and where Neal Cassady and Gary Snyder would come visiting, but most of the time he'd be alone. There was no room for me in this house, because his aloneness would include his mother, stirring her big pots in the kitchen, watching her game shows on the television set he was going to buy her, with a glass of red wine in her hand. It had always been his dream to do what he'd promised his father—settle down in a house with Memere, who'd worked in shoe factories so he could stay home and write his books, who didn't understand but always forgave her no-good, lazy son, who didn't like

Allen, hadn't liked either of his wives; she'd been right about them, too. Memere was the woman he was going to now. "I really like you, though, Joycey," he said.

For the first time, I asked Jack, "Would Memere like me?"

He said, "Maybe. Yeah, she might. She doesn't approve of sex, though, between unmarried people."

Of course not. Neither did my parents. Suddenly the problem seemed clarified.

He was going to Memere the way he'd gone to Tangier, dreaming the whole thing before he ever got there. It was as if the power of Jack's imagination always left him defenseless. He forgot things anyone else would have remembered. Like how lonely and bored he was quickly going to be in Memere's house. Or that maybe Memere didn't even want to move. I was sure old ladies liked to stay in one place, not be trundled around with all their stuff in boxes, back and forth across the country on Greyhound buses.

But somehow I knew I couldn't say any of this—even though he always told me how practical I was and treated me like a worldly person, an authority on publishing, for example. No matter how skeptical you were, you couldn't strike at someone's deepest vision. Why, I was very hard-boiled, really, I thought, compared to Jack.

"You should get yourself a little husband," he said to me with sad generosity.

I said I didn't want that.

"Well, then finish your book, travel with Elise."

I said, "What if I came to San Francisco?"

With a flash of exhilaration I saw that I could do it. I didn't need Jack to take me, only to be at the other end of my destination. I started talking about how I'd begin saving money immediately, how I'd collect Unemployment out there until I found another job, how I'd get my own place in the city where he could come. I was sick of New York anyway, I said. I'd spent my entire twenty-one years in one place, and he was right, that was too long.

Somehow this solution to our relationship never had occurred to Jack. Once again I'd surprised him.

"Well, do what you want, Joycey," he said. "Always do what you want."

It was disconcerting, though, to be left so free. Men were supposed to ask, to take, not leave you in place. I wanted to be wanted. Unlike Alex, Jack took what you gave him, asked no more. For Jack you didn't have to be anything but what you were—just as Ti Gris the cat was only Ti Gris, to be admired in all his hopeless Ti Grisness. Sometimes it was Jack who fed Ti Gris. Crouching motionless at a respectful distance from the plastic bowl, he'd watch with tender attentiveness each tiny ingestion of food. Could leaving in place be a kind of loving?

All I knew two days later when Jack left for Florida was that when I got off the bus in San Francisco at the end of the summer, I'd find him waiting for me in the Greyhound terminal, ready to carry my suitcase through the streets of North Beach until he found me a beautiful cheap room in some hotel where Allen Ginsberg had once lived, where we'd make love on the new bed. And he'd take me out to all the jazz joints that very night, and introduce me to everyone—Neal Cassady, in particular, was going to be crazy about me, because I'd remind him right away of his first wife, a sixteen-year-old blonde runaway named Luanne.

INTERESTINGLY enough, the only woman Jack Kerouac ever actually took with him on the road wasn't me or Edie Parker or Carolyn Cassady or any of the dark *fellaheen* beauties of his longings, but Gabrielle L'Evesque Kerouac, age sixty-two, with her bun of iron-grey hair and her round spectacles and her rosary beads in her old black purse.

As Jack laments the dreariness of bus stations, the awful unendingness of transcontinental highways, the nights of upright, jolted sleep to which he's subjecting his mother, Memere cheerfully looks out the window at the Texas plains, the Rio Grande Valley, the Mojave Desert, keeping the two of them going with the aspirins she's sensibly brought with her, alternated with Cokes. She buys souvenirs and, in a restaurant where she orders oysters, flirts with an old man and writes her address for him on a menu. Memere's thrilled by the small adventure of an overnight stop in a run-down hotel that humiliates

Jack by its cheapness. It's all luxury and gaiety, not hardship. With
her boy Jackie beside her, she's seeing the world at last. What had
she known but work and poverty and Sunday masses? As a child of
fourteen she'd gone into the shoe factories, married at seventeen, had
three babies—a lifetime of sewing and mending, soapsuds and thrift.
In thrift, she'd surpassed even my mother, saving the last inches of
thread on a spool, half a potato, a quarter of an onion, a packet of
needles from 1910. The boxes Jack packed for Memere to bring to
California were full of what the affluent would consider mere debris.
Perhaps to her those few days on the Greyhound bus seemed the
bridal journey she'd never had.

But no house awaited Memere and Jack after all. Only a three-
room apartment without enough furniture and they had to watch
every penny at the supermarket. Memere hated Berkeley, hated the
hills and the morning fog that kept the clothes from drying on the
line, hated the crazy strangers that kept dropping in to lure Jack away
from her, hated the sound of his typewriter behind his shut door. She
missed her daughter and her neighbors and the beautiful Orlando
sunshine. Why couldn't Jackie just live with her in some nice place
there? What was the good of all this foolish moving around? she
asked her son.

"Anxiously awaiting your coming out here now," Jack wrote me
in his letter of June 11, adding that not only he but Neal was plead-
ing with me to hurry up and to bring Elise and Sheila with me, so
that we'd all be ready for a great new season. Berkeley was quiet and
flowery; San Francisco wilder than before. The papers every day were
full of news and editorials about *Howl*, which had been banned for
obscenity and removed from bookstores by the local police.

The main North Beach hangout, The Place, had clippings about
Howl on the bulletin board as well as paintings by local artists and
phone messages and letters that the bartender held for his customers. "You will love this mad joint," Jack wrote. "Nothing like it in New
York." One night he'd gotten into a ridiculous fight there, which he
described with relish. A small bespectacled man had been hitting

his wife. When Jack intervened, he took a swing at him. Holding his assailant by the arms, Jack had simply "dumped him sitting" to the floor.

But the letter ended bewilderingly and sadly: "It's the end of the land, babe, it gives you that lonely feeling—I KNOW that I'll eventually return to NY to live. Mad Jack."

I WANTED to get my bus ticket the minute I read that letter, but I was scared to arrive there penniless. Somehow I had to save two hundred dollars. I gave up my apartment and moved in for the time being with my friend Connie who had worked for Robert Giroux. The change was too much for Ti Gris, who found a way to slide open a window screen and make his getaway from my life at long last. "Well I guess Ti Gris's on his way to China, where he will become an immortal and ride away on a dragon," Jack wrote.

Meanwhile I'd talked Elise into going to California with me. Hadn't we always planned to go adventuring together? She had nothing to lose but her awful typing job. From Tangier, Allen had gone on to Paris with Peter and wouldn't be back till next spring. It was dangerous to wait for him anyway. In Berkeley, Elise could go to graduate school—it would be easy for her to do that, according to Jack. Everything was easy in California, land of blue skies and leafy streets and a million new interesting scenes and people.

"I hope, when you get here," Jack worried, "you'll allow me to be a little bugged in general, I just can't imagine what to do or think anymore. Incidentally, tho, I'd like to draw you or paint you, at leisure . . ."

JUST WHEN I was so eager to abandon New York, it seemed to turn before my eyes into a kind of Paris. The new cultural wave that had crested in San Francisco was rolling full force into Manhattan, bringing with it all kinds of newcomers—poets, painters, photographers, jazz musicians, dancers—genuine artists and hordes of would-be's, some submerging almost instantly, others quickly bobbing to the surface and remaining visible. Young and broke, they converged upon the easternmost edges of the Village, peeling off into the nondescript district of warehouses and factory lofts, and Fourth Avenue with its used bookstores, and the broken-wine-bottle streets of the Bowery. An area with an industrial rawness about it, proletarian, unpretty— quite illegal to live in, but landlords were prepared to look the other way. An outlaw zone that silently absorbed people who'd sneak their incriminating domestic garbage out in the dead of night or hide a bed behind a rack of paintings, always listening for the knock of the housing inspector.

An older group of painters had survived here since the late 1940s. In lofts deserted by the garment industry, where sewing-machine needles could still be found in the crevices of floorboards, they'd dispensed with the confinements of the easel. Possessing space if little else, they'd tacked their canvases across larger and larger stretches of crumbling plaster, or nailed them to the floor. They threw away palettes and used the metal tops of discarded kitchen tables. Paint would rain down on the sized white surfaces—house paint, if there was no money for oils—colors running in rivulets, merging, splashing, coagulating richly in glistening thickness, bearing witness to the gesture of the painter's arm in a split second of time, like the record of a mad, solitary dance. Or like music, some said, like bop, like a riff by Charlie Parker, incorrigible junky and genius, annihilated by excess in 1955, posthumous hero of the coming moment. Or like Jack's "spontaneous prose," another dance in the flow of time. For the final issue of *Black Mountain Review*, he'd jotted down his own manifesto, which many of the New York painters soon would read: "Time being of the essence in the purity of speech, sketching language is undisturbed flow from the mind of personal secret idea-words *blowing* (as per jazz musician) on subject of image."

Substitute *painting, color, stroke*, and it was close in spirit to the way the painters defined themselves in their heated discussions at "The Club," a loft on Eighth Street where they met regularly, or over beers at the Cedar Bar, continuing on into dawn over coffee at Riker's. Blearily they'd stagger back to their studios, switching on the light to stare at the new canvas up on the wall, matching it to the words still spinning in the brain, feeling exhausted or depressed or dangerously exalted—with the rent due, after all, and not enough money for the tube of cadmium red, and no gallery another goddam year.

But Jackson Pollock had broken the ice, they said, broken it for all of them, and then died—in classic American style—in his Oldsmobile, in his new affluence and fame that seemed to mean so little to him by the time he got it that he veered off the road into a tree by the side of Montauk Highway on his way to a party with his teen-age mistress and her girlfriend. Suicide by alcohol, this accident they all still talked about obsessively even a year later. Endless Jackson stories they told, and they journeyed out to Amagansett to the grave marked by a granite boulder that had been outside Pollock's house, with his signature on it in bronze as if he'd signed his death—the name of the artist at the very end completing the painting.

Legend adheres to artists whose deaths seem the corollaries of their works. There's a perversely compelling satisfaction for the public in such perfect correspondences—like the satisfaction the artist feels upon completing an image. It was fitting that Jackson Pollock, whose paintings were explosions of furious vitality, dizzying webs of paint squeezed raw from the tube, who ground cigarette butts into his canvases with seeming brutal disrespect for the refinements of Art, would smash through a windshield at eighty miles an hour. Thirteen years later, Kerouac's quiet death in St. Petersburg would be viewed as improper, slightly embarrassing—at best, supremely ironic. Better to have died like Pollock or James Dean, or like Neal Cassady had—of exposure on the railroad tracks.

Artists are nourished by each other more than by fame or by the public, I've always thought. To give one's work to the world is an experience of peculiar emptiness. The work goes away from the artist into a void, like a message stuck into a bottle and flung into the sea. Criticism is crushing and humiliating. Pollock was hailed as a genius by the time he died, but could he have forgotten the widely repeated witticism that his paintings could have been done by a chimpanzee?

As for praise, somehow it falls short, empty superlatives. The true artist knows the pitfalls of vanity. Dangerous to let go of one's anxiety. But did you *understand*? must always be the question. To like and admire is not enough: did you *understand*? And will you understand the next thing I do—the wet canvas in my studio, the page I left in my typewriter? Unreasonably, the artist would like to know this, too. Praise has to do with the past, the finished thing; the unfinished is the artist's preoccupation.

> Follow roughly outlines in outfanning movement over subject, as river rock, so mindflow over jewel-center need (run your mind over it, *once*) arriving at pivot, where what was dim formed "beginning" becomes sharp-necessitating "ending" and language shortens in race to wire of time-race of work, following law of Deep Form, to conclusion, last words, last trickle—Night is The End.

—Jack Kerouac

It's with a fire that the summer of 1957 comes in, in my memory, a giant conflagration on Eighth Street and Broadway. I remember the night sky filling with smoke and flame and the fire engines clamoring, and that it was a Friday and, being at loose ends, I'd stayed downtown after work. Wanamaker's Department Store was burning—the massive old landmark that had stood for so long like a boundary wall between the Village and the East Side. That Friday night it burned to the ground. The famous clock I'd walked under in January on my way to meet Jack melted like one of Salvador Dali's watches.

What a strange night it was. The summer restlessness, the mobs watching the fire, the smell of ashes everywhere. On East Tenth Street a half-dozen galleries were opening that night for the first time, according to fliers pasted up around the Village. Owned and run by artists, they seemed to have come into being all at once in deserted storefronts. Gradually, the shabby block between Fourth Avenue and the Bowery had become a little country of painters. Franz Kline and Willem de Kooning, men whose names had just become familiar to me, lived on that street, as did many of the totally unknown artists whose works I was about to see in the small new galleries. For me Tenth Street had the charm of foreign territory—to enter it that fiery night was like finding Washington Square all over again. Under the strange dusky orange glare, as passing sirens wailed, groups of people moved from storefront to storefront, talking intensely, laughing, congratulating each other, gulping wine from paper cups, calling out to friends: "Have you seen the stuff at the March yet?" . . . "Hey, I'll meet you at the Camino!" . . . "Is Franz here? Anyone seen Franz?" To get into a gallery you'd first stand back from the narrow doorway to let a rush of others out, and, once inside, you'd be drawn into a slow circular progression from painting to painting and have to look at everything for a least a few moments, whether you liked what you saw or not. That seemed the unspoken rule—everyone's work must be given attention.

I didn't really know what to make of the paintings. What was I supposed to see? Where were the images? My college teachers had taught me always to look for images; but I found very few as recognizable as those in even the most difficult Picassos at the Museum of Modern Art. There was just all this paint. Sometimes you had the impression of tremendous energy or an emotion you couldn't quite put into words; sometimes nothing came to you from the canvas at all. Was this how you decided which ones were good or bad?

But goodness and badness didn't even seem important that night. It was the *occasion* that was important. What I'd wandered into wasn't the beginning of something, but the coming into light of what had been stirring for years among all these artists who'd been known only to each other.

Major or minor, they all seemed possessed by the same impulse— to break out into forms that were unrestricted and new.

Minor Characters, 1983

Gregory Corso
(1930–2001)

If Ginsberg was the link between Beat and hippie, Gregory Corso was the link between Beat and punk. He was the fourth wheel of the movement—Burroughs, Ginsberg, and Kerouac being the trinity. Corso was younger and grew up rough out of Little Italy, an orphanage, and foster care. He was jailed at thirteen and spent most of his time inside until he was twenty-one, but he didn't waste time served, educating himself and immersing himself in poetry. After his release Corso met Ginsberg in a bar and was brought into the early inner circle. I met him at Burroughs's seventieth birthday party, where he arrived handsome in a suede suit with new teeth. When the check went around at the end of the evening he withdrew $100 from the kitty.

Marriage

Should I get married? Should I be good?
Astound the girl next door with my velvet suit and faustus hood?
Don't take her to movies but to cemeteries
tell all about werewolf bathtubs and forked clarinets
then desire her and kiss her and all the preliminaries
and she going just so far and I understanding why
not getting angry saying You must feel! It's beautiful to feel!
Instead take her in my arms lean against an old crooked tombstone
and woo her the entire night the constellations in the sky—

When she introduces me to her parents
back straightened, hair finally combed, strangled by a tie,
should I sit knees together on their 3rd degree sofa
and not ask Where's the bathroom?
How else to feel other than I am,

often thinking Flash Gordon soap—
O how terrible it must be for a young man
seated before a family and the family thinking
We never saw him before! He wants our Mary Lou!
After tea and homemade cookies they ask What do you do for a
    living?
Should I tell them? Would they like me then?
Say All right get married, we're losing a daughter
but we're gaining a son—
And should I then ask Where's the bathroom?

O God, and the wedding! All her family and her friends
and only a handful of mine all scroungy and bearded
just wait to get at the drinks and food—
And the priest! he looking at me as if I masturbated
asking me Do you take this woman for your lawful wedded wife?
And I trembling what to say say Pie Glue!
I kiss the bride all those corny men slapping me on the back
She's all yours, boy! Ha-ha-ha!
And in their eyes you could see some obscene honeymoon going
    on—
Then all that absurd rice and clanky cans and shoes
Niagara Falls! Hordes of us! Husbands! Wives! Flowers! Chocolates!
All streaming into cozy hotels
All going to do the same thing tonight
The indifferent clerk he knowing what was going to happen
The lobby zombies they knowing what
The whistling elevator man he knowing
The winking bellboy knowing
Everybody knowing! I'd be almost inclined not to do anything!
Stay up all night! Stare that hotel clerk in the eye!
Screaming: I deny honeymoon! I deny honeymoon!
running rampant into those almost climactic suites
yelling Radio belly! Cat shovel!

O I'd live in Niagara forever! in a dark cave beneath the Falls
I'd sit there the Mad Honeymooner
devising ways to break marriages, a scourge of bigamy
a saint of divorce—

But I should get married I should be good
How nice it'd be to come home to her
and sit by the fireplace and she in the kitchen
aproned young and lovely wanting my baby
and so happy about me she burns the roast beef
and comes crying to me and I get up from my big papa chair
saying Christmas teeth! Radiant brains! Apple deaf!
God what a husband I'd make! Yes, I should get married!
So much to do! like sneaking into Mr Jones' house late at night
and cover his golf clubs with 1920 Norwegian books
Like hanging a picture of Rimbaud on the lawnmower
like pasting Tannu Tuva postage stamps all over the picket fence
like when Mrs Kindhead comes to collect for the Community
    Chest
grab her and tell her There are unfavorable omens in the sky!
And when the mayor comes to get my vote tell him
When are you going to stop people killing whales!
And when the milkman comes leave him a note in the bottle
Penguin dust, bring me penguin dust, I want penguin dust—

Yet if I should get married and it's Connecticut and snow
and she gives birth to a child and I am sleepless, worn,
up for nights, head bowed against a quiet window, the past behind
    me,
finding myself in the most common of situations a trembling man
knowledged with responsibility not twig-smear nor Roman coin
    soup—
O what would that be like!
Surely I'd give it for a nipple a rubber Tacitus

For a rattle a bag of broken Bach records
Tack Della Francesca all over its crib
Sew the Greek alphabet on its bib
And built for its playpen a roofless Parthenon

No, I doubt I'd be that kind of father
not rural not snow no quiet window
but hot smelly tight New York City
seven flights up, roaches and rats in the walls
a fat Reichian wife screeching over potatoes Get a job!
And five nose running brats in love with Batman
And the neighbors all toothless and dry haired
like those hag masses of the 18th century
all wanting to come in and watch TV
The landlord wants his rent
Grocery store Blue Cross Gas & Electric Knights of Columbus
Impossible to lie back and dream Telephone snow, ghost parking—
No! I should not get married I should never get married!
But—imagine if I were married to a beautiful sophisticated woman
tall and pale wearing an elegant black dress and long black gloves
holding a cigarette holder in one hand and a highball in the other
and we lived high up in a penthouse with a huge window
from which we could see all of New York and ever farther on
        clearer days
No, can't imagine myself married to that pleasant prison dream—

O but what about love? I forget love
not that I am incapable of love
it's just that I see love as odd as wearing shoes—
I never wanted to marry a girl who was like my mother
And Ingrid Bergman was always impossible
And there's maybe a girl now but she's already married
And I don't like men and—
but there's got to be somebody!

Because what if I'm 60 years old and not married,
all alone in a furnished room with pee stains on my underwear
and everybody else is married! All the universe married but me!

Ah, yet well I know that were a woman possible as I am possible
then marriage would be possible—
Like SHE in her lonely alien gaud waiting her Egyptian lover
so I wait—bereft of 2,000 years and the bath of life.

The Happy Birthday of Death, 1960

Bob Kaufman
(1925–1986)

Not just a poet but a griot, *Bob Kaufman composed poems in his head and recited them from memory. What's written here is the text of a poem made not to be read but spoken. He didn't write his poems down; his wife did so that he could stay purely inside the sound, working in the rhythms of jazz, improvising like a musician, and creating poetry on the spot. Kaufman was a son of New Orleans, a scion of the melting pot: German Jewish Catholic African Hoodoo. A merchant sailor, he met Ginsberg and Kerouac at the New School. Kaufman said he coined the word "beatnik." A Buddhist, he took a vow of silence to protest the Vietnam War and didn't speak for ten years, breaking silence the day the war ended with the poem "All Those Ships That Never Sailed."*

Walking Parker Home

Sweet beats of jazz impaled on slivers of wind
Kansas Black Morning/ First Horn Eyes/
Historical sound pictures on New Bird wings
People shouts/ boy alto dreams/Tomorrow's
Gold belled pipe of stops and future Blues Times
Lurking Hawkins/ shadows of Lester/ realization
Bronze fingers—brain extensions seeking trapped sounds
Ghetto thoughts/ bandstand courage/ solo flight
Nerve-wracked suspicions of newer songs and doubts
New York altar city/ black tears/ secret disciples
Hammer horn pounding soul marks on unswinging gates
Culture gods/ mob sounds/ visions of spikes
Panic excursions to tribal Jazz wombs and transfusions
Heroin nights of birth/ and soaring/ over boppy new ground.
Smothered rage covering pyramids of notes spontaneously
    exploding

Cool revelations/ shrill hopes/ beauty speared into greedy ears
Birdland nights on bop mountains, windy saxophone revolutions
Dayrooms of junk/ and melting walls and circling vultures/
Money cancer/ remembered pain/ terror flights/
Death and indestructible existence

In that Jazz corner of life
Wrapped in a mist of sound
His legacy, our Jazz-tinted dawn
Wailing his triumphs of oddly begotten dreams
Inviting the nerveless to feel once more
That fierce dying of humans consumed
In raging fires of Love.

Solitudes Crowded with Loneliness, 1959

Lester Young
(1909–1959)

Lester Young was a great reed man (tenor sax and clarinet) who emerged with the Count Basie Orchestra and became a huge influence on bop and cool jazz as well as a prototypical hipster. A cool cat in a porkpie hat known as "Prez" as in President, a nickname he got from Billie Holiday (he returned the favor by calling her "Lady Day"), Young was a legendary neologist, a coiner of hipster-isms who spoke his own semi-private language. Drafted during World War II, he underwent a brutal year of barracks detention for smoking marijuana. His life was marked by alcohol problems and his playing often suffered. In the film Round Midnight *Dexter Gordon plays a character based on Young and the similarly afflicted Bud Powell. Prez died in 1959 shortly after this interview was conducted, by French jazz critic François Postif.*

LESTERPARIS59

Although he wasn't free until five o'clock in the morning, I was determined to interview Lester. I knew he wasn't very talkative, but he wanted the interview to be taped, and that encouraged me.

One afternoon at six o'clock I knocked at his door. Lester told me to come in: he had been waiting for me.

When he saw my tape recorder he shouted happily. He asked me: "Can I talk slang?" I agreed, and from then on he relaxed. I felt during the interview that he was pleased to be able to speak freely.

YOU WEREN'T **really born in New Orleans?**
Uh, uh. Should I really tell you? I could tell a lie. I was born in Woodville, Mississippi, because my mother went back to the family; so after I was straight, you know, everything was cool, she took me back to New Orleans and we lived in Algiers, which is across the river.

I left when I was ten. They had trucks going around town advertising for all the dances, and this excited me, you know? So they gave me handbills and I was running all over the city until my tongue was hanging out. From there I went to Memphis and then to Minneapolis. I tried to go to school and all that . . . I wasn't interested.

The only person I liked on those trucks in New Orleans was the drummer, you dig?

Drums now? No eyes. I don't want to see them. Everytime I'd be in a nice little place, and I'd meet a nice little chick, dig, her mother'd say, 'Mary, come on, let's go'. Damn, I'd be trying to pack these drums, because I wanted this little chick, dig? She'd called her once and twice, and I'm trying to get straight, so I just said, I'm through with drums. All those other boys got clarinet cases, trumpet cases, trombone cases and I'm wiggling around with all that s—t, and Lady Francis, I could really play those drums. I'd been playing them for a whole year.

How did you get started on tenor?

I was playing alto and they had this evil old cat with a nice, beautiful, background, you know, mother and father and a whole lot of bread and like that, you know, so everytime we'd get a job . . . this was in Salinas, Kansas, so everytime we'd go see him, we'd be waiting ninety years to get us to work while he fixed his face you know, so I told the bossman, his name was Art Bronson. So I said, 'listen, why do we have to go through this? You go and buy me a tenor saxophone and I'll play the m-f and we'd be straight then.'

So he worked with this music store, and we got straight, and we split. That was it for me. The first time I heard it. Because the alto was a little too high.

When did you learn to read music?

When I first came up in my father's band I wasn't reading music; I was faking it, but I was in the band. My father, he got me an alto out of the pawnshop, and I just picked the m-f up and started playing it. My father played all the instruments and he read, so I had to get close to my sister, you dig, to learn the parts.

One day my father finally said to me, Kansas, play your part, and he knew goddamn well I couldn't read. So my sister played her part and then he said, Lester play your part, and I couldn't read a m-f note, not a damn note. He said get up and learn some scales. Now you know my heart was broke, you dig, and I went and cried my little teardrops, while they went on rehearsing. I went away and learned to read the music, and I came back in the band. All the time I was learning to read, I was playing the records and learning the music at the same time, so I could completely foul them up.

I don't like to read music, just soul . . . there you are.

I got a man in New York writing music for me right now, so when I get back it'll be for bass violin, two cellos, viola, French Horn and three rhythm. I'll just take my time with it, if it don't come out right, I'll just say f—k it, no. This is the first time, and I always wanted to do that. Norman Granz would never let me make no records with no strings. Yardbird made millions of records with strings. When I was over here the last time I played with strings, the first winners, I think they were. Germans. Anyway I played with them, and they treated me nice and played nice for me.

Who were your early influences?

I had a decision to make between Frankie Trumbauer and Jimmy Dorsey, you dig, and I wasn't sure which way I wanted to go. I'd buy me all those records and I'd play one by Jimmy and one by Trumbauer, you dig? I didn't know nothing about Hawk then, and they were the only ones telling a story I liked to hear. I had both of them made.

Was Bud Freeman an influence?

Bud Freeman??!! We're nice friends, I saw him just the other day down at the union, but influence, ladedehumptedorebebob . . . s—t! Did you ever hear him (Trumbauer) play "Singing the Blues"? That tricked me right then and that's where I went.

How about Coleman Hawkins?

As far as I'm concerned, I think Coleman Hawkins was the President first, right? When I first heard him I thought that was some great jazz I was listening to. As far as myself, I think I'm the second one. Not braggadocious, you know I don't talk like that. There's only one way to go. If a guy plays tenor, he's got to sound like Hawk or like Lester.

If he plays alto, he's got to be Bird or Johnny Hodges. There's another way, the way I hear all the guys playing in New York, running all over the place.

In Kansas City, when I was with Basie, they told me to go and see Coleman Hawkins, and how great he is; so I wanted to see how great he is, you know. So they shoved me up on the stand, and I grabbed his saxophone, played it, read his clarinet parts, everything! Now I got to run back to my job where there was 13 people and I got to run ten blocks. I don't think Hawk showed at all. Then I went to Little Rock with Count Basie, and I got this telegram from Fletcher Henderson saying come with me. So I was all excited because this was bigtime, and I showed it around to everyone and asked them what I should do. Count said he couldn't tell me, so I decided to split and went to Detroit. But it wasn't for me. The m-f's were whispering on me, everytime I played. I can't make that. I couldn't take that, those m-f's whispering on me, Jesus! So I went up to Fletcher and asked him would you give me a nice recommendation? I'm going back to Kansas City. He said "Oh, yeah" right quick. That bitch, she was Fletcher's wife, she took me down to the basement and played one of those old windup record players, and she'd say, Lester, can't you play like this? Coleman Hawkins records. But I mean, can't you hear this? Can't you get with that? You dig? I split! Every morning that bitch would wake me up at nine o'clock to teach me to play like Coleman Hawkins. And she played trumpet herself . . . circus trumpet! I'm gone!

How did you first go with Basie?

I used to hear this tenor player with Basie all the time. You see we'd get off at two in Minneapolis and it would be one in Kansas City, that kind of s—t, you dig. So I sent Basie this telegram telling him I couldn't stand to hear that m-f, and will you accept me for a job at any time? So he sent me a ticket and I left my madam here and came on.

How did you get along with Herschel?

We were nice friends and things, but some nights when we got on the stand it was like a duel, and other nights it would be nice music. He was a nice person, in fact I was the last to see him die. I even paid his doctor bills. I don't blame him; he loved his instrument, and I loved mine . . .

Why did you leave the Basie band?

That's some deep question you're asking me now. Skip that one, but I sure could tell you that, but it wouldn't be sporting. I still have nice eyes. I can't go around thinking evil and all that. The thing is still cool with me, because I don't bother about nobody. But you take a person like me, I stay by myself, so how do you know anything about me? Some m-f walked up to me and said, "Prez I thought you were dead!" I'm probably more alive than he is, you dig, from that hearsay.

You've known Billie for a long time, haven't you?

When I first came to New York I lived with Billie. She was teaching me about the city, which way to go, you know? She's still my Lady Day.

What people do, man, it's so obvious, you know? If you want to speak like that, what do I care what you do? What he do, what he does, what nobody do, it's nobody's business!

Man, they say he's an old junkie, he's old and funky, all that s—t, that's not nice. Whatever they do, let them do that and enjoy themselves, and you get your kicks yourself. All I do is smoke some New Orleans cigarettes, don't sniff nothing in my nose, nothing. I drink and I smoke and that's all. But a lot of people think I'm this way and I don't like that, I resent that. My business is the musical thing, all the way . . .

Do you think you play modern today?

In my mind when I play, I try not to be a repeater pencil, you dig? Always leave some spaces—lay out. You won't catch me playing like Lester Leaps In and that s—t, but I always go back.

I can play all those reed instruments. I can play bass clarinet. If I brought that out, wouldn't it upset everything? I know both Coltrane and Rollins. I haven't heard Coltrane, but I played with Rollins once in Detroit. I just made some records for Norman with clarinet. I haven't played it for a long time, because one of my friends stole it. That's the way it goes. I made them in 1958, in the Hollywood Bowl. Oscar Peterson and his group.

I developed my tenor to sound like an alto, to sound like a tenor, to sound like a bass, and I'm not through with it yet. That's why they get all trapped up, they say 'Goddam, I never heard Prez play like this'. That's the way I want them to hear. That's MODERN, dig? F—k what you played back in '49—it's what you play today, dig? A lot of them got lost and walked out.

Do you play the same thing everyday?
Not unless you want to get henpecked.

What kind of group would you like to have?
Give me my little three rhythm and me—happiness . . . the four Mills Brothers, ha, ha. I can relax better, you dig. I don't like a whole lotta noise no goddamn way. Trumpets and trombones, and all that—f—k it. I'm looking for something soft; I can't stand that loud noise. Those places, in New York, the trumpets screaming, and the chicks putting their fingers in their ears. It's got to be sweetness, you dig? Sweetness can be funky, filthy, or anything. What ever you want!

The Blues? Great Big Eyes. Because if you play with a new band like I have and are just working around, and they don't know no blues, you can't play anything! Everybody has to play the blues and everybody has them too . . .

Am I independent? Very much! I'd have taken off the other night if I had 500 dollars. I just can't take that b-s, you dig? They want everybody who's a Negro to be an Uncle Tom, or Uncle Remus, or Uncle Sam, and I can't make it. It's the same all over, you fight for your life—until death do you part, and then you got it made . . .

Norman Mailer
(1923–2007)

It took Norman Mailer to move the hipster—rebranded as "the American existentialist"—to the center of American discourse with this knockout manifesto that weaves in race, nuclear weapons, the Holocaust, crime, drugs, and the intellectual legacy of (among others) Karl Marx, Wilhelm Reich, and D. H. Lawrence. He described it afterward as "a trip into the psychic wild." Mailer was too ambitious to be hip and too hot to be cool—he was running for president of the Great American Novel—but he knew the buzz. He'd been on bennies and quit marijuana, complaining it made him "over-brilliant." A founding editor of the Village Voice, *novelist, filmmaker, polemicist, innovator of the New Journalism, eventually a New York mayoral candidate: Mailer could have been hip if he wanted to, but his ambitions lay elsewhere.*

The White Negro

Superficial Reflections on the Hipster

Our search for the rebels of the generation led us to the hipster. The hipster is an *enfant terrible* turned inside out. In character with his time, he is trying to get back at the conformists by lying low . . . You can't interview a hipster because his main goal is to keep out of a society which, he thinks, is trying to make everyone over in its own image. He takes marijuana because it supplies him with experiences that can't be shared with "squares." He may affect a broad-brimmed hat or a zoot suit, but usually he prefers to skulk unmarked. The hipster may be a jazz musician; he is rarely an artist, almost never a writer. He may earn his living as a petty criminal, a hobo, a carnival roustabout or a freelance moving man in Greenwich Village, but some hipsters have found a safe refuge in the upper income brackets as television comics or movie actors. (The late James Dean, for one, was a hipster hero.) . . . It is tempting to describe the hipster in psychiatric terms as infantile, but the style of his infantilism is a sign of the times. He does not try to enforce his will on others, Napoleon-fashion, but contents himself with a magical omnipotence never disproved because never tested. . . . As the only extreme nonconformist of his generation, he exercises a powerful if underground appeal for conformists, through newspaper accounts of his delinquencies, his structureless jazz, and his emotive grunt words.

—"Born 1930: The Unlost Generation" by Caroline Bird
Harper's Bazaar, Feb. 1957

P ROBABLY, WE will never be able to determine the psychic havoc of the concentration camps and the atom bomb upon the unconscious mind of almost everyone alive in these years. For the first time in civilized history, perhaps for the first time in all of history, we have been forced to live with the suppressed knowledge that the smallest facets of our personality or the most minor projection of our ideas, or indeed the absence of ideas and the absence of personality could mean equally well that we might still be doomed to die as a cipher in some vast statistical operation in which our teeth would be counted, and our hair would be saved, but our death itself would be unknown, unhonored, and unremarked, a death which could not follow with dignity as a possible consequence to serious actions we had chosen, but rather a death by *deux ex machina* in a gas chamber or a radioactive city; and so if in the midst of civilization—that civilization founded upon the Faustian urge to dominate nature by mastering time, mastering the links of social cause and effect—in the middle of an economic civilization founded upon the confidence that time could indeed by subjected to our will, our psyche was subjected itself to the intolerable anxiety that death being causeless, life was causeless as well, and time deprived of cause and effect had come to a stop.

The Second World War presented a mirror to the human condition which blinded anyone who looked into it. For if tens of millions were killed in concentration camps out of the inexorable agonies and contractions of super-states founded upon the always insoluble contradictions of injustice, one was then obliged also to see that no matter how crippled and perverted an image of man was the society he had created, it was nonetheless his creation, his collective creation (at least his collective creation from the past) and if society was so murderous, then who could ignore the most hideous of questions about his own nature?

Worse. One could hardly maintain the courage to be individual, to speak with one's own voice, for the years in which one could complacently accept oneself as part of an elite by being a radical were forever gone. A man knew that when he dissented, he gave a note upon his life which could be called in any year of overt crisis. No wonder then that these have been the years of conformity and depression. A stench of fear has come out of every pore of American life, and we suffer from a collective failure of nerve. The only courage, with rare exceptions, that we have been witness to, has been the isolated courage of isolated people.

2.

IT IS ON this bleak scene that a phenomenon has appeared: the American existentialist—the hipster, the man who knows that if our collective condition is to live with instant death by atomic war, relatively quick death by the State as *l'univers concentrationnaire*, or with a slow death by conformity with every creative and rebellious instinct stifled (at what damage to the mind and the heart and the liver and the nerves no research foundation for cancer will discover in a hurry), if the fate of twentieth-century man is to live with death from adolescence to premature senescence, why then the only life-giving answer is to accept the terms of death, to live with death as immediate danger, to divorce oneself from society, to exist without roots, to set out on that uncharted journey with the rebellious imperatives of the self. In short, whether the life is criminal or not, the decision is to encourage the psychopath in oneself, to explore that domain of experience where security is boredom and therefore sickness, and one exists in the present, in that enormous present which is without past or future, memory or planned intention, the life where a man must go until he is beat, where he must gamble with his energies through all those small or large crises of courage and unforeseen situations which beset his day, where he must be with it or doomed not to swing. The unstated essence of Hip, its psychopathic brilliance, quivers with the knowledge that new kinds of victories increase one's power for new kinds of perception; and defeats, the wrong kind of defeats, attack the body and imprison one's energy until one is jailed in the prison air of other people's habits, other people's defeats, boredom, quiet desperation, and muted icy self-destroying rage. One is Hip or one is Square (the alternative which each new generation coming into American life is beginning to feel), one is a rebel or one conforms, one is a frontiersman in the Wild West of American night life, or else a Square cell, trapped in the totalitarian tissues of American society, doomed willy-nilly to conform if one is to succeed.

A totalitarian society makes enormous demands on the courage of men, and a partially totalitarian society makes even greater demands, for the general anxiety is greater. Indeed if one is to be a man, almost any kind of unconventional action often takes disproportionate courage. So it is no accident that the source of Hip is the Negro for he has been living on the margin between totalitarianism and democracy for two centuries. But the presence of Hip as a working philosophy in the sub-worlds of American life is probably due to jazz, and its knife-like entrance into culture, its subtle but so penetrating influence on an avant-garde generation—that postwar generation of adventurers who (some consciously, some by osmosis) had absorbed the lessons of disillusionment and disgust of the twenties, the depression, and the war. Sharing a collective disbelief in the words of men who had too much money and controlled too many things, they knew almost as powerful a disbelief in the socially monolithic ideas of the single mate, the solid family and the respectable love life. If the intellectual antecedents of this generation can be traced to such separate influences as D. H. Lawrence, Henry Miller, and Wilhelm Reich, the viable philosophy of Hemingway fit most of their facts: in a bad world, as he was to say over and over again (while taking time out from his parvenu snobbery and dedicated gourmandize), in a bad world there is no love nor mercy nor charity nor justice unless a man can keep his courage, and this indeed fitted some of the facts. What fitted the need of the adventurer even more precisely was Hemingway's categorical imperative that what made him feel good became therefore The Good.

So no wonder that in certain cities of America, in New York of course, and New Orleans, in Chicago and San Francisco and Los Angeles, in such American cities as Paris and Mexico, D.F., this particular part of a generation was attracted to what the Negro had to offer. In such places as Greenwich Village, a ménage-à-trois was completed—the bohemian and the juvenile delinquent came face-to-face with the Negro, and the hipster was a fact in American life. If marijuana was the wedding ring, the child was the language of Hip for its argot gave expression to abstract states of feeling which all could share, at least all who were Hip. And in this wedding of the white and the black it was the Negro who brought the cultural dowry. Any Negro who wishes to live must live with danger from his first day, and no experience can ever be casual to him, no Negro can saunter down a street with any real certainty that violence will not visit him on his walk. The cameos of security for the average white: mother and the home, job and the family, are not even a mockery to millions of Negroes; they are impossible. The Negro has the simplest of alternatives: live a life of constant humility or ever-threatening danger. In such a pass where paranoia is as vital to survival as blood, the Negro has stayed alive and begun to grow by following the need of his body where he could. Knowing in the cells of his existence that life was war, nothing but war, the Negro (all exceptions admitted) could rarely afford the sophisticated inhibitions of civilization, and so he kept for his survival the art of the primitive, he lived in the enormous present, he subsisted for his Saturday night kicks, relinquishing the pleasures of the mind for the more obligatory pleasures of the body, and in his music he gave voice to the character and quality of his existence, to his rage and the infinite variations of joy, lust, languor, growl, cramp, pinch, scream and despair of his orgasm. For jazz is orgasm, it is the music of orgasm, good orgasm and bad, and so it spoke across a nation, it had the communication of art even where it was watered, perverted, corrupted, and almost killed, it spoke in no matter what laundered popular way of instantaneous existential states to which some whites could respond, it was indeed a communication by art because it said, "I feel this, and now you do too."

So there was a new breed of adventurers, urban adventurers who drifted out at night looking for action with a black man's code to fit their facts. The hipster had absorbed the existentialist synapses of the Negro, and for practical purposes could be considered a white Negro.

To be an existentialist, one must be able to feel oneself—one must know one's rages, one's anguish, one must be aware of the character of one's frustration and know what would satisfy it. The overcivilized man can be an existentialist only if it is chic, and deserts it quickly for the next chic. To be a real existentialist (Sartre admittedly to the contrary) one must be religious, one must have one's sense of the "purpose"—whatever the purpose may be—but a life which is directed by one's faith in the necessity of action is a life committed to the notion that the substratum of existence is the search, the end meaningful but mysterious; it is impossible to live such a life unless one's emotions provide their profound conviction. Only the French, alienated beyond alienation from their unconscious could welcome an existential philosophy without ever feeling it at all; indeed only a Frenchman by declaring that the unconscious did not exist could then proceed to explore the delicate involutions of consciousness, the microscopically sensuous and all but ineffable *frissons* of mental becoming, in order finally to create the theology of atheism and so submit that in a world of absurdities the existential absurdity is most coherent.

In the dialogue between the atheist and the mystic, the atheist is on the side of life, rational life, undialectical life—since he conceives of death as emptiness, he can, no matter how weary or despairing, wish for nothing but more life; his pride is that he does not transpose his weakness and spiritual fatigue into a romantic longing for death, for such appreciation of death is then all too capable of being elaborated by his imagination into a universe of meaningful structure and moral orchestration.

Yet this masculine argument can mean very little for the mystic. The mystic can accept the atheist's description of his weakness, he can agree that his mysticism was a response to despair. And yet . . . and yet his argument is that he, the mystic, is the one finally who has chosen to live with death, and so death is his experience and not the atheist's, and the atheist by eschewing the limitless dimensions of profound despair has rendered himself incapable to judge the experience. The real argument which the mystic must always advance is the very intensity of his private vision—his argument depends from the vision precisely because what was felt in the vision is so extraordinary that no rational argument, no hypotheses of "oceanic feelings" and certainly no skeptical reductions can explain away what has become for him the reality more real than the reality of closely reasoned logic. His inner experience of the possibilities within death is his logic. So, too, for the existentialist. And the psychopath. And the saint and the bullfighter and the lover. The common denominator for all of them is their burning consciousness of the present, exactly that incandescent consciousness which the possibilities within death has opened for them. There is a depth of desperation to the condition which enables one to remain in life only by engaging death, but the reward is their knowledge that what is happening at each instant of the electric present is good or bad for them, good or bad for their cause, their love, their action, their need.

It is this knowledge which provides the curious community of feeling in the world of the hipster, a muted cool religious revival to be sure, but the element which is exciting, disturbing, nightmarish perhaps, is that incompatibles have come to bed, the inner life and the violent life, the orgy and the dream of love, the desire to murder and the desire to create, a dialectical conception of existence with a lust for power, a dark, romantic, and yet undeniably dynamic view of existence for it sees every man and woman as moving individually through each moment of life forward into growth or backward into death.

3.

IT MAY BE fruitful to consider the hipster a philosophical psychopath, a man interested not only in the dangerous imperatives of his psychopathy but in codifying, at least for himself, the suppositions on which his inner universe is constructed. By this premise the hipster is a psychopath, and yet not a psychopath but the negation of the psychopath, for he possesses the narcissistic detachment of the philosopher, that absorption in the recessive nuances of one's own motive which is so alien to the unreasoning drive of the psychopath. In this country where new millions of psychopaths are developed each year, stamped with the mint of our contradictory popular culture (where sex is sin and yet sex is paradise), it is as if there has been room already for the development of the antithetical psychopath who extrapolates from his own condition, from the inner certainty that his rebellion is just, a radical vision of the universe which thus separates him from the general ignorance, reactionary prejudice, and self-doubt of the more conventional psychopath. Having converted his unconscious experience into much conscious knowledge, the hipster has shifted the focus of his desire from immediate gratification toward that wider passion for future power which is the mark of civilized man. Yet with an irreducible difference. For Hip is the sophistication of the wise primitive in a giant jungle, and so its appeal is still beyond the civilized man. If there are ten million Americans who are more or less psychopathic (and the figure is most modest), there are probably not more than one hundred thousand men and women who consciously see themselves as hipsters, but their importance is that they are an elite with the potential ruthlessness of an elite, and a language most adolescents can understand instinctively, for the hipster's intense view of existence matches their experience and their desire to rebel.

Before one can say more about the hipster, there is obviously much to be said about the psychic state of the psychopath—or, clinically, the psychopathic personality. Now, for reasons which may be more curious than the similarity of the words, even many people with a psychoanalytical orientation often confuse the psychopath with the psychotic. Yet the terms are polar. The psychotic is legally insane, the psychopath is not; the psychotic is almost always incapable of discharging in physical acts the rage of his frustration, while the psychopath at his extreme is virtually as incapable of restraining his violence. The psychotic lives in so misty a world that what is happening at each moment of his life is not very real to him whereas the psychopath seldom knows any reality greater than the face, the voice, the being of the particular people among whom he may find himself at any moment. Sheldon and Eleanor Glueck describe him as follows:

> The psychopath . . . can be distinguished from the person sliding into or clambering out of a "true psychotic" state by the long tough persistence of his anti-social attitude and behaviour and the absence of hallucinations, delusions, manic flight of ideas, confusion, disorientation, and other dramatic signs of psychosis.

The late Robert Lindner, one of the few experts on the subject, in his book *Rebel Without a Cause—The Hypnoanalysis of a Criminal Psychopath* presented part of his definition in this way:

> . . . the psychopath is a rebel without a cause, an agitator without a slogan, a revolutionary without a program: in other words, his rebelliousness is aimed to achieve goals satisfactory to himself alone; he is incapable of exertions for the sake of others. All his efforts, hidden under no matter what disguise, represent investments designed to satisfy his immediate wishes and desires. . . . The psychopath, like the child, cannot delay the pleasures of gratification; and this trait is one of his underlying, universal characteristics. He cannot wait upon erotic gratification which convention demands should be preceded by the chase before

the kill: he must rape. He cannot wait upon the development of prestige in society: his egoistic ambitions lead him to leap into headlines by daring performances. Like a red thread the predominance of this mechanism for immediate satisfaction runs through the history of every psychopath. It explains not only his behaviour but also the violent nature of his acts.

Yet even Lindner who was the most imaginative and most sympathetic of the psychoanalysts who have studied the psychopathic personality was not ready to project himself into the essential sympathy—which is that the psychopath may indeed by the perverted and dangerous front-runner of a new kind of personality which could become the central expression of human nature before the twentieth century is over. For the psychopath is better adapted to dominate those mutually contradictory inhibitions upon violence and love which civilization has exacted of us, and if it be remembered that not every psychopath is an extreme case, and that the condition of psychopathy is present in a host of people including many politicians, professional soldiers, newspaper columnists, entertainers, artists, jazz musicians, call-girls, promiscuous homosexuals and half the executives of Hollywood, television, and advertising, it can be seen that there are aspects of psychopathy which already exert considerable cultural influence.

What characterizes almost every psychopath and part-psychopath is that they are trying to create a new nervous system for themselves. Generally we are obliged to act with a nervous system which has been formed from infancy, and which carries in the style of its circuits the very contradictions of our parents and our early milieu. Therefore, we are obliged, most of us, to meet the tempo of the present and the future with reflexes and rhythms which come from the past. It is not only the "dead weight of the institutions of the past" but indeed the inefficient and often antiquated nervous circuits of the past which strangle our potentiality for responding to new possibilities which might be exciting for our individual growth.

Through most of modern history, "sublimation" was possible: at the expense of expressing only a small portion of oneself, that small portion could be expressed intensely. But sublimation depends on a reasonable tempo to history. If the collective life of a generation has moved too quickly, the "past" by which particular men and women of that generation may function is not, let us say, thirty years old, but relatively a hundred or two hundred years old. And so the nervous system is overstressed beyond the possibility of such compromises as sublimation, especially since the stable middleclass values so prerequisite to sublimation have been virtually destroyed in our time, at least as nourishing values free of confusion or doubt. In such a crisis of accelerated historical tempo and deteriorated values, neurosis tends to be replaced by psychopathy, and the success of psychoanalysis (which even ten years ago gave promise of becoming a direct major force) diminishes because of its inbuilt and characteristic incapacity to handle patients more complex, more experienced, or more adventurous than the analyst himself. In practice, psychoanalysis has by now become all too often no more than a psychic blood-letting. The patient is not so much changed as aged, and the infantile fantasies which he is encouraged to express are condemned to exhaust themselves against the analyst's nonresponsive reactions. The result for all too many patients is a diminution, a "tranquilizing" of their most interesting qualities and vices. The patient is indeed not so much altered as worn out—less bad, less good, less bright, less willful, less destructive, less creative. He is thus able to conform to that contradictory and unbearable society which first created his neurosis. He can conform to what he loathes because he no longer has the passion to feel loathing so intensely.

The psychopath is notoriously difficult to analyze because the fundamental decision of his nature is to try to live the infantile fantasy, and in this decision (given the dreary alternative of psychoanalysis) there may be a certain instinctive wisdom. For there is a dialectic to changing one's nature, the dialectic which underlies all psychoanalytic method: it is the knowledge that if one is to change one's habits, one must go back to the source of their creation, and so the psychopath exploring backward along the road of the homosexual, the orgiast, the drug-addict, the rapist, the robber and the murderer seeks to find those violent parallels to the violent and often hopeless contradictions he knew as an infant and as a child. For if he has the courage to meet the parallel situation at the moment when he is ready, then he has a chance to act as he has never acted before, and in satisfying the frustration—if he can succeed—he may then pass by symbolic substitute through the locks of incest. In thus giving expression to the buried infant in himself, he can lessen the tension of those infantile desires and so free himself to remake a bit of his nervous system. Like the neurotic he is looking for the opportunity to grow up a second time, but the psychopath knows instinctively that to express a forbidden impulse actively is far more beneficial to him than merely to confess the desire in the safety of a doctor's room. The psychopath is ordinately ambitious, too ambitious ever to trade his warped brilliant conception of his possible victories in life for the grim if peaceful attrition of the analyst's couch. So his associational journey into the past is lived out in the theatre of the present, and he exists for those charged situations where his senses are so alive that he can be aware actively (as the analysand is aware passively) of what his habits are, and how he can change them. The strength of the psychopath is that he knows (where most of us can only guess) what is good for him and what is bad for him at exactly those instants when an old crippling habit has become so attacked by experience that the potentiality exists to change it, to replace a negative and empty fear with an outward action, even if—and here I obey the logic of the extreme psychopath—even if the fear is of himself, and the action is to murder. The psychopath murders—if he has the courage—out of the necessity to purge his violence, for if he cannot empty his hatred then he cannot love, his being is frozen with implacable self-hatred for his cowardice. (It can of course be suggested that it takes little courage for two strong eighteen-year-old hoodlums, let us say, to beat in the brains of a candy-store keeper, and indeed the act—even by the logic of the psychopath—is not likely to prove very therapeutic, for the victim is not an immediate equal. Still, courage of a sort is necessary, for one murders not only a weak fifty-year-old man but an institution as well, one violates private property, one enters into a new relation with the police and introduces a dangerous element into one's life. The hoodlum is therefore daring the unknown, and so no matter how brutal the act, it is not altogether cowardly.)

At bottom, the drama of the psychopath is that he seeks love. Not love as the search for a mate, but love as the search for an orgasm more apocalyptic than the one which preceded it. Orgasm is his therapy—he knows at the seed of his being that good orgasm opens his possibilities and bad orgasm imprisons him. But in this search, the psychopath becomes an embodiment of the extreme contradictions of the society which formed his character, and the apocalyptic orgasm often remains as remote as the Holy Grail, for there are clusters and nests and ambushes of violence in his own necessities and in the imperatives and retaliations of the men and women among whom he lives his life, so that even as he drains his hatred in one act or another, so the conditions of his life create it anew in him until the drama of his movements bears a sardonic resemblance to the frog who climbed a few feet in the well only to drop back again.

Yet there is this to be said for the search after the good orgasm: when one lives in a civilized world, and still can enjoy none of the cultural nectar of such a world because the paradoxes on which civilization is built demand that there remain a cultureless and alienated bottom of exploitable human material, then the logic of becoming a sexual outlaw (if one's psychological roots are bedded in the bottom) is that one has at least a running competitive chance to be physically healthy so long as one stays alive. It is therefore no accident that psychopathy is most prevalent with the Negro. Hated from outside and therefore hating himself, the Negro was forced into the position of exploring all those moral wildernesses of civilized life which the Square automatically condemns as delinquent or evil or immature or morbid or self-destructive or corrupt. (Actually the terms have equal weight. Depending on the telescope of the cultural clique from which the Square surveys the universe, "evil" or "immature" are equally strong terms of condemnation.) But the Negro, not being privileged to gratify his self-esteem with the heady satisfactions of categorical condemnation, chose to move instead in that other direction where all situations are equally valid, and in the worst of perversion, promiscuity, pimpery, drug addiction, rape, razor-slash, bottle-break, what-have-you, the Negro discovered and elaborated a morality of the bottom, an ethical differentiation between the good and the bad in every human activity from the go-getter pimp (as opposed to the lazy one) to the relatively dependable pusher or prostitute. Add to this, the cunning of their language, the abstract ambiguous alternatives in which from the danger of their oppression they learned to speak ("Well, now, man, like I'm looking for a cat to turn me on . . ."), add even more the profound sensitivity of the Negro jazzman who was the cultural mentor of a people, and it is not too difficult to believe that the language of Hip which evolved was an artful language, tested and shaped by an intense experience and therefore different in kind from white slang, as different as the special obscenity of the soldier, which in its emphasis upon "ass" as the soul and "shit" as circumstance, was able to express the existential states of the enlisted man. What makes Hip a special language is that it cannot really be taught—if one shares none of the experiences of elation and exhaustion which it is equipped to describe, then it seems merely arch or vulgar or irritating. It is a pictorial language, but pictorial like non-objective art, imbued with the dialectic of small but intense change, a language for the microcosm, in this case, man, for it takes the immediate experiences of any passing man and magnifies the dynamic of his movements, not specifically but abstractly so that he is seen more as a vector in a network of forces than as a static character in a crystallized field. (Which latter is the practical view of the snob.) For example, there is real difficulty in trying to find a Hip substitute for "stubborn." The best possibility I can come up with is: "That cat will never come off his groove, dad." But groove implies movement, narrow movement but motion nonetheless. There is really no way to describe someone who does not move at all. Even a creep does move—if at a pace exasperatingly more slow than the pace of the cool cats.

4.

LIKE CHILDREN, hipsters are fighting for the sweet, and their language is a set of subtle indications of their success or failure in the competition for pleasure. Unstated but obvious is the social sense that there is not nearly enough sweet for everyone. And so the sweet goes only to the victor, the best, the most, the man who knows the most about how to find his energy and how not to lose it. The emphasis is on energy because the psychopath and the hipster are nothing without it since they do not have the protection of a position or a class to rely on when they have overextended themselves. So the language of Hip is a language of energy, how it is found, how it is lost.

But let us see. I have jotted down perhaps a dozen words, the Hip perhaps most in use and most likely to last with the minimum of variation. The words are man, go, put down, make, beat, cool, swing, with it, crazy, dig, flip, creep, hip, square. They serve a variety of purposes and the nuance of the voice uses the nuance of the situation to convey the subtle contextual difference. If the hipster moves through his life on a constant search with glimpses of Mecca in many a turn of his experience (Mecca being the apocalyptic orgasm) and if everyone in the civilized world is at least in some small degree a sexual cripple, the hipster lives with the knowledge of how he is sexually crippled and where he is sexually alive, and the faces of experience which life present to him each day are engaged, dismissed or avoided as his need directs and his lifemanship makes possible. For life is a contest between people in which the victor generally recuperates quickly and the loser takes long to mend, a perpetual competition of colliding explorers in which one must grow or else pay more for remaining the same (pay in sickness, or depression, or anguish for the lost opportunity), but pay or grow.

Therefore one finds words like go, and make it, and with it, and swing: "Go" with its sense that after hours or days or months or years of monotony, boredom, and depression one has finally had one's chance, one has amassed enough energy to meet an exciting opportunity with all one's present talents for the flip (up or down) and so one is ready to go, ready to gamble. Movement is always to be preferred to inaction. In motion a man has a chance, his body is warm, his instincts are quick, and when the crisis comes, whether of love or violence, he can make it, he can win, he can release a little more energy for himself since he hates himself a little less, he can make a little better nervous system, make it a little more possible to go again, to go faster next time and so make more and thus find more people with whom he can swing. For to swing is to communicate, is to convey the rhythms of one's own being to a lover, a friend, or an audience, and—equally necessary—be able to feel the rhythms of their response. To swing with the rhythms of another is to enrich oneself—the conception of the learning process as dug by Hip is that one cannot really learn until one contains within oneself the implicit rhythm of the subject or the person. As an example, I remember once hearing a Negro friend have an intellectual discussion at a party for half an hour with a white girl who was a few years out of college. The Negro literally could not read or write, but he had an extraordinary ear and a fine sense of mimicry. So as the girl spoke, he would detect the particular formal uncertainties in her argument, and in a pleasant (if slightly Southern) English accent, he would respond to one or another facet of her doubts. When she would finish what she felt was a particularly well-articulated idea, he would smile privately and say, "Other-direction . . . do you really believe in that?"

"Well . . . No," the girl would stammer, "now that you get down to it, there is something disgusting about it to me," and she would be off again for five more minutes.

Of course the Negro was not learning anything about the merits and demerits of the argument, but he was learning a great deal about a type of girl he had never met before, and that was what he wanted.

Being unable to read or write, he could hardly be interested in ideas nearly as much as in lifemanship, and so he eschewed any attempt to obey the precision or lack of precision in the girl's language, and instead sensed her character (and the values of her social type) by swinging with the nuances of her voice.

So to swing is to be able to learn, and by learning take a step toward making it, toward creating. What is to be created is not nearly so important as the hipster's belief that when he really makes it, he will be able to turn his hand to anything, even to self-discipline. What he must do before that is find his courage at the moment of violence, or equally make it in the act of love, find a little more between his woman and himself, or indeed between his mate and himself (since many hipsters are bisexual), but paramount, imperative, is the necessity to make it because in making it, one is making the new habit, unearthing the new talent which the old frustration denied.

Whereas if you goof (the ugliest word in Hip), if you lapse back into being a frightened stupid child, or if you slip, if you lose your control, reveal the buried weaker more feminine part of your nature, then it is more difficult to swing the next time, your ear is less alive, your bad and energy-wasting habits are further confirmed, you are farther away from being with it. But to be with it is to have grace, is to be closer to the secrets of that inner unconscious life which will nourish you if you can hear it, for you are then nearer to that God which every hipster believes is located in the senses of his body, that trapped, mutilated and nonetheless megalomaniacal God who is It, who is energy, life, sex, force, the Yoga's *prana*, the Reichian's orgone, Lawrence's "blood," Hemingway's "good," the Shavian life-force; "It"; God; not the God of the churches but the unachievable whisper of mystery within the sex, the paradise of limitless energy and perception just beyond the next wave of the next orgasm.

To which a cool cat might reply, "Crazy, man!"

Because, after all, what I have offered above is an hypothesis, no more, and there is not the hipster alive who is not absorbed in his own tumultuous hypotheses. Mine is interesting, mine is way out (on the avenue of the mystery along the road to "It") but still I am just one cat in a world of cool cats, and everything interesting is crazy, or at least so the Squares who do not know how to swing would say.

(And yet crazy is also the self-protective irony of the hipster. Living with questions and not with answers, he is so different in his isolation and in the far reach of his imagination from almost everyone with whom he deals in the outer world of the Square, and meets generally so much enmity, competition, and hatred in the world of Hip, that his isolation is always in danger of turning upon itself, and leaving him indeed just that, crazy.)

If, however, you agree with my hypothesis, if you as a cat are way out too, and we are in the same groove (the universe now being glimpsed as a series of ever-extending radii from the center), why then you say simply, "I dig," because neither knowledge nor imagination comes easily, it is buried in the pain of one's forgotten experience, and so one must work to find it, one must occasionally exhaust oneself by digging into the self in order to perceive the outside. And indeed it is essential to dig the most, for if you do not dig you lose your superiority over the Square, and so you are less likely to be cool (to be in control of a situation because you have swung where the Square has not, or because you have allowed to come to consciousness a pain, a guilt, a shame or a desire which the other has not had the courage to face). To be cool is to be equipped, and if you are equipped it is more difficult for the next cat who comes along to put you down. And of course one can hardly afford to be put down too often, or one is beat, one has lost one's confidence, one has lost one's will, one is impotent in the world of action and so closer to the demeaning flip of becoming a queer, or indeed closer to dying, and therefore it is even more difficult to recover enough energy to try to make it again, because once a cat is beat he has nothing to give, and no one is interested any longer in making it with him. This is the terror of the hipster—to be beat—because once the sweet of sex has deserted him, he still cannot give up the search. It is not granted to the hipster to grow old gracefully—he has been captured too early by the oldest dream of power, the gold fountain of Ponce de León, the fountain of youth where the gold is in the orgasm.

To be beat is therefore a flip, it is a situation beyond one's experience, impossible to anticipate—which indeed in the circular vocabulary of Hip is still another meaning for flip, but then I have given just a few of the connotations of these words. Like most primitive vocabularies each word is a prime symbol and serves a dozen or a hundred functions of communication in the instinctive dialectic through which the hipster perceives his experience, that dialectic of the instantaneous differentials of existence in which one is forever moving forward into more or retreating into less.

5.

IT IS IMPOSSIBLE to conceive a new philosophy until one creates a new language, but a new popular language (while it must implicitly contain a new philosophy) does not necessarily present its philosophy overtly. It can be asked then what really is unique in the life-view of Hip which raises its argot above the passing verbal whimsies of the bohemian or the lumpenproletariat.

The answer would be in the psychopathic element of Hip which has almost no interest in viewing human nature, or better, in judging human nature, from a set of standards conceived a priori to the experience, standards inherited from the past. Since Hip sees every answer as posing immediately a new alternative, a new question, its emphasis is on complexity rather than simplicity (such complexity that its language without the illumination of the voice and the articulation of the face and body remains hopelessly incommunicative). Given its emphasis on complexity, Hip abdicates from any conventional moral responsibility because it would argue that the results of our actions are unforeseeable, and so we cannot know if we do good or bad, we cannot even know (in the Joycean sense of the good and the bad) whether we have given energy to another, and indeed if we could, there would still be no idea of what ultimately the other would do with it.

Therefore, men are not seen as good or bad (that they are good-and-bad is taken for granted) but rather each man is glimpsed as a collection of possibilities, some more possible than others (the view of character implicit in Hip) and some humans are considered more capable than others of reaching more possibilities within themselves in less time, provided, and this is the dynamic, provided the particular character can swing at the right time. And here arises the sense of context which differentiates Hip from a Square view of character. Hip sees the context as generally dominating the man, dominating him because his character is less significant than the context in which he must function. Since it is arbitrarily five times more demanding of one's energy to accomplish even an inconsequential action in an unfavorable contest than a favorable one, man is then not only his character but his context, since the success or failure of an action in a given context reacts upon the character and therefore affects what the character will be in the next context. What dominates both character and context is the energy available at the moment of intense context.

Character being thus seen as perpetually ambivalent and dynamic enters then into an absolute relativity where there are no truths other than the isolated truths of what each observer feels at each instant of his existence. To take a perhaps unjustified metaphysical extrapolation, it is as if the universe which has usually existed conceptually as a Fact (even if the Fact were Berkeley's God) but a Fact which it was the aim of all science and philosophy to reveal, becomes instead a changing reality whose laws are remade at each instant by everything living, but most particularly man, man raised to a neo-medieval summit where the truth is not what one has felt yesterday or what one expects to feel tomorrow but rather truth is no more nor less than what one feels at each instant in the perpetual climax of the present.

What is consequent therefore is the divorce of man from his values, the liberation of the self from the Super-Ego of society. The only Hip morality (but of course it is an everpresent morality) is to do what one feels whenever and wherever it is possible, and—this is how the war of the Hip and the Square begins—to be engaged in one primal battle: to open the limits of the possible for oneself, for oneself alone, because that is one's need. Yet in widening the arena of the possible, one widens it reciprocally for others as well, so that the nihilistic fulfillment of each man's desire contains its antithesis of human co-operation.

If the ethic reduces to Know Thyself and Be Thyself, what makes it radically different from Socratic moderation with its stern conservative respect for the experience of the past is that the Hip ethic is immoderation, childlike in its adoration of the present (and indeed to respect the past means that one must also respect such ugly consequences of the past as the collective murders of the State). It is this adoration of the present which contains the affirmation of Hip, because its ultimate logic surpasses even the unforgettable solution of the Marquis de Sade to sex, private property, and the family, that all men and women have absolute but temporary rights over the bodies of all other men and women—the nihilism of Hip proposes as its final tendency that every social restraint and category be removed, and the affirmation implicit in the proposal is that man would then prove to be more creative than murderous and so would not destroy himself. Which is exactly what separates Hip from the authoritarian philosophies which now appeal to the conservative and liberal temper—what haunts the middle of the twentieth century is that faith in man has been lost, and the appeal of authority has been that it would restrain us from ourselves. Hip, which would return us to ourselves, at no matter what price in individual violence, is the affirmation of the barbarian, for it requires a primitive passion about human nature to believe that individual acts of violence are always to be preferred to the collective violence of the State; it takes literal faith in the creative possibilities of the human being to envisage acts of violence as the catharsis which prepares growth.

Whether the hipster's desire for absolute sexual freedom contains any genuinely radical conception of a different world is of course another matter, and it is possible, since the hipster lives with his hatred, that many of them are the material for an elite of storm troopers ready to follow the first truly magnetic leader whose view of mass murder is phrased in a language which reaches their emotions. But given the desperation of his condition as a psychic outlaw, the hipster is equally a candidate for the most reactionary and most radical of movements, and so it is just as possible that many hipsters will come—if the crisis deepens—to a radical comprehension of the horror of society, for even as the radical has had his incommunicable dissent confirmed in his experience by precisely the frustration, the denied opportunities, and the bitter years which his ideas have cost him, so the sexual adventurer deflected from his goal by the implacable animosity of a society constructed to deny the sexual radical as well, may yet come to an equally bitter comprehension of the slow relentless inhumanity of the conservative power which controls him from without and from within. And in being so controlled, denied, and starved into the attrition of conformity, indeed the hipster may come to see that his condition is no more than an exaggeration of the human condition, and if he would be free, then everyone must be free. Yes, this is possible too, for the heart of Hip is its emphasis upon courage at the moment of crisis, and it is pleasant to think that courage contains within itself (as the explanation of its existence) some glimpse of the necessity of life to become more than it has been.

It is obviously not very possible to speculate with sharp focus on the future of the hipster. Certain possibilities must be evident, however, and the most central is that the organic growth of Hip depends on whether the Negro emerges as a dominating force in American life. Since the Negro knows more about the ugliness and danger of life than the white, it is probable that if the Negro can win his equality, he will possess a potential superiority, a superiority so feared that the fear itself has become the underground drama of domestic politics. Like all conservative political fear it is the fear of unforeseeable consequences, for the Negro's equality would tear a profound shift into the psychology, the sexuality, and the moral imagination of every white alive.

With this possible emergence of the Negro, Hip may erupt as a psychically armed rebellion whose sexual impetus may rebound against the antisexual foundation of every organized power in America, and bring into the air such animosities, antipathies, and new conflicts of interest that the mean empty hypocrisies of mass conformity will no longer work. A time of violence, new hysteria, confusion and rebellion will then be likely to replace the time of conformity. At that time, if the liberal should prove realistic in his belief that there is peaceful room for every tendency in American life, then Hip would end by being absorbed as a colorful figure in the tapestry. But if this is not the reality, and the economic, the social, the psychological, and finally the moral crises accompanying the rise of the Negro should prove insupportable, then a time is coming when every political guidepost will be gone, and millions of liberals will be faced with political dilemmas they have so far succeeded in evading, and with a view of human nature they do not wish to accept. To take the desegregation of the schools in the South as an example, it is quite likely that the reactionary sees the reality more closely than the liberal when he argues that the deeper issue is not desegregation but miscegenation. (As a radical I am of course facing in the opposite direction from the White Citizen's Councils—obviously I believe it is the absolute human right of the Negro to mate with the white, and matings there will undoubtedly be, for there will be Negro high school boys brave enough to chance their lives.) But for the average liberal whose mind has been dulled by the committee-ish cant of the professional liberal, miscegenation is not an issue because he has been told that the Negro does not desire it. So, when it comes, miscegenation will be a terror, comparable perhaps to the derangement of the American Communists when the icons to Stalin came tumbling down. The average American Communist held to the myth of Stalin for reasons which had little to do with the political evidence and everything to do with their psychic necessities. In this sense it is equally a psychic necessity for the liberal to believe that the Negro and even the reactionary Southern white are eventually and fundamentally people like himself, capable of becoming good liberals too if only they can be reached by good liberal reason. What the liberal cannot bear to admit is the hatred beneath the skin of a society so unjust that the amount of collective violence buried in the people is perhaps incapable of being contained, and therefore if one wants a better world one does well to hold one's breath, for a worse world is bound to come first, and the dilemma may well be this: given such hatred, it must either vent itself nihilistically or become turned into the cold murderous liquidations of the totalitarian state.

6.

No MATTER what its horrors the twentieth century is a vastly exciting century for its tendency is to reduce all of life to its ultimate alternatives. One can well wonder if the last war of them all will be between the blacks and the whites, or between the women and the men, or between the beautiful and ugly, the pillagers and managers, or the rebels and the regulators. Which of course is carrying speculation beyond the point where speculation is still serious, and yet despair at the monotony and bleakness of the future have become so engrained in the radical temper that the radical is in danger of abdicating from all imagination. What a man feels is the impulse for his creative effort, and if an alien but nonetheless passionate instinct about the meaning of life has come so unexpectedly from a virtually illiterate people, come out of the most intense conditions of exploitation, cruelty, violence, frustration, and lust, and yet has succeeded as an instinct in keeping this tortured people alive, then it is perhaps possible that the Negro holds more of the tail of the expanding elephant of truth than the radical, and if this is so, the radical humanist could do worse than to brood upon the phenomenon. For if a revolutionary time should come again, there would be a crucial difference if someone had already delineated a neo-Marxian calculus aimed at comprehending every circuit and process of society from ukase to kiss as the communications of human energy—a calculus capable of translating the economic relations of man into his psychological relations and then back again, his productive relations thereby embracing his sexual relation as well, until the crises of capitalism in the twentieth century would yet be understood as the unconscious adaptations of a society to solve its economic imbalance at the expense of a new mass psychological imbalance. It is almost beyond the imagination to conceive of a work in which the drama of human energy is engaged, and a theory of its social currents and dissipations, its imprisonments, expressions, and tragic wastes are fitted into some gigantic synthesis of human action where the body of Marxist thought, and particularly the epic grandeur of *Das Kapital* (that first of the major *psychologies* to approach the mystery of social cruelty so simply and practically as to say that we are a collective body of humans whose life-energy is wasted, displaced, and procedurally stolen as it passes from one of us to another)—where particularly the epic grandeur of *Das Kapital* would find its place in an even more God-like view of human justice and injustice, in some more excruciating vision of those intimate and institutional processes which lead to our creation and disasters, our growth, our attrition, and our rebellion.

Dissent, 1957; Advertisements for Myself, 1959

Frank O'Hara
(1926–1966)

A great poet of the illustrious era of the New York School, Frank O'Hara was a figure of enormous scope—a brilliant art critic and curator who held as much sway among painters as among poets, and a secret virtuoso musician. If Kerouac's poetry had the frenetic quality of hard bop, O'Hara's had the reflective ease of Miles Davis's Kind of Blue. *In his* Personism: A Manifesto, *O'Hara posited a new movement in poetry (which he conceived after a conversation with LeRoi Jones) in which poems are written to one person (not oneself), "unmade telephone calls," achieving a new level of abstraction. "The Day Lady Died" was written July 17, 1959.*

The Day Lady Died

It is 12:20 in New York a Friday
three days after Bastille day, yes
it is 1959 and I go get a shoeshine
because I will get off the 4:19 in Easthampton
at 7:15 and then go straight to dinner
and I don't know the people who will feed me

I walk up the muggy street beginning to sun
and have a hamburger and a malted and buy
an ugly NEW WORLD WRITING to see what the poets
in Ghana are doing these days
                                        I go on to the bank
and Miss Stillwagon (first name Linda I once heard)
doesn't even look up my balance for once in her life
and in the GOLDEN GRIFFIN I get a little Verlaine
for Patsy with drawings by Bonnard although I do

think of Hesiod, trans. Richmond Lattimore or
Brendan Behan's new play or *Le Balcon* or *Les Nègres*
of Genet, but I don't, I stick with Verlaine
after practically going to sleep with quandariness

and for Mike I just stroll into the PARK LANE
Liquor Store and ask for a bottle of Strega and
then I go back where I came from to 6th Avenue
and the tobacconist in the Ziegfeld Theatre and
casually ask for a carton of Gauloises and a carton
of Picayunes, and a NEW YORK POST with her face on it

and I am sweating a lot by now and thinking of
leaning on the john door in the 5 SPOT
while she whispered a song along the keyboard
to Mal Waldron and everyone and I stopped breathing

1959; *Lunch Poems*, 1964

Amiri Baraka (LeRoi Jones)
(b. 1934)

Amiri Baraka was born Everett LeRoi Jones in Newark, where he still lives and works. After serving in the air force—he was discharged on suspicion of being a communist—he settled in Greenwich Village where he joined the avant-garde scene. In 1958 Jones founded Totem Press and the magazine Yugen *with his wife, Hettie Cohen, and worked on the periodicals* The Floating Bear *and* Kulchur. *After a trip to Cuba in 1960 he became increasingly political. His first book,* Preface to a Twenty Volume Suicide Note, *was published in 1961. It has been followed by many others: poetry, plays, fiction, studies of music and politics. He changed his name to Amiri Baraka in 1966. His life has been as diverse as his bibliography. Baraka has been politically active, locally and nationally, has taught at universities, co-authored the autobiography of Quincy Jones, acted in Warren Beatty's* Bulworth, *and he was poet laureate of New Jersey until that office was eliminated due to a controversy over his poem on 9/11, "Somebody Blew Up America." He is now the poet laureate of the Newark Public Schools.*

The Screamers

LYNN HOPE adjusts his turban under the swishing red green yellow shadow lights. Dots. Suede heaven raining, windows yawning cool summer air, and his musicians watch him grinning, quietly, or high with wine blotches on four-dollar shirts. A yellow girl will not dance with me, nor will Teddy's people, in line to the left of the stage, readying their *Routines*. Haroldeen, the most beautiful, in her pitiful dead sweater. Make it yellow, wish it whole. Lights. Teddy, Sonny Boy, Kenny & Calvin, Scram, a few of Nat's boys jamming long washed handkerchiefs in breast pockets, pushing shirts into homemade cummerbunds, shuffling lightly for any audience.

"The Cross-Over,"
Deen laughing at us all. And they perform in solemn unison a social
tract of love. (With no music till Lynn finishes "macking" with any
biglipped Esther screws across the stage. White and green plaid jackets his men wear, and that twisted badge, black turban/on red string
conked hair. (OPPRESSORS!) A greasy hipness, down-ness, nobody
in our camp believed (having social-worker mothers and postman
fathers; or living squeezed in lightskinned projects with adulterers
and proud skinny ladies with soft voices). The theory, the spectrum,
this sound baked inside their heads, and still rub sweaty against those
lesser lights. Those niggers. Laundromat workers, beauticians, pregnant short-haired jail bait separated all ways from "us," but in this
vat we sweated gladly for each other. And rubbed. And Lynn could
be a common hero, from whatever side we saw him. Knowing that
energy, and its response. That drained silence we had to make with
our hands, leaving actual love to Nat or Al or Scram.

He stomped his foot, and waved one hand. The other hung loosely
on his horn. And their turbans wove in among those shadows. Lynn's
tighter, neater, and bright gorgeous yellow stuck with a green stone.
Also, those green sparkling cubes dancing off his pinkies. A-boomp
bahba bahba, A-boomp bahba bahba, A-boomp bahba bahba,
A-boomp bahba bahba, the turbans sway behind him. And he grins
before he lifts the horn, at Deen or drunk Becky, and we search the
dark for girls.

Who would I get? (Not anyone who would understand
this.) Some light girl who had fallen into bad times and ill-repute for
dating Bubbles. And he fixed her later with his child, now she walks
Orange St. wiping chocolate from its face. A disgraced white girl
who learned to calypso in vocational school. Hence, behind halting
speech, a humanity as paltry as her cotton dress. (And the big hats
made a line behind her, stroking their erections, hoping for photographs to take down south.) Lynn would oblige. He would make the
most perverted hopes sensual and possible. Chanting at that dark

crowd. Or some girl, a wino's daughter, with carefully vaselined bow legs would drape her filthy angora against the cardboard corinthian, eying past any greediness a white man knows, my soft tyrolean hat, pressed corduroy suit, and "B" sweater. Whatever they meant, finally, to her, valuable shadows barely visible.

Some stuck-up boy with "good" hair. And as a naked display of America, for I meant to her that same oppression. A stunted head of greased glass feathers, orange lips, brown pasted edge to the collar of her dying blouse. The secret perfume of poverty and ignorant desire. Arrogant too, at my disorder, which calls her smile mysterious. Turning to be eaten by the crowd. That mingled foliage of sweat and shadows: *Night Train* was what they swayed to. And smelled each other in The Grind, The Rub, The Slow Drag. From side to side, slow or jerked staccato as their wedding dictated. Big hats bent tight skirts, and some light girls' hair swept the resin on the floor. Respectable ladies put stiff arms on your waist to keep some light between, looking nervously at an ugly friend forever at the music's edge.

I wanted girls like Erselle, whose father sang on television, but my hair was not straight enough, and my father never learned how to drink. Our house sat lonely and large on a half-Italian street, filled with important Negroes. (Though it is rumored they had a son, thin with big eyes, they killed because he was crazy.) Surrounded by the haughty daughters of depressed economic groups. They plotted in their projects for mediocrity, and the neighborhood smelled of their despair. And only the wild or the very poor thrived in Graham's or could be roused by Lynn's histories and rhythms. America had choked the rest, who could sit still for hours under popular songs, or be readied for citizenship by slightly bohemian social workers. They rivaled pure emotion with wind-up record players that pumped Jo Stafford into Home Economics rooms. And these carefully scrubbed children of my parents' friends fattened on their rhythms until they could join the Urban League or Household Finance and hound the poor for their honesty.

I was too quiet to become a murderer, and too used to extravagance for their skinny lyrics. They mentioned neither cocaine nor Bach, which was my reading, and the flaw of that society. I disappeared into the slums, and fell in love with violence, and invented for myself a mysterious economy of need. Hence, I shambled anonymously thru Lloyd's, The Nitecap, The Hi-Spot, and Graham's desiring everything I felt. In a new English overcoat and green hat, scouring that town for my peers. And they were old pinch-faced whores full of snuff and weak dope, celebrity fags with radio programs, mute bass players who loved me, and built the myth of my intelligence. You see, I left America on the first fast boat.

This was Sunday night, and the Baptists were still praying in their "faboulous" churches. Though my father sat listening to the radio, or reading pulp cowboy magazines, which I take in part to be the truest legacy of my spirit. God never had a chance. And I would be walking slowly toward The Graham, not even knowing how to smoke. Willing for any experience, any image, any further separation from where my good grades were sure to lead. Frightened of post offices, lawyer's offices, doctor's cars, the deaths of clean politicians. Or of the imaginary fat man, advertising cemeteries to his "good colored friends." Lynn's screams erased them all, and I thought myself intrepid white commando from the West. Plunged into noise and flesh, and their form become an ethic.

Now Lynn wheeled and hunched himself for another tune. Fast dancers fanned themselves. Couples who practiced during the week talked over their steps. Deen and her dancing clubs readied *avant-garde* routines. Now it was *Harlem Nocturne*, which I whistled loudly one Saturday in a laundromat, and the girl who stuffed in my khakis and stiff underwear asked was I a musician. I met her at Graham's that night and we waved, and I suppose she knew I loved her.

Nocturne was slow and heavy and the serious dancers loosened their ties. The slowly twisting lights made specks of human shadows, the darkness seemed to float around the hall. Any meat you clung to was yours those few minutes without interruption. The length of the music was the only form. And the idea was to press against each other hard, to rub, to shove the hips tight, and gasp at whatever passion. Professionals wore jocks against embarrassment. Amateurs, like myself, after the music stopped, put our hands quickly into our pockets, and retreated into the shadows. It was as meaningful as anything else we knew.

All extremes were popular with that crowd. The singers shouted, the musicians stomped and howled. The dancers ground each other past passion or moved so fast it blurred intelligence. We hated the popular song, and any freedman could tell you if you asked that white people danced jerkily, and were slower than our champions. One style, which developed as Italians showed up with pegs, and our own grace moved toward bellbottom pants to further complicate the cipher, was the honk. The repeated rhythmic figure, a screamed riff, pushed in its insistence past music. It was hatred and frustration, secrecy and despair. It spurted out of the diphthong culture, and reinforced the black cults of emotion. There was no compromise, no dreary sophistication, only the elegance of something that is too ugly to be described, and is diluted only at the agent's peril. All the saxophonists of that world were honkers, Illinois, Gator, Big Jay, Jug, the great sounds of our day. Ethnic historians, actors, priests of the unconscious. That stance spread like fire thru the cabarets and joints of the black cities, so that the sound itself became a basis for thought, and the innovators searched for uglier modes. Illinois would leap and twist his head, scream when he wasn't playing. Gator would strut up and down the stage, dancing for emphasis, shaking his long gassed hair in his face and coolly mopping it back. Jug, the beautiful horn, would wave back and forth so high we all envied him his connection, or he'd stomp softly to the edge of the stage whispering those raucous threats. Jay first turned the mark around, opened the way further for the completely nihilistic act. McNeeley, the first Dada coon of the age, jumped and stomped and yowled and finally sensed the only other space that form allowed. He fell first on his knees, never releasing the horn, and walked that way across the stage. We hunched together drowning any sound, relying on Jay's contorted face for evidence that there was still music, though none of us needed it now. And then he fell backwards, flat on his back, with both feet stuck up high in the air, and he kicked and thrashed and the horn spat enraged sociologies.

That was the night Hip Charlie, the Baxter Terrace Romeo, got wasted right in front of the place. Snake and four friends mashed him up and left him for the ofays to identify. Also the night I had the grey bells and sat in the Chinese restaurant all night to show them off. Jay had set a social form for the poor, just as Bird and Dizzy proposed it for the middle class. On his back screaming was the Mona Lisa with the mustache, as crude and simple. Jo Stafford could not do it. Bird took the language, and we woke up one Saturday whispering *Ornithology*. Blank verse.

And Newark always had a bad reputation, I mean, everybody could pop their fingers. Was hip. Had walks. Knew all about The Apple. So I suppose when the word got to Lynn what Big Jay had done, he knew all the little down cats were waiting to see him in this town. He knew he had to cook. And he blasted all night, crawled and leaped, then stood at the side of the stand, and watched us while he fixed his sky, wiped his face. Watched us to see how far he'd gone, but he was tired and we weren't, which was not where it was. The girls rocked slowly against the silence of the horns, and big hats pushed each other or made plans for murder. We had not completely come. All sufficiently eaten by Jay's memory, "on his back, kicking his feet in the air, Go-ud Damn!" So he moved cautiously to the edge of the stage, and the gritty Muslims he played with gathered close. It was some mean honking blues, and he made no attempt to hide his intentions. He was breaking bad. "Okay, baby," we all thought, "Go for yourself." I was standing at the back of the hall with one arm behind my back, so the overcoat could hang over in that casual gesture of fashion. Lynn was moving, and the camel walkers were moving in the corners. The fast dancers and practicers making the whole hall dangerous. "Off my suedes, motherfucker." Lynn was trying to move us, and even I did the one step I knew, safe at the back of the hall. The hippies ran for girls. Ugly girls danced with each other. Skippy, who ran the lights, made them move faster in that circle on the ceiling, and darkness raced around the hall. Then Lynn got his riff, that rhythmic figure we knew he would repeat, the honked note that would be his personal evaluation of the world. And he screamed it so the veins in his face stood out like neon. "Uhh, yeh, Uhh, yeh, Uhh, yeh," we all screamed to push him further. So he opened his eyes for a second, and really made his move. He looked over his shoulder at the other turbans, then marched in time with his riff, on his toes across the stage. They followed; he marched across to the other side, repeated, then finally he descended, still screaming, into the crowd, and as the sidemen followed, we made a path for them around the hall. They were strutting, and all their horns held very high, and they were only playing that one scary note. They moved near the back of the hall, chanting and swaying, and passed right in front of me. I had a little cup full of wine a murderer friend of mine made me drink, so I drank it and tossed the cup in the air, then fell in line behind the last wild horn man, strutting like the rest of them. Bubbles and Rogie followed me, and four-eyed Moselle Boyd. And we strutted back and forth pumping our arms, repeating with Lynn Hope, "Yeh, Uhh, Yeh, Uhh." Then everybody fell in behind us, yelling still. There was confusion and stumbling, but there were no real fights. The thing they wanted was right there and easily accessible. No one could stop you from getting in that line. "It's too crowded. It's too many people on the line!" some people yelled. So Lynn thought further, and made to destroy the ghetto. We went out into the lobby and in perfect rhythm down the marble steps. Some musicians laughed, but Lynn and some others kept the note, till the others fell back in. Five or six hundred hopped-up woogies tumbled out into Belmont Avenue. Lynn marched right in the center of the street. Sunday night traffic stopped, and honked. Big Red yelled at a bus driver, "Hey, baby, honk that horn in time or shut it off!" The bus driver cooled it. We screamed and screamed at the clear image of ourselves as we should always be. Ecstatic, completed, involved in a secret communal expression. It would be the form of the sweetest revolution, to hucklebuck into the fallen capital, and

Amiri Baraka (LeRoi Jones)

let the oppressors lindy hop out. We marched all the way to Spruce, weaving among the stalled cars, laughing at the dazed white men who sat behind the wheels. Then Lynn turned and we strutted back toward the hall. The late show at the National was turning out, and all the big hats there jumped right in our line.

Then the Nabs came, and with them, the fire engines. What was it, a labor riot? Anarchists? A nigger strike? The paddy wagons and cruisers pulled in from both sides, and sticks and billies started flying, heavy streams of water splattering the marchers up and down the street. America's responsible immigrants were doing her light work again. The knives came out, the razors, all the Biggers who would not be bent, counterattacked or came up behind the civil servants smashing at them with coke bottles and aerials. Belmont writhed under the dead economy and splivs floated in the gutters, disappearing under cars. But for a while, before the war had reached its peak, Lynn and his musicians, a few other fools, and I, still marched, screaming thru the maddened crowd. Onto the sidewalk, into the lobby, halfway up the stairs, then we all broke our different ways, to save whatever it was each of us thought we loved.

The Moderns: An Anthology of New Writing in America, 1963; *Tales*, 1967

Alexander Trocchi
(1925–1984)

Scottish-born Alexander Trocchi was a merchant seaman during World War II and later studied at the University of Glasgow. After moving to Paris in the early fifties, he edited the literary magazine Merlin *(publishing Henry Miller and Samuel Beckett among others) and hung out with Terry Southern. He wrote pornographic novels (such as* Thongs *and* White Thighs*) published pseudonymously by the Olympia Press and acquired a formidable heroin habit. While living in New York City, the scene of his most interesting work, Trocchi wrote the 1960 novel* Cain's Book*, excerpted here, a fictionalized and self-mythologizing autobiography. Trocchi later lived in London where he operated a bookstore and where he died at fifty-eight.*

from *Cain's Book*

When I was three I went to bed at night with a stuffed white bird. It had soft feathers and I held it close to my face. But it was a dead bird and sometimes I looked at it hard and for a long time. Sometimes I ran my thumbnail along the split in the rigid beak. Sometimes I sucked the blue beads which had been sewn in place of the eyes. When the beak was prised open and wouldn't close again I disliked the bird and sought justifications. It was indeed a bad bird.

THE PAST is to be treated with respect, but from time to time it should be affronted, raped. It should never be allowed to petrify. A man will find out who he is. Cain, Abel. And then he will make the image of himself coherent in itself, but only in so far as it is prudent will he allow it to be contradictory to the external world. A man is contradicted by the external world when, for example, he is hanged.

These thoughts come to mind . . . such is my drugged state, the only witness myself, only the metamorphic Count offering you eternal death, who has committed suicide in an hundred obscene ways, an exercise in spiritual masturbation, a game well played when you are alone ... and I write them down as I try to feel my way into where I left off.

I always find it difficult to get back to the narrative. It is as though I might have chosen any of a thousand narratives. And, as for the one I chose, it has changed since yesterday. I have eaten, drunk, made love, turned on—hashish and heroin—since then. I think of the judge who had a bad breakfast and hanged the lout.

Cain's Book. When all is said and done, "my readers" don't exist, only numberless strange individuals, each grinding me in his own mill, for whose purpose I can't be responsible. No book was ever responsible. (Sophocles didn't fuck anyone's mother.) The feeling that this attitude requires defence in the modern world obsesses me.

God knows there are enough natural limits to human knowledge without our suffering willingly those that are enforced upon us by an ignorantly rationalized fear of experience. When I find myself walled in by the solid slabs of other men's fear I have a ferocious impulse to scream from the rooftops.—Yah bleedin mothahfuckahs! So help me Ah'll pee on you!— Prudence restrains me. But as the past must sometimes be affronted so also must prudence sometimes be overruled. *Caveat.*

I say it is impertinent, insolent, and presumptuous of any person or group of persons to impose their unexamined moral prohibitions upon me, that it is dangerous both to me and, although they are unaware of it, to the imposers, that in every instance in which such a prohibition becomes crystallized in law an alarming precedent is created. History is studded with examples, the sweet leper stifled by the moral prejudice of his age. Vigilance. Dispute legal precedent.

In my study of drugs (I don't pretend for a moment that my sole interest in drugs is to study their effects. . . . To be familiar with this experience, to be able to attain, by whatever means, the serenity of a vantage point "beyond" death, to have such a critical technique at one's disposal—let me say simply that on my ability to attain that vantage point my own sanity has from time to time depended)—in my study of drugs I have been forced to run grave risks, and I have been stymied constantly by the barbarous laws under which their usage is controlled. These crude laws and the social hysteria of which they are a symptom have from day to day placed me at the edge of the gallow's leap. *I demand that these laws be changed.*

The hysterical gymnastics of governments confronting the problem of the atomic bomb is duplicated exactly in their confrontation of heroin. Heroin, a highly valuable drug, as democratic statistics testify, comes in for all the shit-slinging. Perhaps that is why junkies, many of whom possess the humour of detachment, sometimes call it "shit."

We cannot afford to leave the potential power of drugs in the hands of a few governmental "experts," whatever they call themselves. Critical knowledge we must vigilantly keep in the public domain. A cursory glance at history should caution us thus. I would recommend on grounds of public safety that heroin (and all other known drugs) be placed with lucid literature pertaining to its use and abuse on the counters of all chemists (to think that a man should be allowed a gun and not a drug!) and sold openly to anyone over twenty-one. This is the *only* safe method of controlling the use of drugs. At the moment we are encouraging ignorance, legislating to keep crime in existence, and preparing the way for one of the most heinous usurpations of power of all times . . . all over the world . . .

SUCH MIGHT have been my thoughts as I walked away from Sheridan Square where I left Tom Tear. He went into Jim Moore's. Sometimes he sat there for hours, usually in the middle of the night from about twelve till three or four; the countermen liked him and they were generous when he ordered anything. The diner, because it was open all night, was a useful meeting place. The coffee counter is composed of two U's linked by a very short counter which supports the cash register. Its top is of green plastic. The stools are red and chrome. There is a jukebox, a cigarette machine, glass everywhere, and windows . . . that's the advantage of the place, the huge uncurtained windows which look out on to the centre of the square. You can only sit there so long without being seen by your little junkie friends who can see you waiting. It's like being in a goldfish bowl in a display window of a pet shop. (In New York people look in at you through the glass windows of snack bars; Paris cafés spill out onto the street where those who are walking by are open to inspection.) It has also, from another point of view, its disadvantage. If our friends can look in, so can the police, and many of the anonymous men who sit at the counter or who lounge about outside in the small hours could conceivably fink. So it is dangerous to be seen there too often, especially if you are high. Most of us returned there eventually because we were often hung up for shit.

He had asked me to go and have a coffee with him but I knew that once I was inside I would find it difficult to leave. And all of the hours I spent, the hours of vigil I spent in that diner, waiting, were probably the worst.

I walked up Seventh Avenue and turned west on 23rd Street and made directly for the river. The bars were still open so the streets weren't deserted. On 23rd a police car trailed me for a few seconds and then glided past. Without turning my head I caught a glimpse of the man beside the driver, his head turned my way. I wasn't carrying anything that night.

I kept walking past Eighth, Ninth, and I walked up Ninth and turned left a few blocks later. I was walking slowly. Suddenly I was opposite an alley and in the alley about twenty yards away was the dark figure of a man standing close to a wall. He was alone under a small light near a garage door and he was exposing himself to a brick wall.

In terms of literal truth my curiosity was pointless. A man goes to a lane to urinate, an everyday happening which concerns only himself and those who are paid to prevent public nuisance. It concerned me only because I was there and doing nothing in particular as was quite ordinary for me, like a piece of sensitive photographic paper, waiting passively to feel the shock of impression. And then I was quivering like a leaf, more precisely, like a mute hunk of appetitional plasm, a kind of sponge in which the business of being excited was going on, run through by a series of external stimuli; the lane, the man, the pale light, the flash of silver—at the ecstatic edge of something to be known.

THE FLASH of silver comes from earlier; it was a long time ago in my own country and I saw a man come out of an alley. He had large hands. The thought of his white front with its triangle of coarse short hair came to me. I thought of the mane of a wolf, of the white Huns, perhaps because he stooped. Or perhaps because my own ears were pricked back and alert. In his other hand was the glint of something silver. As he walked past me he put his hands in his pockets. I looked after him. I realised I hadn't seen his face. Before I reached the corner he had turned into an adjacent street. I reached the intersection and he was entering a public house. I didn't see him in the bar nor in any of the side rooms. The bar was crowded with workmen, the same caps, the same white scarves, the same boots. He was not in the men's toilet.

Sitting there—an afterthought—I noticed that someone had cut a woman's torso deep in the wood of the door. As big as a fat sardine. There was no toilet paper. I used a folded sheet of the *Evening News*, part of which I tore carefully from the other part which was wet. It was water, and dust had collected. It had been jammed beneath the pipe under the cistern. The ink had run. I felt a necessity to read inside the wet pages. When I peeled them apart I found nothing of interest. A well-known stage actor was to be married. The paper was more than six weeks old. I remembered reading a few days before that he had since died. I couldn't remember whether he left a widow.

I drank one small whiskey at the bar and left. The original impulse to find him had left me. The street was deserted, and the lane. On my way home I wondered why I had followed him. I wasn't after facts, information. I didn't delude myself from the moment I became aware of his shadow, although in self-defence I may have pretended to wonder, to seek safety in the problematic. I can see now I must have known even then it was an *act* of curiosity. Even now I'm the victim of my own behaviour: each remembered fact of the congeries of facts out of which in my more or less continuous way I construct this document is an *act of remembrance*, a selected fiction, and I am the agent also of what is unremembered, rejected; thus I must pause, overlook, focus on my effective posture. My curiosity was a making of significance. I experienced a sly female lust to be impregnated by, beyond words and in a mystical way to confound myself with, not the man necessarily, though that was part of the possibility, but the secrecy of his gesture.

He wore the clothes of a workman, a cap, a shapeless jacket, and trousers baggy at the knees. He might have been a dustman, or a coalman, or unemployed. The hissing gas lamp cast his shadow diagonally across the lane and like a finger into the tunnel. As I came abreast of it I glanced through into the lane and when I saw him I caught my breath. The valve slid open. The faint lust at my belly made me conscious of the cold of the rest of my body. I felt the cool night wind on my face as I sensed my hesitation. It was the way he stood, swaying slightly, and half-hidden, and it was then that I thought of his crotch, and of the stench of goats in the clear night air of the Tartar steppes, of the hairs of his belly, and of the stream of yellow urine from his blunt prick running in a broad, steaming sheet down the stone wall, its precision geometrical, melting the snow near the toes of his big boots. If I had had the nerve I might have approached him then and there instead of following him into the bar, but there was no kinetic quality in my hesitation. It lay on me like an impotence, cloying, turning my feet to lead. It was my cowardice which shattered me. The other knowledge, of the desire, came as no shock. Still, and with a sense of bathos, I found myself moving in pursuit of him when he lurched backwards into full view and passed me at the end of the tunnel where I stood. Did I invent the glint of silver? Endow him with a non-existent razor. The honing of the blade. When I couldn't find him in the bar, and after I had applied my skill to the torso on the wooden door, I returned to the lane and walked through the tunnel towards light. The singing gas lamp evoked memories of sensation, but faintly, and there was no element of anticipation. In the lane I looked over the wall at the windows of the dark tenements above. A pale light showed here and there from behind curtains. Above the level of the roofs the sky was darkening indigo and shifty with thin cloud. I thought: on such a night as this werewolves are abroad and the ambulances of death run riot in the streets. I kicked at the snow on the cobbles. My feet were cold. I walked home with a sense of failure, too familiar even then to shrug off easily. And then, when I entered the flat there was Moira wearing her drop ear-rings, waiting, hoping, at the portal of her day's thoughts, and I walked past her surlily, with no greeting.

MOIRA WAS sitting opposite me. This was before our divorce and before either of us came to America. I had put the incident of the man in the lane out of my mind. It was nearly ten o'clock. Two hours until the New Year. One day followed another. Relief at having attained the limit of the old year made me uneasy. It wasn't as though I were walking out of prison.

Moira was hurt at my isolation. I could sense the crude emotion run through her. It was abrasive. She said I was selfish, that it showed in my attitude, on that of all nights. I knew what she meant.

She felt the need to affirm something and in some way or other she associated the possibility with the passing of the old year. "Thank God this year's nearly over!" she said.

That struck me as stupid so I didn't answer.

"Do you hear what I say?" she demanded.

I looked at her speculatively.

"Well?" she said.

She began to speak again but this time she broke off in the middle. And then she walked across the room and poured herself a drink. She moved from one event to another without ever coming to a decision. It was as though she were trapped outside her own experience, afraid to go in. I don't know what it was she was going to say. She poured herself a drink instead. I watched her from where I was sitting. Her thighs under the soft donkeybrown wool were attractive. She has still got good thighs. Her flesh is still firm and smooth to the touch; belly, buttocks, and thighs. The emotion was there, at all the muscle and fibre. And then she was opposite me again, sipping distastefully at her drink, avoiding my gaze. She was trying to give the impression that she was no longer aware of me and at the same time she sensed the absurdity of her position. That made her uncomfortable. For her the absurd was something to shun. She had a hard time of it, retreating like a Roman before Goths and Vandals.

It occurred to me that I might take her. She didn't suspect. She didn't realise her belly was more provocative when it had been run through with hatred. Hatred contracts; it knitted her thicknesses. She was hotter then, only then. As she began to doubt my love she became a martyr and unlovable. But anger sometimes freed her; her muscles had experienced excitement. . . . To walk across to her. She would pull herself up defensively and refuse to look at me. But her distance was unconvincing. She was not inviolable. That was the moment when I had to be in control of myself, for my lust tended to become acid in my mouth. I preferred her anger to her stupidity. It was something against which I could pit my lust. When I was confronted by her stupidity there took place in me a kind of dissociation, like the progressive separation in milk as it turns sour. I was no longer, as it were, intact, and she was no longer interesting.

I thought of the man in the lane. I had suddenly felt very close to myself, as though I were on the edge of a discovery. I was perplexed when I couldn't find him in the bar. I supposed he must have left while I was in the lavatory. The torso was cut deep in the wood, an oakleaf of varnish left where the pubic hairs were. I touched it with my forefinger, scratching varnish off with my fingernail. It struck me that it was too big. My wife had a big cunt with a lot of pubic hair, but not as big as that. It was heavily packed into her crotch. When I thought of it I always thought of it wet, the hairs close at the chalkwhite skin of her lower belly and embedded like filings in the pores. That made me think of her mother. I don't know why. The torso held my attention. I ran my fingers over it. The pads of my fingers were excited by the rough wood. I felt a slight prickling at the hairs at the back of my neck. I hadn't known wood so intimately before. I participated. I leaned against it. It felt good. That was when I first thought of my wife that night, more particularly, of the elaborate "V" of her sex, standing with my thighs close to the door, touching. I took one drink and left. There was no sign of any man. I looked up and down the street. I felt it was going to snow.

My memory of that New Year's Eve joins those two together, my ex-wife Moira, at her most abject, and the Glasgow proletarian my mother feared, and whose image in the lane under the gaslight, with a thing of silver in one hard hand, elides mysteriously into myself. I often thought it must have been a razor, Occam's perhaps.

It occurred to me she was wearing those new ear-rings her cousin brought her from Spain. That was the second time I noticed the ear-rings that night. She had had her ears pierced a month before. The doctor did it for her. She said she thought drop ear-rings suited her.

It was New Year's Eve. Moira felt she was about to step across a threshold. The ear-rings represented her decision to do so. The date was marked on a calendar. I had wondered why she was wearing them. She had said earlier she didn't want to go to a cinema. Actually I had forgotten the date. I was surprised she was wearing the ear-rings when I got back to the flat.

She was standing in the middle of the room, facing me. I felt she was waiting for me to say something. I had just come in. I was to notice the ear-rings. When I had done so we were to step hand in hand into a new calendar year. But I didn't notice them. I was still thinking of the man in the lane. And Moira herself got in the way, standing in the middle of the room, looking stupid, like she did in public when she thought no one was paying attention to her. Her eyes, as they say, expressed polite interest, indefatigably. At nothing,

nothing. At the beginning I didn't see it. Perhaps it didn't exist at the beginning. I don't know. Anyway, it came to be as obtrusive as her mother's respectability. It had a murderous emphasis. As I say, I didn't see it at the beginning. I even looked the other way. But gradually it became clear to me that she was, among other things, stupid. A stupid bitch. And she had become a boring lay, unimaginative, like a gramophone. And so I didn't notice the ear-rings and my foot was not poised with hers on any threshold and my attention wandered.

I felt she was growing impatient, sitting there, nursing her drink, that she was not sure whether to make a scene, maintain her brittle composure there in the room, or go out quietly. The last move alone would have been authentic . . . or if she had offered me a drink . . . but she was incapable of making it. I think she thought she gave the impression of being dangerous. But Moira was never dangerous, or certainly wasn't at that time. She was not in the least improbable. When the clock struck twelve I heard chairs scraping across the floor of the flat above and the muffled noise of a woman's laughter. When my wife heard it . . . our chimes clock now continued its monotonous tick . . . she stiffened, and at that instant I caught her eye. I had seldom seen her so angry. She lunged out with her foot and kicked over the table. The whiskey bottle splintered on the hearth and the whiskey seeped out underneath the fender on to the carpet where it made a dark stain. For a moment, contemplating it and then me, she tottered like a skittle, and then, bursting into tears, she threw herself out of the room. She had removed her body with her anger. I felt suddenly quite empty.

My mind returned then to the lavatory. I had examined the oakleaf and with my penknife I hewed it down to its proper size. It was no bigger than a pea when I had finished, a minute isosceles triangle with a rough bottom edge to it. I was pleased with the result. Leaning forward then on the handle of my knife, I caused the small blade to sink deeply into the wood at a low centre in the triangle. The knife came away with a small tug. The score, because of the camber of the blade, was most life-like; wedge-shaped, deep. I completed my toilet and returned to the bar. I drank a whiskey. When I left I made straight for the alley.

The flats above formed a tunnel over it where it met the street so that one looked through darkness towards light. Just beyond the darkness, half out of sight round a jutting cornerstone, the man should have stood. I walked along the centre of the lane through the tunnel. The lane, a dead-end, was deserted. The dustbins were already out. I lingered a while. Perhaps I was the stranger you watched apprehensively from your kitchen window. When I left the lane it was already dark and a lamplighter was coming in my direction with his long lighted pole.

THE FLASH of silver . . . the sudden excitement that was almost a nausea . . . the thought of Moira before we left Glasgow . . . the whole complex of the past: I relived it all in that instant I caught sight of the man in the alley on my way back to the scow. The heroin had worn off but I was still pleasantly high from a joint that Tom and I had smoked on the way to Sheridan Square. The street was deserted. The man in the alley, facing the wall, hadn't noticed me yet. I was standing about ten yards from him. Like a man looking on a new continent. I felt the decision at my nostrils, and perhaps it was to communicate that to him, or perhaps it was simply to steady myself in my purpose—I lit a cigarette, cupping my hands over the match and holding them close to my face, causing the skin of my lower face to glow in the shaft of warmth from the match and leaving the skin about my lips tingling minutely in anticipation. The noise of the match striking and the sudden glow in the dark reached him. He froze momentarily and then looked sideways towards me. I could just make out the round yellowish face and the black moustache. There was a tightening pleasure at my entrails. I was quite sure of myself now. A nameless man. And something nameless had taken possession of me. I had simply to be and feel the workings of the nameless purpose in me, to grant, permissively to meet with, sensation unobstructed, rocked gently out of nightmare at him. He was buttoning up, slowly, it might have been reflectively, and then he turned towards me. There was something oblique and crablike in his movement. He was standing there, still under the electric lamp which shone on his shapeless double-breasted jacket at the shoulder and on the right side of his round face. I felt myself moving slowly towards him a foot at a time, looking straight at his face. It seemed that he moved forward to meet me. In a few sensational seconds my front was close to his front and our faces were an inch apart. I felt the warmth of his ear against mine and his hand. Belt, thighs, knees, chest, cheek. A few minutes later we were walking very close together back to my scow at Pier 72.

NEW YEAR'S day. Early. Just after 2 a.m. I had just written:

—My wife will enter as she made her exit, like a bad actor in a bad play, and when I move across to her she will make the gesture of resistance, for my act is her cue to resist; and her face will fix itself in its appallingly stupid lines and break where she smiles as she tumbles and says: "Don't Joe! You'll ladder my stocking!"
She will not expect me to. So I shall catch her out at herself.

I heard them in the hall.

My wife's brother crossed the room after glancing at the shattered whiskey bottle. It still lay where she had thrown it. He was wearing a fawn cashmere coat with a thick blue and white scarf wrapped around his neck so that the head, tilted slightly backwards and bringing the fleshy chin into prominence, gave the impression of having been severed from the body and later cushioned there, neatly, pink, and vaguely apoplectic.

When he greeted me it sounded vaguely like a challenge. Robert was vaguely many things; a challenger, a man embarrassed, an inquisitor; his approach, his whole demeanour—at least towards me—was indirect. He was driven on by his sense of duty but was at the same time, so to speak, afraid to stir up the broth. He would gladly not have known what for a long time he had suspected. He had often said to me that he didn't think I was rotten through and through.

"Otherwise Moira wouldn't love you as she does, now, would she?" But it wasn't much after all. Not enough to dispel his consternation.

"Happy New Year, Joe!"

I took his proferred hand, thanked him, and wished him the same.

Moira, who had come in behind him, was staring angrily at the shattered bottle. Robert, turning towards her and following her gaze, murmured quietly: "Better clean it up, Moira. It'll get trod in."

She burst into tears.

"Now, now, Moira," Robert said to her, moving to her and guiding her by the arm towards the bedroom, "you just go to bed and get rested and let me talk this over with Joe." He followed her into the bedroom. I could hear him expostulating with her, imploring her to be reasonable. I felt sorry for him, for both of them, but I didn't think it was a good idea to go after them. It wouldn't have solved anything.

When he came back he sat down in a chair opposite me. He had taken off his coat and scarf. He held them on his knees as he spoke.

"You might have cleaned it up," he said

"I probably will."

He nodded quickly and, after a moment's hesitation, he went on to say that he wasn't the type of person who interfered with other people's business, that if the war had taught him anything it was that there were two sides to every question. During the war my brother-in-law was a major in the Royal Corps of Signals. The military air, leavened by what I suppose he took to be his modesty, was to some extent still with him. He added that in his professional experience he had learned that it was not always useful to look at everything through one's own eyes; even the Law recognized this in its principle of arbitration, the judge in a Court of Law being neutral in spite of the fact that he was appointed by State. My brother-in-law was a solicitor. He often found it helpful to make a gesture to his authorities, military or judiciary, when he was leading up to his point, presenting creden-

Alexander Trocchi

... **205**

tials. He continued. He would be the first to agree if I objected to his
arbitration on the ground that he was his sister's brother, and therefore not, strictly speaking, neutral. However, he hoped I knew *him*.
And, as he had said before, he had no wish to interfere, especially as
it was the New Year. He paused. He said he thought one should begin
the New Year with a fresh start, not with recriminations. But there it
was. Moira, he meant. The poor girl was deeply hurt. To throw bottles
about, he meant. He knew I would see that. He had always known I
was intelligent. And it wasn't like her to throw bottles about all over
the place. We both knew that. He had said it. He had promised Moira
he would have it out with me. And after all she *was* his sister. Very
dear to him. He knew that she was dear to me also. He had never had
any doubts about that. He would not say he didn't find me difficult to
understand sometimes. A man who didn't work, he meant. Oh, he
knew I was supposed to be writing or something. But after all I wasn't
a child any more. A man of my age. Well, anyway, it was none of his
business and the last thing he wanted to do was to interfere. If Moira
didn't mind working while I sat at home that was her business. But
he didn't like to see her upset. It was the New Year. Bygones should
be bygones. If I was agreed no more needed to be said. He was sure I
would see things his way. I was a reasonable man. He was willing to
shake hands and say no more. What now, agreed?

He allowed these last statements to fall on the silence as a grocer
allows dried peas to fall from his brass scoop, one at a time, his head
cocked, regarding the indicator needle fixedly, until it reaches the
appropriate mark. I didn't mean to keep him waiting. Finally without
saying anything I fetched the unbroken bottle of whiskey and poured
him a drink.

"Happy New Year," I said.

"Happy New Year!"

We clinked glasses and he drank his down with obvious relief.
Then he looked at his watch and said he had to be on his way. Claire
was waiting for him. Claire. I always thought of Claire as strawberries
and cream, cream, red and pink. He looked guilty for her. As well he

might. She would have betrayed him for a dry Martini. She told him she didn't like me.

I helped him on with his coat and he wrapped the scarf round his neck. At the door we shook hands. As he left he turned back for a moment and said he was counting on me. I waved him down the stairs. Back in the room I finished my drink and smoked a cigarette. I might have laughed. But I always found it difficult to laugh alone.

Cain's Book, 1960

Fran Landesman
(1927–2011)

Born Frances Deitsch, she attended the Fashion Institute of Technology in New York City and met Jay Landesman, a former gallery owner who founded the pioneering magazine Neurotica *(among the first to publish Ginsberg and Kerouac) in 1948. They married and moved to St. Louis, Jay's hometown, where he opened a nightclub called the Crystal Palace. Fran to begin to write lyrics, including the classic "Spring Can Really Hang You Up the Most," collaborating on songs with the club's pianist, Tommy Wolf. Together with Jay, who wrote the book (based on his unpublished novel about New York hipster life), they produced the musical* The Nervous Set, *which played on Broadway. One of the show's songs, "The Ballad of the Sad Young Men," became an often-requested gay anthem of the pre-Stonewall era.*

The Ballad of the Sad Young Men

All the sad young men
Sitting in the bars
Knowing neon lights
Missing all the stars

All the sad young men
Drifting through the town
Drinking up the night
Trying not to drown

Sing a song of sad young men
Glasses full of rye
All the news is bad again
Kiss your dreams goodbye

All the sad young men
Seek a certain smile
Someone they can hold
For a little while

Tired little girl
Does the best she can
Trying to be gay
For a sad young man

Autumn turns the leaves to gold
Slowly dies the heart
Sad young men are growing old
That's the cruellest part

While a grimy moon
Watches from above
All the sad young men
Play at making love

Misbegotten moon
Shine for sad young men
Let your gentle light
Guide them home again
All the sad young men

The Nervous Set, 1959;
The Ballad of the Sad Young Men and Other Verse, 1982

John Clellon Holmes
(1926–1988)

Holmes's novel Go, *published in 1952 when he was twenty-six years old, was a roman à clef whose main characters were based on Holmes, Kerouac, Cassady, Ginsberg, Burroughs, and Huncke. His article "This Is the Beat Generation"— a generation to whom he attributed "a feeling of being reduced to the bedrock of consciousness"—popularized the term, apparently coined by Kerouac and inspired by Huncke, when it was published in* The New York Times Magazine *in 1952. Holmes never hit the road, but led a quiet life teaching and writing fiction (including the jazz novel* The Horn*), essays, and poetry. The piece here, from his book* Nothing More to Declare *(1967), is a profile of his friend Jay Landesman.*

The Pop Imagination

WHENEVER I met Jay Landesman in a bar in the old days, I always seemed to arrive first. I waited around, and far from being piqued, I discovered that I was experiencing a pleasant little ping-ping-ping of anticipation. What I was anticipating was laughter.

Black laughter. Like the idea of a cigarette smoking a man, or *Dr. Strangelove*. . . . Absurd laughter. Oh—like a camel in sneakers, beaded Art Nouveau lamps that play "Valencia," Andy Warhol. . . . Pertinent laughter. You know, like, "Laugh? I thought I'd *die*," the cobalt bomb, Lenny Bruce. . . . Laughter accompanied by the sound of hot air escaping from reality's punctured balloons.

When I think of things like this, I always think of Landesman. Not because he was a wit. There wasn't a proper epigram in him. Nor one of those living-room Berles, machinegunning everyone with gags. It was that he saw everything on the bias. It was that everything he did had an air of elaborate burlesque about it.

For instance, his six-button jackets with the multiple vents and triple lapels. His stuffed alligator with the lamp in its jaws. His study in St. Louis that was a facsimile of an old Von Sternberg set in all its claustrophobic proliferation of unrelated dreck. *Neurotica*, for instance—so outrageous in its time that you automatically assumed he must have started it for the same reason that other people suddenly decide to throw a wild party. It was like daring the *Partisan Review*niks to go skinny-dipping. Or ASCA (The Advanced School of Cultural Analysis), with all those spoofing lectures on sports cars, drinking, jazz, conformity and other "aspects," which seemed to be nothing more than a deadpan excuse for Sunday afternoon cocktail parties. Or the Crystal Palace Cabaret Theater in St. Louis, created by Landesman and his brother for the simple reason (one couldn't help but feel) that it didn't already exist, and they needed an arena in which to "make things hot." Or Landesman's musical, *The Nervous Set*, that got to Broadway, perhaps too soon, and died—funny, irreverent, a parody of the Beat Generation. Or was it? You kept remembering lines from it, you kept humming those songs. And you laughed.

You did. You laughed at all this. You said, "Good old Jay. What the hell kind of wild stunt will he pull off next?" You always looked forward to seeing him, and what he pulled off next was always more outlandish than you had anticipated. . . . A Twist Room that must have been one of the first authentic discothèques in America. Or a TV gab-show that opened with a shot of Landesman's firehouse shoes, and then panned up to a wry smile that suddenly admitted, "Talk is cheap." Or a musical version of *Dracula*.

A million laughs, all right. A hip, sardonic mind behind it. No doubt of that. Landesmania, his friends called it. A life style that was a wacky amalgam of Hellzapoppin, Theater of the Absurd, and Pop Art. But serious? You must be kidding. . . . I mean, I once saw him wear magenta Bermudas and a pith helmet. He planned a lecture entitled "Abortive Attempts at Middle-Class Rebellion." He was often heard to say things like, "George Raft in a dinner jacket looks like a stolen Bentley." And take his parties! There was something fiendish about them. . . . Chandler Brossard and James Jones in the same room. Hostility games. Come as your favorite perversion. Confess your first homosexual experience. He was a wrecker, he was frivolous, he was— well, just think of going up to Dorothy Kilgallen on Madison Avenue and saying, "This is Sin Street, Madam, get off it!" Or naming your kids Cosmo and Miles Davis. It was all prankishness, eccentricity, maladjusted *chutzpah*. And yet—

And yet there was that damn underlayer to all of it. His projects all seemed to have a disturbing half-life that lingered in the mind like Strontium-90 in the bone. His personal preoccupations had the maddening habit of becoming cultural tendencies ten years later. You never took him seriously at the time, and you were never sure that he did either, and then all of a sudden everywhere you went in New York during the sixties there was a sort of public version of Landesmania. But where was Landesman? He had moved to England, and he wrote back mysteriously, "I see a kind of blurring of the sexual lines. . . . But no matter how you slice it, ducks, it's all love. . . ." And you started to keep your eyes open, craftily, for that one to reach the surface.

After knowing Landesman for seventeen years, I still find it difficult to explain him to a stranger. A tall, shambling man, who has the warm, inquisitive dark eyes and the self-mocking smile of a secret idealist; who speaks in a glib, exaggerated *patois* of show biz lingo, psychiatric gobbledegook, and Negro and Yiddish slang, all blended into a contagious argot of his own, Landesman has been variously described as "a puppet-master with an aggressive *lack* of talent," "the Mike Todd of dying cities," and "a genie with a certain sense of merchandising." There is a bit of truth in all these estimates, but the whole truth is not there.

For myself, I would say that Landesman possessed, years before it was either chic or marketable, what would now be called the Pop Imagination. In a culture where everything is mass-produced, quick-frozen, readymade, precooked or painted-by-the-numbers, he was the first person I knew who refused such a society's categorical choice of either remaining an esthete or becoming a vulgarian. For any and all evidences of a unique and unconventional point of view interested him, and he looked for these evidences in junk shops, movie houses, and newsstands (wherever his own quirky eye led him), as well as in bookstores, art galleries and theaters. In that Stone Age (ten or fifteen years back), when enlightened people sat in their Eames chairs, under their Calders, talking about T. S. Eliot, Landesman was already living in a thicket of Victorian bric-a-brac, and publishing Allen Ginsberg. I suspect his reasons for doing both were very much the same: he believed in indulging his own curiosity, and only things that were counter, wry, eccentric, special and excessive stimulated him.

Having grown up into (and through) a family antique business, Landesman believed that artifacts were sometimes more evocative of their times than ideas. Things had an uncanny aura to him, and clutter made him feel at ease. The first sight that confronted you on entering his New York apartment was a huge sculpture of Noah's Ark fashioned from half the gunwale of a cat boat. Over his desk in St. Louis hung a spray-painted jock strap in a gilt frame, and he always worked warmly insulated behind mountains of books, magazines, record albums and any other nameless effluvia that had caught his eye. As a consequence, it was impossible to imagine him living for long in the functional Gobi of a modern house, and he could be pain-fully hilarious when a guest in one.

Equally, eccentricity of attire was evidence of soul to him, and one ceased being surprised when he turned up in "horrible" candy-striped seersuckers and a string tie that hung down to his crotch, or sporting a denim sack suit in an advanced state of rumple. Such props were as expressive of his personal vision of things as anything he said, for, as he once confided with a dim smile, "Every time I see a man in jodhpurs and an opera hat—and it only happens two or three times a month these days, I always go up and speak to him, because that man isn't going to hang you up about the weather." Sometimes this flair for the eccentric was only inches this side of outright perversity ("the three-lapel jacket—yes, that was a very important project"), but most of the time Landesman was that unique phenomenon in a status-drunk society: a man who knew that the only really hip style is the next one, the one that hasn't been established yet.

He had an omnivorous interest in popular culture, and long before it was High Camp to collect back issues of *Batman* and idolize the horror movies of Tod Browning, he was publishing articles that anatomized the one, and scouring the most dismal reaches of Brooklyn for screenings of the other. Like many of us in the late forties, he felt that the fine arts were so tyrannized by one or another version of the New Criticism that they had become little more than lifeless appendages of it, but, unlike a lot of people in later years, he shifted his attention to the popular arts without sacrificing his sense of the culture as a whole.

The idea that there is something intrinsically worthwhile about the soup cans, science-fiction movies, mammoth billboards and electronic noise that inundates our civilization (an extremely fashionable idea just recently) would have struck Landesman as being hopelessly frivolous. These things were interesting to him only insofar as they indicated the condition of our imaginations, a condition that could not be perceived if we celebrated the signs of its poverty merely for themselves. "Popular culture never lies," he used to say. "Not about the people who consume it," among whom I'm sure he would have included Susan Sontag as well as the stenographer down the hall.

For it was popular culture's unconscious embodiment of inner fantasies that attracted Landesman. He revelled in it, he let it stimulate his rarer appetites for the bizarre, but he never patronized it in the manner of Camp, and his ear was always cocked for the psychic throb within it—seismographic evidences of which filled the pages of *Neurotica*.

As its editor, Landesman's greatest gift probably lay in getting other people to track down and amplify the whispers he had heard. This wasn't laziness, nor inability to do the job himself, but simply a canny understanding that what he could best contribute to the magazine was a general intuition about the culture, and a Hawkshaw-knack for ferreting out people who could particularize that intuition into usable knowledge. Though there were several assistant editors, all of whom did most of the comma-shifting and phrase-haggling, the magazine showed little of their influence—with the single exception of Legman. For Landesman knew precisely what he wanted from the start. He wanted articles like "The World of the Borderline Fetishist," and "Psychiatrist: God or Demitasse?" and "The Unique Mores of the Bar and Tavern Social Milieu"—all of which existed in the beginning only as titles, to which the articles themselves were more or less jerry-written by other people later.

Also he knew the audience he was trying to reach. "I'm not publishing for the three dozen hard-core scatologists along 42nd Street or the little magazine crowd that tells their Shrinks that, of *course*, they consider *Neurotica* too sick to read. I want to get to the five thousand people who really make this society go—the opinion-makers, the guys with the crazy power, the Sell-Outs who are responsible for running the mess in the first place."

It is highly debatable whether *Neurotica* ever succeeded in achieving this aim (despite the fact that, to my knowledge, it is the only little magazine whose entire run of issues was republished in book form a full decade after its demise), but certainly, in Legman, Landesman found someone with the same muckraking appetites, and they worked together like a couple of unemployed dynamiters trying to blow up the Time-Life Building with a firecracker. I tagged along behind them, as did others.

But for all the barefoot crusades of those *Neurotica* days, it is the sheer excitement, the high pitch of fun, that I have remembered longest. It is the laughter that rose through the smoke to the ten-foot ceiling of Landesman's brownstone apartment on West 53rd Street, where we worked together through the late mornings, writing "Alfred Towne's" exposés of homosexuality in American culture. It is Landesman in his undershirt deciding that we should describe "Towne" as "a midwesterner who has left the country," and the afternoons we fueled our gleeful outrage (at what "Towne" humorlessly insisted on calling "the effeminization of values") with lunchtime gin and staggering corned beef sandwiches from the Stage Delicatessen around the corner. It is remembering how laboriously we fashioned our Mile Wide Hints about such-and-such a conductor; and how lecherously we stripped our scandalous aspersions (concerning so-and-so's penchant for drag) down to their last veil; and with what giggling thoroughness we mapped that murky territory of innuendo just this side of libel.

It all seems a little silly today, a little farfetched (though "fearless" articles almost identical to those "Alfred Towne" published in *Neurotica* and *The American Mercury* still appear all these fifteen years later), and yet from those hoarse and smoky afternoons I think we both distilled, for ourselves at least, a sense that we were engaging the real Scene that lay buried somewhere under the glum hypocrisies and lofty nonsense that passed for a serious culture then.

And, anyway, those afternoons led inevitably toward five o'clock, and five o'clock inevitably brought people: Anatole Broyard with that week's facsimile of the Broyard-girl—blonde, tooled, wordless—changing as little, version to version, as Anatole changed from year to year; Robert Lowry as big and bearish in his corduroys as a grizzly with the face of a panda; Marshall McLuhan (when he was in town) improvising ideas like a combination Spengler, Picasso and Mort Sahl; little, zany William Poster with his clear, darting eye for subtle values; Chandler Brossard as difficult to crack as a horse chestnut and just as tart when you did; Paul Mazursky doing his funny Brando imitations while Stanley Radulovich did his serious ones; Carl Solomon yoinking around so frenziedly on a pogo stick that one night he put the end of it right through the floor into the restaurant below—and all their girls, and their friends' girls, and their friends' friends, and even nameless others who may have just heard the hubbub and walked in the door.

These five o'clocks always got to be ten o'clocks somehow, and we found ourselves in Birdland, or up at the Park Palace in Spanish Harlem, or in Glennon's practicing what Landesman called "futility rites," or down at Louis' in the Village. Landesman was tablehopping, or mamboing with great flung feet and stabbing hands. Landesman was ankling off to phone, or being loudly paged by the bartender, having told half a dozen people just where he would be, and when to call.

Mostly, he was always somewhere near the center of a throng of people when I saw him, but one night I found him alone in his apartment, except for a dark-gold girl named Fran, her face luminous with the hip chick's soulfulness; a girl who bore an astonishing resemblance to Zelda Fitzgerald—only lovelier, softer, more remote; a girl who looked as if she had been tagged early, and *become* herself in the act of surviving it; the kind of girl with a certain pang behind her intelligence and her chic; the kind of girl you marry if you know your own hangups well enough. A month or so later, Landesman did just that, and almost immediately they became "Jay and Fran" to everyone who knew them, one name all but unpronounceable without the other.

Soon after this, Landesman grew bored with hunting the culture's various psychic Snarks, for, unlike Legman, he was not imprisoned by a single perception, and world-changing was not his wine. That singular geiger counter in his head was geared to himself and his personal interests (which he took to be representative), and when there was no click in his current life, he always began to look elsewhere.

Also, by 1951, there was Fran, and their marriage; there was a growing need for a setting where the results of an action could be immediately seen, and there was New York that is never hospitable to this need. In one of those abrupt decisions that make us look at our friends through new eyes, Landesman gave *Neurotica* to Legman, and he and Fran moved back to St. Louis.

Thereafter, the trait that had distinguished everything that Landesman had done surfaced in him rapidly, until it became clear that what drove him (and drives the Pop Imagination generally) was an overriding theatrical sense—a sense of how to put a point of view on display, how to isolate a falsehood so that it could be seen, how to reveal a subtle truth through sheer exaggeration. Landesman's need was to enliven life by "staging" it, to strike creative sparks by rubbing people and ideas together, and, above all, to satisfy a curiosity that was as gluttonous as a Dempster Dumpster. To Landesman, existence was a series of Happenings, or he got glum. Ultimately, his need was for a theater, and St. Louis became that theater for him.

What followed was the Crystal Palace ("the most gorgeous saloon in America"), and the plays, and ASCA, and the TV show. What followed were the lyrics that Fran began to write one day that were set to music by Tommy Wolf, Alec Wilder, and Roy Kral (those sad, wry, sexy leider—like "Listen Little Girl," "Fun Life," and "Spring Can Really Hang You Up the Most—" that resembled nothing so much as the fragrant, whimsical, intimate contents of an evening purse, belonging to a girl who is as interesting to talk to as to lie with, spilled out on the dressing table of another, inevitable dawn), and the need for a showcase in which these songs could be displayed. And what followed that was *The Nervous Set*, with book by Landesman, and all the other shows that made St. Louis, for a few brief years, a town that people visited for more than beer and baseball.

When I conjure up such a visit, I am sitting in Landesman's living room, or in the patio behind his house, or in any one of a dozen apartments nearby that he and his brother kept for "their people"; music is providing its throbbing insulation against the discordant world outside (more than likely little-known show tunes, or bossa nova, or good rock); martinis are being stirred in a huge pitcher, making that velvety sound of ice cushioned by gin; there are half a dozen people around, all of whom give off the indescribable air of being members of Landesman's *troupe*; children yodel at a TV program upstairs; later (I know) there will be a dinner party somewhere under a chandelier or among enormous imitation trees, during which everyone will be brighter and wittier and sexier than he really is, and later still, Gaslight Square and the Palace, Lenny Bruce or Samuel Beckett, and crowds of people who seem to know me simply because I know Landesman.

I am sitting there, nicely mulled, astonished by the realization that I am in the midst of a community within a community—a community with its own theaters, bars, restaurants, apartments and galleries, all reflecting the same life style, the same brand of restless and bizarre intelligence. I am amazed, because I have never known its exact like before, but I am also happily expectant (the way I used to be at Billy Wilder movies, the way I still am when I listen to Thelonious), for I know that no matter what happens in the hours ahead, it will be funny, hip, mordant, noisy and meaningful: the stuff of a good memory.

Landesman's sense of theater permeated this whole community, and infected anything he spent five minutes on. He always answered the phone with a crisp, "Jay L-a-n-d-esman here!" lingering sonorously on his own name, as one does every time one says a name like Walther von der Vogelweide. He introduced outlandish soubriquets for everyone, some of them so maddeningly adhesive that they simply absorbed the actual person, like a kind of verbal Venus flytrap. I remember, for instance, a five-foot-two chutney salesman who was known to me only as The Lord God, a buxom flip of a girl from the Ozarks called Dearest Little, and a hip-talking layout man invariably referred to as F. Scott Fredsegal.

The cocktail hour was orchestrated like an *opéra-bouffe*—music, and booze, and just the right mix of jarring people, all of it calculated to produce an unexpected and sometimes scandalous denouement. Gossip flitted around the room in a balletic counterpoint that intensified the odd feeling of theatricality. There was something overheated and incestuous about these liquid twilights, for Landesman believed that strong personalities, acting on one another in an artificial setting, inevitably would generate the kind of drama out of which recognitions came, and he frankly manipulated "his people" toward this end.

There were animosities a-plenty; there was a more or less continual game of musical beds going on; new "stars" were taken up, old ones dropped; games of charades somehow always ended in group therapy sessions; parties quickly became psychodramas; and there are people from those days who probably have no desire to ever hear the name Landesman again. In my opinion, however, Landesman's

John Clellon Holmes

habit of playing the social Diaghilev was ultimately more creative than destructive (how thin the line!). For its spur was not merely boredom, but rather a desire to break through all the masks, and heighten his sense of life as being openended, dangerous with possibilities, free; a sense that later drew him naturally toward Zen, LSD and consciousness-expansion in general. In any case, people seemed to "perform" a little beyond their usual talents when they were around Landesman. At least, most of them still refer to those days with the unmistakable accents we reserve for the description of an enlarging experience, and Landesman spoke to a vein of ironical decadence which, in those pious, prosperous years, ran deep in all of us. For in the struggle of progress versus decay, Landesman frankly opted for the latter, and this, I believe, was the closest he came to having a guiding principle. It was also the dark secret of his appeal.

Out of the loftiest of intentions, the lust for progress has created the shallowest of worlds, and even the most optimistic of social engineers must sometimes wake up after midnight, disturbed by a vague but persistent nostalgia for something that is not covered in the manuals. As a result, people of my generation instinctively gravitated to the margins, the corners, the backstreets of contemporary experience, hoping to gain a little human time before the automated bulldozers of the future arrived. A lot of us felt twinges of guilt about this, but there was no arguing with the fact that, though we were *for* progress, it profoundly depressed us; and as the steel and glass "environments" went up, we tended to withdraw to whatever "neighborhoods" were left.

Landesman was usually there before us, getting out the gin, and busily poking at the pomposities of a culture so traduced that it equated the Good only with the Useful. This was why he had gone back to St. Louis in the first place, for St. Louis in the fifties was a dying city (hopelessly stratified by outmoded social distinctions, its growth paralyzed by civic ordinances that were as hoary as its architecture), and its prevailing mood can best be compared to the mood of pre-Castro Havana: lethargy, somnolence and a faint whiff of corruption hung in the air that wafted off the big river. It was precisely the sort of scene in which a canny and energetic provocateur could make his move, and almost before they knew it, the burghers and the debutantes found a minor, but authentic, cultural renaissance flourishing under their very noses—*Krapp's Last Tape* instead of the usual *South Pacific*, and "Squareville U.S.A.: A New Look At Main Street" in place of the standard lecture on rubbernecking in Angkor Wat.

For a while a few luxuriant poinsettias bloomed among the crumbling buildings and the blistered streets. But cultural renaissances cannot hold out for long against America's twin fixations of the moment—urban renewal and civic betterment—and St. Louis eventually voted for progress as represented by the wrecker's ball and the touring company. You *knew* a Broadway musical was good (hadn't you read about it in *The New Yorker*?), and every city, with any pride in itself, was erecting those distinctive air-conditioned saltine boxes. But how did you *know* what to feel about the murky and controversial plays the Landesmans put on? And those old waterfront buildings, some of them going back a hundred and fifty years or more—they were only eyesores that never ceased to remind you that you lived in a backward little city in Hicksville. So as the Saarinen Arch (The Gateway to the West) relentlessly went up, Landesman's flamboyant banner, on which might have been emblazoned the frank admonition, "Onward and Downward!" fluttered to the pavement. And in another of those abrupt uprootings, which were the surest sign that it was never comfort that he prized, but creative *room*, he went east. All the way east. All the way to London.

Landesman chose decay, I firmly believe, because of what he knew. He knew himself, and he knew what interested him, and he knew in what exotic mulch those interests had a chance of coming to full flower. Also, he knew precisely how he had to live to prevent the contradictions in his nature (an artist's nature, even though he sometimes lacked an art—that is to say, a reckless, inquisitive, ultimately unsatisfiable nature) from becoming stalemated in a struggle that he knew he could only *lose*. For underlying his imagination, his theatricality, and his "decadence," was something considerably more rare: a man cursed with a keenly contemporary sensibility and all its exaggerated appetites, living out, in himself, most of the psychic displacements and realignings, which, in this time, often suggest that a new and wider human consciousness is on the road to its Bethlehem to be born.

Beyond this, one can only speculate, but my speculation tells me that it was a radical notion of sex that stood behind most of Landesman's "projects." For when I think of him, I always think of that black, iconoclastic humor that we all possessed, or at least recognized instantly, in those days; that humor which said, "It isn't that way. That isn't the way it is. We all know how it *really* is"; that humor dubbed "sick" by a society so Orwellian that it actually confused the diagnosis with the disease. I think Landesman knew, as well, that in a situation so existentially false that black humor is the only intelligent saving response, that humor always tends to reflect the secret intuition that sexuality is somehow the last sanctuary of the Real; a final frontier that no passports, visas or customs can prevent us from crossing in order to discover (in the danger and the dark on the other side) what it is like to be fully and mysteriously alive. I think Landesman ceaselessly experimented, dared to "act out," engineered new and disturbing situations, and always put *himself* on the line, because he worked at his life the way writers work at a book, and always assumed (often wrongly) that everyone else was as seriously involved in the search as he.

For, above all, I think he *was* serious. He was serious about marriage, for instance—so serious that he tried to discover a new sort of basis on which it could survive in an Age of Splitsville, a basis that would embody *all* the contradictory urges of love and power, ego and self, which (far from representing abnormality in our century) are the very norm from which we must begin; and his marriage to Fran, which survived enough upheavals to wreck any relationship with the slightest bit of deceit in it, was probably the single marriage that I knew about that I would have made book would last. If, as he got older, he was less and less concerned with challenging the powers that be, influencing the age and competing in the arena (hadn't we all seen the "issues" come and go, despite the tireless energy and high hopes that were expended on them?), it was probably because he eventually came to believe that there was no direction left for us to take, except down into the cavern of ourselves where all the "issues" start. And if he became more hedonistic, less success-driven, and occasionally an advocate of avant-garde sex mores, I think it was because he suspected that the most farreaching revolution of our generation would probably turn out to be the Sexual Revolution—predicated, as it was, on a conception of the totally unsuppressed human being, and promising, as it did, an end to the duality of which all the "issues" were only the bitter, cerebral end products.

"What I really want," he once said, "is reasonably simple. I want economic security, I want to be around beautiful women who smell good, and I want to stay creative. It seems to me, more and more, that this means adjusting, not to the society, but to the springs of life itself—insofar as you can know them by knowing yourself. Beyond that, I guess what I want is to do everything twice." Knowing him, there is nothing very unreasonable in this.

To me, Landesman represented a side of my generation, and its experience, that I have only come to fully appreciate as we have all gotten older and less amusing. The game-playing, style-enamoured, pomposity-puncturing side. The side that practiced its "futility rites" with so much energy, and wit, and unconscious courage. The funny, hip, mordant, noisy, meaningful side. Not the deepest side perhaps; too impatient and too facile, too continually *aware* of everything, to pause for the probe to ultimate causes. But a side that lived intensely up to its times, nevertheless.

In any case, on those flawless spring mornings when anxiety or exhilaration makes me feel that only a drink in a sunny, uncrowded, old-fashioned barroom will put an egg in my day, I always think of phoning Landesman, and urging a lunch. The talk won't be solemn or profound, but its surface will shimmer with a mind that knows where we have been, and where we are now; a mind that has always found life interesting and a little absurd, but has never lost its taste for the adventure. The people who will turn up later are likely to be tough-minded, attractive, and up on things. They will carefully consider what to drink, and make the smart decision. They will pull their own weight, and won't have to have anything explained to them. And for a few hours, I will have a very keen sense of all of us there together—heirs of a fairly bad world, who have lived through it with some grace, and not made it any worse.

Sometime during those hours, Landesman is bound to say to me: "We've got us a big talk coming one of these days, Johnnie . . . ," always a sign to me that he is feeling warm, expansive, hurried and affectionate. And I will think (as I always do) that we really have no need of that talk. I know where he is going, and I know why. His restless eye—for the fun, and the nerves, and the girls of his time—has always given him away.

Nothing More to Declare, 1967

Seymour Krim
(1922–1989)

When I was twelve years old I wanted to be a beatnik because of the character Maynard G. Krebs *on* The Many Loves of Dobie Gillis. *By the time I was fourteen my inspiration was Seymour Krim's paperback anthology* The Beats— *a collection of what he called "fantastic crazy nutty grim honest liberating fertilizing writing"—which made that scene look more glamorous than* Peter Gunn. *There's no greater advocate than a convert and Krim, who came to Beat from the mainstream milieu of* Commentary *and* The Hudson Review, *brought to the scene the enthusiasm of a St. Paul. You can feel it in "Making It!," from* Views of a Nearsighted Cannoneer. *It worked for me. Thanks Seymour, thanks Maynard.*

Making It!

W HEN HAS an inside phrase like "making it" or so-and-so's "got it made" shot with such reality through the museum of official English? In this terse verbal shorthand lies a philosophy of life that puts a gun in the back of Chase Manhattan rhetoric and opens up, like a money-bag, the true values that make the Sammys and Susies of modern city life run today. *You've got it made.* How the words sing a swift jazz poem of success, hi-fi, the best chicks (or guys), your name in lights, pot to burn, jets to L.A. and London, bread in the bank, baby, and a fortress built around your ego like a magic suit of armor! *You've got it made.* Royalties pouring in, terraces stretching out, hip movie starlets strutting in butt-parade, nothing but Jack Daniels with your water, your name in Skolsky's column, Tennessee for lunch, dinner with—somebody who swings, sweetheart! And tomorrow the world (as a starter).

Middle-class ideals of success once curled the lip of the intellectual; today he grins not, neither does he snide. Columbia professor, poet, painter, ex-Trotskyite, Partisan Review editor, G. E. engineer, Schenley salesman—they all live in the same world for a change and that world says, go! The Marxist, neo-Christian, romantic, humanitarian values of 20 years ago are great for the mind's library and its night-time prayer mat; but will they fill the cancerous hunger in the soul for getting what *you* want today? Softies become tough, toughies get harder, men dig that they'd rather be women, women say to hell with lilacs and become men, the road gets rougher (as Frankie lays his smart-money message on us) and you've got to move, hustle, go for the ultimate broke or you'll be left with a handful of nothing, Jack and Jill! What happened to the world out *there*, the one you always thought you loved and honestly-couldn't-get-enough-of-without-wanting-a-sou-in-return for your pure and holy feelings? *Baby, that world went up in the cornball illusions of yesterday! Forget it just like it never knew you were alive. This bit about being a fine writer, a dedicated actor, a movie-maker with Modern Museum notions of heaven, a musician because you truly love it, a painter because you die when you smell the color? Don't make me laugh—it's not good for the stitches, dad. This world (nuts, this rutting universe!) is a Mt. Everest, kiddo, and you've got to start climbing now or the dumbwaiter of this age will slam you down into the black basement. Use whatever you've got and use what you* ain't *got, too!*

Throughout the jumping metropolis of New York one sees vertical fanaticism, the Thor-type upward thrust of the entire being, replacing pale, horizontal, mock-Christian love of fellow-creature; the man or woman who is High Inside, hummingly self-aware, the gunner and the gunnerette in the turret of the aircraft that is Self, is watching out for number one with a hundred new-born eyes. He or she has been slicked down by the competition to a lean, lone-eagle, universe-supporting role. Hey Atlas, did you ever think that common man and woman would be imprisoned under the burden of your heroic weight and find it the ultimate drag rather than the ultimate god-like stance, without value, nobility or purpose? The ancient symphonies of Man have lost their meaning. It is hopelessness that drives the modern whirlwind striver to put such emphasis on personal achievement.

In every brain-cell of intellectual and artistic life the heat is on in America today no differently than it is in business. Values? Purpose? Selectivity? Principles? *For the birds, Charley! I want to make it and nothing's going to stand in my way because everything is crap, except making it! I want* my *ego to ride high,* my *heart to bank the loot of life,* my *apartment to swing,* my *MG to snarl down the highway,* my *pennant to wave above the scattered turds of broken dreams for a better world! Why don't you level and say you want the same, you hypocrite? Be honest for Chrissakes!*

With the blessings of psychiatry, enlightened (so-called) selfishness has become the motto of hip city life; the once-Philistine is admired for his thick skin and wallet; the poor slob who translates Artaud but can't make his rent, a girl, or hold his own at a party is used as a dart-board for the wit of others—not by the "enemy," either, but by his very Village brothers who have forsaken a square idealism for a bite-marked realism. The only enemy today is failure, failure, failure, and the only true friend is—success! How? In what line? Whoring yourself a little? Buttering up, sucking up, self-salesmanship, the sweet oh-let-me-kiss-your-ass-please smile? *Don't be naive, friend. You think this hallucinated world is the moonlight sonata or something? You think anyone cares about your principles or (don't make me puke!) integrity or that they make the slightest ripple in the tempest of contemporary confusion? Go sit at home, then, you model saint and keep pure like the monks with your hands on your own genitalia! Because if you want to make it out in the world, baby, you have to swing, move, love what you hate and love yourself for doing it, too!*

The one unforgivable sin in city life today is not to *make it*. Even though the cush of success may seem hollow to the victor as his true self sifts the spoils, alone and apart from the madding cats who envy him, he knows that his vulnerable heart could not bear the pain of being a loser. Wasn't success drummed at him every day in every way in relation to women, status, loot—Christ, the image of himself in his own eyes? Didn't he see those he admired in his tender years flicked off like so many flies because they'd never made a public victory of their talents? My God, man, what else could he do except be a success (or kill himself)—the world being what it is?

For *making it* today has become the only tangible value in an environment quaking with insecurity and life's mockery of once-holy goals, which the bored witch of modern history has popped over the rim of the world for sport, like an idle boy with paper pellets. *How can you buy grand abstractions of human brotherhood for that daily fix needed by your ego when Dostoievsky and Freud have taught us we hate our parents, brothers, sisters and wives, as well as friends? Oh, no, you can't snow us, you peddlers of fake hope! We know you for what you are: vaseline-tongued frustrates who wanted to make it and lost. Man, how the wound shows behind your pathetic rationalizations!*

The padded values and euphemisms of a more leisurely time have been ruthlessly stripped away under the hospital light of today's world; honesty, integrity, truthfulness, seem sentimental hangovers from a pastoral age, boy-scout ideals trying to cope with an armored tank of actuality that is crumpling the music-box values of the past like matchsticks. It is not Truth that is pertinent today, in the quaint dream of some old philosopher; it is the specific truths of survival, getting, taking, besting, as the old order collapses like a grounded parachute around the stoney vision of the embittered modern adult. *What is left but me?* mutters the voice of reality, *and how else can I save myself except by exhausting every pore in the race with time?* We see in America today a personal ambition unparalled in fierce egocentricity, getting ahead, achieving the prize, making a score—for the redemption of self. Are the ends good? Does it matter to the world? Will it pass muster at the gates of judgment? *Such questions are ridiculous: they presume a God above man rather than the god of life who thumps within my chest for more, faster, bigger, conquests for me, me, ME!*

As the individual stands his lonely vigil in the polar night of the desolation of all once agreed-upon values—as they have receded like the tide, rolling back into the past—where else, he cries, can he turn but to his own future? Who else will help him? What can he or she do but mount the top of personal fulfillment in a world that has crumbled beneath the foot? Upon the neon-lit plains of the modern city comes the tortured cry of a million selves for a place in the sun of personal godhood. As one by one the lights of the old-fashioned planets Peace, Love, Happiness, have flickered and gone out, plunging all into the spook jazzglow of a new surrealist dawn, the only believable light comes from the soul-jet of need that burns in the private heart. *Let the lousy world crash like a demented P-38! What can I do about it? I'm merely a pawn of this age like you. Man, my only escape-hatch is making it at the highest pitch I can dream of!*

An individualism just short of murder has replaced the phantom of socialism as the idols of the recent past shrink into mere trophies on the mocking walls of history. In an existence so dream-like, uncertain, swift, the only nailed-down values that remain are those that can be seen in the bank-book of life. *Can honors be taken away from me? Fame? Money? The beauty I can possess (by name or dollar) in both flesh and leather? No! Don't croon to me of art or soul in a world that has flipped loose from its moorings, seen the futility of truth, the platitude of spiritual hope, the self-deception in innocence, the lack of discrimination in goodness, the pettiness of tears! You live only once, Jack, and if you don't swing with the fractured rhythms of this time—if you hide behind the curtains of a former, simpler, child's world of right and wrong—you condemn yourself to the just sneers of those who dig the real world as it is! Baby, there is no significance today but YOU and the sooner you wake up to the full horror of this fact, the better!*

By time-honored esthetic and moral standards the knowing modern man, and woman, is a barely polite gangster; his machine-gun is his mind, ideas his bullets, power and possession his goals. The reduction of the real to the usable has been whittled into a necessity by the impossible number of potential choices within himself: he knows, after juggling more thoughts than he can reach conclusions about, that he must snap down the lid on fruitless speculation and use the precious energy for making warheads on the spears of practicality.

Victims of their own subjective desperation, pigmies under the heavens of thought that dot the roof of their minds with a million perverse stars, converge upon the external prizes of life like hordes released from prison: eager to bury the intolerable freedom of the mind's insanity in the beautiful sanity of—making it! *Yes, yes, I will convert the self that bugs me into an objective victory in the steel and weighable world! I will take the scalding steam of my spirit and hiss it outward like an acetylene torch upon the hard shale of life, and cut diamonds for myself! You say this therapy of mine adds brutality to the gutter of modernity, that I care only for my private need at the expense of the world? That my fuel is desperation and that I'm marvellously indifferent about adding my shot of cruel self-interest to an already amoral environment? I don't deny it. Survival at its highest conception* means *making it! To live you must conquer if you're normal enough to hate being stuck with your futile being and smart enough to know you must trade it for success!*

For what else is there? Dying at parties, as I used to, when I saw some headliner bring the fawn out of even the best people, who swooned around this living symbol of magic? Eating my heart out because I didn't have the admiration, the quiff, the loot, the attention *I and all human beings demand out of life? Suppose I do know how cheap and unlike my original ideal it all is? You want it too, you envious bastard, you know you do! Spit it out that the ego is the world today for all of us and that without its gratification living is a hell, a roasting on the skewer of frustration as you watch others grab the nooky! Jack, life is too far gone—too man-eat-man—for your wistful moralizing and pansy references to the cathedrals of the past. It's only the present that counts in a world that has no forseeable future and I'm human enough to want to swing my way to the grave—sweetheart, you can have immortality!*

In an age that has seen the abandonment, because they are too costly, of cherished political and personal hopes, hypodermic realism inside and business-like efficiency outside becomes the new style. The address-book replaces the soul, doing is the relief of being, talking of thinking, getting of feeling. *I've got to numb myself in action, exhaust* this inner fiend, or else all the hopelessness of this so-called life of mine will come bursting through its trap-door and overwhelm me! I've got to swing, plan, plot, connive, go and get and get some more, because what else is there, Buster? The frenzied tempo of achievement is matched only by the endless desert within; the futility-powered desperado drives himself ever forward, trying to find in action some publicly-applauded significance that is freezingly absent in solitude. Does it matter that he finds his buddies who have made it as rocket-desperate and unsatisfied as himself?

Hell no. Doesn't the world admire us and isn't it obvious that it's better to be miserable as a storm-trooper than as a Jew? Wasn't my picture in Look, wasn't I on Mike Wallace's show and didn't I turn down an invitation from Long John? Doesn't my answering-service hum with invitations, haven't I made it with that crazy-looking blonde who sings at the Persian Room as well as that distinguished lady novelist who lives near Dash Hammett's old apartment on West 10th? Don't I jive with Condon as well as Wystan Auden, Jim Jones (when he's in town) as well as Maureen Stapleton, Bill Zeckendorf, Bill Rose, Bill Styron, Bill Faulkner, Bill Basie, Bill Williams, Bill de Kooning, Bill Holden—just on the Bill front? Don't I get tips on the market, complimentary copies of Big Table as well as Holiday, didn't I put down Dali at that party for being square and get a big grin from Adlai Stevenson for doing so?

Man, I know what I'm doing! I'm swinging instead of standing still, I'm racing with a racing age, I'm handling 17 things at once and I'm scoring with them all! Life's too wild today, sonny, to worry about the fate of the race or private morality or nun-like delicacies of should-I or should-I-not; anyone with brains or even imagination is a self-driven marauder with the wisdom to know that if he hustles hard enough he can have a moat full of gravy and a penthouse-castle high over life's East River! I'm bartering my neuroses for AT&T (not crying over them to Beethoven's Ninth like you, you fake holy man!) and bemoaning my futile existence with Mumm's Extra Dry and the finest hemp from Laredo and my new Jackson Pollock and my new off-Broadway boff and my new book and my new play and my new pad and this TV show they're gonna build around me and—Jesus, I've got it made!

.... while down below the lusting average man and woman sweats in jealousy at the sight of these dexedrine angels, the very inspiration of what he and she can become if only they too can put that last shred of shame behind them and swing, extrovert yourself, get with it, make that buck, make that chick, make that poem, make this crazy modern scene *pay off*, O my heart, so I too can sink my teeth in the sirloin and wear the pearls of hell!

Views of a Nearsighted Cannoneer, 1961

Del Close
(1934–1999)

Del Close was an actor first, coming up in a St. Louis troupe that included Mike Nichols and Elaine May. In New York he did stand-up, acted on Broadway in The Nervous Set, and in 1959 cut a comedy record called How to Speak Hip. It was hipster self-criticism, goofing on the nouveau hep, and it was a big hit. Even as satire it converted many of its audience to the groovy pose. Close later went to Second City, directed The Committee theater troupe in San Francisco, rode with Ken Kesey's Merry Pranksters, and was "house metaphysician" at Saturday Night Live. He's best known as a mentor to Dan Aykroyd, John Belushi, John Candy, Chris Farley, Tina Fey, Bill Murray, Amy Poehler, Gilda Radner, and Harold Ramis.

Dictionary of Hip Words and Phrases

Ace: A dollar. Also, a friend. "I'm tight with him, he's my ace buddy."
Action: What's happening. "What's shakin' baby, where's the action?"
Axe: Musical instrument. Also, any tool with which you make your living.
Amp: Ampule.
Amphetamine: A powerful stimulant.
Amphetamine head: Habitual user of amphetamine. They are noted for their never ending stream of chatter, their misguided energy, and their unreliability.
Baby: A friendly form of address used for persons of either sex.
Bad: Good. "Monk blows bad piano, man." Also, occasionally, bad. "He's a bad face, man, and I don't want him around."
Bad News: A dreary, unpleasant, or dangerous person. "Here comes Mr. Bad News."
Bag: Very general term for set of circumstances, a complex of behav-

iour patterns, etc. "I'm going to Mexico to study the teachings of Gurdjeiff." "Oh, you're in that bag!"

Ball: Pleasurable experience. "It was great, I had a ball."

Beatnik: A term coined by Herb Caen of San Francisco to describe the self-proclaimed members of the Beat Generation living in the North Beach area. A much abused term, now mostly applied to teenage bohemians, or anything else that's funny looking or whom you don't happen to like. Similar to "Communist" in that respect.

Beat, to: To steal. "He beat me for my short." He stole my car.

Behind: Under the influence of. "I get very goofy behind lush, so I don't drink." Also, as a result of: I'm very strung out behind no sleep.

Bill: One hundred dollars.

Blow: To play any musical instrument. "He blows bad guitar." Also, to make: "My old lady blows nutty scrambled eggs." Also, to lose: "Be here by 5:00 or you'll blow the gig." "I blew my watch." I lost my watch.

Boss: Very good. "That Mercedes is a boss short."

Box: Phonograph.

Boxed: High, stoned.

Bread: Money. "Lay some bread on me, baby, I'm up tight."

Bug: To annoy or irritate. "Don't bug me, Jim."

Burned, to be: To be cheated or swindled. "What happened to that project in which we invested twenty dollars a piece?" "I'm sorry, boys. I got burned, what can I tell you." Also: angry.

Burn down: To create an atmosphere in which no "action" is possible. "Nothing's happening on East 3rd Street, man, all those uncool people burned it down."

Bring down: A depressing person or thing.

Busted: Arrested for a reason. "Charlie the Gizzard took a fall, man,—he got tapped in that big bust last June."

Cat: Male hipster.

Changes, tough: hard times.

Changes: Originally, musical chord changes. Now, refers to psychological or emotional changes. "Man, when you came through that door in that ape suit, I went through a terrible change."

Changes, to put through: To do purposeful violence to a person's state of mind. To disorient. To startle and amaze. See "Put on" and "Riff."

Chick: Girl.

Chops: Embouchure, or lips. Extended to mean any part of the body used to play an instrument. A pianist's chops are his hands. A tap-dancer's chops are his feet. And his shoes are his axe.

City: A suffix used for emphasis. "You went to the Elk's meeting—what was it like?" "What can I tell you? It was Clyde city."

Clyde: An offensive square, a hick.

Come down: To return to normal from a high.

Come on, to: How one presents oneself. To say that someone "comes on strong" means that he has an overdeveloped personality. Also, to make sexual overtures. "So I was trying to sound her. But she said 'Don't come on with me, baby, my old man's outside.'"

Connection: The man you buy it from. Whatever "it" may be. The "Man."

Cook: To do what you do well. "When he started blowing piano, I couldn't see nothing happening, but now he's starting to cook."

Cool: Safe, good, all right, yes, appropriate. An outlook. An attitude. A type of jazz. "Cool it" means stop it, leave, relax, change the subject, etc.

Cop: To obtain, either by purchase or by theft. Many hip expressions owe their validity to being more inclusive in meaning than their English equivalents. See "Old lady."

Cop out: Excuse, shield, cover story.

Count: The amount. "Was it a good count?" "No, man, I got burned."

Crazy: Obsolete term of approval.

Crib: Apartment, "pad." Musicians' term.

Cut, cut out: Leave, "split."

Dig: Understand, appreciate. Also, to look at or listen to. To pay attention. Often used as interjectory verbal punctuation, to command attention or to break up thoughts. "Dig. We were walking down Tenth Avenue, you dig it, and dig! Here comes this cop. So dig, here's what we did."

Do up: To use up or to destroy. "We did up the dope and then we did up the car."

Down home: Oddly enough, a phase of approval. A "down home stud" is a man endowed with the old-fashioned virtues of honesty and integrity. Down to earth. Solid. Also funky, earthy.

Drag: A person or thing that is boring or depressing. "What a drag. What a bring down. I'm drug with this party, I'm going to cut out."

Dues: The disadvantages you will put up with in order to get what you want. The punishment for unwise behaviour.

Eye, the: The television set.

Eyes: Desire. "I got big eyes for some scoff, man, starving." Or, more simply, "I'm gonna split, you eyes?" Meaning: Do you want to come?

Face: Person. "He's a West Coast face."

Fall, to take a: To be arrested.

Fall by: Visit.

Fall in: Enter.

Fall out: Go to sleep suddenly. "Like, when you said 'Fall by,' we thought we'd fall over and fall in on you, but blew it, we fell out."

Far Out: Weird, difficult to understand, strangely motivated. "He's a very far out cat. He sleeps in a bath full of jellied consomme."

Fink: An informer. Lowest form of animal life.

Flick: Movie.

Flip: To go crazy. Less literally, to "flip" over something means to like it a great deal.

Forget it: Expression of contempt.

Freak: Someone who likes something very much, or exclusively. A girl who only goes for musicians is a "musician freak." "I can't smoke these cigarettes, man, I'm a menthol freak."

Freak scene: Swinging, but not monogamously.

Freaky: Strange, odd, funny.

Full, full-out: Complete, or utter. "It was a full shuck," "She's a full-out freak."

Funky: Earthy, down home. When pronounced "Fonky" it means very earthy, very down home.

Fuzz: The police. Originally a pickpockets' term, stemming from the fact that police had nothing in their pockets but fuzz.

Gas: Superlative. "It was a gas, I mean it was a wig."

Geets: Home-made telephone slugs.

Get in the wind: To leave, cut out.

Good people: A good person. "I dig Charley, man, he's good people."

Grease: Money. Also means to eat, or food.

Groove behind, to: To like or enjoy. "I groove behind raspberry sherbet."

Groovy: Coming back into use as a complimentary adjective. "She's a groovy chick."

Hangup: A fascinating object or concept. Also, a psychological block or personality quirk.

Head: Originally, a marijuana smoker, or "tea head." Now very similar in meaning to "freak." A greedy person is a "greed head."

Heat: Police.

High: Intoxicated by narcotics, marijuana, stimulants, depressants, what you will. "Shoe polish is a nutty high."

Hincty: Paranoid, overly nervous about the police. "You bring me down when you go into your hincty bag."

Hip: To know, to be aware.

Hipster: A fully paid-up member of Hip society.

Hippy: A junior member of Hip society, who may know the words, but hasn't fully assimilated the proper attitude.

Hippie-dip: Derogatory term for hippy.

Holding: To have on one's person whatever is needed, usually drugs or money.

Hooked: Addicted.

Hook: A mania. A Satyr may be said to have a "terrible chick hook."

Horn: The telephone. "Get on the horn, call me up."

Hung up: Neurotic. Also, to be in a position in which one is robbed of choice, frustrated. Also, fascinated.

Hustle: To work in a field other than your own. "Are you gigging steady?" "No man, I'm hustling." Scuffling.

Hustler: A survival artist, usually with no visible source of income, often engaged in small-time illegal activity.

In Front: Before. In advance. "I want the bread in front."

Into something: Someone who is putting good creative ideas into his work may be said to be "into something." A high compliment.

Jim: An uncomplimentary form of address. A one word putdown. "Cool yourself, Jim."

Jive: A fearsome insult. Originally in three words. Now, the second two words are usually left unspoken. "You jive . . ." "I can't stand all them jive people."

Joint: Marijuana cigarette.

Juice: Liquor.

Juice-head: A habitual drunk, a lush.

Juiced: Drunk.

Junkie: A narcotics addict.

Later: Goodbye. Also, a derogatory term similar to "Forget it." "Later for that, man."

Lay on: To give. "Lay a deuce on me 'til Tuesday." Lend me two dollars.

Like: A form of verbal punctuation. The extensive use of this word would seem to indicate that the hipster is unconsciously aware of the fact that he can never communicate exactly what he wants to say, and that what he is saying is at best an approximation of what he intends to communicate.

Loose wig: To be free to "swing" creatively is to have a loose wig.

Make: To take. "I make mescaline about twice a year."

Make, to: "I made him for fuse by the way he came on." I guessed that he was probably a police officer because of the way he behaved.

Make it, to: To be good. "Trane really makes it, man."

Make it with, to: To have an affair with someone is to "make it" with him or her. "I'm making it with Jenny now. Man, she really makes it!"

Man: A neutral form of address for either sex.

Man, the: The police. Also, the connection.

Mother: Friendly form of address. "There you go, mother."

Nod: A brief nap. "It's uncool to nod on the street corner waiting for the light to change."

Nutty: Nice, good, attractive. Also, a phrase of agreement, or assent.

Ofay: Negro term for white person. Pig Latin for "foe."

Old lady: Lover or wife.

Old Man: Lover or husband. This is a significant attitude, drawing as little distinction as possible between lover and marital partner.

Off, to: To steal. "Dig the chandelier? I offed it from a church."

Off the wall: Weird, unlikely, far out.

Out: Similar to, but more complimentary than "far out"—"They're a nutty group, man, they blow some out sounds."

Pad: A Hip home or apartment.

Pick up on, to: To pay attention to, to listen to. "Let's go pick up on some sounds." Also, to take, or "make." "I been clean for a month, I would dig to pick up on some pot." To discover. "Ever since Roge picked up on Islam he's been a different cat."

Pin: To examine with full attention. "I tight pinned him, and I make him a full-out fraud."

Pinned: Pupils dilated. "Am I pinned?"

Popped: Arrested, "busted."

Pot: Marijuana.

Pound, a: Five dollars.

Put down: To reject, to denigrate. Also, an insult. "What a terrible put-down!"

Put on: A favourite sport of the Hipster, occasionally vicious. A variety of practical joke in which the victim is not aware that he is being "had." See also, Riff.

Reefer: Once meant marijuana cigarette, now refers to a quantity of marijuana. The difference in this case between hip and non-hip depends on the article. It is un-hip to ask for "a reefer," but "Have you got any reefer?" is acceptable. Under certain circumstances, of course.

Riff: Originally, an improvised instrumental solo. Now, a conversational solo. "Harold blew a nutty riff about the alligators in the New

York subways." A "riff" can be used in a "put on." "Man, I never know whether you're coming on straight, or just riffing at me."

Roach: The unsmoked remains of a "joint."

Salty: Angry.

Salty, to jump: To "come on" in an angry way.

Scarf: To eat.

Scoff: To eat. "Scarf" and "scoff" are also used as nouns. "Let's pick up some scarf."

Score: To make a successful deal with the connection. Also, to succeed with a girl.

Scuffle: To hustle.

Shades: Sun glasses.

Shaking: Happening. "What's shaking?"

Short: Car.

Short line: Very little money. "I'm hung up behind very short line." "It's a fun gig, but short line." —It's a good job, but the pay is small.

Shuck: A con, fraud, or put on.

Scam: A practical improvisation. "How are we going to decorate this coffee house on forty-three bucks?" "Take it off your wig, we'll scam it." Don't worry about it, we'll scuffle something together. Also, a synonym for shuck. A fraud may be called a "full scam."

Scene: Where the happenings happen. "When I came back in from the coast, all my buddies had split the scene." Also, a party. "Call up some people. We'll make a scene."

Sides: Records.

Slam: Jail. Or, "the slammer."

Something else: Something very good indeed.

Sound: To ask. "I sounded him about a gig, but nothing's happening." —I asked him about a job, but there were no openings.

Sounds: Music. "Have you got any sounds at your pad?" Do you have a radio or a phonograph?

Split: To leave.

Square: Conventional, unimaginative. A Babbitt.

Straight: High, or stoned. "Fall by and I'll straighten your head for you." Also, not high, not stoned—down. To "get straight" means to get whatever you need. "Need any bread?" "No, baby, I'm straight." To "straighten" someone means to give him the correct information, what he needs or to give him

Straights: Civilian cigarettes.

Stone: Complete, as in "full." "She's a stone freak." "He's a stone pro."

Stoned: Very high.

Stash: A secret hiding place for illicit goods. Often elaborate or imaginative.

Strung out: Far gone, physically or mentally. When one's source of supply is cut off, one is "strung out."

Stud: A male.

Swing, to: To be happy or successful or both. To enjoy oneself. To "groove."

Taking care of business: Attending to the annoying but essential practical details of existence without losing one's ability to "swing." The phrase, "He takes care of business" often has the ring of admiration.

Taste: A sample.

Tapped: Arrested.

There you go: A greeting, "Hello."

Tight: On close, friendly terms. "I'm tight with him." He's a good friend of mine.

Tossed: Searched by the police. "The man tossed my short and they found a roach. That's how I got tapped."

Tough: Very good.

Tough changes: Hard times.

Tube, the: Television.

Turn on: To get high. Also, to become interested in something. "I got turned on to Stendahl in high school, and I dig him out, man, he's too much."

Twisted: High. "Straight."

Uncool: Dangerously uncautious.

Up tight: In a difficult position.

Viper: Marijuana smoker.

Wasted: Very high. Also, to inflict physical damage on someone is to "waste" him. "He got into his violent bag, you dig it? so I told him 'Don't come on with me, Jim, I'll do up your head' so he did anyway, so I wasted him."

What's shaking?: What's happening?

Wheels: Car.

Wig: Mind. "You can't stop his wig, man, he's got ideas!"

Wig, to: To flip happily. "I told him the good news, and he wigged out."

Zonked: Very high, stoned, twisted, wasted, turned around, smashed, boxed.

How to Speak Hip, 1961

Lenny Bruce
(1925–1966)

Lenny Bruce didn't write, he talked. At first he talked like his mother, Sally Marr, who worked as a stand-up comic and impressionist. But the more he talked the more he turned into Lenny. He worked as an emcee in strip clubs, in real dives. Biographer Albert Goldman noted that it was precisely the barrel-bottom nature of his gigs that allowed him to completely escape his inhibitions and riff where no one had riffed before. Bruce was the first free-association comic rock star, and he never met a subject he shrank from, even as his candor earned him arrests. Here he tells the terrible truth about drugs. Lenny did "Pills and Shit" almost fifty years ago. In it he predicted pot would be legal in ten years. He was off by forty years. And he was dead at forty.

Pills and Shit: The Drug Scene

OH! I got busted since I've seen you. I'm going to lay that on you first. I got two arrests. One: illegal use and possession of dangerous drugs—which is a lie. They're *not*, they're *friendly*.

Lemme get serious with that for a moment. That's how weird I am: I could never discuss or support anything I'm involved with.

I don't smoke pot at all. I don't dig the high. The reason I don't smoke shit is that it's a hallucinatory high, and I've got enough shit going around in my head; and second, it's a *schlafedicker* high, and I like being *with* you all the time. So therefore I can talk about pot, and champion it.

Marijuana is rejected all over the world. Damned. In England heroin is alright for out-patients, but marijuana? They'll put your ass in jail.

I wonder why that is? The only thing I can think of is De Quincy— the fact that opium is smoked and marijuana is smoked, and there must be some correlation there. Because it's not a deterrent. In all the codes you'll always see, "Blah-blah-blah with all the narcotics *except* marijuana." So the legislature *doesn't* consider it a narcotic. Who does?

Well, first: I think that there's no *justification* for smoking shit. Alcohol? Alcohol has a medicinal justification. You can drink rock-and-rye for a cold, pernod for getting it up when you can't get it up, blackberry brandy for cramps, and gin for coming around if she didn't come around.

But marijuana? The only reason could be: *To Serve The Devil—Pleasure!* Pleasure, which is a dirty word in a Christian's culture. Pleasure is Satan's word.

> CONDEMNING VOICE: What are you doing! You're *enjoying* yourself? Sitting on the couch smoking shit and *enjoying* yourself? When your mother has *bursitis!* And all those people in China are suffering, too!
>
> GUILTY VOICE: I'm enjoying it a *little* bit, but it's bad shit, anyway. And I got a headache and I'm eating again from it.

IF WE were to give Man A three glasses of whiskey a day, and Man B were to smoke the necessary amount of marijuana to produce a euphoria like that the alcohol brings, and we do this now for ten years straight, stop them cold one day—Pow!

The guy who juiced will suffer some absence syndromes—he'll need a taste, physically need a taste. The guy that smoked the pot will suffer no discomfort. He is not addicted. Healthwise, the guy who juiced is a little screwed up; and the pot smoker may have a little bronchitis. Maybe.

SINCE MARIJUANA is not a deterrent, no more than cigarettes, it seems inhumane that they *schlep* people and put them in jail with it.

> "Well, maybe marijuana's not *bad* for you, but it's a stepping stone. It leads to heavier drugs—heroin, etc."

Well, that syllogism has to work out this way, though: The heroin addict, the bust-out junkie that started out smoking pot, says to his cell-mate:

"I'm a bust-out junkie. Started out smoking pot, look at me now. By the way, cell-mate, what happened to you? There's blood on your hands. How'd you get to murder those kids in that crap game? Where did it all start?"

"Started with bingo in the Catholic Church."

"I see."

NOW LEMME tell you something about pot. Pot will be legal in ten years. Why? Because in this audience probably every other one of you knows a law student who smokes pot, who will become a senator, who will legalize it to protect himself.

But then no one will smoke it anymore. You'll see.

DO ME a favor. I don't want to take a bust. The code reads that *I* talk, *you* smoke, *I* get busted. So don't smoke—drop a few pills, but don't smoke.

DID YOU see the *Post* reviews? It said that

"His regulars consist of mainlining musicians, call girls and their business managers."

Isn't that a little bit libelous?

I KNOW that Californians are very concerned with the modern. Seven years ago there was a narcotics problem in New York, fifteen years ago in Los Angeles. Now in L.A. it's been like this:

They have a rehabilitation center, and they got this group to attack these narcotic drug addicts. Now, this group is attacking, and getting good at attacking. They mobilize. They get good at it, and better and better and better. First they learn the orthodox way to attack. Then, by hanging out with these deterrents, these felons, they learn *un*orthodox ways. They become bitchy-good attackers—unorthodox, orthodox—and they're wailing their ass off.

Suddenly:

CALIFORNIA LOSING ITS WAR
AGAINST DRUG ADDICTS

There are eighteen hundred empty beds at the rehabilitation center.

"*Schmuck*, you're winning!"

"No, we're *losing*. We gotta fill up the beds!"

"You didn't make one win? In fifteen years?"

"No. We're losing, we're losing!"

Well, I assume there's only one junkie left.

NARCOTICS? Now they've finished with heroin—I think in 1951 there were probably about fifty narcotic officers and seven thousand dope fiends in this state. Today, probably, there are about fifteen thousand narcotics officers and four dope fiends. Fifteen thousand Nalline testing stations, loop-o meters, and they got four dopey junkies left, old-time 1945 hippies.

O.K. One guy works for the county, undercover; the other guy works for the federal heat. O.K. So, finally, finally they went on strike:

JUNKIE: Look, we don*wanna* use dope any more. We're *tired*!

AGENT: Come on, now, we're just after the guys who sell it.

JUNKIE: *Schnook*, don'tya remembuh me? Ya arrested me last week. I'm the undercover guy for the federals.

It's like Sambo, running around the tree. *He* works for the federals, *he* works for the county.

AGENT: Look, we're after the guys who sold it to you. O.K.?

JUNKIE: But *nobody* sold it to me. I bought it from *him*, I told you that . . .

AGENT: Well, will ya just point out one of the guys?

JUNKIE: Don't you *know* him? There's four of us! I told ya that.

AGENT: Just tell us the names of the guys. Cooperate now. Tell us everybody.

JUNKIE [*gives up*]: O.K. He was a Puerto Rican. Drove a green Buick. Hangs out in Forster's.

AGENT: We'll wait for him.

JUNKIE: O.K.

Three days with the investigation:

AGENT: Is that him?

JUNKIE: No, I think it's, hm, ah, I think he was Hawaiian, anyway.

AGENT: O.K. Don't forget. If you hear from him—

JUNKIE: O.K. I'll call ya the first thing.

AGENT: O.K.

So now they've finished up that nonsense, and the guy says:

"You mean to tell me that you guys are gonna screw up our rehabilitation program? If *you're* not using any dope, you certainly *know* some people that need help."

JUNKIE: We don't know anybody. We don't know *anybody*. *Please. I can't use any more dope.* I don't *like* it any more.

AGENT: Well, you really are selfish. You don't care about anybody but yourself. Do you know we have a center to rehabilitate people with fifteen hundred empty beds?

JUNKIE: I know, I'm shitty that way. I'll try.

I LOVED that when he got arrested. He was a dope fiend—Bela Lugosi. It was the worst advertisement for rehabilitation: he was a dope fiend for seven years; he cleaned up; and dropped dead.

THERE'RE NO more narcotic drug addicts, so we're moving now to dangerous drugs. Dangerous drugs—no opiates, nothing to send you to that lethal mania, but the mood elevators, the amphetamines.

The big connections of the dangerous drugs are Squibb and Park-Lilly, Olin Mathison and Merc and Wyeth. Do they know that? Does the legislature know that? I wonder why they're not apprised of that situation. Dangerous drugs—that's the legal phrase—relates to all these medications that are mood elevators, not made for sores or boils. They are made not in Guatemala, but in factories and for a purpose.

Then I said, "These senators, they come from the South. South-erners don't take pills. Nor do Southern doctors prescribe pills." I'll bet you that when all those people were dying of spinal meningitis at Moffitt Field—and heretofore sulpha drugs had worked—you won-dered what happened. Guys are dying there:

"They're spitting out the pills!"

"They're *what*? Whatsa matter with you guys? You're *dying* and you're spitting out the sulpha drugs!"

"Look. I'm a Lockheed worker, and I read all about it in the *Herald Express*, about those dangerous drugs. I'm not filling my body fulla those poisons! I got spinal meningitis, I'll get rid of it the natural way—take an enema, I'll sweat and I'll run around. Not gonna take none of that horseshit."

O.K. now, dangerous drugs. Now, the insanity in that area is that the reason that heroin is *verboten* is that it's no good for people. It destroys the ego, and the only reason we get anything done in this country is that you want to be proud of it and build up to the neigh-bors. And if the opiate *schleps* all that away, then the guy goes up to the guy who builds a new building and he'll say,

DETACHED HIPPY VOICE: Hey, that's cool.

And that's it. So it's no good. And that's why it's out.

You know what I'd like to investigate? Zig-zag cigarette papers. Yeah. Bring the company up:

DEEP AGGRESSIVE VOICE: Now we have this report, Mr. Zig-zag . . . Certainly it must have seemed unusual to you, that Zig-zag papers have been in business for sixteen years, and Bugler tobacco has been out of business for five years! . . .

This committee comes to the conclusion . . . that the people are using your Zig-zag cigarette papers, to . . . roll marijuana tobacco in it.

"Oh, shit."

"That's right. Lots of it—rolling it and smoking it."

Dig. The beautiful part about it is that so many neighborhood grocery stores have been kept in business for years—the *schmucks* don't know that, right?

> YOUNG VOICE [*trying to sound nonchalant*]: O.K. I'll have Delsey toilet tissues, and, ah, another six cans of soup, and a broom, and, ah . . . some cigarette papers.
>
> OLD JEWISH VOICE: I dunno, ve stay in business so long, it's terrific. All the markets—but ve screw em, we chahge top prices, and the people come in here anyway. They *like* me.

O.K. Where does this go on? At a place called Alfie's. Alfy's. Open 24 Hours. Cigarettes, cigars, old Jewish man behind the counter:

> YOUNG WISE GUY: Pa?
>
> ANCIENT JEW: Yuh?
>
> WISE GUY: Pa, do you sell many cigarette papers here?
>
> OLD JEW: Uh.
>
> WISE GUY: What do you assume that people are doing with the cigarette papers they're buying?
>
> OLD JEW: De're rollink cigarettes.
>
> WISE GUY: They're rolling cigarettes? In these flamboyant times you assume people are *rolling* cigarettes?
>
> OLD JEW: Uhhh, so vut are you doink mit cigarette papuhs?
>
> WISE GUY: You don't know?
>
> OLD JEW: No.
>
> WISE GUY: They're rolling *pot*!
>
> OLD JEW: Vus?
>
> WISE GUY: Pot.
>
> OLD JEW: *Vus machts du* pop?
>
> WISE GUY: Marijuana, *schmuck*!
>
> OLD JEW: Marijuana? Hey! Uh, agh, *vus?* Hey—

Always talking to some *schmuck* in the back who's not there.

> —you heard dot? Marijuana. All dese years I never knew dot. Marijuana. Sig-sag papuhs, marijuana, roll the marijuana, *meschugenah*, marijuana.

Next an eighty-year-old pensioner walks to the stand:

OLD PENSIONER: "Hullo? Hullo? Solly, in the bek? Hullo? Ding-
alingalingalinga?"

OLD JEW: Hullo.

PENSIONER: Listen, gimme a peckege Bugler's and some Sig-
sag papuhs.

OLD JEW: *Vus?* Sig-sag papuhs? Justa momunt . . . [*Aside*] Hullo,
policeman? Is gecamein a junkie!

All right. The kid, six years old, played by George McCready:

"Well, let's see now. I'm all alone in my room, and it's Saturday,
and Mother's off in Sausalito freaking off with Juanita, so I'll
make an airplane. Yes. What'll I do . . . I'll make, ah, an Me-110,
that's a good structure. I'll get the balsa wood . . . cut it out there
. . . there we go . . . rub it up . . . Now, I'll get a little airplane glue,
rub it on the rag, and, uh, uh, . . . hmmmmmm, I'm getting
loaded! . . . Is this possible? Loaded on airplane glue? Maybe
it's stuffy in here. I'll call my dog over.

"Felika! Felika, come here, darling, and smell this rag. Smell
it! You freaky little doggy . . . smell the rag Felika . . . Felika!
Felika! IT WORKED! I'M THE LOUIS PASTEUR OF JUNK-
IEDOM! I'm out of my skull for a dime!

"Well, there's much work to be done now . . . horse's hooves
to melt down, noses to get ready . . ."

CUT TO, the toy store. The owner, Albert Wasserman. The kid walks
in:

tinglelingleling!

KID [*affected innocent voice*]: Hello Mr. Shindler. It's a lovely
store you've got here . . . Ah, why don't you let me have a nickel's
worth of pencils, and a big boy tablet, hm? A Big-Little Book?
Some nail polish remover, and, ah, [*voice changes to a driven
madness*] *two thousand tubes of airplane glue!*

OWNER [*old Jew*]: Dot's very unusual! Ve haff nefer sold so
much airplane glue before. I'm an old man—don't bring me
no heat on the place! And save me a taste, you know? I vouldn't
burn you for no bread, you know?

Cut to Paul Cotes, Confidential File:

"This is Paul Cotes, Confidential File, and next to me, ladies and gentlemen of the viewing audience on television, is a young boy who's been sniffing airplane glue. Could be your kid, anybody's kid, whose life has been destroyed by the glue. I hope you can sleep tonight, Mr. LePage. Pretty rotten, a young kid like this. What's your name, sonny?"

"I'm Sharkey, from Palo Alto."

"Well, it's obvious that Sharkey feels a lot of hostility for the adult world. Sharkey, how did it all start, kid? How did you start on this road to ruin? With airplane glue."

"Well, I foist started chippying round wit small stuff—like smellin' sneakuhs, doity lawndry, Mallowmar boxes . . ."

"A little Kraft-Ebbing in there . . . That's very interesting, Sharkey. You've been sniffing it for six months?"

"At'sright."

"Are you hooked?"

"No. I'm stuck."

THIS SCHMUCK here was hooked on morphine suppositories. Like that? Honest to God. If heroin is a monkey on the back, what's a morphine suppository?

When I was in England all these faggots were strung out on sleeping pill suppositories. *Emmis.* So I says to this cat, I says, "Do they really make you sleep, man?"

He says, "Are you kidding? Before you get your *finger* outta your *athth* you're *athleep*, Mary."

That's a beautiful ad:

BEFORE YOU GET YOUR FINGER OUT OF YOUR ASS—
YOU'RE ASLEEP!
NEBYALTAL

"What is *that*? What did he need *that* for?"

"He's *weird*, that's all. He's on it, that's all. He's on it."

"How can you tell?"

"You can tell when they're on it. He's standing on it right now. He *has* to have it. They gotta have it. They kill their mothers for it in the mornings. They got the strength of a madman."

How does he take it?

[*Deep bass voice, with pride*]: "I take it in the suppository form."

Haha! I got high just before the show:

[*Urgently*] "Get it up there, Phil!"

"O.K."

"Hurry up! Hurry up! Somebody's coming!"

Now the reason why I take it in the suppository form is that I have found that even with the most literate doctors, it's not the *substance*, it's the *method of administration*, because if this man would take a ton of opiates through a suppository, the imagery is: "If he takes rubicane in the arm, it's monstrous; but the guy takes it in the ass—what can it be? The *tuchus* . . ."

THIS IS a benzedrex inhaler. I know the inventor, who invented amphetamine sulphate, which was originally used for just shrinking the mucus membrane, you know, the air passage, but some fellows found out that you could crush these benzedrine inhalers and— you've done it—and put them in coca-colas, and it would become a cerebral depressant. So, somehow they took out the benzedrine and put in benzedrex.

The old thing—one guy ruined it for the rest.

Now, if you notice, it has a date when it's exhausted. Your nose? No. The inhaler. Smith, Klein and French.

Now it's sort of weird, you know. I put this, and you know, sniff it up there. But it's about a year old, and it's probably exhausted; so I don't know if I just did that, or sticking things in my nose, you know? Or maybe I'm just hooked on smelling my pocket!

Actually, is it lewd? That goes back to taste. You know that it's just not good taste to blow your nose in public or put one of these in your nose in public. And I've never done it in front of anybody. But I just feel like I wanna do it tonight.

For the first time, being recorded on tape, a man sticking a Smith Klein French inhaler in his nose!

"Ladies and gentlemen, we're here at Fax No. Two. A hush is going over the crowd. He's reaching in his pocket. His neck is tightening. Some ladies sitting ringside, traumatically, are sweating. He's taking it out, giggling nervously. Will he stick it up there? Nervous laughs emit from the crowd. He's a degenerate. Two D.A.R. women are throwing up. There go the people from the Mystery Bus Tour."

'We want our $5.75 back!'

"There he goes, folks, he's sniffing!

'Hi, Howard, hi! Zowie! We're really high now, Howard. We certainly are. We've solved the world's problems.'"

And you're only twelve months old, you little bugger!

EXPLOITATION FILMS present: I WAS A TEEN-AGE REEFER-SMOKING PREGNANT YORTSITE CANDLE. With Sal Mineo and Natalie Wood. See Sal Mineo as the trigger-happy Arty, the kid who knew but one thing—how to *love*, how to *kill!* And see Fatlay Good as Theresa, the girl who knew the other thing, tenderness, and love. And see Lyle Talbot as Gramps, who liked to watch. A picture with a message, and an original Hollywood theme—narcotics.

The film opens as we find Nunzio locked in the bathroom with the stuff, the *baccala*, the marijuana. Cut to the exterior—Youngstown kitchen, there's the wife, you know, the factory-worker wife, the whole bit. He comes home,

WIFE [*delighted*]: Put me down, you big nut! Oh, tee hee . . .

That scene, you know? Looking at her,

HUSBAND [*tenderly*]: Where's our son, where's Ralph?

WIFE [*concerned*]: He's in the bathroom again. And I dunno whatsamatter with him. He's nervous and listless, and he's not bothering with any of his friends, and he's falling off in his studies . . .

HUSBAND: In the bathroom again, eh? Tsk Tsk. Hmmm . . . [*knocks on the door*] Ralph? What are you doing in there?

RALPH [*sucking in a big drag, then trying to hold it in as he answers*]: Usta minud, I beyout in a minud.

WIFE: He's got asthma.

HUSBAND: Will you stop with that, you nitwit! He's on the stuff! O.K. Suddenly we hear a knock at the door, a whistle; and he takes the marijuana, throws it in the toilet, rushes to the door—there's no one there! He's thrown it away! It's *gone*, it's *too late*! Beads of perspiration are breaking out on his forehead.

RALPH: It's gone! There's only one thing left to do—*smoke the toilet!*

The Essential Lenny Bruce, 1967

Mort Sahl
(b. 1927)

Mort Sahl was the first stand-up comic whose schtick was intellectual. Not goof intellectual like Irwin Corey, but the campus type with button-down, V-neck and newspaper. Sahl was a new type, a liberal middle-class hipster, riffing on politics. He was like a clean version of Lenny but then when JFK, for whom he'd written jokes, got assassinated Sahl went all out, reading the Warren Commission Report on stage and getting laughs. He got a lot, but he also brought down heat from the officious media and was marginalized as one of those conspiracy kooks, especially when he was deputized by New Orleans D.A. Jim Garrison. Sahl's one-man Broadway show was canceled in 1967 on the eve of opening night, but he never backed down.

The Billy Graham Rally

All right.
Now are there any groups
Which we have not offended
In some small way?
I've gone into every field except theism.
I do that on the next show.
And I'll tell you about
The Billy Graham rally in New York.
Which I went to in your interest.
Kind of consumer's test.

And I did, I went to see him.
And he's pretty wild.
And I thought it quite significant
That his annual report is in the paper

254

For the '57 Crusade to Save Souls,
And it didn't get into the religious section
On Saturday or Sunday
But it's on the financial page.
Well, he did very well.
There's nothing wrong with, you know,
Paying your way.

So, at any rate . . . that isn't what I meant!
I thought I heard some bowling upstairs.
So, at any rate . . .
He does that all the time.
You got the wrong connotation.
I think too many of you are free-associating, you know.
Graham does that all the time.
He's alway's reading and looking up, you know.
Which even people in the field will admit
Is an assumption.
We don't *know*.
I mean, we think it, right?

He does that.
And he always says to his audience,
"Do you believe?"
And the audiences always say—
You know, they are very vociferous;
They're kind of a cross between
The Bonus March and Jazz at the Philharmonic.
Anyway, he always says to them,
"Do you believe?"
And the audience always lays it on him,
You know, like, *"YOU KNOW IT!"*
Sure.

And then a couple of minutes later
He'll be into original sin or something,
And all of a sudden he'll stop—
You know, like they never said it—
And he'll say, *"Do you believe?"*
And then they lay it on him again.
He does this all the time, you know.
So he obviously is insecure in these areas.

So I'll have more to say about him later.
I don't want to give all this away.
But it's really weird.
It was a very weird rally.

And this rally,
You read about this kook who went out,
This kind of weird guy went out
And started collecting money with the others.
He's not really an usher.
And he's putting money in the bag and everything.
And nobody knew
Because the sun was in back of him
Forming a nimbus.

And I was meanwhile
Taking pictures of Graham like crazy
Because I wanted to show something
To the folks back home.
And then later on I developed the roll
And it was blank.
Which is really weird.

Anyway, so then this guy collected all the bread
And he started to split with the money.

And these two policemen caught him
At the gate at the rally
And they brought him
To Billy Graham's feet for salvation.
And he said, "What are you doing with the money?"
And he said, "I took the money
In an effort to get closer to God. . . ."
By eliminating the middleman, of course.

The Future Lies Ahead, 1958;
Breaking It Up!: The Best Routines of the Stand-Up Comics, 1975

Bob Dylan
(b. 1941)

Folk singer. Unusual voice. Groovy vines. Thirty-five studio albums, twelve live. Probably greatest songwriter in English and maybe the hippest man alive. Has been since he got booed at Newport for using an electric guitar. Around that time ('65–'66) he was doing prose poetry too, in a surrealist vein, which when finally published in 1971 as Tarantula *failed to have the impact of the songs. Dylan stayed away from the written word until 2004 when* Chronicles: Volume One, *a luminous memoir of Beat funky folky bohemia, was published to considerable acclaim. I couldn't put it down. It wasn't surprising that it was superbly written but it was amazing that he could remember it all.*

from *Chronicles: Volume One*

WHEN I wasn't staying at Van Ronk's, I'd usually stay at Ray's place, get back sometime before dawn, mount the dark stairs and carefully close the door behind me. I shoved off into the sofa bed like entering a vault. Ray was not a guy who had nothing on his mind. He knew what he thought and he knew how to express it, didn't make room in his life for mistakes. The mundane things in life didn't register with him. He seemed to have some golden grip on reality, didn't sweat the small stuff, quoted Psalms and slept with a pistol near his bed. At times he could say things that had way too much edge. Once he said that President Kennedy wouldn't last out his term because he was a Catholic. When he said it, it made me think about my grandmother, who said to me that the Pope is the king of the Jews. She lived back in Duluth on the top floor of a duplex on 5th street. From a window in the back room you could see Lake Superior, ominous and foreboding, iron bulk freighters and barges off in the distance, the sound of foghorns to the right and left. My grandmother had only one leg and had been a seamstress. Sometimes on weekends my parents would drive down from the Iron Range to Duluth and drop me off at her place for a couple of days. She was a dark lady, smoked a pipe. The other side of my family was more light-skinned and fair. My grandmother's voice possessed a haunting accent—face always set in a half-despairing expression. Life for her hadn't been easy. She'd come to America from Odessa, a seaport town in southern Russia. It was a town not unlike Duluth, the same kind of temperament, climate and landscape and right on the edge of a big body of water.

Originally, she'd come from Turkey, sailed from Trabzon, a port town, across the Black Sea—the sea that the ancient Greeks called the Euxine—the one that Lord Byron wrote about in *Don Juan*. Her family was from Kagizman, a town in Turkey near the Armenian border, and the family name had been Kirghiz. My grandfather's parents had also come from that same area, where they had been mostly shoemakers and leatherworkers.

My grandmother's ancestors had been from Constantinople. As a teenager, I used to sing the Ritchie Valens song "In a Turkish Town" with the lines in it about the "*mystery Turks and the stars above*," and it seemed to suit me more than "La Bamba," the song of Ritchie's that everybody else sang and I never knew why. My mother even had a friend named Nellie Turk and I'd grown up with her always around.

There were no Ritchie Valens records up at Ray's place, "Turkish Town" or otherwise. Mostly, it was classical music and jazz bands. Ray had bought his entire record collection from a shyster lawyer who was getting divorced. There were Bach fugues and Berlioz symphonies— Handel's *Messiah* and Chopin's A-Major Polonaise. Madrigals and religious pieces, Darius Milhaud violin concertos—symphonic poems by virtuoso pianists, string serenades with themes that sound like polka dances. Polka dances always got my blood pumping. That was the first type of loud, live music I'd ever heard. On Saturday nights the taverns were filled with polka bands. I also liked the Franz Liszt records—liked the way one piano could sound like a whole orchestra. Once I put on Beethoven's *Pathetique* Sonata—it was melodic, but then again, it sounded like a lot of burping and belching and other bodily functions. It was funny—sounded almost like a cartoon. Reading the record jacket, I learned that Beethoven had been a child prodigy and he'd been exploited by his father and that Beethoven distrusted all people for the rest of his life. Even so, it didn't stop him from writing symphonies.

I'd listen to a lot of jazz and bebop records, too. Records by George Russell or Johnny Coles, Red Garland, Don Byas, Roland Kirk, Gil Evans—Evans had recorded a rendition of "Ella Speed," the Leadbelly song. I tried to discern melodies and structures. There were a lot of similarities between some kinds of jazz and folk music. "Tattoo Bride," "A Drum Is a Woman," "Tourist Point of View" and "Jump for Joy"—all by Duke Ellington—they sounded like sophisticated folk music. The music world was getting bigger every day. There were records by Dizzy Gillespie, Fats Navarro, Art Farmer and amazing ones by Charlie Christian and Benny Goodman. If I needed to wake up real quick, I'd put on "Swing Low Sweet Cadillac" or "Umbrella Man" by Dizzy Gillespie. "Hot House" by Charlie Parker was a good record to wake up to. There were a few souls around who had heard and seen Parker play and it seemed like he had transmitted some secret essence of life to them. "Ruby, My Dear" by Monk was another one. Monk played at the Blue Note on 3rd Street with John Ore on bass and the drummer Frankie Dunlop.

Sometimes he'd be in there in the afternoon sitting at the piano all alone playing stuff that sounded like Ivory Joe Hunter—a big half-eaten sandwich left on top of his piano. I dropped in there once in the afternoon, just to listen—told him that I played folk music up the street. "We all play folk music," he said. Monk was in his own dynamic universe even when he dawdled around. Even then, he summoned magic shadows into being.

I liked modern jazz a lot, liked to listen to it in the clubs . . . but I didn't follow it and I wasn't caught up in it. There weren't any ordinary words with specific meanings, and I needed to hear things plain and simple in the King's English, and folk songs are what spoke to me most directly. Tony Bennett sang in the King's English and one of his records was laying around—the one called *Hit Songs of Tony Bennett*, which had "In the Middle of an Island," "Rags to Riches" and the Hank Williams song "Cold, Cold Heart."

The first time I heard Hank he was singing on the *Grand Ole Opry*, a Saturday night radio show broadcast out of Nashville. Roy Acuff, who MC'd the program, was referred to by the announcer as "The King of Country Music." Someone would always be introduced as "the next governor of Tennessee" and the show advertised dog food and sold plans for old-age pensions. Hank sang "Move It On Over," a song about living in the doghouse and it struck me really funny. He also sang spirituals like "When God Comes and Gathers His Jewels" and "Are You Walking and a-Talking for the Lord." The sound of his voice went through me like an electric rod and I managed to get a hold of a few of his 78s—"Baby, We're Really in Love" and "Honky Tonkin'" and "Lost Highway"—and I played them endlessly.

They called him a "hillbilly singer," but I didn't know what that was. Homer and Jethro were more like what I thought a hillbilly was. Hank was no burr head. There was nothing clownish about him. Even at a young age, I identified fully with him. I didn't have to experience anything that Hank did to know what he was singing about. I'd never seen a robin weep, but could imagine it and it made me sad. When he sang "the news is out all over town," I knew what news that was, even though I didn't know. The first chance I got, I was going to go to the dance and wear out my shoes, too. I'd learn later that Hank had died in the backseat of a car on New Year's Day, kept my fingers crossed, hoped it wasn't true. But it was true. It was like a great tree had fallen. Hearing about Hank's death caught me squarely on the shoulder. The silence of outer space never seemed so loud. Intuitively I knew, though, that his voice would never drop out of sight or fade away—a voice like a beautiful horn.

Much later, I'd discover that Hank had been in tremendous pain all his life, suffered from severe spinal problems—that the pain must have been torturous. In light of that, it's all the more astonishing to hear his records. It's almost like he defied the laws of gravity. The *Luke the Drifter* record, I just about wore out. That's the one where he sings and recites parables, like the Beatitudes. I could listen to the *Luke the Drifter* record all day and drift away from myself, become totally convinced in the goodness of man. When I hear Hank sing, all movement ceases. The slightest whisper seems sacrilege.

In time, I became aware that in Hank's recorded songs were the archetype rules of poetic songwriting. The architectural forms are like marble pillars and they had to be there. Even his words—all of his syllables are divided up so they make perfect mathematical sense. You can learn a lot about the structure of songwriting by listening to his records, and I listened to them a lot and had them internalized. In a few years' time, Robert Shelton, the folk and jazz critic for the *New York Times*, would review one of my performances and would say something like, "resembling a cross between a choirboy and a beatnik...he breaks all the rules in songwriting, except that of having something to say." The rules, whether Shelton knew it or not, were Hank's rules, but it wasn't like I ever meant to break them. It's just that what I was trying to express was beyond the circle.

ONE NIGHT, Albert Grossman, the manager of Odetta and Bob Gibson, came into the Gaslight to talk to Van Ronk. Whenever he came in, you couldn't help but notice him. He looked like Sidney Greenstreet from *The Maltese Falcon*, had an enormous presence, dressed always in a conventional suit and tie, and he sat at a corner table. Usually when he talked, his voice was loud, like the booming of war drums. He didn't talk so much as growl. Grossman was from Chicago, had a non–show business background but didn't let that stand in his way. Not your usual shopkeeper, he had owned a nightclub in the Windy City and had to deal with district bosses and various fixes and ordinances and carried a .45. Grossman was no hayseed. Van Ronk told me later that Grossman had discussed with him the possibility of Dave playing in a new super folk group that he was putting together. Grossman had no illusions or doubts that the group was going to go straight to the top, be immensely popular.

Eventually, Dave passed on the opportunity. It wasn't his cup of tea, but Noel Stookey would accept the offer. Grossman changed Stookey's name to Paul and the group that Grossman had created was Peter, Paul and Mary. I had met Peter earlier back in Minneapolis when he was the guitarist for a dance troupe that came through town, and I'd known Mary ever since I first got into the Village.

It would have been interesting if Grossman had asked me to be in the group. I would have had to change my name to Paul, too. Grossman did hear me play from time to time, but I didn't know what he made of me. It was premature for that anyway. I wasn't yet the poet musician that I would become, Grossman couldn't get behind me just yet. He would, though.

I WOKE up around midday to the smell of frying steak and onions on a gas burner. Chloe was standing over the stove and the pan was sizzling. She wore a Japanese kimono over a red flannel shirt, and the smell was assaulting my nostrils. I felt like I needed a face mask.

I had planned to go see Woody Guthrie earlier, but when I woke up the weather was too stormy. I had tried to visit Woody regularly, but now it was getting harder to do. Woody had been confined to Greystone Hospital in Morristown, New Jersey, and I would usually take the bus there from the Port Authority terminal, make the hour-and-a-half ride and then walk the rest of the half mile up the hill to the hospital, a gloomy and threatening granite building—looked like a medieval fortress. Woody always asked me to bring him cigarettes, Raleigh cigarettes. Usually I'd play him his songs during the afternoon. Sometimes he'd ask for specific ones—"Rangers Command," "Do Re Me," "Dust Bowl Blues," "Pretty Boy Floyd," "Tom Joad," the song he'd written after seeing the movie *The Grapes of Wrath*. I knew all those songs and many more. Woody was not celebrated at this place, and it was a strange environment to meet anybody, least of all the true voice of the American spirit.

The place was really an asylum with no spiritual hope of any kind. Wailing could be heard in the hallways. Most of the patients wore ill-fitting striped uniforms and they would file in and out walking aimlessly about while I played Woody songs. One guy's head would be constantly falling forward on his knees. Then he'd raise up and he would fall forward again. Another guy thought he was being chased by spiders and he twirled in circles, hands slapping his arms and legs. Someone else who imagined he was the president wore an Uncle Sam hat. Patients rolled their eyes, tongues, sniffed the air. One guy, continually licking his lips. An orderly in a white gown told me that the guy eats communists for breakfast. The scene was frightful, but Woody Guthrie was oblivious to all of it. A male nurse would usually bring him out to see me and then after I'd been there a while, would lead him away. The experience was sobering and psychologically draining.

On one of my visits, Woody had told me about some boxes of songs and poems that he had written that had never been seen or set to melodies—that they were stored in the basement of his house in Coney Island and that I was welcome to them. He told me that if I wanted any of them to go see Margie, his wife, explain what I was there for. She'd unpack them for me. He gave me directions on how to find the house.

In the next day or so, I took the subway from the West 4th Street station all the way to the last stop, like he said, in Brooklyn, stepped out on the platform and went hunting for the house. Woody had said it was easy to find. I saw what looked to be a row of houses across a field, the kind he described, and I walked towards it only to discover I was walking out across a swamp. I sunk into the water, knee level, but kept going anyway—I could see the lights as I moved forward, didn't really see any other way to go. When I came out on the other end, my pants from the knees down were drenched, frozen solid, and my feet almost numb but I found the house and knocked on the door. A babysitter opened it slightly, said that Margie, Woody's wife, wasn't there. One of Woody's kids, Arlo, who would later become a professional singer and songwriter in his own right, told the babysitter to let me in. Arlo was probably about ten or twelve years old and didn't know anything about any manuscripts locked in the basement.

I didn't want to push it—the babysitter was uncomfortable, and I stayed just long enough to warm up, said a quick good-bye and left with my boots still waterlogged, trudged back across the swamp to the subway platform.

Forty years later, these lyrics would fall into the hands of Billy Bragg and the group Wilco and they would put melodies to them, bring them to full life and record them. It was all done under the direction of Woody's daughter Nora. These performers probably weren't even born when I had made that trip out to Brooklyn.

I wouldn't be going to see Woody today. I was sitting in Chloe's kitchen, and the wind was howling and whistling by the window. I could look out on the street and see in both directions. Snow was falling like white dust. Up the street, towards the river, I watched a blonde lady in a fur coat with a guy in a heavy overcoat who walked with a limp. I watched them for a while and then looked over to the calendar on the wall.

March was coming in like a lion and once more I wondered what it would take to get into a recording studio, to get signed by a folk record label—was I getting any closer? "No Happiness for Slater," a song off The Modern Jazz Quartet's record, played in the apartment.

One of Chloe's hobbies was to put fancy buckles on old shoes and she suggested wanting to do it to mine.

"Those clodhoppers could use some buckles," she said.

I told her, no thanks, I didn't need any buckles.

She said, "You got forty-eight hours to change your mind." I wasn't going to change my mind. Sometimes Chloe tried to give me motherly advice, especially about the opposite sex . . . that people get into their own fixes and not to care about anybody more than they care about themselves. The apartment was a good place to hibernate.

Once I was in the kitchen listening to Malcolm X talking on the radio. He was lecturing on why not to eat pork or ham, said that a pig is actually one third cat, one third rat, one third dog—it's unclean and you shouldn't eat it. It's funny how things stick with you. About ten years later I was having dinner at Johnny Cash's house outside of Nashville. There were a lot of songwriters there. Joni Mitchell, Graham Nash, Harlan Howard, Kris Kristofferson, Mickey Newberry and some others. Joe and Janette Carter were also there. Joe and Janette were the son and daughter of A.P. and Sarah Carter and cousins to June Carter, Johnny's wife. They were like the royalty of country music.

Johnny's big fireplace was blazing and crackling. After dinner, everybody sat around in the rustic living room with high wooden beams and wide plate-glass windows that overlooked a lake. We sat in a circle and each songwriter would play a song and pass the guitar to the next player. Usually, there'd be comments made like "You really nailed that one." Or "Yeah, man, you said it all in them few lines." Or maybe something like "That song's got a lot of history in it." Or "You put all yourself into that tune." Mostly just complimentary stuff. I played "Lay, Lady, Lay" and then I passed the guitar to Graham Nash, anticipating some kind of response. I didn't have to wait long. "You don't eat pork, do you?" Joe Carter asked. That was his comment. I waited for a second before replying. "Uh, no sir, I don't," I said back. Kristofferson almost swallowed his fork. Joe asked, "Why not?" It's then that I remembered what Malcolm X had said. "Well, sir, it's kind of a personal thing. I don't eat that stuff, no. I don't eat something that's one third rat, one third cat and one third dog. It just doesn't taste right." There was an awkward momentary silence that you could have cut with one of the knives off the dinner table. Johnny Cash then almost doubled over. Kristofferson just shook his head. Joe Carter was quite a character.

There weren't any Carter Family records up at the apartment, either. Chloe slapped some steak and onions on my plate and said, "Here, it's good for you." She was cool as pie, hip from head to toe, a Maltese kitten, a solid viper—always hit the nail on the head. I don't know how much weed she smoked, but a lot. She also had her own ideas about the nature of things, told me that death was an impersonator, that birth is an invasion of privacy. What could you say? You couldn't say anything back when she said stuff like that. It's not like you could prove her wrong. New York City didn't faze her at all. "A bunch of monkeys in this town," she'd say. Talking to her you'd get the idea right away. I put on my hat and coat, grabbed my guitar and started bundling up. Chloe knew that I was trying to get places. "Maybe someday your name will get around the country like wildfire," she'd say. "If you ever get a couple of hundred bucks, buy me something."

I shut the door behind me and went out into the hallway and down the spiral cascading staircase, got to the marble-floored landing at the bottom and went out through the narrow courtyard entryway. The walls smelled of chloride. I walked leisurely through the door and up to the sidewalk through the latticed iron gate, threw a scarf around my face and headed for Van Dam Street. On the corner, I passed a horse-drawn wagon full of covered flowers, all under a plastic wrap, no driver in sight. The city was full of stuff like that.

Folk songs played in my head, they always did. Folk songs were the underground story. If someone were to ask what's going on, "Mr. Garfield's been shot down, laid down. Nothing you can do." That's what's going on. Nobody needed to ask who Mr. Garfield was, they just nodded, they just knew. It was what the country was talking about. Everything was simple—seemed to make some kind of splendid, formulaic sense.

New York City was cold, muffled and mysterious, the capital of the world. On 7th Avenue I passed the building where Walt Whitman had lived and worked. I paused momentarily imagining him printing away and singing the true song of his soul. I had stood outside of Poe's house on 3rd Street, too, and had done the same thing, staring mournfully up at the windows. The city was like some uncarved block without any name or shape and it showed no favoritism. Everything was always new, always changing. It was never the same old crowd upon the streets.

I crossed over from Hudson to Spring, passed a garbage can loaded with bricks and stopped into a coffee shop. The waitress at the lunch counter wore a close-fitting suede blouse. It outlined the well-rounded lines of her body. She had blue-black hair covered with a kerchief and piercing blue eyes, clear stenciled eyebrows. I was wishing she'd pin a rose on me. She poured the steaming coffee and I turned back towards the street window. The whole city was dangling in front of my nose. I had a vivid idea of where everything was. The future was nothing to worry about. It was awfully close.

Chronicles: Volume One, 2004

Jack Smith
(1932–1989)

Jack Smith's 1963 Flaming Creatures *was declared obscene by a New York criminal court, although Smith, the ultimate underground movie visionary, might have been the only person who found it erotic. Andy Warhol got his filmic concept from Smith—as well as the word "superstar" and performers such as Maria Montez. Smith in turn acted for Warhol and for Robert Wilson, who likewise owes some of his aesthetic, style, and tempo to Smith's influence. Jack Smith didn't care about money; he lived for his art, and his apartment, which he held on to precariously, was a priceless work of art itself and the scene of legendary midnight performances. This essay—his impassioned tribute to the star of 1940s escapist classics* Cobra Woman, White Savage, *and* Siren of Atlantis—*demonstrates that everything Jack Smith did was conceived with astonishing, if twisted, complexity.*

The Perfect Filmic Appositeness of Maria Montez

"In Paris I can do no wrong, they love me there."
                                        —Maria Montez
a few years later:
"Elle ne dessert pas le nom d'actrice."
                                        —A Paris paper reviewing a film
                                        she made there.

AT LEAST in America a Maria Montez could believe she was the Cobra woman, the Siren of Atlantis, Scheherazade, etc. She believed and thereby made the people who went to her movies believe. Those who could believe, did. Those who saw the World's Worst Actress just couldn't and they missed the magic. Too bad—their loss. Their magic comes from the most inevitable execution of the conventional pattern of acting. What they can appreciate is what most people agree upon—GOOD PERFS. Therefore you can have GOOD PERFS & no real belief. GOOD PERFS that give you no magic—oh I guess a sort of magic, a magic of sustained efficient operation (like the wonder that the car motor held out so well after a long trip).

But I tell you Maria Montez Moldy Movie Queen, Shoulder pad, gold platform wedgie Siren, Determined, dreambound, Spanish, Irish, Negro?, Indian girl who went to Hollywood from the Dominican Rep. Wretch actress—pathetic as actress, why insist upon her being an actress—why limit her. Don't slander her beautiful womanliness that took joy in her own beauty and all beauty—or whatever in her that turned plaster cornball sets to beauty. Her eye saw not just beauty but incredible, delirious, drug-like hallucinatory beauty.

The vast machinery of a movie company worked overtime to make her vision into sets. They achieved only inept approximations. But one of her atrocious acting sighs suffused a thousand tons of dead plaster with imaginative life and a truth.

Woman and yet imaginator/believer/child/simple pathetically believing with no defenses—a beautiful woman who could fantasy—do you know of a woman like that? There aren't any. Never before, never since—this was an extraordinary unique person. Women—people—don't come in combinations that can/can't happen again:
fantasy—beauty
child—siren
creature—straight etc because each is all these plus its opposite—and to dig one woman is to mysteriously evoke all others and not from watching actresses give PERFS does one feel anything real about woman, about films, about the world, various as it is for all of us, about men. But to see one person—OK if only by some weird accident—exposing herself—having fun, believing in moldiness (still moldy, but if it can be true for her and produces delight—the delight of technicolor movies—then it would be wonderful if it could be true for us).

And in a crazy way it is all true for us because she is one of us. Is it invalid of her to be the way she is? If so, none of us are valid—a position each one of us feels a violation of oneself if taken by another person (whatever our private thots may be). If you think you are invalid you may be the person who ridicules Montez movies. To admit of Maria Montez validities would be to turn on to moldiness, Glamourous Rapture, schizophrenic delight, hopeless naivete, and glittering technicolored trash!

> "Geef me that Coparah chewel!"
> "Geef me that Coparah chewel!"
> —line of dialogue from *Cobra Woman*,
> possibly the greatest line of dialogue in any
> American flic.

> "Juvenile . . . trash . . . "
> —Jesse Zunser, N.Y. reviewer.

Juvenile does not equal shameful and trash is the material of creators. It exists whether one approves or not. You may not approve of the Orient but it's half of the world and it's where spaghetti came from. Trash *is* true of Maria Montez flix but so are jewels, Cobra jewels and so is wondrous refinement—

Night—the villain/high priest enters the bedroom of the old queen (good) and stabs her in her bed. Seen thru a carved screen in bkgrnd—at that moment—the sacred volcano erupts (orange light flashes) Old queen stares balefully (says something?) and dies. Now the cobra priestess (the evil sister) and the high priest can seize Jon Hall betrothed to/and the good sister (rightful ruler) and imprisons them with no opposition. Persecution of Cobra Island—Crushing offerings demanded for King Cobra—

(Chunk of scenario synopsized)

There is a (unsophisticated, certainly) validity there—also theatrical drama (the best kind)—also interesting symbolism, delirious hokey, glamour—unattainable (because once possessed) and juvenile at its most passionate.

If you scorn Montez-land (now gone anyway so you are safe from its contamination) you are safely out of something you were involved in once and you resent (in direct ratio to your scorn, even to rage) not being able to go back—resent the closed, rainbow colored gates, resent not being wanted there, being a drag on the industry.

Well, it's gone with the war years (when you know that your flic is going to make money you indulge in hokey—at these times when investments must be certain you must strictly follow banker-logic), Universal probably demolished the permanent Montez-land sets. Vera West committed suicide in her blackmail swimming pool. Montez dead in her bathtub from too much reducing salts. The colors are faded. Reel-Art Co. sold all her flix to TV.

Montez-land (created of one woman's belief—not an actress') was made manifest on this earth, changed the world—15 to 20 flix they made around her—OK vehicles (the idea of vehicles shouldn't be condemned because it has been abused), vehicles that were medium for her belief therefore necessary, a justice, a need felt—Real—as investment, as lots of work for extras, hilarious to serious persons, beloved to Puerto-Ricans, magic for me, beauty for many, a camp to homos, Fauve American unconsciousness to Europeans etc.

Can't happen again. Fantasies now feature weight lifters who think now how lucky and clever they were to get into the movies & the fabulous pay . . . , think something like that on camera—it's contagious & you share those thots (which is a magical fantasy too but another article on "The Industry"). All are now safe from Maria Montez outrages! I suppose the color prints are destroyed now. Still, up until about 5 yrs ago, (when they were bought up by T.V.), Montez reissues cropped up at tiny nabes—every week one or another of them played somewhere in N.Y.C. At that time they were 12 to 17 years old. When they are shown now on TV they are badly chopped up, with large chunks missing. The pattern being repeated—their irresistibility resulting in their being cut & stabbed & punished. All are now safe from Montez embarrassment—the tiny nabes are torn down, didn't even make supermarkets—the big nabes have to get back investments so can't be asked (who'd ask) to show them. The art houses are committed to seriousness and importance, essays on celluloid (once it was sermons on celluloid), food for thought imported from THE CONTINENT. No more scoldings from critics . . .

At this moment in movie history there is a feeling of movies being approved of. There is an enveloping cloud of critical happiness—it's OK to love movies now. General approval (nobody knowing who starts it—but it's OK for you and everybody else). It's a pretty diffuse and general thing. Maria Montez flix were particular—you went for your particular reasons, dug them for personal reasons—had specific feelings from them & about them. It was a peculiarly idiosyncratic experience and heartily despised by critics. Critics are writers. They like writing—and written characters. Maria Montez's appeal was on a purely intuitive level. She was the bane of critics—that person whose effect cannot be known by words, described in words, flaunts words (her *image* spoke). Film critics are writers and they are hostile and uneasy in the presence of a visual phenomenon. They are most delighted by bare images that through visual barrenness call thought into play to fill the visual gap. Their bare delights are "purity and evocative." A spectacular, flaming image—since it threatens their critichood need to be able to write—is bad and they attack it throwing in moral extensions and hinting at idiocy in whoever is capable of visually appreciating a visual medium. Montez-land is truly torn down and contemporary sports-car Italians follow diagrams to fortunes, conquests, & murders to universal approbation.

> Maria Montez was a very particular person:
> Off screen she was:
> A large, large boned woman
> 5' 9"
> Oily
> Skin dark,

> & gave impression of being
> dirty
> Wore Shalimar perfume

It is a reminder of one's own individuality to value a particular screen personality. It is also a nuttiness (because gratuitous). But you will have nuttiness without Maria Montez—want more—need all you can get—need what ever you don't have—& need it badly—Need what you don't need—need what you hate—need what you have stood against all through the years. Having a favorite star has very human ramifications—not star-like entirely. Stars are not stars, they are people, and what they believe is written on their foreheads (a property of the camera). Having a favorite star is considered ludicrous but it is nothing but non verbal communication the darling of the very person who doesn't believe anything real can exist between a star and a real person. Being a star was an important part of the Montez style. Having Maria Montez as a favorite star has not been gratuitous (tho it was in 1945) since it has left a residue of notions, interesting to me as a film-maker and general film aesthete. No affection can remain gratuitous. Stars who believe nothing are believable in a variety of roles, not to me tho, who have abandoned myself to personal tweakiness.

Those who still underrate Maria Montez, should see that the truth of Montez flix is only the truth of them as it exists for those who like them and the fact that others get anything out of them is only important because it is something they could miss and important because it is enjoyment missed. No one wants to miss an enjoyment and it is important to enjoy because it is important to think and enjoying is simply thinking—Not hedonism, not voluptuousness—simply thought. I could go on to justify thought but I'm sure that wouldn't be necessary to readers of magazines. There is a world in Montez movies which reacting against turns to void. I can explain their interest for me but I can't turn them into good film technique. Good film technique is a classical attribute. *Zero de Conduite*—perfect film technique, form, length, etc., a classical work—Montez flix are none of these. They are romantic expressions. They came about because (as in the case of Von Sternberg) an inflexible person committed to an obsession was given his way thru some fortuitous circumstance. Results of this sort of thing TRANSCEND FILM TECHNIQUE. Not barely—but resoundingly, meaningfully, with magnificence, with the vigor that one exposed human being always has—and with failure. We cause their downfall (after we have enjoyed them) because they embarrass us grown up as we are and post adolescent/post war/post graduate/post-toasties etc. The movies that were secret (I felt I had to sneak away to see M. M. flix) remain secret somehow and a nation forgets its pleasures, trash,

> Somebody saved the Marx Bros. by finding
> SERIOUS MARXIAN BROTHERS
> ATTRIBUTES.

Film for these film romanticists (Marx Bros., Von Stroheim, Montez, Judy Canova, Ron Rice, Von Sternberg, etc.) a place. Not the classically inclined conception a strip of stuff (Before a mirror is a place) is a place where it is possible to clown, to pose, to act out fantasies, to not be seen while one gives (Movie sets are sheltered, exclusive places where nobody who doesn't belong can go) Rather the lens range is the place and the film a mirror image that moves as long as the above benighted company's beliefs remained unchallenged, and as far as their own beliefs moved them.

If Maria Montez were still alive she would be defunct. She would be unable to find work (Maybe emasculated mother type parts) She'd be passé, dated, rejected. A highly charged idiosyncratic person (in films) is a rare phenomenon in time as well as quantity. Unfortunately their uniqueness puts a limitation upon itself. Uniqueness of Quantity calling into existence a uniqueness of time to limit itself. We punish such uniqueness, we turn against it—give it only about 5 years (the average life of a star). Once lost these creatures cannot be recovered tho their recovery would be agreeable. Who wouldn't welcome back Veronica Lake who is by this time a thing in the air, a joke, a tragedy, a suffering symbol of downfall, working as a barmaid at Martha Washington Hotels—shorn. We lose them—our creatures. When some rudeness/cutting off of hair out of fear of wartime machinery/makes the believer disbelieve, the believer joins us in our wanting but not being able to believe and is through, first because of the cynicism of movie fans and secondly because of the resultant breakdown of their fantasy.

Corniness is the other side of marvelousness. What person believing in a fantasy can bear to have its other side discovered. Thru accidents, rudenesses, scandals, human weaknesses have cut short those who made movie worlds (movies as place) that were too full to have room for anything but coincidences, politeness & benightings. But denial is short lived. So will our denial of our personal films. Someday we will value these personal masterpieces. We don't have to do injustice to the film of cutting, camera movement, rhythm, classical feelings, structured, thought loaded (for there's the moldiness of the foreign darling, that it disobeys its own most central rule—that technique by itself can evoke as does poetry). Yet plots that demand serious definite attention spell out the evocation for the images.

ON A very obvious level too much dialogue (still a violation even if it is no longer Hollywood-moronic) on an unsuspected level—much use of story furthering (different than Hollywood) images, rich with story furthering detail (more sophisticated than Hollywood details), rich with (more tour de force than H) cutting—all these exist not to create a film for itself but exactly the same effect as Hollywood Oprobriums—a film for a plot—all these tools of film STILL force an emphasis on the story because they each are used still to force an emphasis on the story and we only have a Hollywood disguised in sandals, Rivieras, pallazzos, ascots, etc. A new set of cliches that we aren't familiar enough with yet to see as cliches. European films are not necessarily better than the most Hollywood of our flix, they are only different and that superficially—certainly not more filmic because they are every bit as/plot story word/orientated. This we will see clearly when we start to get tired of their particular set of thought & story cliches. And we must, because these are always oppressive in a film—are the oppressive parts of movies as we know them because they dissipate the film challenge—to use our eyes. To apprehend thru our eyes.

The whole gaudy array of secret-flix, any flic we enjoyed: Judy Canova flix (I don't even remember the names), *I walked with a Zombie, White Zombie, Hollywood Hotel,* all Montez flix, most Dorothy Lamour sarong flix, a gem called *Night Monster, Cat & the Canary, The Pirate,* Maureen O'Hara Spanish Galleon flix (all Spanish Galleon flix anyway), all Busby Berkely flix, *Flower Thief,* all musicals that had production numbers, especially Rio de Janeiro prod. nos., all Marx Bros. flix. Each reader will add to the list.

Above kind of film is valid only when done by one who is its master—not valid in copies. Only valid when done with flair, corniness, and enjoyment. These masterpieces will be remembered because of their peculiar haunting quality—the copies will drop away from memory and the secret film will be faced. We still feel the disgust and insult of the copies and react against the whole body including the originals. The secret films were the most defenseless since they afford to ignore what bad copies caused us to come its demand in order to protect ourselves from the bad copies. And they being the pure expressions have had to take all the blame.

A bad copy film has a way of evoking a feeling of waste that is distressing. Waste of time in months, money in millions—we spent our *own* best part of a dollar—and hope for more film excitement was made guilty in lying sequels—squandered money. The guilt has come to be applied to the flix that were copied. (Who will ever admit having enjoyed a Judy Canova flic?) The flix of the 30's and 40's (even I detest flix of the 50's) are especially guilty because they haven't acquired the respectability of antiquareanism. Anyway the secret flic is also a guilty flic.

These were light films—if we really believed that films are visual it would be possible to believe these rather pure cinema—weak technique, true, but rich imagery. They had a stilted, phony imagery that we choose to object to, but why react against that phoniness. That phoniness could be valued as rich in interest & revealing. Why do we object to not being convinced—why can't we enjoy phoniness? Why resent the patent "phoniness" of these films—because it holds a mirror to our own, possibly.

The primitive allure of movies is a thing of light and shadows. A bad film is one which doesn't flicker and shift and move through lights and shadows, contrasts, textures by way of light. If I have these I don't mind phoniness (or the sincerity of clever actors), simple minded plots (or novelistic "good" plots), nonsense or seriousness (I don't feel nonsense in movies as a threat to my mind since I don't go to movies for the ideas that arise from sensibleness of ideas). Images evoke feelings and ideas that are suggested by feeling. Nonsense on one given night might arouse contemptuous feeling and leave me with ideas of resolution which I might extend to personal problems and thus I might be left with great sense. It's a very personal process— thoughts via images and therefore very varied. More interesting to me than discovering what is a script writer's exact meaning. Images always give rise to a complex of feelings, thots, conjectures, speculations, etc. Why then place any value on good or bad scripts—since the best of scripts detracts most from the visual realm than in the literary. Visual truths are blunt, whereas thots can be altered to suit & protect. The eye falls into disuse as a receiver of impressions & films (images) mean nothing without word meanings.

Our great interest in films is partly the challenge it presents us to step into the visual realm. A personality type star appeals to, informs the eye. Maria Montez was remarkable for the gracefulness of her gestures and movement. This gracefulness was a real process of moviemaking. Was a real delight for the eye—was a genuine thing about that person—the acting was lousy but if something genuine got on film why carp about acting—which HAS to be phoney anyway—I'd

RATHER HAVE atrocious acting. Acting to Maria Montez was hoodwinking. Her real concerns (her conviction of beauty/her beauty) were the main concern—her acting had to be secondary. An applying of one's convictions to one's activity obtains a higher excellence in that activity than that attained by those in that activity who apply the rules established by previous successes by others.

The more rules broken the more enriched becomes the activity as it has had to expand to include what a human view of the activity won't allow it to not include.

What is it we want from film?

> A vital experience
> an imagination
> an emotional release
> all these & what we want from life
> Contact with something
> we are not, know not,
> think not, feel not, understand not,
> therefore: An expansion.

Because Maria Montez who embodies all the above cannot be denied—was not denied—that mass of thoughts we have about film must be added to, to include her acting, since anybody's acting is only the medium of soulful exchange and is not important in itself except at the point that the acting student learns to forget its rules; In Maria Montez's case a high fulfillment was reached without ever having known the rules and those who adore rules could only feel offence, and expressed it in ridicule.

M. M. dreamed she was effective, imagined she acted, cared for nothing but her fantasy (she attracted fantasy movies to herself—that needed her—they would have been ridiculous with any other actress—any other human being) Those who credit dreams became her fans. Only actress can have fans and by a dream coming true she became and actually was and is an actress.

(Go to the T. D. of the NYPL—go to the actress dept., ask for stills of "Maria Montez." Six Gigantic Volumes of delirious photos will come up on the dumb waiter.)

But in my movies I know that I prefer non actor stars to "convincing" actor-stars—only a personality that exposes itself—if through moldiness (human slips can convince me—in movies) and I was very convinced by Maria Montez in her particular case of her great beauty and integrity.

I finish this article—a friend, Davis Gurin, came to tell me "I came to tell you, tonight I saw a young man in the street with a plastic rose in his mouth declaiming—I am Maria Montez, I am M. M." A nutty manifestation, true—but in some way a true statement. Some way we must come to understand that person. Not worth understanding perhaps—but understanding is a process—not the subject it chooses. But that process has a Maria Montez dept. as well as a film dept. and you bought this magazine for a dollar.

Film Culture, Winter 1962–63

William S. Burroughs
(1914–1997)

Although he was a close friend and role model for the younger Allen Ginsberg and Jack Kerouac, William S. Burroughs created a revolution in literature almost single-handedly. His early novels Junky *and* Queer *were the last word on the underground cultures of drugs and homosexuality that helped forge the Beat sensibility. Burroughs was indebted to Ginsberg as an editor, his collaborator Brion Gysin for the "cut-up technique," and to a surprising extent to L. Ron Hubbard, having participated in Scientology until he was declared a "clear." These influences are visible in this excerpt from* Nova Express *(from the "cut-up trilogy":* The Soft Machine, The Ticket That Exploded, *and* Nova Express), *but it was Burroughs's particular genius to explore and understand the state of language in the late twentieth century and to map the means of control used to manipulate the human race by more or less invisible overlords. Here as elsewhere Burroughs set himself up as an enemy of the mythos of progress and a dissenter against the future.*

Last Words

LISTEN TO my last words anywhere. Listen to my last words any world. Listen all you boards syndicates and governments of the earth. And you powers behind what filth deals consummated in what lavatory to take what is not yours. To sell the ground from unborn feet forever—

"Don't let them see us. Don't tell them what we are doing—"

Are these the words of the all-powerful boards and syndicates of the earth?

"For God's sake don't let that Coca-Cola thing out—"

"Not The Cancer Deal with The Venusians—"

"Not The Green Deal—Don't show them that—"

"Not The Orgasm Death—"

"Not the ovens—"

Listen: I call you all. Show your cards all players. Pay it all pay it all pay it *all* back. Play it all pay it all play it *all* back. For all to see. In Times Square. In Piccadilly.

"Premature. Premature. Give us a little more time."

Time for what? More lies? Premature? Premature for who? I say to all these words are not premature. These words may be too late. Minutes to go. Minutes to foe goal—

"Top Secret—Classified—For The Board—The Elite—The Initiates—"

Are these the words of the all-powerful boards and syndicates of the earth? These are the words of liars cowards collaborators traitors. Liars who want time for more lies. Cowards who can not face your "dogs" your "gooks" your "errand boys" your "human animals" with the truth. Collaborators with Insect People with Vegetable People. With any people anywhere who offer you a body forever. To shit forever. For this you have sold out your sons. Sold the ground from unborn feet forever. Traitors to all souls everywhere. You want the name of Hassan i Sabbah on your filth deeds to sell out the unborn?

What scared you all into time? Into body? Into shit? I will tell you: *"the word."* Alien Word *"the."* *"The"* word of Alien Enemy imprisons *"thee"* in Time. In Body. In Shit. Prisoner, come out. The great skies are open. I Hassan i Sabbah *rub out the word forever.* If you I cancel all your words forever. And the words of Hassan i Sabbah as also cancel. Cross all your skies see the silent writing of Brion Gysin Hassan i Sabbah: drew September 17, 1899 over New York.

Prisoners, Come Out

"DON'T LISTEN to Hassan i Sabbah," they will tell you. "He wants to take your body and all pleasures of the body away from you. Listen to us. We are serving The Garden of Delights Immortality Cosmic Consciousness The Best Ever In Drug Kicks. And *love love love* in slop buckets. How does that sound to you boys? Better than Hassan i Sabbah and his cold windy bodiless rock? Right?"

At the immediate risk of finding myself the most unpopular character of all fiction—and history is fiction—I must say this:

"Bring together state of news—Inquire onward from state to doer—Who monopolized Immortality? Who monopolized Cosmic Consciousness? Who monopolized Love Sex and Dream? Who monopolized Life Time and Fortune? Who took from you what is yours? Now they will give it all back? Did they ever give anything away for nothing? Did they ever give any more than they had to give? Did they not always take back what they gave when possible and it always was? *Listen:* Their Garden Of Delights is a terminal sewer— I have been at some pains to map this area of terminal sewage in the so called pornographic sections of *Naked Lunch* and *Soft Machine*— Their Immortality Cosmic Consciousness and Love is second-run grade-B shit—Their drugs are poison designed to beam in Orgasm Death and Nova Ovens—Stay out of the Garden Of Delights—It is a man-eating trap that ends in green goo—Throw back their ersatz Immortality—It will fall apart before you can get out of The Big Store—Flush their drug kicks down the drain—*They are poisoning and monopolizing the hallucinogen drugs—learn to make it without any chemical corn*—All that they offer is a screen to cover retreat from the colony they have so disgracefully mismanaged. To cover travel arrangements so they will never have to pay the constituents they have betrayed and sold out. Once these arrangements are complete they will blow the place up behind them.

"And what does my program of total austerity and total resistance offer *you*? I offer you nothing. I am not a politician. These are conditions of total emergency. And these are my instructions for total emergency if carried out *now* could avert the total disaster *now* on tracks:

"*Peoples of the earth, you have all been poisoned.* Convert all available stocks of morphine to apomorphine. Chemists, work around the clock on variation and synthesis of the apomorphine formulae.

Apomorphine is the only agent that can disintoxicate you and cut the enemy beam off your line. Apomorphine and silence. I order total resistance directed against this conspiracy to pay off peoples of the earth in ersatz bullshit. I order total resistance directed against The Nova Conspiracy and all those engaged in it.

"The purpose of my writing is to expose and arrest Nova Criminals. In *Naked Lunch, Soft Machine* and *Nova Express* I show who they are and what they are doing and what they will do if they are not arrested. Minutes to go. Souls rotten from their orgasm drugs, flesh shuddering from their nova ovens, prisoners of the earth to *come out.* With your help we can occupy The Reality Studio and retake their universe of Fear Death and Monopoly—

"(Signed) INSPECTOR J. LEE, NOVA POLICE"

POST SCRIPT Of The Regulator: I would like to sound a word of warning—To speak is to lie—To live is to collaborate—Anybody is a coward when faced by the nova ovens—There are degrees of lying collaboration and cowardice—That is to say degrees of intoxication—It is precisely a question of *regulation*—The enemy is not man is not woman—The enemy exists only where no life is and moves always to push life into extreme untenable positions—You can cut the enemy off your line by the judicious use of apomorphine and silence—*Use the sanity drug apomorphine.*

"Apomorphine is made from morphine but its physiological action is quite different. Morphine depresses the front brain. Apomorphine stimulates the back brain, acts on the hypothalamus to regulate the percentage of various constituents in the blood serum and so normalize the constitution of the blood." I quote from *Anxiety and Its Treatment* by Doctor John Yerbury Dent.

Pry Yourself Loose and Listen

I WAS traveling with The Intolerable Kid on The Nova Lark—We were on the nod after a rumble in The Crab Galaxy involving this two-way time stock; when you come to the end of a biologic film just run it back and start over—Nobody knows the difference—Like nobody there before the film.* So they start to run it back and the projector blew up and we lammed out of there on the blast—Holed up in those cool blue mountains the liquid air in our spines listening to a little high-fi junk note fixes you right to metal and you nod out a thousand years.† Just sitting there in a slate house wrapped in orange flesh robes, the blue mist drifting around us when we get the call—And as soon as I set foot on Podunk earth I can smell it that burnt metal reek of nova.

"Already set off the charge," I said to I&I (Immovable and Irresistible)—"This is a burning planet—Any minute now the whole fucking shit house goes up."

* Postulate a biologic film running from the beginning to the end, from zero to zero as all biologic film run in any time universe—Call this film X1 and postulate further that there can only be one film with the quality X1 in any given time universe. X1 is the film and performers—X2 is the audience who are all trying to get into the film—Nobody is permitted to leave the biologic theater which in this case is the human body—Because if anybody did leave the theater he would be looking at a different film Y and Film X1 and audience X2 would then cease to exist by mathematical definition—In 1960 with the publication of *Minutes To Go*, Martin's stale movie was greeted by an unprecedented chorus of boos and a concerted walkout—"We seen this five times already and not standing still for another twilight of your tired Gods."
† Since junk *is* image the effects of junk can easily be produced and concentrated in a sound and image track—Like this: Take a sick junky—Throw blue light on his so-called face or dye it blue or dye the junk blue it don't make no difference and now give him a shot and photograph the blue miracle as life pours back into that walking corpse—That will give you the image track of junk—Now project the blue change onto your own face if you want The Big Fix. The sound track is even easier—I quote from *Newsweek*, March 4, 1963 Science section: "Every substance has a characteristic set of resonant frequencies at which it vibrates or oscillates."—So you record the frequency of junk as it hits the junk-sick brain cells—
"What's that?—Brain waves are 32 or under and can't be heard? Well speed them up, God damn it—And instead of one junky concentrate me a thousand—Let there be Lexington and call a nice Jew in to run it—"
Doctor Wilhelm Reich has isolated and concentrated a unit that he calls "the orgone"—Orgones, according to W. Reich, are the units of life—They have been photographed and the color is blue—So junk sops up the orgones and that's why they need all these young junkies—They have more orgones and give higher yield of the blue concentrate on which Martin and his boys can nod out a thousand years—Martin is stealing *your orgones.*—You going to stand still for this shit?

So Intolerable I&I sniffs and says: "Yeah, when it happens it happens fast—This is a rush job."

And you could feel it there under your feet the whole structure buckling like a bulkhead about to blow—So the paper has a car there for us and we are driving in from the airport The Kid at the wheel and his foot on the floor—Nearly ran down a covey of pedestrians and they yell after us: "What you want to do, kill somebody?"

And The Kid sticks his head out and says: "It would be a pleasure Niggers! Gooks! Terrestrial dogs"—His eyes lit up like a blow torch and I can see he is really in form—So we start right to work making our headquarters in The Land Of The Free where the call came from and which is really free and wide open for any life form the uglier the better—Well they don't come any uglier than The Intolerable Kid and your reporter—When a planet is all primed to go up they call in I&I to jump around from one faction to the other agitating and insulting all the parties before and after the fact until they all say: "By God before I give an inch the whole fucking shit house goes up in chunks."

Where we came in—You have to move fast on this job—And I&I is fast—Pops in and out of a hundred faces in a split second spitting his intolerable insults—We had the plan, what they call The Board Books to show us what is what on this dead whistle stop: Three life forms uneasily parasitic on a fourth form that is beginning to wise up. And the whole planet absolutely flapping hysterical with panic. The way we like to see them.

"This is a dead easy pitch," The Kid says.

"Yeah," I say. "A little bit too easy. Something here, Kid. Something wrong. I can feel it."

But The Kid can't hear me. Now all these life forms came from the most intolerable conditions: hot places, cold places, terminal stasis and the last thing any of them want to do is go back where they came from. And The Intolerable Kid is giving out with such pleasantries like this:

"All right take your ovens out with you and pay Hitler on the way out. Nearly got the place hot enough for you Jews didn't he?"

"Know about Niggers? Why darkies were born? Antennae coolers what else? Always a spot for *good* Darkies."

"You cunts constitute a disposal problem in the worst form there is and raise the nastiest whine ever heard anywhere: 'Do you love me? Do you love me? Do you love me???' Why don't you go back to Venus and fertilize a forest?"

"And as for you White Man Boss, you dead prop in Martin's stale movie, you terminal time junky, haul your heavy metal ass back to Uranus. Last shot at the door. You need one for the road." By this time everybody was even madder than they were shit scared. But I&I figured things were moving too slow.

"We need a peg to hang it on," he said. "Something really ugly like virus. Not for nothing do they come from a land without mirrors." So he takes over this news-magazine.

"Now," he said, "I'll by God show them how ugly the Ugly American can be."

And he breaks out all the ugliest pictures in the image bank and puts it out on the subliminal so one crisis piles up after the other right on schedule. And I&I is whizzing around like a buzz saw and that black nova laugh of his you can hear it now down all the streets shaking the buildings and skyline like a stage prop. But me I am looking around and the more I look the less I like what I see. For one thing the nova heat is moving in fast and heavy like I never see it anywhere else. But I&I just says I have the copper jitters and turns back to his view screen: "They are skinning the chief of police alive in some jerkwater place. Want to sit in?"

"Naw," I said. "Only interested in my own skin."

And I walk out thinking who I *would* like to see skinned alive. So I cut into the Automat and put coins into the fish cake slot and then I really see it: Chinese partisans and well armed with vibrating static and image guns. So I throw down the fish cakes with tomato sauce and make it back to the office where The Kid is still glued to that screen. He looks up smiling dirty and says:

"Wanta molest a child and disembowel it right after?"

"Pry yourself loose and listen." And I tell him. "Those Tiddly Winks don't fuck around you know."

"So what?" he says. "I've still got The Board Books. I can split this whistle stop wide open tomorrow."

No use talking to him. I look around some more and find out the blockade on planet earth is broken. Explorers moving in whole armies. And everybody concerned is fed up with Intolerable I&I. And all he can say is: "So what? I've still got . . . /" Cut.

"Board Books taken. The film reeks of burning switch like a blow torch. Prerecorded heat glare massing Hiroshima. This whistle stop wide open to hot crab people. Mediation? Listen: Your army is getting double zero in floor by floor game of 'symbiosis.' Mobilized reasons to love Hiroshima and Nagasaki? Virus to maintain terminal sewers of Venus?"

"All nations sold out by liars and cowards. Liars who want time for the future negatives to develop stall you with more lying offers while hot crab people mass war to extermination with the film in Rome. These reports reek of nova, sold out job, shit birth and death. Your planet has been invaded. You are dogs on all tape. The entire planet is being developed into terminal identity and complete surrender."

"But suppose film death in Rome doesn't work and we can get every male body even madder than they are shit scared? We need a peg to evil full length. By God show them how ugly the ugliest pictures in the dark room can be. Pitch in the oven ambush. Spill all the board gimmicks. This symbiosis con? Can tell you for sure 'symbiosis' is ambush straight to the ovens. 'Human dogs' to be eaten alive under white hot skies of Minraud."

And Intolerable I&I's "errand boys" and "strikebreakers" are copping out right left and center:

"Mr. Martin, and you board members, vulgar stupid Americans, you will regret calling in the Mayan Aztec Gods with your synthetic mushrooms. Remember we keep exact junk measure of the pain inflicted and that pain must be paid in full. Is that clear enough Mr. Intolerable Martin, or shall I make it even clearer? Allow me to introduce myself: The Mayan God of Pain And Fear from the white hot plains of Venus which does not mean a God of vulgarity, cowardice, ugliness and stupidity. There is a cool spot on the surface of Venus three hundred degrees cooler than the surrounding area. I have held that spot against all contestants for five hundred thousand years. Now you expect to use me as your 'errand boy' and 'strikebreaker' summoned up by an IBM machine and a handful of virus crystals? How long could you hold that spot, you 'board members'? About thirty seconds I think with all your guard dogs. And you thought to channel my energies for 'operation total disposal'? Your 'operations' there or here this or that come and go and are no more. *Give my name back.* That name must be paid for. You have not paid. My name is not yours to use. Henceforth I think about thirty seconds is written."

And you can see the marks are wising up, standing around in sullen groups and that mutter gets louder and louder. Any minute now fifty million adolescent gooks will hit the street with switch blades, bicycle chains and cobblestones.

"Street gangs, Uranian born of nova conditions, get out and fight for your streets. Call in the Chinese and any random factors. Cut all tape. Shift cut tangle magpie voice lines of the earth. Know about the Board's 'Green Deal?' They plan to board the first life boat in drag and leave 'their human dogs' under the white hot skies of Venus. 'Operation Sky Switch' also known as 'Operation Total Disposal.' All right you board bastards, we'll by God show you 'Operation Total Exposure.' For all to see. In Times Square. In Piccadilly."

Nova Express, 1964

Ed Sanders
(b. 1939)

Ed Sanders was a bridge between the Beats and the sixties rock and roll generation. A classical scholar, in 1962 he founded Fuck You, a Magazine of the Arts *and in 1964 he started a band, the Fugs, with Tuli Kupferberg and Ken Weaver. They released their first album,* The Village Fugs Sing Ballads of Contemporary Protest, Point of Views, and General Dissatisfaction, *in 1965, the same year Sanders opened the Peace Eye Bookstore, a center of the alternative universe that was the East Village. The Peace Eye was raided by police in 1966 and Sanders was charged with obscenity. In 1976 he published the manifesto* Investigative Poetry, *a title that defines a polymathic career that includes books on the Manson family trial, Allen Ginsberg, and Egyptian hieroglyphics. This is an excerpt from Sanders's hilarious and educational memoir* Tales of Beatnik Glory.

Siobhan McKenna Group-Grope

T HE TAN FOG of particulate dooky lay low 'tween the high clouds and the barren skyline cenotaphs of New York City. Within the closure of lower Manhattan, in tenement slums of the poor, a poetry reading was held in late September of 1961 at The House of Nothingness on Tompkins Square North. It was an open reading—one where any and all were allowed to read their works.

In warm weather the readings were held out back in the court where there was a beautiful rectangular garden of raked white sand with a triad of small boulders bunched in the sand at one end. The garden was molded after a similar garden in a Zen temple in Kyoto.

There were seven humans—three women, four men, who were walking through the streets after the reading toward an apartment at 704 East 5th Street just off Avenue C. Each of them had read their poetry. That is, when they arrived at Nothingness, each had approached the person running the readings and had placed his/her name on the reading list. There were twenty-three readers that September night, divided into three approximately one-hour sets. Readers were requested to limit themselves to ten minutes each but occasionally someone droned through a 115-quatrain translation of the Pyramid Texts of King Unas so that after, say, fifteen minutes, people began to shift impatiently at their tables. In all truth the majority of those attending had come clutching spring-binders of their own verse to read and viewed time-hogs with disapproval.

Of the seven walking through the midnight East Side, three were editors of their own poetry magazines. They knew each other's work intimately and discussed it whenever they met, which was just about every day. Their life was the world of poetry and poetry publications and the recounting of the anecdotes of poet-life. They lifted a common nose of disdain upon the rest of the world, especially television and newspapers with their ceaseless spew of right-wing death.

In spite of the horror, terror and vileness of the *res publica*—the ennui, the mental spasms that sent them down plateaus of nothingness constrained to watch the blobs convulse and mull and melt—in spite of it, they met that fall after the readings to listen to poetry records, and, while lyrics softly babbled from the speaker, did lie down toward the Galaxy to pluck the vast lyre of grass-grope. For no right-wing government can prevent the sneers and derision of the people smoking pot in private.

Compared with the bunch-punches of the psychedelic years to come, it was tenderly innocent—but it was thought to comprise an historical first, the premiere instance in Western Civilization of such activities.

They specialized in Caedmon/Spoken Arts records—committing skin-clings to the best minds of three generations, including Dylan Thomas, e.e. cummings, Marianne Moore, Delmore Schwartz, William Carlos Williams, Edith Sitwell, and even T.S. Eliot, although it is to be admitted that Eliot reading *Murder in the Cathedral* made it somewhat difficult to keep up the stoked fires of fornication. (A complete list of poets, to whose verse were held the parties, is appended.)

It was actress Siobhan McKenna's reading of Irish poetry that the group played again and again in their fuckings. God, it turned them on. They exhausted their love-surge listening to Siobhan McKenna. They talked about writing her a letter inviting her to attend one of their midnight specials the next time she should visit New York. They were especially excited to find out that McKenna had performed as Lady Macbeth in Gaelic at a theatre in Galway.

"Let's find out if she had made a recording of the play in Gaelic!" someone exclaimed, bright-eyed with eagerness.

There was no theory behind the group-gropes—unless the theory of the heated bottom. "Who loves himself loves me who love myself"—the bard sang; and that was the gropers' theory. They didn't discuss it really—but fell down regardless into the furrows of the avoidance of coma. If anyone asked, "Why do you think we do this?"—someone carried the hookah-tip over to the person or toppled them onto the mattress with a grope-tackle.

Some were hesitant, waxing bold later. Others the reverse. It was like that Ezra Pound poem, *E. P. Ode Pour L'Election de Son Sépulchre*, Part IV, only as applied to phonographic fornication. Ava, for instance, wrote long-line poems of religious nature and wore extremely demure attire, but once the police lock was poked into place, became a torrid participant. Brash-mouthed Bill however, who was a veritable Tourette's disease of obscene expletives, became almost unparticipatingly shy, although he was eager to hop around the mattresses with an ancient box camera. For the most part, the seven relaxed into a common soul and grew to know each others' bodies and desires and energies to a labyrinthine degree.

When the sex-hungry poets arrived at the pad: Ava, Bill, Rosebud, Nelson, Rick, Trudy, and a human named Obtak who considered himself to be the reincarnation of Shelley, they drank a round of yohimbine-bark tea that Rick had made during the day after a street-scrounge for mirrors. Right away they stacked the poetry records atop the turntable. Rick had a gentle thing about mirrors and that afternoon he'd collected as many as he could find in the Bowery area from thrown-away dressers. He hauled up five cracked, pitiful specimens which he lined around the mattresses. That was his chief thrill, to watch others reflected fucking in mirrors, at the same time listening, say, to Edith Sitwell, while Ava massaged his pornic area with a banana skin.

There was a small offset press in the back room on which Ava printed a monthly verse-paper. Ava and Obtak had to work awhile in the room fixing the inking mechanism which had become mal-adjusted so that only the left side of the page was being printed. When it was fixed, they fell fucking beneath the machine on a blue air mattress, unable to wait for the poesy. Someone in the bedroom put on an e. e. cummings/Luciano Berio composition. After a few minutes, Ava and Obtak came out of the press room, Ava laughing, "I guess it's time to go to bed." She leaned against the bathtub and whipped off her blue velour pullover, dropped her jeans skirt, flaming over to turn on the water. She took a bath with the assistance of Nelson, and then appeared at the mattress, dabbing at her hair-ends with a towel.

There were two mattresses side by side, one double-sized, one single. Before anything they smoked a lot of grass, via the toilet roll dope blow. They took the cardboard inner cylinder and Rick punched a small hole into the top of it, inserting a thick burning bomber in the aperture. At both ends mouths were positioned. One end sucked his/her lungs full of dope. Then, on signal, he/she blew the lungful through the tube into the sucking mouth-lungs of the other, in a fast whoosh. Then it was off to the zone.

There were variations of this, for instance when Bill inserted his cock through the roll when there was a lit roach burning perpendicu-larly and several of them took a toke.

For serious bedside smoking, however, there was a five-tube hoo-kah made out of a jug from an office water cooler. The toke-tubes were long lengths of rubber lab tubing wrapped in velvet ribbons. The carved burl was kept packed with grass and throughout the festivities anyone could lean over from the mattress and snerk.

They started with an arpeggio of e. e. cummings, Marianne Moore, Dylan Thomas, and a flash of *Howl*. Then it was the McKenna hour. Siobhan McKenna's voice, soft, full, beautiful, triggered off a cross-mattress grope spasm that turned the arms and legs of the lovers into a quick frenzy of motion like a dropped fistful of jackstraws. When she read Yeats's *The Stolen Child*, with the chorus in Gaelic, three suffered orgasm immediately. "Siobhan! Siobhan!"—Bill moaned, as he was engaged in E3- with Obtak, Ava, Rick, and Nelson. E3- was a term used by them to denote concomitant double-handed beatoff plus fellatio by Ava, with simultaneous impletion of Ava from the back.

There were numerous combinations but usually they paired and trio'd off by the end of the records. Ava and Nelson slept together. They always seemed to pair off and indeed, of them all, were the only ones to live together. Ava pushed her slight frame against him. Soon she was atop and seesaw bumping. She was able to come that way, rocking, rubbing forward, sliding into the happiness. Next to the frenzying Ava/Nelson, Rick and Rosebud lay side by side, Rick bringing her to a moaning cliff-leap by means of an extraordinary device fashioned from a furry pipe cleaner.

Obtak and Trudy, she side, he at her back, eyes shut tight, making it on the single mattress. Trudy was able to lift her leg and move it back and forth across the partner's chest during conjunction.

As for Bill, he usually fell asleep after a single act of love culminating in a long warbling scream they called the "yohimbine yodel." Bill had read a poem that night at The House of Nothingness titled *Homage to the Buttock*. Later on, Bill and Ava were seeing how hard they could whack themselves together and the pops filled the air from the pubic cymbals. Perhaps thinking of his poem, Ava whisper-urged him to climb upon, nay, to impinge himself within, her buttocks. He became confused and soon had to stop, thinking she had bidden buttockal pain upon herself because of his poem—for verily there are few who trod the paths of Mt. Bulgar.

He continued to think so except that he gradually learned that she genuinely was an adept of buttockery. Forever he remembered her lying topless upon her stomach on the sleeping bag on the air mattress in blue tights and Rick pushed his hand upon her behind and into the inward-curving, rotating the muscles circularly. "Don't stop, don't stop"—she whispered. "That arouses me more than anything all night."

Bill and Trudy loved Dylan Thomas, especially when he read *Fern Hill*. It drove them crazy. That night they played it over and over, seven times, until Bill was constrained to utter his famed yohimbine yodel after which he was soon asleep.

Hours oozed. They talked. They smoked. They wrote. They ate. Some departed. Some slept. Some kissed till dawn. And the gatherings went on each Monday for ten weeks before their Galaxy spiraled into dissolution. One went one way, one another.

During the ensuing decade, the seven ran into each other occasionally—at Orly Airport, in domes of meditation Colorado mountains, and so forth. "Remember those nights of Siobhan McKenna?"

"I sure do."

And always the friendship. bloomed. to renew again. the pleasures. of former. commingling.

Recorded poets grope-list:
1. *Yeats (Siobhan McKenna reading)*
2. *e. e. cummings*
3. *Ezra Pound*
4. *T. S. Eliot*
5. *Dylan Thomas*
6. *Edith Sitwell*
7. *A. Ginsberg*
8. *Marianne Moore*
9. *W. C. Williams*

10. *Delmore Schwartz*
11. *Arthur Rimbaud (Germaine Bree reading)*
12. *E. A. Poe*
13. *Lawrence Ferlinghetti*
14. *Edna St. Vincent Millay*
15. *W. H. Auden.*

Tales of Beatnik Glory, 1975; expanded edition, 1990

Rudolph Wurlitzer
(b. 1937)

*A descendant of the jukebox tycoon, Rudy Wurlitzer began writing while a young merchant seaman. After stints at Columbia and in the U.S. Army, he became Robert Graves's secretary in Majorca, absorbing Graves's lessons in the craft of writing. His first novel (*Nog*) and first screenplay (for Jim McBride's* Glen and Randa*) both date from 1969. Later screenplays include* Two-Lane Blacktop *(Monte Hellman),* Pat Garrett and Billy the Kid *(Sam Peckinpah),* Walker *(Alex Cox),* Candy Mountain *(Robert Frank), and* Little Buddha *(Bernardo Bertolucci). His novels—after* Nog *came* Flats, Quake, Slow Fade, *and* The Drop Edge of Yonder—*found a fiercely appreciative readership. Thomas Pynchon said of* Nog: *"The novel of bullshit is dead."*

from *Nog*

YESTERDAY AFTERNOON a girl walked by the window and stopped for sea shells. I was wrenched out of two months of calm. Nothing more than that, certainly, nothing ecstatic or even interesting, but very silent and even, as those periods have become for me. I had been breathing in and out, out and in, calmly, grateful for once to do just that, staring at the waves plopping in, successful at thinking almost nothing, handling easily the three memories I have manufactured, when that girl stooped for sea shells. There was something about her large breasts under her faded blue tee shirt, the quick way she bent down, her firm legs in their rolled-up white jeans, her thin ankles—it was her feet, actually; they seemed for a brief, painful moment to be elegant. It was that thin-boned brittle movement with her feet that did it, that touched some spot that I had forgotten to smother. The way those thin feet remained planted, yet shifting slightly in the sand as she bent down quickly for a clam shell, sent my heart thumping, my mouth dry, no exaggeration, there was something gay and insane about that tiny gesture because it had nothing to do with her.

I went to Smitty's, a roadhouse a quarter of a mile down the beach. When I came back, she was gone. I could not sit in my room. The walls closed in on me. I could see the walls closing in on me, and my situation, if that is what it is, a situation, seemed suddenly so dull and hopeless; this cheap thrown-together guest house of imitation redwood on the California coast with its smell of mold and bad plumbing, the inane view from my window of driftwood and seaweed, flat predictable waves, corny writings in the sand, pot-bellied fishermen and bronzed godlike volleyball players. I had to pull out, I thought, I was beginning to notice things, lists were forming, comparisons were on the way. And now I don't have the octopus. I suppose that is what there is to tell about. Then I'll move on. Last night there was a storm, and I abandoned the octopus. I didn't really abandon the octopus, it's still in the bathysphere on the truck bed, and the truck bed is still up on blocks, but it's not the same any more. I'm going to move on alone.

I have money and I can make money. I want to say that now. I'm not reprobate, nor am I a drain on anyone. My great aunt left me two thousand a year, and I have, or had, an octopus and a truck. A man sold me the octopus and truck in Oregon. I met him in a bar in one of those logging towns on the Coast where the only attractive spot is the village dump, which at least has the advantage of facing the sea. Nog, he was apparently of Finnish extraction, was one of those semi-religious lunatics you see wandering around the Sierras on bread and tea, or gulping down peyote in Nevada with the Indians. He was dressed in black motorcycle boots, jeans and an old army shirt with sergeant chevrons still on the sleeves. His face was lean and hatchet-edged, with huge fuzzy eyes sunk deep in his skull like bullet holes. He kept complaining about a yellow light that had lately been streaming out of his chest from a spot the size of a half dollar. We drank and talked about the spot and the small burning sensation it gave him early in the morning and about his octopus. He had become disillusioned about traveling with the octopus and had begun having aggressive dreams about it. He wanted to sell it. We bought a bottle and walked out beyond the town into logged-off hills that looked like old battlefields. A low mist hung over a struggling second growth of redwood and Douglas fir. The tracks of giant caterpillar tractors wound everywhere. Pits and ditches were scattered about like shell holes. Thousands of frogs croaked and salamanders hung suspended between lids of green slime and rotting logs. I felt vaguely elated, like a witness to some ancient slaughter.

Nog lived in what had once been a water tank in the middle of a rough field. The octopus was there, all right. It was sitting inside a bathysphere on a truck bed. Nog had built a mold out of plaster of Paris for the tentacles and another one for the obese body with its parrot-like beak and bulging eyes. Then he had poured liquid latex rubber into the molds. The bathysphere was carefully fashioned out of a large butane gas tank and stolen pieces of metal from a nearby bridge. There were three portholes from which you could watch the octopus move its eight tentacles around in the bubbling water. Nog had been traveling to all the state and county fairs through the West and Midwest, charging kids a dime and adults a quarter. Most people believed the octopus was real, but whenever there was a loud doubt Nog would tell them the truth. He would never give money back, and occasionally there would be fights. In Bird City, Utah, the bathysphere had been tipped over by three men who had just been on a losing softball team. He was weary of the whole thing, he kept repeating. We sat down on a bench in front of his house, and he filled me in on octopus lore. The crowd appreciated the devilfish myth the most, and it was important to tell them how dangerous octopi are and how they can drown and mangle a human or sink a small boat. One should never tell them the truth, which is that octopi are quite friendly. I refused any more information. We sat quietly and it grew dark. Finally Nog said that he had stopped knowing how to entertain himself. He said he guessed that was my trouble, too, but that I should take a chance with the octopus. He suggested I transform it into a totem that I didn't mind seeing every day.

I bought the octopus, and for a year I traveled through the country with it.

Nog is not quite clear enough. I have to invent more. It always comes down to that. I never get a chance to rest. I have never been able, for instance, to understand the yellow light streaming from his chest. But now that the octopus has faded away, Nog might emerge into a clearer focus. Those were sentimental and fuzzy days, those trips through the West with the octopus, and sometimes I find myself wishing more of it were true. (I find, when I ruminate like this, that I invent a great deal of my memories—three now, to be exact—because otherwise I have trouble getting interested.) But I have gotten faster with myself and more even-tempered since I met Nog. Perhaps not even-tempered but certainly more dulcet. I think about trips, bits and pieces of trips, but I no longer try and put anything together (my mind has become blessedly slower), nor do I try as much to invent a suitable character who can handle the fragments. But I don't want to get into all that. There is always the danger that I might become impressed by what once was a misplaced decision for solitude.

I'm thinking about trying the East. I will go to New York and get a small room on the top of a hotel.

When I was on the road with the octopus I did a lot of reminiscing about New York. New York was, in fact, my favorite memory for four or five months, until it got out of hand and I had to drop it. I lived in a comfortable duplex apartment on top of an old hotel overlooking a small park and harbor. I was sort of an erotic spy on myself then, but managed to survive, at least for those four or five months, by keeping an alert and fastidious watch on the terrifying view outside. I watched ships glide and push into huge docks, and far below, through silvery leaves, the quiet violence in the park. At night I stayed up with the fantastic lights of cars and subways as they flowed over the concrete ramps that weaved around the hotel. I lived precariously in the center of brutal combinations of energy, and gradually, as I closed in on myself, the bridges transformed into massive spider webs imprisoning the subways as they rumbled like mechanical snakes across the black river. The subways shot off green and yellow sparks in defense, in specific relays of time, always getting through. I had to drop that memory. But now, with more miles and memories in control, I might attempt New York.

From my window I can see the beach. An old couple digs razor-backed clams, and a small boy writes "David Salte Hates the Slug" on the sand with a large knotted stick. It has never been enough for me to have a stick and some sand to draw in. I am not indifferent enough. I am too self-engrossed to play in the sand. But yesterday afternoon I was *trying* to at least get ready to play, trying to find the right approach, the right kind of silence, when the girl walked by. That touch of elegance ruined my confidence. It made me dwell on the time I have spent just getting by, made me hate the octopus and the kingdom of the octopus, the small towns, the long monotonous highways, the squalid fairgrounds. It made me take a walk on the beach.

It's a glorious beach, I suppose; usually empty, very wide and sandy. In back there are warm and green mountains, and most of the time the sea is well-behaved, although it was rough then and it had begun to rain. I began to think of beaches. I have been on eighty-seven beaches in the last fifteen years. Before that it is easier to be vague. Lately I have been reviewing each beach, although it isn't a satisfactory way of getting through the day. Too much of my life has been spent on beaches: Cannes, Far Rockaway, Stinson Beach, one beach in Ireland, two in Crete, Lido, Curaçao, Luquillo, Curadado, Malibu, Deya, Nice, Tangiers, Cob, the Virgin Islands—to name a few. I never run into the water. I am actually afraid of moving water. Nor do I get a suntan. I lie in one place, usually on my stomach, and do nothing. For me, beaches are profane.

So there I was, reaching the end of the beach, thinking about beaches, when I saw the girl again. She was standing near a black rock, a yellow shawl wrapped around her face, staring inanely at the sea. I walked up to her, and standing a little apart and to the rear of her, I too stared at the sea. The waves were rushing in and out, quite furious now, sucking at the stones. I looked at her. She seemed not to have noticed me, and for this I was grateful. I was happy enough just to stand there, next to her, for my former feelings about her foot were quite in control. In fact, I inspected her feet and it didn't seem possible that one of them should have acted as such a catalyst. Her feet were like her face, too broad and splotchy, rather crude and used up. Her dull features reassured me so much that I thought I might be able to stay on for another few months.

She turned toward me.

I have never been able to connect with strange women except if they are in distress or in some way hung up. She looked abysmally happy.

"You live in the boarding house, don't you?" she asked. "Yes, I think you're the only one who is permanent there."

I wasn't able to answer, a common fault of mine.

"What do you do? I mean, we've all been wondering what you do. You look frail and timid, like some great thinker or something. That's what I think, anyway. My husband thinks you're recovering from some romantic disease. Who's right, him or me?"

She sat down on the black rock. The rain was drenching us. I was unprepared for such a downpour, being dressed in white seersucker pants, white paisley shirt and finely-woven linen shoes. I stood near her, waiting, but resolved not to give out with any information. If pressed, I might improvise on one of my memories. One should have an electric mind, I decided right there, not a tepid half-awake coping mind.

"Walk me down the beach," the girl said. "I'm so wet. We're *both* so wet. You don't mind, do you? I'll tell you a secret, we call you Dr. Angst because of the gloom on your face. You don't mind, do you?"

I walked with her. I was, in fact, deeply offended, not by being called Dr. Angst but by being noticed that much. Words began to spill out of me, quite out of my control. "Why try to know anything about a place? The customs, the size, the weather, the people, the economy, the politics, the fish, the suntan techniques, the games, the swimming. It is better to stay indoors and not mess around with useless experiences. A small room in a boarding house. Anonymous. Eat each meal at a plastic counter. Smitty's will do. Do nothing, want nothing, if you feel like walking, walk; sleeping, sleep. Do you know how hard that is? No memories; if they start to intrude, invent them. Three is sufficient. I use only three. New York for adventure, beaches for relaxation, the octopus and Nog for speculation. No connections. Narrow all possibilities. Develop and love your limitations. No one knows you. Know no one. Natural rhythms, my dear. That's the ticket."

She had wandered off to pick up a mussel shell. She came skipping back. "I use them for collages. I paste them in; shells, colored pieces of glass, driftwood, anything." She giggled. "Did you know that today is the Fourth of July?"

"No."

"We're having a party. You're invited. Everyone is coming. Well, not *everyone*, but Timmons and Harry and the man who runs the gift shop and one or two others. My husband too, of course."

I put my arm around her. Her behavior seemed to allow for such an embrace as long as nothing called her attention to it. But she stepped away, giving me a quizzical glance. I am unable to cope with quizzical glances.

"I know you," I said decisively, trying to struggle away. "Ten years ago in New York; I don't remember your name, but I *might* have even slept with you. It scares me, stumbling onto a part of my past like that. You were more emaciated then, of course, with your hair very ratty. You were carrying a sign in some kind of demonstration when I met you, that's you, very political. Am I right?"

"I'm from Baltimore," she said with a quick glance down at her awful feet. "I've never seen a demonstration of any kind. We moved out here when Ollie got a job working with an agricultural firm. They transferred him. We like it fine."

"I won't press," I said. I have retained a certain amount of old-fashioned dignity. "Who you are and what you do are your problems."

We walked on in silence. The silence, in fact, was fierce. And, I was proud to think, not one piece of information had I given away. No history, therefore no bondage. I have known myself to give out with facts, numbers, names, stories. I am that nervous sometimes. But as I said before, I am faster now. It was a joy to walk beside her with only her self-conscious distrust of me to handle. She was thinking I was only a little weird, possibly diseased; she was too simple, too nice to think anything more. And I'm too haggard to produce sexual fears; my ears are too huge and my lips too thin and uncontrolled.

We pressed on in the rain. I was all for delaying the walk as much as possible, but she was too determined to get home. Just before the house she had proudly marked as hers, we passed an old man in a First World War hat, struggling with a heavy log. He was bent and puffing as he tried to shift the log on top of a low makeshift sea wall.

I stopped. He was remarkably ugly and defiant.

"Colonel Green," the girl said. "He lives in that big three-story house next to ours. He has a grandson in there and some kind of a woman, but they hardly ever show themselves. It's not a good policy to talk to him. He comes out in every storm. A maniac about the sea. He must be eighty, honest, and Ollie says that all that's keeping him alive is this crazy war he has going against the sea. Everyone thinks he's a blight on the community."

"Grab hold," Colonel Green ordered. He marched up and shouted in my ear. "Goddamn water rising at three hundred miles an hour. Too dumb to see it? Flood the whole town before anyone shifts ass to do anything about it. Fact. Lift her up."

I helped him lift the log onto the sea wall. He was dressed in a yellow mackintosh and big fishing boots. His furiously weathered face was sunk deep into his neck, and his tiny blue eyes, like two pale robin's eggs, protruded into the night, unblinking and beautiful.

"People," he yelled again into my ear.

I helped him with another log. We labored and swore, but the log kept slipping back onto the sand. Finally the colonel ordered a halt and sat down on the sea wall, wheezing and kicking the wet sand with his boots. I could only pick out every third or fourth word the colonel said, the wind was so strong and his voice had sunk to such a rasp. "Hear . . . no retreat . . . only . . . bastard sea . . . kicking up higher . . . iron woman . . . What . . . ? What . . . ? What . . . ?"

I went up and yelled in his ear. "Right. A huge operation. Biggest operation in years. Massive. Mounting up out there. Ready to initiate general collapse. *Any*time."

We yelled back and forth. Then he punched me amiably in the stomach, and we struggled with the log. This time we made it. After another rest, we walked down to the sea for a better evaluation. "Jeep," the colonel yelled, coming up to my ear again and grasping me by the neck so I wouldn't turn away. He only had, after all, so many words in him. "Good thick sand tires. Drag every piece of maverick wood to the stronghold. Dig in! Protect the road!"

I nodded and followed him up the beach to his house. Before very long, however, I took a sharp turn to the left and ducked out of his line of march. As it happened, I was unfortunate enough to be standing in front of the girl's large bay window. She was standing with several other people, looking gaily down at me. I didn't, of course, want to have anything to do with anyone. The evening had already been too much of a lark. It might possibly set me back for months. I wanted only to get to bed and pull the covers over my head. A few sips of whiskey, that would do me fine. Just to listen to the storm with a memory or two. To go over once again a few details about the octopus. My clothes were drenched. I had long ago taken off my shoes and shirt. I was suffering from chills. They were waving. But I wasn't going anywhere. I had done very well that night. I had talked far too much but was rather amazed at how well I had managed. Nothing had been said. It was all right.

A hand grabbed the upper part of my arm and escorted me into the house.

"It's about time," a low, modulated, terrifically friendly voice

roared. "I'm Ollie, of course. *Glad* to have you aboard. You're quite
the stranger around here. I won't even ask what you were doing with
that old maniac out there. It looks like we got to you just in time.
What's that? Look here, Sarah, this poor fella has had it. Get him
some dry clothes. Better still, get him into my terrycloth bathrobe.
That's it. Get in there now. That's the boy."

I followed Sarah into the bedroom. She smiled at me, and I took
off my clothes.

"Now wait," she said, very fast. "Listen. I don't know you. That
bathrobe. The bathrobe is hanging in the bathroom."

I went into the bathroom and stood, shivering, behind the door.
I too was a little ill at ease. After all, at first sight I've been told I'm
not exactly pleasing to look at. "I was a track man," I yelled into the
bedroom. "Four-forty under fifty-five seconds. I assure you." There
was no answer. There didn't seem to be anything else to do but to give
out with some information. "Slipping out from New York, everything
going too fast. Left and wandered out to Coast. Met Nog and bought
octopus. Traveled to county and state fairs, developing wonderful
aversion to people and trips in general but at the same time a growing obsession with octopus. Hard to even talk about it. Was afraid
to let go, surrender it, walk away. Settled down here just to sit, you
understand, wanting nothing at all. Waiting it out. Then thinking of
beaches, developing that memory up to par with other two. Beaches,
you understand, beaches where most of life has dribbled away, past
beaches, future beaches and now right here a . . ."

I ventured a peek out the door, but she had left the bedroom. I
preferred to think she hadn't heard me; that, indeed, she had never
heard me. I could still slip out. The terrycloth bathrobe was hanging
behind the door. I put it on and turned to investigate the bathroom. It
was a beautiful bathroom. There was a huge green tile tub, a new toilet
and washbowl. I opened the cabinet over the washbowl. I couldn't
stop looking at the objects on the top two shelves: suntan oil, Anacins,
cold cream, three pink hair curlers, two yellow toothbrushes, one of
which was very dirty, Dramamine pills, Itolsol eye bath, Ban, Kolex
cold capsules, Ammens Medicated Powder and a small box of Ben-

zedrine pills. I stared at each object and then went over them again. A bottle of hydrogen peroxide fell from one of the lower shelves. I dumped the contents of every bottle in the cabinet into the bathtub except for the Benzedrine pills, which I put into the pocket of the terrycloth bathrobe. I turned the water on. It was a reviving thing to do. Then I turned the water off and stepped into the bedroom. The bedroom was painted a pale mauve. There was a king-sized bed, three small watercolors of clipper ships, a dresser, a sewing machine, two night tables and a television set. It was pleasant. I felt very relaxed. I got into bed and pulled the covers over my head.

I thought of Nog. He would be wandering over the Sierras probably, that yellow light streaming from his chest. I haven't been able to think too clearly about the octopus since I had come to the beach. I had given it a chance, it wasn't as if I had deserted it. I had driven through the Northwest, the Southwest and the Midwest. Thousands of people had looked at it, and many had even thought it was real. I had made money. But once off the road I could never go out behind the boarding house and look at it up on the truck bed. It was the last thing to throw away. Lately I've imagined its eight tentacles wrapped around my head slowly smothering me.

I must have fallen asleep. A hand shook me. "Now look. It's perfectly all right if you come in and use my terrycloth bathrobe and even take a nap in the middle of my bed, but why violate my bathroom?"

I slipped my head under the covers.

Ollie pulled the covers off the bed. I looked up at his face. It wasn't too bad a face. It was broad and handsome in a puffy way. Ollie was about to say something when Sarah took him by the hand and led him to the doorway. They whispered together. Finally Sarah came back and said, sweetly, "I'll bet you would like to join the party. We're going to have fireworks. Please, it will be fun."

Between the two of them I was escorted to the edge of the living-room rug. There were only five people. There might have been more in other rooms, but I counted five. I took care not to notice anything else. I sat down.

"The last time was in New York," I said.

"Is that right," a fat man said. He was eating an egg- and shrimp-salad sandwich and drinking bourbon and water.

"New York is an active place. Not as much action as you might have been led to believe, but still, an active place. I lived in a sort of penthouse. Beautiful furniture. Turn-of-the-century stuff."

"What exactly is your line?" I was asked.

"I'm a cultural impresario. Nog is the name. I'm investigating cephalopods or, as they say here, octopi or octopuses. Timid creatures, really, much maligned."

The man excused himself and went into the next room.

The wind battered against the window. I remember that very well, the wind battering against the window and the hum of conversation. I pulled the curtain over the bay window to protect the room from the terrible racket of the storm.

There was boisterous talk about fireworks and drinking and last year's Fourth of July party.

Sarah advanced toward me, smiling bravely, "Having fun?" she asked.

"Of course I'm having fun," I replied.

"Would you mind telling me what you do?" she asked.

It was obvious that they were closing in on me. I was forced to throw out a series of delaying actions.

"You may ask," I said, being extremely polite. "Of course you may ask. I'm making a survey of the West Coast. Marine animals mostly. Did you know fossils of cephalopods have been found in rocks that are believed to be at least four hundred million years old? They are harmless. Most people don't want to know that, but they are harmless, even rather stupid . . . I am also making a survey of the Sierras and another, more general survey on Los Angeles, Sacramento, Portland, Seattle, San Francisco, Oakland, and Santa Barbara, to name a few. I am also, on the side, so to speak, investigating totems."

I remember dancing.

I remember sitting for a long stretch, looking at television.

I was able to become more anonymous. I ate roast beef and drank Seven-Up.

I remember no more until I was asked down to the game room by Ollie. "Now, Mr. Mysterious," he said, laughing and slapping me on the back. "You can tell me what you do."

"A survey of beaches," I replied quickly. "Taking ten to fifteen years. The best years of my life consumed in this project. All over the Western world. Marvelous and fantastic stories. Over eight beaches noted so far, actually eighty-seven. To name a few: Far Rockaway, Montauk, Las Palmas, Harrison's Landing, Brighton, Antibes, Westhampton, Orient, Marblehead, Malibu, Coventry, Truro, the whole of the Ceylonese coast, Tangier, Tunis and Ceuta, that whole stretch, Ibiza and Formentera, Vancouver and two beaches in Rhodes and Hydra, three in Crete and only one in all of Ireland. The beach here, the present one, is calm, wide and sandy, few sharks, and a good class of swimmers. Weather mostly good. Except, of course, for tonight. Tonight there is a storm."

He handed me a Ping-Pong racket. We played Ping-Pong.

At first I just shoveled the ball back, trying to be polite. I managed to get the ball close to his racket. But then he grew angry and shouted at me to play ball. I put little twists on the ball and chopped back on the serve. He slammed back harder. Several times it appeared that he wanted to say something, but we were playing so hard there was no time to talk. I kept him hopping. There were backhand smashes for him to contend with, forehand chops, tricky cross-court serves, sleezy slices. Balls sprayed around the room, but he had a plentiful supply from a large wicker basket that hung from the ceiling on a wire chain. We played even harder, and I rolled up the sleeves of my terrycloth bathrobe. Finally, wheezing and perspiring, he stood still, squeezing a Ping-Pong ball in his hand. He appeared to be stuck in some way. There was nothing else to do but grab the basket of Ping-Pong balls and fling them at him. That started him off. He yelled. I threw my paddle, catching him in the throat. Then I tipped over the table. He was left sitting on the floor.

I walked out of the game room and into the storm.

Colonel Green was still working on the sea wall. He had managed to move one more log.

"Getting you down?" I yelled at him. "Worst storm in years. Watch battle fatigue. Absolutely all right."

The colonel surveyed the beach, his hands on his hips.

"Crashing . . . now . . . 1937 . . . the drift . . . up later . . . no help . . . tatters . . . tatters . . ."

I grabbed the end of a log. "Where do you get these logs?" I yelled. "What do you do, push them back when the storm is over?"

"Selfish . . . 1937 . . . four-door sedan . . . stand tall . . ."

We labored some more but couldn't move the log. I went back to my room and went to bed.

What I should have done was get rid of the octopus, what I have been trying to do is get rid of the octopus, what I am beginning just now to remember was that I did get rid of the octopus. I see it now for the first time. I either took it back to the party and put it in the bathtub or danced with it on the beach. No, I did bring it back to the beach but not to dance with. I took off my terrycloth bathrobe and ran down to the truck and got the octopus out of the bathysphere, its tentacles waving all over me. Struggling in the rain and wind, I dragged it back and pulled it up on the sea wall. Such a spectator gave the colonel enough of a jolt to finish the sea wall. Then together we threw it in the sea, and I went home and went to bed. It was something like that, I can remember something like that, a storm, a party and then the octopus. There was an octopus, although I know deep down that the octopus is still up on blocks. I know, too, that nothing happened and I haven't traveled with the octopus. But I shall move on anyway, perhaps to New York. I remember great things about New York.

Nog, 1969

Brion Gysin
(1916–1986)

I'm declaring the British-born Brion Gysin an honorary American, as a Beat founding father and a son of Canadians. A painter foremost, he was expelled at age nineteen from the Surrealist Group by André Breton; published A History of Slavery in Canada; *studied Japanese calligraphy; and moved in 1950 to Tangier, where his circle included Paul Bowles and William Burroughs. Moving back to Paris in 1958 he took up residence in what became known as The Beat Hotel. With Burroughs he developed the "cut-up technique" of rearranging existing text to create new text, and with Ian Sommerville invented "the dreamachine," a stroboscopic device based on the frequency of alpha waves. He was the actual source of the Alice B. Toklas brownie recipe. This is a chapter from Gysin's Saharan novel,* The Process.

from *The Process*

I AM OUT in the Sahara heading due south with each day of travel less sure of just who I am, where I am going or why. There must be some easier way to do it but this is the only one I know so, like a man drowning in a sea of sand, I struggle back into this body which has been given me for my trip across the Great Desert. "This desert," my celebrated colleague, Ibn Khaldoun the Historian, has written, "This desert is so long it can take a lifetime to go from one end to the other and a childhood to cross at its narrowest point." I made that narrow childhood crossing on another continent; out through hazardous tenement hallways and stickball games in the busy street, down American asphalt alleys to paved playgrounds; shuffling along Welfare waiting-lines into a maze of chain-store and subway turnstiles and, through them, out onto a concrete campus in a cold gray city whose skyscrapers stood up to stamp on me. It has been a long trail a-winding down here into this sunny but sandy Middle Passage of my life in Africa, along with the present party. Here, too, I may well lose my way for I can see that I am, whoever I am, out in the middle of Nowhere when I slip back into this awakening flesh which fits me, of course, like a glove.

I know this body as if it were a third party whose skin I put on as a mask to wear through their "Land of Fear" and I do go in a sort of disguise for, like everyone else out here in this blazing desert where a man is a fool to show his face naked by day, I have learned to wrap five or six yards of fine white muslin around my head to protect the mucus of my nose and throat against the hot, dry wind. All you can see of me is my eyes. For once, I look just like everyone else. No need for me to open these eyes. I know what is out there—nothing but the very barest stripped illusion of a world; almost nothing, nothing at all.

Bundled up like a mummy, I huddle here under my great black burnous, a cape as big as a bag for an animal my size, shape and color. It also serves as a portable tent smelling of woodsmoke and lanolin, under which I fumble for the two pencil-thin sections of my *sebsi*, my slim wooden keef-pipe from Morocco, to fit them together. A fine flesh-pink clay pipe head, no bigger than the last joint of my little finger, snuggles up over a well-fitted paper collar shaped wet with spit. I try it like a trumpet; airtight, good. My keef-pouch from Morocco is the skin of a horned viper sewn into a *metoui* and stuffed with great grass. I check with my thumb the tide of fine-chopped green leaf which rolls down its long leather tongue, milking most of the keef back into the pouch. What remains, I coax into the head of my pipe with the beckoning crook of my right forefinger.

A masterpiece matchbox the size of a big postage stamp leaps into the overturned bowl of my left hand, riding light but tight between the ball of my thumb and my third finger. I make all these moves not just out of habit but with a certain conscious cunning through which I ever-so slowly reconstruct myself in the middle of your continuum; inserting myself, as it were, back into this flesh which is the visible pattern of Me. Yet, I know this whole business is a trap which may well be woven of nothing but words, so I joggle the miniature matchbox I hold in my hand and these masterpiece matches in here chuckle back what always has sounded to me like a word but a word which I cannot quite catch. It could be a rattling Arabic word but my grasp of Arabic is not all that good and no one, not even Hamid, will tell me what the matches say to the box. I hold the box up to my ear as I shake it again, trying to hear what the box stutters back. If I remember correctly, Basilides in his "Game" reduced all the Names proposed by the Gnostics to one single rolling, cacophonic, cyclical word which he thought might well prove to be a Key to the heavens: *Kaulakaulakaulakaulakaulakau . . ."* Can the matches match that?

I love these little matches bought back in Tanja. Each match is a neat twist of brown paper like a stick dipped in wax, with a helmet-shaped turquoise-blue head made to strike on the miniature Sahara of sandpaper slapped onto one side of the box. Matchbox is clamped into the claw of left thumb and middle finger. This indifferent caliper proves suddenly sadist as it rams poor matchbox back onto himself, with little-finger of right hand clear up his ass. Little-finger holds him impaled; proffering a drawerful of identical matches to caliper, who solemnly selects one little brother, pinching him tight. Matchbox is closed with a small, scraping sigh against the heel of right hand. Little-finger withdraws from the rape to help snub poor match against the backslide of his box; striking and exploding his head.

I elbow my way out of this cocoon of felted camel-hair smelling of woodsmoke to thrust forward this pipe, pouch and matches just as we go over a bump and I open my eyes. I am not alone. We are five passengers in here, where we should be only four in the blistering metal cabin of this truck whose red-hot diesel is housed in with us, too. Two seats on either side of it are called First-Class Transportation, while Third-Class is out on the back on top of the cargo of sacks beneath a cracking tarpaulin. In the front seat, Driver, who looks like a chipmunk with the toothache because of the way his sloppy turban hangs under his chin, crouches over the wheel like a real desert rat.

Black Greaser, his number-two man, has been playing a long windy tune on a flute made out of a bicycle-pump and the bump nearly rams the flute down his throat. An anonymous vomiting man, like a doll leaking wet sawdust and slime, flops out the far window carsick while, here right beside me, crammed into my seat with me when we are not up in the air, is Middleman; Stowaway. We rise shoulder to shoulder and I hope he lands back on the diesel and burns.

He has risen up in the air without losing his cross-legged Sufi saint pose, as if to show me he knows how to levitate. I shoot up my own dusty eyebrows at him as much as to say: *So can I!* because he glares at my pipe with all the baleful ferocity of a carnivorous bird. He feels I pollute him with my keef-smoke—too bad! We both drop back into my seat. I paid First-Class Transportation for these broken springs; no need to share them with him. Yesterday, or the day before, or one of those days back along our trail, he suddenly jumped up from behind a bare dune in the middle of nowhere, flagging us down. I had spotted him up there ahead of us and was just saying to myself: "Is that a man or a bush?" when he started up, skipping and waving his arms. Driver changed gear without daring to stop in the sand from which this little old stick of a man hopped up quick as a bird when Black Greaser threw open the door, grandly waving him into my seat with me. He is a Hadj, just back from the pilgrimage to Mecca; a new little saint. Black Greaser let his whole ugly face fall apart in a welcoming grin: "No baggage, Father?"

The little old man twitched aside the yards of gray-green muslin piled on top of his head and swathing his bearded face: "No baggage. This is the way I came and—*Inch' Allah!*—this is the way I shall return."

I push back the window of opalescent glass frosted by the blasting of sand, to thrust the whole length of my slender pipe out like a periscope into the bouncing air of the dazzling desert through which we churn night and day no faster than a funeral. When I lean out the window, the light out there hits me like a blow. Shading my eyes, I look down into the granular shallows of flowing sand on whose current we ride until I am dizzy and sick. Everything visibly crawls; even the cloth of my sleeve when I look at it close. I glance up and out with my eyes clenched against the all but intolerable brightness of the blazing desert where the mirage sizzles across the horizon like a sweep of glittering marshes, thickly grown with tall rushes whipped by the wind. Air ignites and flames up around the truck like the billowing breath of a blast furnace searing my lungs. The water should lie not more than a half hour's distance away—or so you might think. Hour after hour, day after day, we bore on through the sands without reaching those marshes.

All this ululating emptiness aches in my ears like the echo of a shell. Now and again, I swear I can hear the lowing and bellowing of invisible herds of longhorn cattle but, of course, there are none. When I listen even further down into myself, I contact something else which shakes my whole intimate contact with Me. When I try to tune out the constant moaning roar of the wind, my whole being vibrates to a sound down below the threshold of hearing. My sinuses, antrums, the cords of my throat and the cavities of my chest, the very hollows of my bones hum in a register too low for my ear but, for no known reason, I tremble, I quake. This, so they tell me, is the voice of Ghoul and Ghoul is the Djinn of the Desert, Keeper of the Land of Fear. Grains of sand in their incalculable billions of billions are grinding, grinding together, rolling and sliding abrasively in dunes as big as New York and as high, vibrating this ocean of air through which we paddle like sick fish on their flight from some distant dynamite blast. At that, a very American thought suddenly strikes me: they do have an atomic center out here in the Sahara. Could this air be radioactive, perhaps? Or, is that just the black breath of Ghoul?

FAR AWAY back up north in the green hills of Morocco, which I call home since I began to merge almost against my will into this scene with Hamid my Moroccan mock-guru, everyone around the keef cafés is always talking and singing of the Sahara but not one man in ten knows where it begins or ends or how to get into this desert. "It

lies down that way, many days marching," they say, swinging their
long slim keef-pipes around vaguely south. Yet, every last man sitting there on a straw mat on the floor feels he owns the whole sweep
of the Sahara desert, personally, inside his own Muslim head. Let
some paleface tourist appear on the scene and they will all proclaim
themselves competent "guides," if you please; when not one of them
can read even a map. In my forlorn American way, I thought to teach
Hamid the lay of the land and, to this end, I pulled my poor self
together to make an expedition up out of the damp grotto in which
Hamid and I were living in the native quarter of Tanja, in the impasse
of a narrow alley in a section of the Medina below even the tight-
packed little pedestrian square of cafés called the Socco Chico; in
other words, lost.

I adjusted my shades and smoked one last pipe for the road before
I stepped cautiously out into the mainstream of mankind in the
swarming alley as narrow as a corridor that is our street. At first, the
entire Medina of Tanja feels like one mysteriously rambling mansion
packed full of maniacs but, eventually, what looks like a terrifying
trap to a tripper gets to feel like your very own house. I cut into the
traffic and kept my head down as I whipped around corners with
my eyes glued to the ground; so as not to be noticed, I hoped. I slid
through alleys so wide I could touch the walls on both sides with my
elbows and I had to flatten myself into doorways to let heavily-laden
donkeys and porters push past. The whole point of this game, best
known to Old Tanja Hands, is to get from one side of the Socco Chico
to the other without crossing it; invisible to all traders and touts. My
own cunning route, first shown me by Hamid of course, is a turnoff
between the old *Hotel Satan* and *Casa Delerium*, once a whorehouse
in better days. This way, you can bypass not only the Socco Chico
but also steep Siaghine Street running up out of it; lined as it is with
neon-lit bazaars, swarming with tourists and tramps.

I meant to drop by the American Library on my way up to the
Boulevard in the New Town of Tanja but, when I caught sight of
myself in a mirror in a shop window, I thought: Uh-uh, better not! I

managed to make myself look a little more human before I got to the
Café de Paris on the Place de France. I drew up in front of a raggedy
man who sells raggedy books in the street. On an earlier trip, I had
spotted his stock of old dog-eared French guidebooks and road maps
of North Africa, put out by Michelin, the makers of tires. As I bent
over his wares, I picked up on the fact that I was getting scanned from
behind their newspapers by the whole row of white American and
British operatives seated, as always, out on the terrace of the Café de
Paris. They had their telepathic finders out feeling all over me as I
bought, for one dirham, a map which is now out of print. I scuttled
back down to the Socco and called Hamid out of his cavernous keef
café to drag him home for a bout of instruction in the map.

*#151 Morocco, Algeria and Tunisia (1 centimeter for 20 kilometers
or 1/2,000,000).* On this map, one handspan to the right along the
Mediterranean shore lies Woran. With your thumb on Woran, your
little-finger lands on Algut. If you pivot due south from that white
city on the cliffs, your thumb will fall on Ghardaïa, the mysterious
desert capital of the Dissident Mozabites. All that can take at least
three or four days of travel from the bright blue Straits of Gibraltar,
along the lush coastal valleys, over green hills and mountains so high
they are covered with snow. On the far side of these are plains marked
in brown to denote almost no annual rainfall at all and they must be
crossed before you get to even the fringe of the bright golden Sahara.
The trouble with this map is that it has two big insets of Woran and
Algut, shown in some detail at a scale of 1/500,000, and these effec-
tively obscure the desert trails to the south.

I trundled myself back up to the Boulevard again next day, or was
it next week? Anyway, one fine day when I could tear myself away
from the great smells of Hamid's cooking and manage to part the
curtain of keef which hung over our door, I fell out into the street
and worked my way back to the Boulevard bookstall, where I bought,
unobserved, an old guide to Algeria and the Michelin map #152—a
great prize. This pretty, pictorial map was printed to illustrate the
glorious exploit of General Leclerc, who marched a Free French army

from Dakar all the way north to Tunis across the Sahara by way of
Lake Chad. Not even the Romans could have brought off such a feat
but Hamid shows little interest in anything done by the French or the
Roumis, in general. Being Black, I am not a real Roumi to Hamid.
On the other hand, Hamid looks down on all Blacks as the natural
slaves of the Arabs; even though his own hair is curly enough to give
him trouble finding a barber, back in the States. Hamid shuts me up
when I tell him I am Black. "You're not Black, you're American! *Safi!*
Enough!"

Hamid suddenly became fascinated by the form he began to see
in my map. He pointed out that the Great Desert is in the shape of
a camel stretching its neck right across Africa, from the Atlantic to
the Red Sea. He laughed like a lunatic to see that the western butt-
end of his camel was dropping its Mauretanian crud on the Black
Senegalese—"Charcoal Charlies," Hamid calls them, having picked
up the term in the port. The head of Hamid's camel drinks its fill in
the sweet waters of the Nile. The eye of the camel, naturally enough, is
that fabled city of Masr, where the Arab movies are made and all the
radios ring out over streets paved with gold. Us poor Nazarenes call
the place Cairo, for short. Suddenly, somewhere down on the lower
middle belly of Hamid's camel, about four knuckles north of Kano
in northern Nigeria, I dowsed out a big carbuncle. With no more
warning than that, my whole heart rushed out to this place which was
pictured as an outcropping of extinct ash-blue volcanoes jutting up
out of the bright yellow sands. I noted that the whole area was called
the Hoggar and it seemed to boast only one constantly inhabited
place, whose name I made out to be Tam. I was truly surprised to hear
myself calmly boasting to Hamid, as if I were AMERICAN EXPRESS:
"I'll be in this place, here, this time next year."

"*Inch' Allah!* if God wills," Hamid corrected me automatically and
then, as if he were indeed the Consul of Keef, who was sending me out
on this mission, he went on: "I'll get them to cut you a green passport
of keef to see you through everything. I'll see that you get the best
of the crop from Ketama and I'll bring it down from the mountain

myself with the blessings of Hassan-i-Sabbah, the Father of Grass. On your way, you're bound to run into some other Assassins."

"But, Hamid," I laughed: "I am not an Assassin at all!"

"We are Assassins, all of us," he gravely replied.

The Process, 1969

Ishmael Reed
(b. 1938)

A poet, novelist, playwright, and essayist, Ishmael Reed has been an indelible presence in African American literature since the 1960s. He has written ten novels, including the 1972 hoodoo novel Mumbo Jumbo *excerpted here, which I consider one of the most important American novels. Reed has also published six volumes of poetry and eight collections of essays. He taught at U.C. Berkeley for thirty-five years, and has edited thirteen literary anthologies. A delightful late bloomer, after collaborating as lyricist and vocalist on three albums with producer Kip Hanrahan and a host of legendary musicians, including Allen Toussaint, David Murray, Taj Mahal, Eddie Harris, and Bobby Womack, he recently debuted as a jazz pianist heading up the Ishmael Reed Quintet.*

from *Mumbo Jumbo*

A TRUE SPORT, the Mayor of New Orleans, spiffy in his patent-leather brown and white shoes, his plaid suit, the Rudolph Valentino parted-down-the-middle hair style, sits in his office. Sprawled upon his knees is Zuzu, local doo-wack-a-doo and voo-do-dee-odo fizgig. A slatternly floozy, her green, sequined dress quivers.

Work has kept Your Honor late.

The Mayor passes the flask of bootlegged gin to Zuzu. She takes a sip and continues to spread sprawl and behave skittishly. Loose. She is inhaling from a Chesterfield cigarette in a shameless brazen fashion.

The telephone rings.

The Mayor removes his hand and picks up the receiver; he recognizes at once the voice of his poker pardner on the phone.

Harry, you'd better get down here quick. What was once dormant is now a Creeping Thing.

The Mayor stands up and Zuzu lands on the floor. Her posture reveals a small flask stuck in her garter as well as some healthily endowed gams.

What's wrong, Harry?

I gots to git down to the infirmary, Zuzu, something awful is happening, the Thing has stirred in its moorings. The Thing that my Grandfather Harry and his generation of Harrys had thought was nothing but a false alarm.

The Mayor, dragging the woman by the fox skins hanging from her neck, leaves city hall and jumps into his Stutz Bearcat parked at the curb. They drive until they reach St. Louis Cathedral where 19th-Century HooDoo Queen Marie Laveau was a frequent worshiper; its location was about 10 blocks from Place Congo. They walk up the steps and the door's Judas Eye swings open.

Joe Sent Me.

What's going on, hon? Is this a speakeasy? Zuzu inquires in her cutesy-poo drawl.

The door opens to a main room of the church which has been converted into an infirmary. About 22 people lie on carts. Doctors are rushing back and forth; they wear surgeon's masks and white coats. Doors open and shut.

1 man approaches the Mayor who is walking from bed to bed examining the sleeping occupants, including the priest of the parish.

What's the situation report, doc? the Mayor asks.

We have 22 of them. The only thing that seems to anesthetize them is sleep.

When did it start?

This morning. We got reports from down here that people were doing "stupid sensual things," were in a state of "uncontrollable frenzy," were wriggling like fish, doing something called the "Eagle Rock" and the "Sassy Bump"; were cutting a mean "Mooche," and "lusting after relevance." We decoded this coon mumbo jumbo. We knew that something was Jes Grewing just like the 1890s flair-up. We thought that the local infestation area was Place Congo so we put our anti-pathetic substances to work on it, to try to drive it out; but it started to play hide and seek with us, a case occurring in 1 neighborhood and picking up in another. It began to leapfrog all about us.

But can't you put it under 1 of them microscopes? Lock it in? Can't you protective-reaction the dad-blamed thing? Look I got an election coming up—

To blazes with your election, man! Don't you understand, if this Jes Grew becomes pandemic it will mean the end of Civilization As We Know It?

That serious?

Yes. You see, it's not 1 of those germs that break bleed suck gnaw or devour. It's nothing we can bring into focus or categorize; once we call it 1 thing it forms into something else.

No man. This is a *psychic epidemic*, not a lesser germ like typhoid yellow fever or syphilis. We can handle those. This belongs under some ancient Demonic Theory of Disease.

Well, what about the priest?

We tried him but it seized him too. He was shouting and carrying on like any old coon wench with a bass drum.

What about the patients, did you ask any of them about how they knew it?

Yes, 1, Harry. When we thought it was physical we examined his output and drinking water to determine if we could find some normal germ. We asked him questions, like what he had seen.

What *did* he see?

He said he saw Nkulu Kulu of the Zulu, a locomotive with a red green and black python entwined in its face, Johnny Canoeing up the tracks.

Well Clem, how about his feelings? How did he feel?

He said he felt like the gut heart and lungs of Africa's interior. He said he felt like the Kongo: "Land of the Panther." He said he felt like "deserting his master," as the Kongo is "prone to do." He said he felt he could dance on a dime.

Well, his hearing, Clem. His hearing.

He said he was hearing shank bones, jew's harps, bagpipes, flutes, conch horns, drums, banjos, kazoos.

Go on go on and then what did he say?

He started to speak in tongues. There are no isolated cases in this thing. It knows no class no race no consciousness. It is self-propagating and you can never tell when it will hit.

Well doc, did you get other opinions?

Who do you think some of those other cases are? 6 of them are some of the most distinguished bacteriologists epidemologists and chemists from the University.

There is a commotion outside. The Mayor rushes out to see Zuzu rejoicing. Slapping the attendants who are attempting to placate her. The people on carts suddenly leap up and do their individual numbers. The Mayor feels that uncomfortable sensation at the nape and soon he is doing something resembling the symptoms of Jes

Grew, and the Doctor who rushes to his aid starts slipping dipping gliding on out of doors and into the streets. Shades of windows fly up. Lights flick on in buildings. And before you know it the whole quarter is in convulsions from Jes Grew's entrance into the Govi of New Orleans; the charming city, the amalgam of Spanish French and African culture, is out-of-its-head. By morning there are 10,000 cases of Jes Grew.

The foolish Wallflower Order hadn't learned a damned thing. They thought that by fumigating the Place Congo in the 1890s when people were doing the Bamboula the Chacta the Babouille the Counjaille the Juba the Congo and the VooDoo that this would put an end to it. That was merely a fad. But they did not understand that the Jes Grew epidemic was unlike physical plagues. Actually Jes Grew was an anti-plague. Some plagues caused the body to waste away; Jes Grew enlivened the host. Other plagues were accompanied by bad air (malaria). Jes Grew victims said that the air was as clear as they had ever seen it and that there was the aroma of roses and perfumes which had never before enticed their nostrils. Some plagues arise from decomposing animals, but Jes Grew is electric as life and is characterized by ebullience and ecstasy. Terrible plagues were due to the wrath of God; but Jes Grew is the delight of the gods.
So Jes Grew is seeking its words. Its text. For what good is a liturgy without a text? In the 1890s the text was not available and Jes Grew was out there all alone. Perhaps the 1920s will also be a false alarm and Jes Grew will evaporate as quickly as it appeared again broken-hearted and double-crossed (++)

Mumbo Jumbo, 1972

Bobbie Louise Hawkins
(b. 1930)

*A prolific poet, prose writer, and monologist, Bobbie Louise Hawkins has pro-
duced many stories, essays, and memoirs that have been collected in* Own Your
Body *(1973),* My Own Alphabet *(1989),* Bijou *(2005),* Selected Prose *(2012),
and other books. She has released two performance CDs,* Live at the Great
American Music Hall *and* Jaded Love. *Hawkins was the wife of poet Robert
Creeley from 1957 to 1975 and his book* For Love *is dedicated to her.*

Frenchy and Cuban Pete

I N 1947 Albuquerque got its first stripper club. That was a good year
for Albuquerque. The first Jewish Delicatessen opened on Central
Avenue right downtown. And a lot of a very different kind of person
started going to the University of New Mexico on the G.I. Bill.

The G.I. Bill changed the look of Joe College U.N.M. drastically. A
large part of the influx, particularly in the painting department, were
Jews from New York. That look blew me over. Everytime I saw somebody looking great it turned out later that he or she was a Jew. For
awhile I got worried about it. Or rather I got worried about whether
I should be worried about it. That all my friends were Jews. Then I
thought what the hell go along with it.

I sat through evening after evening of conversations so abstract
that the only thing clear was that they all knew what they were talking
about. And it was fascinating. You have to realize that the talk I had
been understanding wasn't worth the effort. A presumptuous snob at
seventeen is what I was, out of desperation. What these people were
talking about involved rampant energy, arms waving, real anger for
intellectual reasons and a dynamic. They were so knowledgeable.

One of them who wanted to make love to me but never did gave me a Modern Library copy of *Sons and Lovers* for my birthday. I mean I was getting so much sustenance off of them that not being able to follow the mesh of their reasoning and not recognizing the names of their heroes was trivial; hardly to be thought of. And there were consistent small bonuses like eating my first hot pastrami on rye.

Anyway to return to the history of the city, that was growing a town, that's supposed to have been the first year the Mafia made their move in on the overall action. It was a stripper club west of town, out Central heading for the desert.

The building was a junker; cement block with patterns. Inside, the room was a huge barnlike square, with a dance floor orchestra section intruding off one wall so the tables were jammed into the remaining three sides.

Every couple of hours there would be a floor show. The exotic dancer was naked on her left side with a little pasty on her nipple and a g-string. Her right side was dressed up like a red and black devil. She was split right down the center and the act was watching the right side get it on with the left side. A lot of the time it really looked like two people, the right side being aggressive, the left side fighting it off, but being progressively overcome, even attracted. Hitting the floor at the same time and working up to a grand climax with all the lights going black to give her/it a chance to get up and walk away. Saving the image from a tawdry exit.

And then Cuban Pete and Frenchy would come on for a comic turn. Cuban Pete was a short fat Greek with a mass of black curls and an accent. He wore a straw hat and a blouse with huge ruffled sleeves. The straw hat worked as a hand prop. He'd take it off with a flourish, give it a shimmy-shake at the end of his arm to make a point, and to enter, and to exit. Frenchy was six feet tall with a high bleached pompadour and spike heels, and almost nothing else. She was a walking example of what was legally allowed. She would station herself like so many pounds on the hoof in front of the band microphone as if she meant to sing. Thank God she never did. Cuban Pete would have a hand mike with yards of cable to let him meander among the tables while they went through their act.

They were rotten. The jokes were so bad that the only way you knew when one was over was the band would go "*Ta-Taaaa!*" Then we'd all break up. "*Ta-Taaaa!*" was the real punch line. It let you see where you would have laughed if it had been funny.

One of their routines was Cuban Pete would be out among the clientele yelling back, "Hey Frenchy! How you like that movie I take you to last night?" "Oh!" she'd say, her nose like a trumpet, "Clark Gable was wonderful!"

"How you like that?" Cuban Pete would ask us. "I say how you like that movie I take you to last night and she says Clark Gable was wonderful!" He would try again. "Hey Frenchy, how you like that movie I take you to last night?"

"Oh!", she'd answer, "Clark Gable was wonderful!"

"How you like that?" throwing his arms wide in mock despair so the ruffles would ripple.

"I want to ask you just one thing."

"What you say?"

"I want to ask you just one thing."

"She wants to ask me something. O.K. Frenchy. What you want to know?"

"I want to know if you're jealous of Clark Gable?"

"How you like that! I ask her how she like the movie and she wants to know am I jealous of Clark Gable!"

A long pause to build suspense, then—

"You gah-dam right I am!"

Ta-Taaaa

THERE WAS another routine that Frenchy walked or rather marched through with two other women. The orchestra played a rousing medley of *Over There* and *I'm a Yankee Doodle Dandy* and such like songs, and Frenchy would come marching onto center dance floor with a Marine's hat on. The other women represented the Army and the Navy. All three of them wore red satin brassieres and very short blue and white striped skirts. They marched into a triangle with Frenchy out front, all of them keeping a time-step, marching in place. Then the two girls in back marched toward each other and wheeled in unison toward the bandstand where they came by an enormous American flag which they opened out to make a backdrop for Frenchy. They marched around her wrapping her in the flag. The highlight was when all the lights went out and the flag and costumes glowed in the dark.

Ta-Taaaa

I DID have a lover at that time. He was studying acting. I was studying painting. He would talk to me like two artists talking together.

He was also really tender. I had had an abortion three months before and I was basically scared about making love. I also had the Texas-Baptist blues riding hard on me . . . down the drain . . . seventeen and used up . . . etc.

It wasn't the idea of getting pregnant again that scared me, though that was certainly there. It was more like feeling raw and misused in my spirit and my body, and he helped me over that. It was a real piece of luck for me that somebody that decent and good-hearted happened along just then.

He used to make toasted cheese sandwiches with apple jelly spread on the top for us to eat in bed, talking.

Anyway, sometime along in there I started knowing the vocabulary and hearing the repetitions and one night at two in the morning some type, in the self-righteous tones we all know to our sorrow, said "You've got to qualify your terms," and I started crying and couldn't stop.

For a month or so I couldn't stand groups of people but then I gradually regained my perspective.

You know the brainwash goes that loss of innocence is a one-timer and thereafter you're left sadder and wiser. But in my experience it's cyclical; the place like the San Andreas Fault where your life makes a necessary dimensional shift. And it's not such a loss, more often it's a trade.

And the pain of it is the least interesting thing about it.

Frenchy and Cuban Pete and Other Stories, 1977

Richard Brautigan
(1935–1984)

Richard Brautigan was famed as the poet laureate of the hippies, and he looked the part, but Brautigan was not a hippie, he was an anomaly. After a traumatic childhood in Tacoma, Washington, Brautigan briefly found his footing in high school but at the age of twenty, apparently motivated by hunger, he invited arrest by throwing a rock through a police station window. He was subsequently hospitalized and subjected to electroshocks which seemed to stimulate his muse. After his release Brautigan became a street poet in San Francisco and published his unique works in underground papers. When his Trout Fishing in America *was published in 1967 it sold over four million copies. Brautigan published ten works of fiction and as many poetry collections during his life, but his success brought him little peace except for the comparative serenity he found on his travels in Japan. He suffered bouts of depression and was a heavy drinker. Living alone in Bolinas, California, he committed suicide at the age of forty-nine.*

The Kool-Aid Wino

WHEN I was a child I had a friend who became a Kool-Aid wino as the result of a rupture. He was a member of a very large and poor German family. All the older children in the family had to work in the fields during the summer, picking beans for two-and-one-half cents a pound to keep the family going. Everyone worked except my friend who couldn't because he was ruptured. There was no money for an operation. There wasn't even money to buy him a truss. So he stayed home and became a Kool-Aid wino.

One morning in August I went over to his house. He was still in bed. He looked up at me from underneath a tattered revolution of old blankets. He had never slept under a sheet in his life.

"Did you bring the nickel you promised?" he asked.

"Yeah," I said. "It's here in my pocket."

"Good."

He hopped out of bed and he was already dressed. He had told me once that he never took off his clothes when he went to bed.

"Why bother?" he had said. "You're only going to get up, anyway. Be prepared for it. You're not fooling anyone by taking your clothes off when you go to bed."

He went into the kitchen, stepping around the littlest children, whose wet diapers were in various stages of anarchy. He made his breakfast: a slice of homemade bread covered with Karo syrup and peanut butter.

"Let's go," he said.

We left the house with him still eating the sandwich. The store was three blocks away, on the other side of a field covered with heavy yellow grass. There were many pheasants in the field. Fat with summer they barely flew away when we came up to them.

"Hello," said the grocer. He was bald with a red birthmark on his head. The birthmark looked just like an old car parked on his head. He automatically reached for a package of grape Kool-Aid and put it on the counter.

"Five cents."

"He's got it," my friend said.

I reached into my pocket and gave the nickel to the grocer. He nodded and the old red car wobbled back and forth on the road as if the driver were having an epileptic seizure.

We left.

My friend led the way across the field. One of the pheasants didn't even bother to fly. He ran across the field in front of us like a feathered pig.

When we got back to my friend's house the ceremony began. To him the making of Kool-Aid was a romance and a ceremony. It had to be performed in an exact manner and with dignity.

First he got a gallon jar and we went around to the side of the house where the water spigot thrust itself out of the ground like the finger of a saint, surrounded by a mud puddle.

He opened the Kool-Aid and dumped it into the jar. Putting the jar under the spigot, he turned the water on. The water spit, splashed and guzzled out of the spigot.

He was careful to see that the jar did not overflow and the precious Kool-Aid spill out onto the ground. When the jar was full he turned the water off with a sudden but delicate motion like a famous brain surgeon removing a disordered portion of the imagination. Then he screwed the lid tightly onto the top of the jar and gave it a good shake.

The first part of the ceremony was over.

Like the inspired priest of an exotic cult, he had performed the first part of the ceremony well.

His mother came around the side of the house and said in a voice filled with sand and string, "When are you going to do the dishes? . . . Huh?"

"Soon," he said.

"Well, you better," she said.

When she left, it was as if she had never been there at all. The second part of the ceremony began with him carrying the jar very carefully to an abandoned chicken house in the back. "The dishes can wait," he said to me. Bertrand Russell could not have stated it better.

He opened the chicken house door and we went in. The place was littered with half-rotten comic books. They were like fruit under a tree. In the corner was an old mattress and beside the mattress were four quart jars. He took the gallon jar over to them, and filled them carefully not spilling a drop. He screwed their caps on tightly and was now ready for a day's drinking.

You're supposed to make only two quarts of Kool-Aid from a package, but he always made a gallon, so his Kool-Aid was a mere shadow of its desired potency. And you're supposed to add a cup of sugar to every package of Kool-Aid, but he never put any sugar in his Kool-Aid because there wasn't any sugar to put in it.

He created his own Kool-Aid reality and was able to illuminate himself by it.

Trout Fishing in America, 1967

Andy Warhol
(1928–1987)

The prime mover of Pop Art, Andy Warhol had ambitions that extended in every direction. He was a filmmaker, a magazine publisher, a creator of advertising, an actor, a model, theater producer, manager of the Velvet Underground, and TV host. When Barney Rosset of Grove Press suggested he write a novel he accepted the challenge and undertook to use a tape recorder to follow one of his superstars, Ondine, for twenty-four hours. (In the end the book added on three further sessions, so that the text covers a period from August 1965 to May 1967.) Four stenographers transcribed the tapes with varying degrees of accuracy and these transcripts, complete with multiple errors, were published unedited except for some random rearrangements introduced by Warhol and the changing of almost all names. Among the characters in this episode from a: a novel *are D (Drella or Andy Warhol), and O (Ondine or Robert Olivo), RR (Rotten Rita or Kenneth Rapp), and SPF (Sugar Plum Fairy or Joe Campbell), a triumvirate of amphetamine-fueled opera freaks who frequented the Silver Factory. The essence of hipsterism is argot and in these conversations we hear an unusually exotic blend of hip talk, speedfreak lingo and the slang of the gay underground.*

from *a: a novel*

DOUGIE—What are you gonna do with this?   O—We're gonna write a novel. It's a novel. It's   being transcribed by three girls.   DOUGIE—What is it all about?   O—Me!   (Rita laughing like a face in the fun house)   O—Look at The Duchess; the next one you won't believe. (*music is drowning the voices*)   RR—Oh me, oh me, oh mye, corpuscles (?) both of you come over here. Good. I just wanted to know one, oh I shouldn't ask you anyway. Ondine, may I just ask one question. Is it cool to uh, to take out, to take our drugs and shoot and everything in front of the taxi-driver?   O—Certainly.   RR—Oh

how wonderful. O—Certainly. RR—Does he mind? O—He
better not. I'm gonna go in and do the test now. Come with me,
come come with me; this is an official arrest. Oh, Rotten, Rotter uh.
The Mayor and myself both are, we we think your spirit is marvelous.
This is a rather unusual group to stumble into. Can we see something that will prove to us that you're not RR—The police. O—the
police? Or J.F.K. is disguise or something. Do you have, I'll take your
word if you say that that's all we have to take, but we're going to take
drugs here and rather vilently. (*laughing*) Dougie or SPF—Are
you gonna tie up? O—No, I'm not gonna tie up, but I don't like
zane business, but we're going to give ourselves pokes. So-called.
I'm sorry, don't let this cut. Keep it under your hats, darling. RR—
Innoculations please. Stretch that out. Innoculations. O—And if
you witness these things your promise not to, it doesn't offend you
does it? SPF—He's getting terse. O—You don't have a two, may I
see your radio, I mean your wristwatch? May I see it? RR—Now he
not only has us, but he's got us on tape which we don't stand a chance.
You and your big mouth; you just put us up for six years. You cock-
sucker. O—He's calling Officer Joe Bolton. RR—I fired him. He's
okay. O—I think you're all right. All right Rotten? I'll take you on
face value, but don't get upset if one of us, Dougie—Face? O—I,
no, no no, not just face alone. Faith. They have trouble understanding. But they're new. Oh well, all right. You're not going to arrest
these two innocent children are you? B—What's wrong with those
two? O—Dorso is, this is a murderous Negress. Now watch out for
her. SPF—She's an Indian. O—She's not an Indian. Sugar! Sugar!
Go in there and fuck them up. Don't let them get upset. SPF—I'm
not letting them. O—You two are, by the time we come in there
with pokes you have to be ready for them. (*Finale—applause*) D—
Oh Ondine, where are you? Ondine? (*music*) (*Ondine talking*) Oh
Ondine, pleeese. O—Let me try it. D—Oh I no no, but you hold
it. Huh? O—Listen Rotten, I know it's awful to ask you to hold the,
would you? Cause Drella's been holding it for so long and he's just,
he shouldn't have to. That's not the needle. That's the vitamin B 12.

Dougie—My attitudes towards narcotics   SPF—Narcotics!?   O—
These are not narcotics.

SPF—These are not narcotics.

O—Do you call vitamin B 12 a narcotic? But keep this next to your
mouth when you speak. Rita, are you all right in there?

Dougie—Avenue D.

SPF—Isn't that funny. I was on 6th street and Avenue C.

O—Suddenly a tear came to my eye thinking of my first experience
on the lower east side.

D—Really?

O—Oh he does so; he looks like Brooklyn too.

SPF—No no.

O—Oh he looks like a New York boy.

SPF—Do you know the last couple of nights what we were up to?

O—Dear, you were in the midst of a festival night. We were down,
they were beating drums and singing about Pan American Day.
That's how the lower east side, but the lower east side was, Brooklyn was different too. I mean. What do you think of us? Is'nt it
wonderful to find such freedom in the midst of New York City?
Did you think that Wagner would permit such nonsense. It's really
that Rita is our Mayor. Do you see that silence? Isn't she a gorgeous
creature. Isn't she divine. You'd never know that she was so foul.

D—Isn't Billy 24?

O—Billy's twenty-f-, no he's 27.

D—Oh he is?

O—I don't know. Billy, aren't you 27? How old are you? Oh. He's 25.

DD—Tea bag?

O—She thinks you said tea bag.

B or RR—Yeah!

O—May I say one thing From what you said you have a tolerant
attitude.

RR—. . . get some chicken and turkey sandwiches; that's a wonderful
idea.

O—No, you said; yes, that's a delightful idea. Dodo, would you hold this for me for a second? And with God's help I will put it away. What do you feel about me? Isn't there a twinge somewhere? I doubt—How do you feel about homosexuality Is it permissable?

Dougie—I think if it's one's prerogative to be homosexual, fine, but everybody does not have to share his beliefs.

O—Don't you see Venus being contacted (*A succulent inverted sigh.*) Look at this, a hand-maiden, a gorgeous Indian maiden. I hate them; I live next dor to them.

Dougie—Is a drug that's supposed to give you a charge.

SPF—Yeah.

Dougie—Um, I think it's something that one becomes addicted to. I think it's something that one has very little control over after a certain period of time.

SPF—Yeah, well that's not altogether true though, because I mean lots of people are addicted to a lot of things they have no control over. In fact, they don't even try y'know?

Dougie—Like smoking?

SPF—Oh well like eating chocolate pudding every night.

Dougie—Yes but

SPF—Do you know my stepfather ate chocolate pudding and ground chuck steak every night for years and years and years.

Dougie—You mean he lived to be a ripe old age?

SPF—No, he's, I don't know. Well I mean he was addicted to that y'know, he really was. And he decided to stop, but he couldn't, he couldn't. Say an addict decided to stop.

Dougie—Well let's take chocolate pudding and narcotics. And you take both of those men; strap them down.

SPF—Did you say pot head?

Dougie—No, narcotics.

SPF—What do you call narcotics?

D—Ondine.

Dougie—Narcotics.

SPF—What? What's a narcotic?

Dougie—To me a narcotic is a man who takes drugs.

SPF—Any kind of drugs? I mean aspirins are drugs.

Dougie—Takes drugs to feel high, takes drugs to feel no pain, takes drugs to make him do what he really wants

SPF—Narcotics are opiates. Aren't narcotics opiates?

D—Oh, I really don't know. I don't think about it.

SPF—And opiates are addicting.

Dougie—I'm not really deeply familiar. I have never read on it y'know.

SPF—Narcotics are opiates and opium nerivatives, and they are addicting like opium, uh, methadrine, heroine y'know.

Dougie—Yeah.

SPF—And then you have a few other things that are addicting like cocaine, that's addicting after awhile. But the rest of the things are not narcotics, like pot or amphetamine are stimulates like benzedrine; they are not addicting and yet people do take these things.

Dougie—Yes.

SPF—And pot's not addicting you know.

Dougie—No, not pot.

SPF—And I'm scared shit of needles. Do you like needles?

D—Uhh, no I

SPF—The whole thing about needles upsets me. I think very graphically of muscle tissue and the cold steel forcing it's way through and the blood, skin, and. It's frightening.

DD—It's a good thing that you couldn't see yourself.

SPF—Why?

D—When?

DD—When you were filled with

SPF—Filled with what?

D—Needles.

DD—Needles.

SPF—(*walking away*) I was never filled with needles. I never have had a needle in my life.

DD—I didn't say filmed, I said filled.

D—Was he really very serious?

SPF—I was never

DD—I was too! But it was a good thing you couldn't see yourself.

SPF—I was unconscious and I did'nt know about the needles.

DD—It was a god thing you couldn't see them.

SPF—In a hospital you see I don't mind needles. I mean they're slightly unpleasant in a hospital, but you know when you tie up

DD—I never had any experiences.

SPF—and the eye dropper and the fountain of blood rushes towards y'know it's all just a little bit afraid. Have you ever seen anyone want to gouge their vein? I mean searching for a vein?

DD—No, I have not. I have not.

SPF—Gouging with a safety pin?

DD—No no, but you have your junkie friends that are here.

SPF—Have you ever seen that? Gouging themselves with a safety pin and stuffing the shit in their arm?

D—Oh I

SPF—You know that's frightening! I mean it's not frightening to them because they realize what's happening. They associate needles with pleasure. I don't associate them at all. (*Conversation and music.*)

SPF—I mean sleeping pills are the greatest test because with sleeping pills you just fade out. I mean you've gone to sleep and then. I mean if you are gonna do away with yourself I think an overdose is *the* way to do it—the way to die.

D—Oh I uh, I actually think just uh staying up and getting a heart attack is the best way.

SPF—Heart attack.

DD—Staying up? But how long do you have to stay up?

SPF—Don't you realize how painful that is?

D—What? A heart attack?

SPF—First of all, you have a stroke which means that you can't talk or walk.

D—Not all the time.

SPF—For twenty-five years.

D—Not all the time.

SPF—Twenty-five you won't be able to walk.

D—Oh Ondine! what are you doing?

(*Delightful music.*)

D—Oh, tomorrow's Friday, oh.

SPF—I worry about you.

D—What?

SPF—I worry about you.

D—Oh.

O—Are you going out for sandwiches you think? I, ooh, OW! Oh, I'm sorry.

RR—Listen, I would like to order. I think we should get Reubens on the telephone.

O—Yes, let's.

a: a novel, 1968

Gerard Malanga
(b. 1943)

A poet and photographer, Gerard Malanga was Andy Warhol's painting assistant and general handyman during the Silver Factory period, as well as the handsome, leading-man superstar of the early Factory's films, and the whip dancer of Warhol's Exploding Plastic Inevitable, a Happening starring the Velvet Underground. Malanga was also the only character in Warhol's a: a novel to appear under his own name. But before all that he was a poet, mentored by Pulitzer Prize winner Richard Eberhart. Malanga has written more than a dozen poetry books, and his portrait photos—many of which have become iconic—have been widely published. This is a poem from a 1971 book with one of the most timely titles of all time: Chic Death.

Photos of an Artist as a Young Man

for Andy Warhol

He lies on bed— white walls
behind him:
furniture scarce.
Illustration of shoe
horn hangs on wall behind
and above him. He has
dark hair. He holds Siamese
cat in arms. It's 1959.

"I grew up in Pittsburgh
after the war: ate soft
boiled eggs every day for two years:
attended Carnegie Tech;
went to New York: lived

with ten dancers on the upper West Side;
free lanced in shoe illustration
with I. Miller Shoe."

Beyond the slow introduction
to refinement, the development of character,
it's not easy to breathe. He is
the invisible and unimaginable journey
through colors silk-screened on canvas
what he or the boy may have seen
years before, standing there
in the field, young, innocent, speechless.

Chic Death, 1971

Nick Tosches
(b. 1949)

Like many of the interesting writers of his generation, Nick Tosches started out writing for rock and roll magazines like Fusion *and* Creem *where writers were allowed to let it all hang out with writing as experimental as the music it covered. Tosches has made a specialty out of profiles of dangerous characters, from Jerry Lee Lewis to Arnold Rothstein to Sonny Liston, and dangerous institutions, from the Vatican to the record business. Along the way he acquired a bit of a dangerous aura himself. Here is a selection from* Dino: Living High in the Dirty Business of Dreams, *which transforms Dean Martin from a cliché into an unintentional hero.*

from *Dino*

SINATRA AND MARTIN: There was something about them that brought out the biggest gamblers. What the Sands paid them, they brought back in spades. It was common knowledge: "Dean Martin is back in the Copa Room," said *Variety* in December 1959, "and the casino execs are happy—because Dino pulls in the same type heavy player as does Frank Sinatra, another of Jack Entratter's surefires."

It was not just the dirty-rich *giovanostri* and *padroni* who were drawn to them, to their glamour, to the appeal of darkness made respectable. The world was full, it seemed, of would-be wops and woplings who lived vicariously through them, to whom the imitation of cool took on the religiosity of the Renaissance ideal of *imitatio Christi*. The very songs that Sinatra and Dean sang, the very images they projected, inspired lavish squandering among the countless men who would be them. It was the Jew-roll around the prick that rendered them ithyphallic godkins, simulacra of the great ones, in their own eyes and in the eyes of the teased-hair lobster-slurping *Bimbo sapiens* they sought to impress.

Both Dean and Frank owned stock in the Sands. By the summer of 1961, Sinatra would hold a nine-percent piece of the operation. Of the other sixteen licensed Sands stockholders, only Jack Entratter, who had succeeded Jake Freedman in 1958 as president, with twelve percent, Freedman's widow, Sadie, with ten percent, and the Sands' vice-president and casino manager, Carl Cohen, with nine and a half percent, owned larger shares; one, Russian-born Hy Abrams, who had been a partner of Bugsy Siegel in the original Flamingo and moved to the Sands in 1954, held an equal, nine-percent piece. Dean, who was granted a gaming license on July 20, 1961, was one of three one-percent owners. His privileged price for that percentage was $28,838, which by then was less than a week's pay.

Despite their immense popularity and the success of Sinatra's albums, neither Dean nor Frank was selling many singles as the decade drew to a close. Sinatra had done well with "Witchcraft" in 1958; Dean had done better that year with "Volare." Since then, neither had broken into the Top Twenty. Sinatra's best-selling record of 1959, "High Hopes," had risen only so far as number thirty. On January 2, 1960, at a news conference in the Senate Caucus Room, John F. Kennedy announced his candidacy for the Democratic presidential nomination. "High Hopes," with new lyrics tailored by Sammy Cahn, would become Kennedy's campaign song. Along the way, it would become the anthem of a time's dumb optimism.

High hopes were what Sinatra had. He envisioned Kennedy, somehow, as his man. He envisioned too an empire of his own—his own casino, his own record company, God only knew what else. And Dean was along for the ride.

JFK and the Rat Pack: These were the symbols, image and spirit, of that carefree time. Even their smiles were alike. In January, while Kennedy got his campaign formally underway, the Rat Pack made the movie that would become its most celebrated legacy.

In 1956, Peter Lawford had been told an idea for a story about a precision-timed robbery sweep of the Las Vegas Strip. Sinatra had bought the rights to the story, with Lawford retaining a share, and hired Harry Brown and Charles Lederer to write a screenplay from it. As it developed, *Ocean's Eleven* became the tale of eleven World War II army buddies reunited for one last maneuver, a multi-million-dollar five-casino heist. Sinatra, who made the picture through his own Dorchester Productions, played ringleader Danny Ocean. They were all in it: Dean, Sammy, Lawford, Joey Bishop. Angie Dickinson played Danny Ocean's wife. Richard Conte, Henry Silva, Akim Tamiroff, and Buddy Lester had key roles. George Raft showed up as a casino owner. Shirley MacLaine had a cameo scene with Dean.

"I used to be Ricky Nelson," Dean tells her. "I'm Perry Como now."

Lewis Milestone, who was already a seasoned professional when he made *All Quiet on the Western Front* in 1930, was hired to direct.

"They say this is hard work, this acting. What bullshit," Dean said. "Work? Work my ass."

Dean and Richard Conte—Nick Conte, as those close to him knew him—got along well. Conte's background at the fringes of Jersey City's *malavita* was not dissimilar to Dean's; and both were the sons of old-fashioned Italian barbers. The production and the partying flowed together. From January 26 through February 16, the Rat Pack filmed by day and took the stage of the Sands by night. To Jack Entratter, the sign outside—it would appear at the closing credits—was like a dream come true:

FRANK SINATRA

DEAN MARTIN

SAMMY DAVIS JR.

PETER LAWFORD

JOEY BISHOP

The newspapers had been full of the upcoming Paris summit conference being planned by Eisenhower, Khrushchev, and De Gaulle. Well, Sinatra declared, they would have their own summit conference of cool. Newspapers across the country began publicizing it as the Rat Pack Summit. By the night they opened, every hotel room in Las Vegas was booked for the duration. Entratter was more than happy to go along with their setup: At least one of them would perform every night; sometimes two or three or four of them, sometimes all five.

Even Kennedy himself showed up at ringside one night. Sinatra introduced him from the stage. Dean came out: "What did you say his name was?" Then Dean picked up little Sammy and held him out to Sinatra: "Here. This award just came for you from the National Association for the Advancement of Colored People." Later, Kennedy joined the Rat Pack upstairs for drinks. Lawford took Davis aside and whispered to him:

"If you want to see what a million dollars in cash looks like, go into the next room; there's a brown leather satchel in the closet. It's a gift from the hotel owners for Jack's campaign."

There were broads that night as well: blowjobs on the house, all around, for the New Frontiersman and his Democratic crew. One of the women Sinatra introduced to Kennedy was a twenty-five-year-old would-be starlet named Judith Campbell. Sinatra had been fucking her for a while. So had Johnny Rosselli, the West Coast's lord of darkness. Now Campbell would begin a two-year affair with Jack Kennedy. Sinatra liked the idea: the two men bonding their friendship through a woman.

Most mornings, they would come offstage at half past one or a quarter to two, drink till dawn, and begin filming.

"It wasn't that it wasn't professional," Angie Dickinson said of the movie making; "but you'd have to look hard to find a camera to prove to you that they weren't playing. They really had fun together. The director was very easy. He knew exactly who was signing his check."

On their closing night, old-time movie-gangster Jack LaRue was introduced in the audience among a crowd of other celebrities. "Why don't you come up here and kill somebody?" Dean called out to him. Later, when he stumbled on a sentence, he remarked, "I got my nose fixed, and now my mouth doesn't work." He urged the audience, "On your way out, please buy a copy of my latest book, *The Power of Positive Drinking.*"

They took the train to Los Angeles that night, and resumed filming at Warner Brothers the next morning.

Ocean's Eleven was completed on March 23. Three weeks later, *Who Was That Lady?* opened at the Criterion in New York. In it, *Variety* had noted, "Martin strengthens the false impression that he isn't acting at all. It should be so easy!" The *Times* did not much care for it— these were the days when the paper of record found Jack Kerouac's *Pull My Daisy* "truly arresting"—but did declare that "Mr. Martin, especially, is fine." On May 9, with André Previn conducting, Dean recorded the soundtrack album for *Bells Are Ringing.* A day later, with Nelson Riddle, he recorded "Ain't That a Kick in the Head," the song that James Van Heusen and Sammy Cahn had written for *Ocean's Eleven*. In mid-June—they could not draft him now—he underwent an operation on his hernia at Cedars of Lebanon Hospital. *Bells Are Ringing* opened at Radio City Music Hall on June 20, two days before he was released from the hospital.

The *Daily News* called *Bells Are Ringing* "a knockout, even better entertainment than it was on the stage." Dean, as Holliday's "partner in singing, dancing and romancing," was "a perfect choice."

HIGH HOPES. That summer, the Rat Pack sang "The Star-Spangled Banner" to open the Democratic national convention in Los Angeles. The delegates from Mississippi loudly protested Sammy Davis's presence on the stage. But Mississippi had the lowest average income level and the fewest television sets per capita of any state. Jack was not playing to them. His bleeding heart went out to the downtrodden of that state, but only through the wonder of television could they truly experience the integrity of that heart and the probity of the share-cropper's friend. As every black man in Hyannis Port knew, young John Kennedy was a man whose sense of justice was real. Television conveyed that reality, as it conveyed all realities.

Dean, who earlier in the year had brought the realities of Fabian and André Previn together on his NBC show, found himself becoming more involved in the shadow play that surrounded Sinatra's infatuation with the prince of the New Frontier. Jack Kennedy's kid brother Bobby, a worse spoiled brat than he, was chief counsel to the McClellan Senate committee's investigations into labor racketeering. Bobby's holy war against Jimmy Hoffa and the Teamsters had stirred trouble far and wide. It seemed that the little rabbit-mouthed *irlandese* was out to crucify not only the new head of the Teamsters but every wop in America along with him. One of those who had been called before the committee in 1959 was Sam Giancana, boss of the Chicago mob, whom both Dean and Sinatra knew from his earliest days of power following the death of Charlie Fischetti. Wearing sunglasses and a cheap hairpiece, Sam had sat there holding a three-by-five-inch card bearing the words of the Fifth Amendment, whose protection he invoked in response to every question Kennedy put forth. The heat had not diminished, and it came to be believed that the only way to get Bobby Kennedy's nose out of everybody's business was through Jack. The Teamsters, of course, could not publicly endorse Jack, though Hoffa himself became one of the believers in the hope of his intercession. But, through Giancana, a large donation to Kennedy's presidential campaign was drawn from the Teamsters pension fund and passed to Jack beneath the blind eyes of his brother Bobby, who took time out from his wop-hunting to serve as Jack's campaign manager. There were also disbursements from the campaign fund made through Sinatra to Skinny D'Amato in Atlantic City. Under Giancana's guidance, D'Amato was to purchase the influence of several West Virginia election officials known to him through the 500 Club.

Giancana, cheap hairpiece and all, was far from a fool. He led Sinatra to think that the donation in support of Kennedy, as well as the influence-buying in West Virginia, was prompted to a great degree by the faith in Kennedy that Sinatra had expressed to him. By giving the impression that he was relying on Sinatra's judgment and that he was doing Sinatra a favor—Sinatra would be able to further ingratiate himself to Jack by taking credit for the donation and new-found support—Giancana rendered Sinatra beholden to him. Not only, Giancana figured, would he now be able to use Sinatra as a money-maker toward his own ends, Sinatra would be able to deliver that other one, that aloof bastard, that unreachable *menefreghista*, toward those same ends as well.

The McGuire Sisters, the three singing daughters of an Ohio minister, had risen to national prominence with a string of hits in 1954, the year that Sam Giancana had become a widower. Sam, who knew the act from the Chez Paree, had run into Phyllis McGuire in Las Vegas in early 1960, about the time that Kennedy announced his candidacy. She was twenty-nine, recently divorced, drinking, and gambling heavily; the days of the McGuire Sisters' big hits were past. She became Giancana's lover. Not long after they began their romance, Sinatra introduced Giancana to Judy Campbell, the woman who was now Kennedy's mistress. Again, he liked the idea. Now the three of them, Frank, Jack, and Sam, were sharing the same *braciole*.

High hopes: a casino of his own. Elmer "Bones" Remmer, the San Francisco gangster who owned the Cal-Neva Lodge, at Crystal Bay on the Nevada side of Lake Tahoe, had gotten in trouble with the Treasury Department, trouble that went deeper than the $800,000 he owed the Internal Revenue Service. Control of the Cal-Neva had passed to Bert "Wingy" Grober, who had his problems too. In June 1960, there was talk of Grober's reducing his stake in the troubled casino. On July 13, 1960, the day Kennedy won the Democratic nomination in Los Angeles, it was announced in Carson City that a group of four men had applied for permission to take over a fifty-seven-percent, majority interest in the Cal-Neva Lodge. Those four men were Frank Sinatra, Dean Martin, Sinatra's longtime friend, piano player, and legbreaker, Hank Sanicola, and Skinny D'Amato. Under the plan, Wingy's interest would be reduced to eighteen percent. Sanicola would hold sixteen percent; D'Amato, thirteen; Dean, three. Sinatra's proposed twenty-five-percent interest, the largest piece, would be shared in secret with Sam Giancana, whose behind-the-scene machinations had enabled the four men to strike an above-board takeover price with Wingy of only $250,000.

On that same night of July 13, as Kennedy's nomination was being announced, Dean opened at the Sands.

"I'd like to tell you some of the *good* things the Mafia is doing," he said. There was a momentary hush, then a long, slow wave of rising laughter.

His singing had begun to take on a new tone. He was no longer merely selling the lie of romance. Stabbing sharply and coldly here and there into the songs with lines of wry disdain, he was exposing his own racket as well, selling the further delusion of their sharing in the secret of that lie itself. It was an elaboration on his tried and true style of singing to the men rather than the women, of singing to them as if they alone could truly understand him. It was also a natural emanation of the way he felt. He simply no longer cared. He began more songs than he finished, dismissing most of them with a wisecrack partway through. Some, with the help of lyricist Sammy Cahn, were simply reduced to gross parody.

"If you think I'm going to get serious, you're crazy. If you want to hear a serious song, buy one of my records."

In the first week of August, *Ocean's Eleven* was previewed at the Fremont Theatre in Las Vegas. The *Los Angeles Examiner* declared it "something you should keep your children away from." *The New Yorker* dismissed it as "an admiring wide-screen color travelogue of the various effluvia—animate and inanimate—of Las Vegas." But *Variety*'s prediction proved true: despite "serious weaknesses in both material and interpretation," it would "rake in chips, thanks to cast." *Ocean's Eleven* became the ninth biggest money-maker of the year, behind such formidable pictures as *Psycho*, *Spartacus*, *Exodus*, *La Dolce Vita*, *Butterfield 8*, and *The Apartment*.

On September 13, the Nevada Gaming Control Board issued a

recommendation for approval of the Cal-Neva takeover. Dean by then had finished another film: *All in a Night's Work*, produced by Hal Wallis and directed by Joseph Anthony, who had done *Career*. Shirley MacLaine once again had the female lead; Cliff Robertson played a romantic ringer in the background. As in *Career*, Wallis found MacLaine "difficult," but Dean "was never a problem." *All in a Night's Work*, as *Variety* later put it, was an "essentially predictable, featherweight comedy," excellently directed and with a strangely classical score by André Previn. "Never for one moment," *Variety* said, "is Martin believable in the role of the youthful publishing tycoon, but his easy-going manner and knack for supplying the comedy reaction gets him by."

On November 1, Sinatra joined Dean on "The Dean Martin Show," which was presented as "Honoring Frank Sinatra." Seven days later, John F. Kennedy was elected president. It was close: a plurality of only 118,574 votes, the narrowest presidential victory of the century.

"Listen, honey, if it wasn't for me, your boyfriend wouldn't even be in the White House," Sam Giancana would tell Judy Campbell.

"Frank won Kennedy the election," Skinny D'Amato would say.

But it was television that won it for him. It was Nixon's poor appearance before the debate cameras that gave Kennedy the votes he needed to scrape by.

The following night, November 9, Dean returned to the Sands: "I just talked to Jack this morning and he made me secretary of liquor." He was, *Variety* reported, "hotter than ever" and "one of the most potent lures for gamblers." He was also "more relaxed than ever—in fact he appears to be imitating his imitators."

Camelot opened in New York on December 3. The show was beloved of the new president, and his administration came to be known by its name: the Camelot years. Jack and Jackie became the fairyland royalty of the land of whiter whites.

High hopes: a record company of his own. Capitol's current contract with Sinatra's Essex Productions company, binding him to release his recordings exclusively through Capitol, would lapse to a nonexclusive basis in February. In early December, it was announced that Sinatra would then begin releasing his records through a new company of his own. On December 19, he made his first recording for his new company, which now had a name: Reprise Records.

Dino: Living High in the Dirty Business of Dreams, 1992

Hunter S. Thompson
(1937–2005)

*After spending years at the low end of the journalism food chain, as sports-
writer, copyboy, newspaper stringer, and writer for underground newspapers,
Hunter S. Thompson spent a year riding with the Hell's Angels, which resulted
in his first book,* Hell's Angels: The Strange and Terrible Saga of the Outlaw
Motorcycle Gangs. *The success of that book gave him entrée into respectable
venues such as* Esquire *and* Harper's, *then* Rolling Stone. *Few cultural publications have exhibited less tolerance for humor than* Rolling Stone, *but they
almost made up for it by giving Hunter S. Thompson carte blanche—even if
many times owner Jann Wenner jerked Thompson's leash and ended up killing
stories that might have been masterpieces, such as his take on the fall of Saigon.
Thompson's* Rolling Stone *debut chronicled his run for sheriff of Aspen, Colorado, and marked the beginning of the gonzo journalism that gave us* Fear and
Loathing in Las Vegas, *excerpted here. Thompson's style was the entheogenic
apotheosis of the New Journalism.*

from *Fear and Loathing in Las Vegas*
A Night on the Town . . . Confrontation at the
Desert Inn . . . Drug Frenzy at the Circus-Circus

SATURDAY MIDNIGHT . . . Memories of this night are extremely
hazy. All I have, for guide-pegs, is a pocketful of keno cards and
cocktail napkins, all covered with scribbled notes. Here is one: "Get
the Ford man, demand a Bronco for race-observation purposes . . .
photos? . . . Lacerda/call . . . why not a helicopter? . . . Get on the
phone, *lean* on the fuckers . . . heavy yelling."

Another says: "Sign on Paradise Boulevard—'Stopless and Topless'
. . . bush-league sex compared to L.A.; *pasties* here—total naked public humping in L.A. . . . Las Vegas is a society of armed masturbators/

gambling is the kicker here/sex is extra/weird trip for high rollers . . .
house-whores for winners, hand jobs for the bad luck crowd."

A LONG time ago when I lived in Big Sur down the road from Lionel
Olay I had a friend who liked to go to Reno for the crap-shooting. He
owned a sporting-goods store in Carmel. And one month he drove
his Mercedes highway-cruiser to Reno on three consecutive weekends—winning heavily each time. After three trips he was something
like $15,000 ahead, so he decided to skip the fourth weekend and
take some friends to dinner at Nepenthe. "Always quit winners," he
explained. "And besides, it's a long drive."

On Monday morning he got a phone call from Reno—from the
general manager of the casino he'd been working out on. "We missed
you this weekend," said the GM. "The pit-men were bored."

"Shucks," said my friend.

So the next weekend he flew up to Reno in a private plane, with
a friend and two girls—all "special guests" of the GM. Nothing too
good for high rollers. . . .

And on Monday morning the same plane—the casino's plane—
flew him back to the Monterey airport. The pilot lent him a dime to
call a friend for a ride to Carmel. He was $30,000 in debt, and two
months later he was looking down the barrel of one of the world's
heaviest collection agencies.

So he sold his store, but that didn't make the nut. They could wait
for the rest, he said—but then he got stomped, which convinced him
that maybe he'd be better off borrowing enough money to pay the
whole wad.

Mainline gambling is a very heavy business—and Las Vegas makes
Reno seem like your friendly neighborhood grocery store. For a loser,
Vegas is the meanest town on earth. Until about a year ago, there was
a giant billboard on the outskirts of Las Vegas, saying:

> DON'T GAMBLE WITH MARIJUANA!
> IN NEVADA: POSSESSION—20 YEARS
> SALE—LIFE!

So I was not entirely at ease drifting around the casinos on this Saturday night with a car full of marijuana and head full of acid. We had several narrow escapes: at one point I tried to drive the Great Red Shark into the laundry room of the Landmark Hotel—but the door was too narrow, and the people inside seemed dangerously excited.

We drove over to the Desert Inn, to catch the Debbie Reynolds/ Harry James show. "I don't know about you," I told my attorney, "but in my line of business it's important to be Hep."

"Mine too," he said. "But as your attorney I advise you to drive over to the Tropicana and pick up on Guy Lombardo. He's in the Blue Room with his Royal Canadians."

"Why?" I asked.

"Why *what*?"

"Why should I pay out my hard-earned dollars to watch a fucking corpse?"

"Look," he said "Why are we out here? To entertain ourselves, or to *do the job?*"

"The job, of course," I replied. We were driving around in circles, weaving through the parking lot of a place I thought was the Dunes, but it turned out to be the Thunderbird . . . or maybe it was the Hacienda . . .

My attorney was scanning *The Vegas Visitor*, looking for hints of action. "How about "'Nickel Nick's Slot Arcade?'" he said. "'Hot Slots,' that sounds heavy . . . Twenty-nine cent hotdogs . . .'"

Suddenly people were screaming at us. We were in trouble. Two thugs wearing red-gold military overcoats were looming over the hood: "What the hell are you doing?" one screamed. "You can't park *here!*"

"Why not?" I said. It seemed like a reasonable place to park, plenty of space. I'd been looking for a parking spot for what seemed like a very long time. Too long. I was about ready to abandon the car and call a taxi . . . but then, yes, we found this *space*.

Which turned out to be the sidewalk in front of the main entrance to the Desert Inn. I had run over so many curbs by this time, that I hadn't even noticed this last one. But now we found ourselves in a position that was hard to explain . . . blocking the entrance, thugs yelling at us, bad confusion. . . .

My attorney was out of the car in a flash, waving a five-dollar bill. "We want this car parked! I'm an old friend of Debbie's. I used to *romp* with her."

For a moment I thought he had blown it . . . then one of the door-men reached out for the bill, saying: "OK, OK. I'll take care of it, sir." And he tore off a parking stub.

"Holy shit!" I said, as we hurried through the lobby. "They almost had us there. That was quick thinking."

"What do you expect?" he said. "I'm your *attorney* . . . and you owe me five bucks. I want it now."

I shrugged and gave him a bill. This garish, deep-orlon carpeted lobby of the Desert Inn seemed an inappropriate place to be haggling about nickel/dime bribes for the parking lot attendant. This was Bob Hope's turf. Frank Sinatra's. Spiro Agnew's. The lobby fairly reeked of high-grade formica and plastic palm trees—it was clearly a high-class refuge for Big Spenders.

We approached the grand ballroom full of confidence, but they refused to let us in. We were too late, said a man in a wine-colored tuxedo; the house was already full—no seats left, at *any* price.

"Fuck seats," said my attorney. "We're old friends of Debbie's. We drove all the way from L.A. for this show, and we're goddamn well going in."

The tux-man began jabbering about "fire regulations," but my attorney refused to listen. Finally, after a lot of bad noise, he let us in for nothing—provided we would stand quietly in back and not smoke.

We promised, but the moment we got inside we lost control. The tension had been too great. Debbie Reynolds was yukking across the stage in a silver Afro wig . . . to the tune of "Sergeant Pepper," from the golden trumpet of Harry James.

"Jesus creeping shit!" said my attorney. "We've wandered into a time capsule!"

Heavy hands grabbed our shoulders. I jammed the hash pipe back into my pocket just in time. We were dragged across the lobby and held against the front door by goons until our car was fetched up. "OK, get lost," said the wine-tux-man. "We're giving you a break. If Debbie has friends like you guys, she's in worse trouble than I thought."

"We'll see about this!" my attorney shouted as we drove away. "You paranoid scum!"

I drove around the Circus-Circus Casino and parked near the back door. "This is the place," I said. "They'll never fuck with us here."

"Where's the ether?" said my attorney. "This mescaline isn't working."

I gave him the key to the trunk while I lit up the hash pipe. He came back with the ether-bottle, un-capped it, then poured some into a kleenex and mashed it under his nose, breathing heavily. I soaked another kleenex and fouled my own nose. The smell was overwhelming, even with the top down. Soon we were staggering up the stairs towards the entrance, laughing stupidly and dragging each other along, like drunks.

This is the main advantage of ether: it makes you behave like the village drunkard in some early Irish novel . . . total loss of all basic motor skills: blurred vision, no balance, numb tongue—severance of all connection between the body and the brain. Which is interesting, because the brain continues to function more or less normally . . . you can actually *watch* yourself behaving in this terrible way, but you can't control it.

You approach the turnstiles leading into the Circus-Circus and you know that when you get there, you have to give the man two dollars or he won't let you inside . . . but when you get there, everything goes wrong: you misjudge the distance to the turnstile and slam against it, bounce off and grab hold of an old woman to keep from falling, some angry Rotarian shoves you and you think: What's happening here? What's going on? Then you hear yourself mumbling: "Dogs fucked the Pope, no fault of mine. Watch out! . . . Why money? My name is Brinks; I was born . . . born? Get sheep over side . . . women and children to armored car . . . orders from Captain Zeep."

Ah, devil ether—a total body drug. The mind recoils in horror, unable to communicate with the spinal column. The hands flap crazily, unable to get money out of the pocket . . . garbled laughter and hissing from the mouth . . . always smiling.

Ether is the perfect drug for Las Vegas. In this town they love a drunk. Fresh meat. So they put us through the turnstiles and turned us loose inside.

THE CIRCUS-CIRCUS is what the whole hep world would be doing on Saturday night if the Nazis had won the war. This is the Sixth Reich. The ground floor is full of gambling tables, like all the other casinos . . . but the place is about four stories high, in the style of a circus tent, and all manner of strange County-Fair/Polish Carnival madness is going on up in this space. Right above the gambling tables the Forty Flying Carazito Brothers are doing a high-wire trapeze act, along with four muzzled Wolverines and the Six Nymphet Sisters from San Diego . . . so you're down on the main floor playing blackjack, and the stakes are getting high when suddenly you chance to look up, and there, right smack above your head is a half-naked fourteen-year-old girl being chased through the air by a snarling wolverine, which is suddenly locked in a death battle with two silver-painted Polacks who come swinging down from opposite balconies and meet in mid-air on the wolverine's neck . . . both Polacks seize the animal as they fall straight down towards the crap tables—but they bounce off the net; they separate and spring back up towards the roof in three different directions, and just as they're about to fall again they are grabbed out of the air by three Korean Kittens and trapezed off to one of the balconies.

This madness goes on and on, but nobody seems to notice. The gambling action runs twenty-four hours a day on the main floor, and the circus never ends. Meanwhile, on all the upstairs balconies, the customers are being hustled by every conceivable kind of bizarre shuck. All kinds of funhouse-type booths. Shoot the pasties off the nipples of a ten-foot bull-dyke and win a cotton-candy goat. Stand in front of this fantastic machine, my friend, and for just 99¢ your likeness will appear, two hundred feet tall, on a screen above downtown Las Vegas. Ninety-nine cents more for a voice message. "Say whatever you want, fella. They'll hear you, don't worry about that. Remember you'll be two hundred feet tall."

Jesus Christ. I could see myself lying in bed in the Mint Hotel, half-asleep and staring idly out the window, when suddenly a vicious nazi drunkard appears two hundred feet tall in the midnight sky, screaming gibberish at the world: *"Woodstock Über Alles!"*

We will close the drapes tonight. A thing like that could send a drug person careening around the room like a ping-pong ball. Hallucinations are bad enough. But after a while you learn to cope with things like seeing your dead grandmother crawling up your leg with a knife in her teeth. Most acid fanciers can handle this sort of thing.

But *nobody* can handle that other trip—the possibility that any freak with $1.98 can walk into the Circus-Circus and suddenly appear in the sky over downtown Las Vegas twelve times the size of God, howling anything that comes into his head. No, this is not a good town for psychedelic drugs. Reality itself is too twisted.

GOOD MESCALINE comes on slow. The first hour is all waiting, then about halfway through the second hour you start cursing the creep who burned you, because nothing is happening . . . and then ZANG! Fiendish intensity, strange glow and vibrations . . . a very heavy gig in a place like the Circus-Circus.

"I hate to say this," said my attorney as we sat down at the Merry-Go-Round Bar on the second balcony, "But this place is getting *to* me. I think I'm getting the Fear."

"Nonsense," I said. "We came out here to find the American Dream, and now that we're right in the vortex you want to quit." I grabbed his bicep and squeezed. "You must *realize*," I said, "that we've found the main nerve."

"I know," he said. "That's what gives me the Fear."

The ether was wearing off, the acid was long gone, but the mescaline was running strong. We were sitting at a small round gold formica table, moving in orbit around the bartender.

"Look over there," I said. "Two women fucking a polar bear."

"Please," he said. "Don't *tell* me those things. Not now." He signaled the waitress for two more Wild Turkeys. "This is my last drink," he said. "How much money can you lend me?"

"Not much," I said. "Why?"

"I have to go," he said.

"Go?"

"Yes. Leave the country. Tonight."

"Calm down," I said. "You'll be straight in a few hours."

"No," he said. "This is serious."

"George Metesky was serious," I said. "And you see what they did to him."

"Don't fuck around!" he shouted. "One more hour in this town and I'll kill somebody!"

I could see he was on the edge. That fearful intensity that comes at the peak of a mescaline seizure. "OK," I said. "I'll lend you some money. Let's go outside and see how much we have left."

"Can we make it?" he said.

"Well . . . that depends on how many people we fuck with between here and the door. You want to leave quietly?"

"I want to leave *fast*," he said.

"OK. Let's pay this bill and get up very slowly. We're both out of our heads. This is going to be a long walk." I shouted at the waitress for a bill. She came over, looking bored, and my attorney stood up.

"Do they *pay* you to screw that bear?" he asked her.

"What?"

"He's just kidding," I said, stepping between them. "Come on, Doc—let's go downstairs and gamble." I got him as far as the edge

of the bar, the rim of the merry-go-round, but he refused to get off until it stopped turning.

"It won't stop," I said. "It's not *ever* going to stop." I stepped off and turned around to wait for him, but he wouldn't move . . . and before I could reach out and pull him off, he was carried away. "Don't move," I shouted. "You'll come around!" His eyes were staring blindly ahead, squinting with fear and confusion. But he didn't move a muscle until he'd made the whole circle.

I waited until he was almost in front of me, then I reached out to grab him—but he jumped back and went around the circle again. This made me very nervous. I felt on the verge of a freakout. The bartender seemed to be watching us.

Carson City, I thought. Twenty years.

I STEPPED on the merry-go-round and hurried around the bar, approaching my attorney on his blind side—and when we came to the right spot I pushed him off. He staggered into the aisle and uttered a hellish scream as he lost his balance and went down, thrashing into the crowd . . . rolling like a log, then up again in a flash, fists clenched, looking for somebody to hit.

I approached him with my hands in the air, trying to smile. "You fell," I said. "Let's go."

By this time people *were* watching us. But the fool wouldn't move, and I knew what would happen if I grabbed him. "OK," I said. "You stay here and go to jail. I'm leaving." I started walking fast towards the stairs, ignoring him.

This moved him.

"Did you see that?" he said as he caught up with me. "Some sonofabitch kicked me in the back!"

"Probably the bartender," I said. "He wanted to stomp you for what you said to the waitress."

"Good *god*! Let's get out of here. Where's the elevator?"

"Don't go *near* that elevator," I said. "That's just what they *want* us to do . . . trap us in a steel box and take us down to the basement." I looked over my shoulder, but nobody was following.

"Don't run," I said. "They'd like an excuse to shoot us." He nodded, seeming to understand. We walked fast along the big indoor midway—shooting galleries, tattoo parlors, money-changers and cotton-candy booths—then out through a bank of glass doors and across the grass downhill to a parking lot where the Red Shark waited.

"You drive," he said. "I think there's something wrong with me."

Fear and Loathing in Las Vegas:
A Savage Journey to the Heart of the American Dream, 1971

Richard Meltzer
(b. 1945)

Another graduate of the rock and roll press, Richard Meltzer got his start at Boston's Crawdaddy! *and worked his way through* Rolling Stone *(where he was found too funny),* Creem, *and* The Village Voice. *His first book,* The Aesthetics of Rock, *was a fantastic mash-up of academic convention and utterly bebop free-association with some Dada flavoring and 220 footnotes. Equally brilliant was Meltzer's sequel* Gulcher, *taking Ezra Pound's* Kulchur *one step further along the ledge. The excerpt here shows Meltzer's unique form of poetic meditation on any given subject. He has written more than a dozen books, as well as lyrics for Blue Öyster Cult and his own groups, such as VOM and Smegma.*

Luckies vs. Camels: Who Will Win?

IT'S EASY with a pack of Camels, it's easy to tell which side is the front and which is the back. The front is the side with the camel's back on it—commonly called the hump and he's got only one, hence he's a dromedary—and the camel's left side and the camel's left side of his face and portions of all four legs and his tail. And three trees and two pyramids. And the back is the side with the buildings in town where people live (they don't live in pyramids, only dead pharaohs live there if you can call it a life).

But on the pack of Lucky Strikes both sides are identical. They both say "It's toasted" plus the Lucky Strike in a circle. Actually it's inside of four concentric circles and maybe more but there still is one way to tell which is the front. The front is the side that's facing you when the thing on top with the Indian and the letter A and "20 cigarettes" all in blue is facing you too. When the left side of the Indian's head is facing your direction and his nose is above his mouth. Otherwise it's upside down and it's the back of the pack, not the front.

Both packs have the surgeon general's warning about health on the same side and both of them have only one word beginning with a lower case piece of type and that's the word *to*. The rule is: "The only words in a title supposed to be small are articles, prepositions and conjunctions." Well *to* is a preposition—even Lenny Bruce knows that—and you know what? The word *that* (capitalized on the packs) is—as used—a conjunction rather than a relative pronoun so they're doing it all wrong and it's even worse than Winston tastes good like a cigarette should. Worse cause it's got the support of the prestigious surgeon general's office behind it.

But all that's quickly forgotten when it comes time for the showdown. People have always been saying that the difference between a good cigarette and a great cigarette is in the know-how. Well they may know how but you've gotta know how too. And you've gotta know how to. To light the cigarette right. And the right way is the same way as for a cigar. First if it was a cigar you'd remove the cigar band by ripping it while it's still on the cigar instead of slipping it off with a pull and a tug so you don't tear the tobacco leaf. Well a seegar is not a cigareet and vice versa so you don't have to worry about no bands, just the lighting part. And in the lighting part you take the cig (whether it's an ar or an arette) and hold it twixt the fingers horizontal with a tangent drawn to the surface of the earth below your feet. In the other hand is the match which has been lit for proper use. Hold the flame so that it's below the end of the cig you want lit but hold it low and slowly approach the cig. Don't ever let the actual flame come in contact with the cig or something bad's gonna happen to the taste of the smoke. It'll taste chemical cause chemicals are what goes into the making of the match. Just let the *heat of the match* light the cig, not the flame itself. One or more attempts may be necessary before you get it down pat but you'll notice the difference already and that's what know-how is.

Now the most important part of the smoke is when it's leaving your respiratory system out through the nose. It's crucial cause exit is the last part of the smoke you'll remember if your memory is good and if it isn't good you shouldn't be smoking. It's that tingle of warmth on the inner surface of the nostrils that does it. Like when it's in your lungs and in your mouth it's just another something in your lungs or mouth. You don't really experience the heat, same goes for the throat too. But you feel the heat to optimum watchamacallit *only in the nose* along the linings. And if the heat isn't important there's no reason to set the Lucky or Camel as the case may be on fire at all, you could just as easily keep it in the ice box with the cold ham.

And the facts are that in the battle of the nose Camels are stronger to the nose, Luckies are weaker. But while Camels may be stronger, Luckies happen to be weaker. One's less weak and the other's less strong and one's more strong and the other's more weak and both are either Camels or Luckies.

Next in priorities is which is packed firmer. Luckies.

Next is which one holds moisture on the mouth end of the paper better and longer. This is important as a matter of comfort, lip comfort to be exact. Lips count too and you're not enjoying smoking pleasure if it isn't comfortable for the lip. Also worth considering in this behalf is where the moisture comes from, it comes from the tongue. It comes from the salivary glands but it's by way of the tongue. So what happens indirectly is that if a cigarette paper requires a lot of moisture to stay wet then the tongue will be getting dry in the process of keeping the lip satisfied. So while it's said that a good tobacco blend is one that won't raw the tongue (this is debatable to say the least and what's wrong with *raw*?) the fact of the matter is it's the paper too that plays a role.

The winner in the holds water longest and bestest is Camels.

Next on the agenda is will the smoke be okay if you light the wrong end and which end is wrong? The wrong end is the end with the writing on it. It's not wrong because it's not *supposed* to be lit on that end, it's wrong on account of the inconvenience caused the smoker. Cause the lettering end is the end nearest the open end of the pack and so you just plant your teeth on it and pull it out. If you had to take the time to take it out with your mitts it would be too long. So it's the wrong end. It's also the wrong end because soon after it's lit the lettering will disappear from oxidation and you won't be able to tell what brand it is.

Both brands smoke okay when you light the wrong end.

Okay next consideration is can you light them from the middle in an emergency? Yes, both will light from the middle in an emergency, in a non-emergency too. But the main emergency may be if it isn't an emergency to begin with so you get uncautious and burn your nose in so doing. The Lucky lights faster in the middle than the Camel.

Which burns faster? Well if you light both of them at exactly 4:58:05 and you lay them down unimpeded and come back at 5:07:21 you'll notice something remarkable as a tender suspender. On the one hand there's more ash on the Camel and on the other there's also more unburned portion on the Camel too! In other words they started at the same length but something extraordinary has transpired in the interim. The logical explanation is there however, it's a very good one. It's that the Lucky burns faster and it also pulls its ash with it as it burns along! So it's a most friendly cigarette, it's one that refuses to reject even its dismembered grotesque burnt end and so it wins that part of the race although that part of the race was unscheduled. Plus it already won the burns fastest part so it has two big points.

Now which has a better draw? A tie.

(A subsidiary competition with no bearing in the final decision: which is better for lighting the other without a match? To be entirely within the confines of truth it must be said that Luckies light Camels better than Camels light Luckies but you could easily turn it around cause it's not always better to give than receive. Hence inconclusive.)

Easiest on the eyes. Neither.

Pleasantest for inhaling. If mellowness is the criterion then it's Camels. If the firewood feeling is the criterion then it's Luckies. If you take out the tobacco from both and roll your own then it's as close to mellow firewood as you can get and no fire extinguisher is needed. It's a tossup here.

Now it might be stressed that tobacco manufacturers and cigarettes in particular have never (never) done anything for the armless smoker. He or she has to keep it in there tight or it falls out and gets dirty so he or she has to start a new one so as not to infect the mouth with germs. So the cig gets smoked way down to a tiny butt because the person cannot even see how far down the smoke has gone without a mirror. Thus it's important that the butt be good. Camel butts are better butts, no problem here.

CONGRATULATIONS LUCKIES FOR WINNING!

Gulcher: Post-Rock Cultural Pluralism (1649–1993), 1990

David Rattray
(1936–1993)

A sadly under-known poet, elegant essayist, and distinguished translator, David Rattray was an extraordinary scholar, fluent in French, German, Italian, Latin, Greek, and Sanskrit, among other tongues. He interviewed Ezra Pound for The Nation *while an undergraduate at Dartmouth, studied at the Sorbonne, and earned a master's in Comparative Literature at Harvard. While living in France, he became an expert on Antonin Artaud, retracing his footsteps and producing the best Artaud translations in English. Rattray also translated Roger Gilbert-Lecomte, René Crevel, and Friedrich Hölderlin, among others. His poems are collected in* Opening the Eyelid *(1990). Rattray also spent years as an editor for* The Reader's Digest, *a seeming oddity, but he produced numerous scholarly books for* The Reader's Digest Press. *This excerpt is from* How I Became One of the Invisible, *an anthology of his work assembled when Rattray was suffering from terminal brain cancer. He died at the age of fifty-seven.*

How I Became One of the Invisible

IN ORDER to become one of the invisible, I had to go through an ordeal technically known as throwing oneself in the arms of God. This consisted of going out in the empty desert with nothing but the clothes that one was wearing and a bag containing certain things. Some of us stayed there for months, others years, many forever.

One night I made up my mind. Pedro, who had already gone, walked out a ways with me in the moonlight.

"Keep on until dawn," he advised. "Then dig a hole just big enough to lie down in. Watch out for snakes and bugs. Wrap up. Try to sleep. Whatever you do, stay out of the sun. There is a cloth in your bag. Put it over your nose and mouth. The air out there is very clean but too hot to breathe. Travel at night. Locate plants; stay with them. Never leave one until you have figured out where the next one will be. Make a slit to suck out the moisture. Eat whatever you can chew, and pretty soon the plants will start coming out, just like stars. Follow them. If a plant makes you nervous, eat just a bit. Find out what it does. You will run into some that give strength, more than you ever dreamed of. At first you are going to feel miserable. You will want to die. Sand sticking to your clothes will rub your skin raw, get in your mouth and down your throat. You will be half blind. You'll think all the time; your mind will race. You will have strange dreams. You will find yourself doing things you would never think of doing anywhere else. You will imagine you are going crazy. All this for a little walk in the sand. There are many animals. Start with the iguana. By the time you learn to get an iguana out of a hole you'll also know how to keep him fresh. Break his back, tie the legs, block the jaws, drop him in the bag. Two days later, still fresh. You will find the desert as crowded as any habitat on earth. After the reptiles, animals and birds, you will meet a few other things. Devils, actually. When you tame your first devil you can eat scorpions if you choose. At that point you can also start going out in broad daylight. You'll get tanned black all over, no matter what you wear. Lions and tigers will sit at your knees. Crocodiles, elephants, hippopotami will ferry you across the river that sometimes rushes through the center of this desert for a day and then vanishes as suddenly as it appeared. When it's time for you to leave, there will be a sign in the sky. All of us witness it. You will feel something like a sudden draft of air. Turn round and face it and you'll see a cloud of white dust pouring out of the sun. An iridescent arc will appear to the east. Within a few seconds the whole sky will glow with luminous crescent-shaped figures, the biggest of which will form itself into a circle round the sun. This will in turn be intersected by a second ring centered on the zenith, its circumference coinciding also with the sun's position. The smaller arcs will fall into concentric patterns about these two grand rings, filling the whole sky with lights. Then you will imagine yourself inside a prism that is vibrating like a gong. You will long to vanish in thin air, to disappear in that sound.

"Then, at the points, three of them, where the two grand circles intersect (east, north, west) you will witness something truly extraordinary: an extra sun at each. Four suns and a whole sky on fire. When you have seen those four suns, turn around and tell your devils to pull their pants up and point you straight to the nearest town."

Four years later, Pedro and I found ourselves together again for the first time, sitting at a table by a mirror in the Café Estrella in Pochutla. The cafe faced out on the marketplace, opposite the jail. Glancing in the mirror, I could see that both of us were skeletally thin, and our eyes bright and bloodshot. In my hair and beard there were traces of gray that I had never seen before. Pedro was beardless still. Both of us wore the crazy-quilt of rags known in that part of the world as la túnica polimita de Joselito ("Little Joseph's coat of many colors").

I found myself staring into a bowl of black coffee, breathless with rapture. Oblivious to me, Pedro worked at carving a pipestem, shaping it from a stick of wood known as jewelwood. Having roughed out a pentagonal star at one end of the pipe, Pedro took up an ice pick and hollowed out the inside a bit farther, then resumed where he had left off on the star.

Not even the most flagrant of the invisible had ever yet had any serious trouble in Pochutla, so the town was a favorite stopping place. There was what we called a supervisor there, an old man who could if need be go to the authorities on our behalf. But the local Commander's friendliness to us had always been so genuine, though distant, that none of us had ever needed help from the Pochutla supervisor since the previous Commander's day. (The present incumbent was his nephew.) Not that the old Commander had been harsh, only his role in those times had been a much more serious one than that of his successor, or at least he had taken it more seriously.

A generation earlier, the town had been invaded by a group of wandering midgets who were tinkers and bootleggers by trade. They sold and also drank absinthe in enormous quantities. The reason they had come to Pochutla was that the tomb of a long-dead saint named Pepe was there. During his lifetime some two generations before that, the midgets' forebears had frequented and revered him. Now their tribe was dying out, and they decided to camp next to his tomb, having long claimed him as their patron and protector. Pepe was always said to be the wormwood-eater's friend. Once settled in, next door to the tomb, they set up shop as repairmen and traffickers as usual.

Late one night, the old Commander decided to get rid of them. Soldiers roused the midgets at bayonet point; they were given one hour to pack and leave. That same night the old Commander had a dream in which Pepe rebuked him. The saint looked just as he had in life, except in the dream his white beard reached all the way down to the ground. When Pepe finished, the old Commander noticed that a crack had opened at his feet and smoke was rising from it. He leaped out of bed, shouting.

Soldiers went after the midgets. When they were overtaken and persuaded, with much kindness, to come back, the old Commander entertained them in the street in front of his house and (remembering the dream) said over and over:

"Pepe is your friend. He loves you . . ."

We invisibles encountered real trouble only when we allowed ourselves to be seduced by the attractions of the city. There we were viewed as untouchables.

In the capital, for instance, because a newspaper publisher whose brother was a senator had denounced our order as an anachronistic and malodorous impropriety, policemen kicked and punched those of us they had arrested until they were themselves exhausted. Then in the middle of the night the victims would be pushed, more dead than alive, into the back of a truck and driven out to an empty spot on the highway to be discharged with warnings never to return.

For his part, Pedro had long since resolved never again to visit the big city. We were now staying at a settlement in the salt swamps south of Pochutla, some ten miles inland from the sea, an area so flat that from the top of a stepladder placed anywhere one saw the ocean glistening in the distance like a curved blade. Between oneself and it, there was an unending expanse of reeds running in all directions, billowy yellow, and bounded on the east by the snaky brown, blue and white outlines of the mountains which defined the approaches to the Wilderness bordering Pochutla to the south.

The swamp settlement served only as a rest stop for transients, and as in all such places there were only a few permanent visitors, a supervisor, and a handful of old men who had decided to remain until their death.

Built on an island of dry ground, the red mud huts we were living in formed a circle round an inner square at the center of which there was an immense and ancient olive tree, its trunk and branches forming an umbrella beneath which we spent long days outdoors in dry weather.

Squatting in two parallel rows facing one another, we played the pebble game. As the game proceeded, both spectators and players kept up a continuous nasal drone the whole time, punctuated only by the click of the pebbles and the beat of a drum played by an aged resident.

The purpose of this game was twofold: it could be used for gambling or as a method of divination, thus resembling almost any other game. However, we set no store by material possessions and had no interest at all in predicting future events. Nevertheless, we surrendered ourselves body and soul to this game of nonexistent stakes and meaningless prognostications. Quitting for the day, an hour or so before sunset, one of us might tell his brothers how he had been to the bottom of a sea teeming with luminous fishes and plants, while another, who could have told how his soul had been ravished into the center of a rainbow, said nothing. At other times, the lives of various paragons of preceding generations were related. One whose name was Serafin I often heard cited as a prodigy.

Serafin had worn woolen clothes exclusively. He refused to put on any garment that was not one hundred percent wool. He wore his hair long, never married and renounced worldly things. All that he had was his mother. Her he honored with absolute obedience. Serafin traveled constantly, but never set out without his mother's permission, and he always returned on the exact date set by her. He smoked tobacco mixed with rifa, was afraid of the dark and could not sleep by himself. Nor could he endure the neighing of horses or the braying of donkeys. He had the gift of second sight. When an inhabitant of any of the villages through which he passed in his wanderings was about to die, Serafin was likely to appear briefly and then, wraithlike, vanish. This always happened at dawn, so that the mere sight of him at that hour came to be taken as a sign that someone must die within the day. Serafin had a prodigious memory. It was said that he had spent some months in a flying saucer where he met with scientists from another planet who taught him their language, their names and the names of their cities.

The evening meal was the only meal of the day in our settlements. The fare varied according to season and the number of people on hand. Sometimes it consisted of nothing more than a pot of boiled mallow root. We were not prevented by this diet, however, from enjoying happy dreams during the hours of darkness. Each night we gathered round the fire with our pipes, some in small groups round a waterpipe, others sitting alone or in pairs with the smaller pocket pipes. We filled the pipes with the ground-up leaves and flowers of the rifa plant (sometimes mixed with a pinch of Mixtec tobacco) and thus made up for our indifference to the pleasures of eating with an unbounded appetite for the joys of smoking rifa, so much so that the inhabitants of the region had a saying to the effect that if there were no more rifa left on the face of the earth, the invisibles would nonetheless have a little something left over.

On the question of how this plant first came to be discovered, we used to tell the story of a king of old who was out walking one day with his top adviser and noticed a plant whose distinctive odor aroused his curiosity. Uprooting it, he dried the stems, flowers and leaves, then ground them up. Later, after taking them in a mixture of cloves and honey, he was filled with a mysterious bright, warm feeling. When the adviser asked whether he was satisfied with the experiment, the king replied.

"*ana h'tloc a rifa* (I was looking for precisely this!)."

Thus both the name of rifa ("precisely this!") and rifa itself were discovered on the same day.

Mixtec tobacco, which we not only sometimes mixed in pipes with rifa for smoking but often chewed while trekking cross-country, was the only kind we ever used. This tobacco was endowed with the most energetic properties, twenty to thirty times more powerful than the ordinary leaf. Our order had used it for the past thousand years, ever since one of the invisible was initiated by a hermit who made him a gift of some cured leaves, together with the following charm:

> Chew me and be strong,
> Drink my juice, your every member
> Will tingle all day long;
> Smoke me and remember.

Not that the introduction of tobacco was without serious consequences for us. Because of it, a number of heterodox brethren withdrew to hermitages near or actually within the Wilderness, where—typically—each would build himself a hut, live by fruit-gathering and clear a patch of ground, with his sole object to grow tobacco plants, to live in their midst and to chew and smoke them day and night.

All of us without exception had two pipes, one pocket and one water. The waterpipe consisted of a long stem inserted in a fat earthenware bowl, which rested on the ground, with a hollowed-out smokehole of conventional type, whereas the pocket pipe was simply a length of hollowed wood with a small metal bowl.

We thought of these two pipes as a pair of demons, the waterpipe a female and the pocket pipe a male. This demonic couple we imagined to be in league to bewitch their owner and keep him in a state of enslavement, for the pocket pipe was forever glued to its owner's lips while on the road or otherwise employed, and the waterpipe was the companion of our nights next to the embers of a lone campfire or with our brothers in the darkness of a cave, smokehut or hostelry.

So important were these pipes that nobody ever willingly traveled without both male and female. One of us, an aged man named Dáfnis, whose twofold beard overspread his weathered chest as whitely as the wings of the Pentecostal dove, losing his male pipe in the neighborhood of Candelárias, even went so far as to declare that he would not proceed one step farther, but built himself a hut where he kept a black she-goat which he named Lucky.

On market days, Dáfnis would appear in the center of Candelárias, accompanied by the black goat. Setting up his waterpipe he would hold forth for hours, surrounded by a crowd of locals who listened attentively to everything he said. Snapping his fingers at the end of a peroration, Dáfnis would send the pipe circulating from mouth to mouth. He would then point out, for the general edification, that Lucky the goat was perfectly clean, and above all not covered with flies:

"This," he would affirm, pointing to the pipeful of rifa, "knocks them out of the air!"

Dáfnis concluded by forcing the goat to eat a large bolus of concentrated rifa. He then also put the mouthpiece of the pipe to the animal's lips, shouting:

"Find me a husband for this woman!"

The goat endured all this with perfect docility but soon exhibited signs of agitation, at which bystanders would nudge one another and grin.

After a few years Dáfnis and Lucky disappeared, leaving an empty hut behind. It was generally assumed that the black goat had at last presented her master with a compatible mate for the widowed waterpipe.

We all lavished particular fantasy on the embellishment of our female pipes, tying colored rags of every description round the bowls—ribbons, bits of coral and cowrie shells, snailshells, brass buttons, picture buttons and likenesses of the Virgin Mary and the saints, pearls of every grade, policeman's whistles, bells, little mirrors, locks of hair tied up at one end with a length of scarlet thread, pierced coins, scapularies, tin soldiers, Maltese crosses, holy medals, gold watchbands; and yet none of this ostentation ever led us into vanity or an infatuation with physical beauty. We never forgot that by the very act of dressing up the female pipe we were channeling away from ourselves the energies of an ogress who delighted not only in enslaving her owner but in obliging him to go to work in order to fit her out in finery—"ogre brocade" we called it.

"A bonfire smothered in ashes" is what a famous recluse of our order once called the settlement where Pedro and I were staying. It maintained a close bond with another, identical in organization but high in the mountains some forty miles to the southeast, close to the Wilderness. One could reach the mountain settlement by a trail running straight, and it did run straight as the proverbial die, from Candelárias. It was said of the two that their fates were joined and that whatever happened, good or bad, to either must infallibly happen to the other. Both were wide open, their rule being absolute hospitality with no distinction being made between good, bad, rich, poor, visible, or invisible. Thieves, robbers, even murderers had more than once enjoyed the enigmatic privilege of our welcome. On one occasion within living memory, our swamp settlement had gone so far as to harbor an escaped mass murderer for a little more than a year before he finally vanished.

It was a well known fact that in both places our gardens had never been molested by birds or insects; our pantries had never seen rats, mice or cockroaches; there were no flies anywhere; and the cats never took anything but what was set before them.

How I Became One of the Invisible, 1992

Iris Owens
(1929–2008)

Seeking a literary life in Paris in the fifties, Barnard graduate Iris Owens found it, taking up with Alexander Trocchi, who converted her to his way of making a living, writing pornographic novels for the Olympia Press's notorious Traveller's Companion Series. Under the name Harriet Daimler she wrote such works of literary naughtiness as Innocence, Darling, The Pleasure Thieves, *and* The Woman Thing. *Under her own name Owens wrote two novels, both semi-autobiographical embellishments of her adventurous life:* After Claude *(1973), the brilliant opening of which is excerpted here, and* Hope Diamond Refuses *(1984). Iris was a friend of mine and few tongues inspired more fear and laughter in close proximity.*

from *After Claude*

I LEFT CLAUDE, the French rat. Six months of devotion wasted on him was more than enough. I left him as the result of an argument we had over a lousy movie, a sort of Communist version of Christ's life, except it didn't seem Communistic to me, whatever that is. Everyone was poor all right, and Mary didn't sport her diamond tiara, but otherwise it was the same old religious crap about how wonderful it is to be a pauper after you're dead. It took them a good half hour to nail Christ to this authentic cross with wooden pegs and a wooden mallet, thump thump, nice and slow so if your thing happens to be palmistry you could become the world's leading authority on the fortunes of Jesus Christ. Then, in case we thought we were watching a routine crucifixion, the sky turned black, thunder and lightning, the Roman troops, played by Yugoslavia's renowned soccer team, squirmed around on their picnic blankets, pondering whether to throw the dice or pack it up.

"Do you think they'll have to call off the game?" I nudged my

French boyfriend, which was when I saw that the idiot was having himself a full-blown Catholic seizure.

Claude glowered at me, and in the gloom of the theater, conveniently illuminated by the flashes of divine lightning occurring on the screen, I got a strobe picture of his features: dark, intense frog eyes, abundant black curly hair foaming out of his head, and finally, his full lips, sealed in a hurt pout. Claude had two expressions: that one, which accompanied his profound moods, and the other one, sleepy eyes, mouth relaxed and puffed as if he were blowing out invisible candles, which was the face he woke up with and starred in most of the day.

He might have answered me, but all human exchange was drowned in a clout of heavenly thunder that simultaneously wiped out Christ and the critical faculties of the stunned audience. The houselights went up, and I found myself in this ward of catatonics.

"Thank God," I said, as we staggered toward the aisle. "I thought that fag would never die." You can't imagine the looks I got from the shell-shock victims. Claude, who wasn't in such great shape himself, made a dazed push for the door.

We left the theater with the rest of the zombies and filed out into the hell of Manhattan's Upper West Side, me wondering how I had allowed Claude to con me into penetrating enemy territory for the privilege of undergoing that exquisite torture. It was hot, New York summer hot, the airless streets pressure-cooked into a thick layer of grease and scum, which reminded me of the best part of the movie which was that it had been cool in there. I lit my first Marlboro in three hours, since the so-called art house considered it very unartistic to smoke anywhere but in the balcony, and Claude, a non-smoker, was happy only in the third row of the orchestra. As a film connoisseur, he deemed it his duty to sit as close to the screen as his neck muscles would tolerate

"Boy," I said, drawing the smoke into my deprived lungs, "it's all fixed or the guy who invented air conditioning would certainly have won the Academy Award by now."

"Why the hell don't you ever shut up? It's a drag to take you any-where."

I gathered from Claude's tone that I had committed a crime, but the only offense I could think of was that of retaining my sanity throughout the endless dirge.

Claude, who had learned his English in England, spoke with one of those snotty, superior accents, stuffed into a slimy French accent, the whole mess flavored with an occasional American hipsterism, making him sound like an extremely rich, self-employed spy. I forgive myself for not instantly despising him, because one: it's not my style to pass hasty judgments on people, and two: it was my luck to meet him under circumstances that made anyone not holding a knife to my throat look appealing.

All around us, the shuffling movie patrons seemed to be snapping out of their trances, because a babble of words rose out of them, and instead of mounting into a riot, instead of rushing back into the theater and pulling up the rows of moth-eaten seats, there was just this Greek chorus about how authentic, how beautiful their recent ordeal had been.

"Authentic," I snorted at Claude. "What makes the director so sure Christ had rotten teeth and acne?" Because, believe me, his close-ups had been unsparing.

"Shut up. Stop attracting attention. It's embarrassing to take you anywhere."

"What is it with you, Claude? Can't we go to a crummy movie without you getting hysterical about the impression I'm making?"

Claude marched smartly ahead of me, and I was practically run-ning, as well as shouting, to keep in touch with him. In a normal neighborhood, we might have aroused suspicion, but up there, it just passed as a harmless purse snatching.

"Slow up," I yelled, when he reached the corner of Broadway and Ninety-fifth Street, because it's not one of my favorite fantasies to be abducted by six muscular militants to go play White Goddess in the back room of guerrilla headquarters. Claude waited, but not necessarily for me. He was searching nervously up and down the hostile streets. I knew he was having a crisis about whether to spend three dollars plus on a taxi ride down to the Village or to risk a knifing/mugging expedition on the IRT, a soul-searching choice for a Frenchman to make.

"Decide, sweetheart," I said, when I caught up to him. "Your money or your life?"

Claude pretended not to hear me, an act of male intelligence that never fails to impress me, and waved at a cab with a glowing off-duty sign. Since we were obviously desirable tenants, uncluttered by kids, pets, or luggage, the taxi came to a screeching halt at the corner. Any halfwit knows that New York taxis don't back up, so we did the hundred-yard dash like two grateful hitchhikers. There followed a brief but searching interview which established that we were all going in the same general direction. The sullen driver unlocked the back door, and Claude shoved me inside and proceeded to give the most detailed directions to our residence on Morton Street, all in his greasy headwaiter's accent, lest, God forbid, the bandit employ his own initiative and take us down the cool, quick extravagance of the West Side Highway. One additional dime spent in a taxi was Claude's idea of death by fire. The driver, hate in his heart, went careening down Broadway as if he were rushing plasma to a beheading.

What with the drenching heat, the harrowing race, and the agony of the meter ticking away Claude's lifeblood, our night might have had a peaceful dissolve into grief and silence, but being as I am the plaything of an infantile god, I found myself not in the usual filthy junk heap but in a portable crypt. Our driver, a full fanatic, had festooned the dashboard and windshield with thorned Christs, weeping Marys, pierced dripping hearts, and a display of blue wax flowers that you wouldn't want to put on your mother's grave. Scattered amidst the gore was the family album. Framed photographs of assorted mental defectives, smiling cripples, consumptives, and proudly uniformed degenerates, all looking straight ahead with the fixed stares of hostages facing a firing squad.

Since I am essentially a lighthearted person who tries to see the humor in this freak show called life, I jabbed Claude in the ribs and said, "Who do you suppose he has buried under the seat?"

"That's not funny," Claude answered, holding himself grimly in the throes of his recent religious exaltation. Claude kept his classic profile, which he tended to think of as a work of art transported across the ocean for the elevation of American females, turned away from me. He stared out the window, his heavy lids dropped over his dark eyes, the streetlights and headlights fleetingly reflected in the narrow slits between his long eyelashes.

"I didn't intend it to be funny. I intended it to be deep and tragic, like that deep and tragic movie that's destroyed your mind."

It appeared that we weren't going to embark on a stimulating discussion of why certain directors should be shot, so I leaned back on the cracked plastic cushions and lit a Marlboro. God know you're not allowed to smoke in a hearse. At the first hint of smoke, the driver whirled around and fixed his mean, crazy, little eyes on me.

"Lady, can't you read signs?"

The fact is I can't, but even if I could, it would have taken an Indian scout to spot a sign in his jungle of relics. He helped me out by pointing to a small printed announcement stapled to his sunvisor which dealt, in essence, with the driver's medical condition and the diagnosis that he would die from the cigarette you smoked. However, what really influenced me was a tattoo on his thick, hairy forearm that I had somehow overlooked. It was a blue tombstone floating in a red cross, inscribed, "In Memory of My Dear Mother," and under that the precise date on which he had killed her. Needless to say, I didn't wish to offend anyone in such perpetual mourning, so I flipped the cigarette out the window.

"Good," Claude said, with a short, nasty laugh.

It was all too much, and I felt my divine patience wearing thin. "What is it with you?" I demanded. "Why are you being so goddamn hostile tonight? Did I ask to come to this funeral? Or, for that matter, did I ask to go to that fag movie? Yes, fag," I emphasized into his rigid profile.

"Get off me," he muttered. "It's bloody hot, and I can't breathe with you screaming obscenities into my face."

"Who's screaming? Who's being obscene? Since when did fag become obscene? Yesterday it was your favorite word." I felt entitled to say that because, according to Claude, everyone, with the possible exception of his heroes Mick Jagger and Mao Tse-tung, was a fag.

"Ugh," I said, "are you defending the movie? All those muscle men floating around in their bathrobes, clutching at each other, and that hairy, rough trade ape, John the Baptist, the way his insane eyes lit up when he spotted Christ coyly dipping into the Jordan? If you want my opinion, I think Christ should have flung back his ringlets and dived into John's caveman sarong, slurp slurp, which would have made it a more gripping movie and, for my money, more authentic, too."

Now, Claude is one of these men who think no answer is the most eloquent answer of all. Why use words is his motto, when you have eyebrows to raise, lips to tighten, and an array of Gregory Peck facial tics to express all human intelligence? It was my job to divine the precise meanings of his various spasms, which was hard work in a well-lighted living room but slavery in the confines of a darkened taxicab. Not that Claude didn't enjoy the sound of his own voice. Don't misunderstand me. He could talk for hours, days, but only on carefully selected topics, such as every disappointing course of his most recent meal. But discourse? Converse? Exchange ideas? Never, and certainly not with that brain-damaged segment of the population called women.

"Speaking of women," I moved in closer to facilitate face reading, "how'd you like Mary? Wasn't she swell? So quiet, so sad, so refined. Never pushing Jesus to become a dentist, make something of himself. In fact, now that I think of it, did she have a single line in the picture?"

Claude's reply came through his perfect, white, clenched teeth.

"I told you to get the fuck off me." A request which was declined, not by me but by the driver, who slammed on his brakes in order to avoid hitting a station wagon that had cravenly stopped for a red light. I was flung across Claude's chest.

"Will you tell that maniac to slow down?"

Claude gave me his rotten smile, as if to suggest that he and the cab driver had partaken of an immortality pill, and fastidiously rubbed the front of his shirt, where my touch had contaminated him.

"Tell him yourself. What is this sudden timidity? Am I the only person you feel free to yell at and insult?" Claude, his eyes glued to the meter, was stuttering with rage.

"Who's insulting you? That's very interesting. You treat me like I'm a leper and tell me *I'm* insulting *you*. The only insult I'm aware of was made to J. Christ, assuming that he wasn't a Jewish mama's boy, willing to go to any lengths to get out from under Mary's potato latkes. Of course he had an especially heavy problem, with her wrapping her head in blankets and swearing he was conceived in her ear. Honestly, Claude, if I were a Catholic, I'd picket the theater."

"But you're not Catholic, are you?" He turned a furious face to me. "You're just Harriet, wonderful Harriet with the big Jewish mouth." Scratch a Frenchman and find a German storm trooper.

"Jewish! Since when did my mouth become Jewish?"

If there's one slur I resent, it's having my personal powers, good or bad, credited to a factor over which I have no control. If my mouth is so Jewish, then pray tell me why my Jewish parents have never understood one single statement I've made to them? The only possible explanation is that I was stolen from the Cossacks at an impressionable age and artfully trained by my Jewish kidnappers to suffer from frequent heartburn and moronic motion pictures.

I forced myself to disregard Claude's irrelevant attack and focus on what could really be upsetting him. I knew he was upset. I hadn't spent six grueling months catering to Claude's sexual appetites without having a pretty good idea of the pervert's moods. Furthermore, he'd been having these childish tantrums for the past two weeks. Curiously enough, two weeks was the longest stretch of unbroken time that Claude and I had spent together, since his job as assistant director of a French television news crew kept him hopping around the country. That was a clue, but what did it mean? I didn't want to face the depressing possibility that two weeks with the same woman created a sexual and emotional threat that Claude simply could not meet. The wretched movie seemed my only available opening into Claude's dilemma. I figured if we could come to some agreement about the film, we could go on from there to the real issues.

"Claude darling, let's not waste our breath on that piece of garbage. Admit you were as bored as I. I mean, two solid hours of crawling, trudging, groaning, it could depress even a normal person. Everyone mumbling and dragging around like a pack of junkies. And Salome's dance. I ask you? Every religious sect agrees it was a sexy dance, but Mr. Authentic is so determined to stupefy his public that he finds a pudgy twelve-year-old that your raving child molester would scorn, he stuffs her in a cardboard poncho, she does a few clumsy umbrella steps, and King Herod, equally obese, rushes her a gourmet dish, namely the head of John the Baptist. It makes you wonder if the sins Christ was ranting about all had to do with overeating. Are we to believe that Christianity was nothing more than the feeble beginnings of Weight Watchers?"

Claude, his arms tightly wrapped around his chest, his crossed legs encased in tight white jeans, said, "I don't want to discuss the movie."

"I couldn't agree more. To hell with the rotten movie. Admit it was torture, so we can talk about us."

Claude sighed.

"Stop suffering so much," I cried. "It's getting all over the taxi."

A tiny, stubborn, human part of me needed to hear that Claude hated the movie, because, believe me, it's no holiday for a woman of my refined tastes to discover she's living with a fool.

I closed my eyes as the taxi shot across Fourteenth Street, barely scraping past a crosstown bus. The driver reacted the way all cab drivers react when they cross Fourteenth Street, which is as though they've entered the Inferno. He couldn't have been more lost or confused. This was the point at which Claude was struck with the terrible possibility of the meter suddenly doubling. He all but rested his head in the goon's lap, guiding him down Seventh Avenue and into Bleecker Street, as if he were docking the *Queen Mary*. We never got driven to the door, because that meant circling an entire city block. The taxi came to a shuddering halt at the corner of Bleecker and Morton, Claude breathlessly absorbed in calculating a ten percent tip. The cabbie grudgingly dropped coins, one by one, into Claude's extended palm, neither of the men considering my prolonged exposure to heat prostration. The transaction completed, Claude went dashing down the street without waiting for me. I scurried after him, already concerned with other matters, such as how I could get to the top floor of our brownstone without being spotted by the psychopath who occupied the ground-floor apartment and spent her days and nights watching for me with murder in her heart.

After Claude, 1973

Lester Bangs
(1948–1982)

Lester Bangs started writing for Rolling Stone *in 1969 with an unsolicited review, and despite his humorously cranky style he lasted four years there before being fired by Jann Wenner. He moved to Detroit, joining the staff of the upstart journal* Creem, *where he poured more wit and energy into album reviews than were contained in the records themselves. He flaunted an attitude every bit as bad as the rock stars he took on as a critic and interviewer. His lengthy argumentative engagement with Lou Reed is the stuff of legend. Bangs was portrayed by Philip Seymour Hoffman in the film* Almost Famous, *which was directed by a rock writer he had mentored, Cameron Crowe. Lester suffered "death by misadventure" (involving the prescription and over-the-counter drugs he preferred) in 1982, at the age of thirty-four. Here he takes on his favorite sparring partner.*

How to Succeed in Torture Without Really Trying,

or, Louie Come Home, All Is Forgiven

THIS IS not Round Three.

By now I am sure there are many of you out there who may have grown a bit weary of this Lou Reed subject. To tell the truth, I'm almost getting bored with Lou myself, and he is certainly not my hero anymore. My new hero is President Amin of Uganda.

You may, however, wonder how such an album as *Metal Machine Music* could be sold, first by the artist to his record company, then by said record company to the "hard rock" consumers of America.

In case you just got here or think *Metal Machine Music* refers to something in the neighborhood of Bad Company, let me briefly

explain that what we have here is a one-hour two-record set of nothing, absolutely nothing but screaming feedback noise recorded at
various frequencies, played back against various other noise layers,
split down the middle into two totally separate channels of utterly
inhuman shrieks and hisses, and sold to an audience that was, to put
it as mildly as possible, unprepared for it. Because sentient humans
simply find it impossible not to vacate any room where it is playing.
With certain isolated exceptions: mutants, mental patients, shriek
freaks, masochists, sadists, amphetamine addicts, hate buffs, drug-
numbed weirdos too walled off by chemicals to feel anything, other
people whose nervous systems are already so bent out of shape that
it sounds perfectly acceptable, the last category possibly including
the author of this article, who likes *Metal Machine Music* so much
that he acquired (did not buy) an 8-track RCA cartridge (on which
are imprinted the words "SPECIAL VALUE!") so that he can listen
to it in his car.

The release of *Metal Machine Music* is nothing if not an event in
the history of the recording industry, and we at *Creem* are proud to
celebrate it. Not since the halcyon days of Bruce Springsteen has there
been a public so divided. (That 98% of them are on one side glowering
and spitting at the other 2 percent means nothing; we at *Creem* will
always stand up for the rights of minority groups, and you won't find
many groups smaller, nor more fervent, than *MMM* fans.) As of this
writing, it looks like *MMM* is gonna be a heavyweight contender in
our *Creem* Readers' Poll categories both of "Disappointment of the
Year" and "Ripoff of the Year." Then again, every once in a while a
ballot rolls in like that from one Carole Pressler of Rocky River, Ohio,
who not only voted *MMM* as all three of the Top Albums of 1975, but
voted for sides A and D as Top Two Singles of the year, and side B as
Best Rhythm & Blues Single.

Yes, these people actually exist, and it would be unfair both to
them and to Lou to star *Metal Machine Music* in a snuff film. Which
is exactly what RCA is doing right now. But let's not jump the groove,
we gots to hear it *all*. This postmortem begins when I get a call from

a lovely agent named after a British hypnotic sedative who says she is doing free-lance publicity for Lou. She tells me that Lou feels bad about the "misunderstandings" involved in the release of *Metal Machine Music*, wants to clear them up and apologize to all the fans who may have been taken unaware. (But that's just the *point!* spits the Imp of the Perverse.) She then tells me Lou is preparing a new album, the long-awaited *Coney Island Baby*, whose song titles alone should give sufficient indication of its content and tone: "Glory of Love," "A Gift to the Women of the World," "Crazy Feelings," "She's My Best Friend," "Charley's Girl" (single), "Nobody's Business," "Born to Be Loved," "Oo-ee Baby," "You Don't Know What It's Like," and "A Sheltered Life," which, she informs me with tongue so far in cheek it's lapping the Jersey shoreline, is "reggae."

Okay. I'm nobody's dummy. I'm everybody's dummy. I believe everything I read, see, and hear. If minions close to the cell say Lou is gonna make an album of sensitive songs for friends and lovers, I say it's right on that the dude should make so as to release concomitant with Valentine's Day. So I call the old geezer up at the latest hotel he's holed up in, Room 605 in the Gramercy Park. Above-mentioned agent told me to call him "three-ish," so I called three-ish, and the operator told me the line was busy. So I waited a few minutes and tried again. Same results. And again. And same still. Meanwhile Louie's girl is calling me on the other line telling me he just rang her up to ask where the fuck is the interviewer. So I call the hotel back, all of this red tape long distance, mind you, and still busy, so I tell the bitch at the desk to buzz in on the creep and tell him Bangs wants to talk to him. I get dead air. So call back yet *again*, buzz, click, chrk, clack, and there he is: "Boy, do you *believe* the operators in this fucking place?"

"Sure," I tell him. "I figured anybody that would put out an album like *Metal Machine Music* was the same kind of person as would tell somebody to call 'em up at a specified time and then give out with a busy signal."

I meant it as a Boy Howdy, but he squared off to fight straightaway: "Fuck you," etc., etc., etc. I told him poppa don't take no mess, this is halftime, so cessation of hostilities. He relaxes his guard, unzips his Frankenstein jumpsuit, and out steps: Jimmy Stewart! A sincere, friendly, helpful, likeable fellow. *This* is the real Lou Reed: a down-home Long Islander who lies through his teeth so good we might as well run the pone poacher for president. "*Metal Machine Music* is probably one of the best things I ever did," he beams, "and I've been thinking about doing it ever since I've been listening to LaMonte [Young, whose name Lou couldn't even remember to spell right on the back of the album]. I had also been listening to Xenakis a lot. You know the drone thing? Well, doing it with a band, you always hadda depend on other people. And inevitably you find that one person is stronger than another."

Note the tone of humility. Still, I had to demur in the direction of this particular piece of music having no direction. Like, each side is sixteen minutes and one second, ending as abruptly as they begin, with tape slice.

"I did it like that because I wanted to cut it hot," said Lou. "And since you're dealing in certain types of distortion up to a certain level of harmonics, I had to have the grooves as wide as possible, because the closer they are, the lower your gain."

"Then why didn't you make it eight minutes on a side," I said, "like an old Elvis album?"

"That would have been a ripoff. It was marketed wrong as it was. There was an information breakdown. They wanted to put it out on Red Seal, and I said no, because that would have been pretentious. I wasn't going to put it out at all. But a friend of mine at another record company asked to hear it, and said why don't you play it for [appellation deleted]. He was the head of classical music at RCA. I think *Metal Machine Music* got him fired. I played it for him and he loved it. I thought he must be mad, but he said we really must put it out. He bypassed the A&R people there and went right to Glancy, said 'We have to have it out on Red Seal.' I said no way. He said why. I said 'Because it seems dilettantish and hypocritical, like saying "The really smart, complicated stuff is over here, in the classical bin, meanwhile the shit rock 'n' roll goes over here where the shmucks are.'" I said 'Fuck you, if you want it out you put it out on the regular label with all the other stuff. All you do is put on a disclaimer.' Which didn't happen, unfortunately. In other words if a kid saw the cover where I'm standin' with a microphone and said, 'Wow, a live album!' they'd say 'What a ripoff!' What they shoulda had was a disclaimer that said before you buy it listen to it for two minutes, because you're not gonna like it, and I said in the liner notes you're not gonna like it."

Breathes there a fan with soul so jade he'd not grant Lou the mantle of an Honest Man. A Patrician, even. Yet vexatious vanity hath wrought a whoozis azzole tryina fool. He may not be a knickerbocker but he shore do can lie. And quoth high sware in frae. Gibberish is as gibberish does, and gibberish stands and beats its monkey footpalms 'pon the strand at 6th Ave. and 44th St. When you try to ask people at RCA about *Metal Machine Music*, they get uptight. They ask not to be quoted, then they launch a fusillade of Styrofoam to the effect that Lou is an artist and an intellectual they respect greatly, thus subclause respecting his right to "experiment." Then they fervently assert that I would be doing Lou and everybody else a favor if I would just let *Metal Machine Music* die a quiet death and slip away forgotten, because, of course, his next album is "the best thing he's ever done" and everybody's gonna love it.

I tell them that I think that sort of attitude is unfair to Lou and his fans. They sit there on the long-distance lam telling me that if I really care about Lou as much as they suspect I do, I won't want to hurt him by digging this *thing* up *now*. Get the picture? "An act of necrophilia," one of the anonymous RCA execs called my labors here. He also concurred, albeit under his breath, when I pronounced *MMM* a sort of schizophrenic ultimatum. He made strange noises when I brandished this album as prima facie evidence in the case against this curious practice known as "Artist Control." Only one RCA employee stonewalled. Ernie Gilbert, new A&R director of Red Seal: "I profess total and complete ignorance."

But a picture begins to emerge. Lou took this thing to the very top of the corp. The guy who headed Red Seal when he first walked in with his machine tapes now works for another company, was not fired as Lou had said, and while demanding that his identity be held in strict secrecy is not afraid of speaking the truth on this caper: "Well, as soon as he came walking into my office I could see this guy was not too well connected with reality. If he was a person walking in off the street with this shit I woulda threw him out. But I hadda handle him with kid gloves, because he was an artist in whom the company had a long-term commitment. He's not my artist, I couldn't get his hackles up, I couldn't tell him it was just a buncha shit. So I told him it was a 'violent assault on the senses.' Jesus Christ, it was fuckin' torture music! There were a few interesting cadences, but he was ready to read anything into anything I said. I led him to believe it was not too bad a work, because I couldn't commit myself. I said I'm not gonna put it out on the Red Seal label, and then I gave him a lotta classical records in the hope that he'd write better stuff next time. All I heard of it after that was that he was supposed to write a very strong disclaimer, which I guess he never did."

So now we have our scenario. Just imagine that wired little weasel, marching through the offices of one of the biggest media conglomerates in the world with his machine music tapes in his hand, not just confident but downright *cocky* that what he had here was the greatest (had to be, since most unbearable) masterpiece in musical history. Lou took *Metal Machine Music* straight to the top, to Kenneth Glancy, president of RCA Records, and worked his way down from there. Office to office, and every one he goes into he just presses the button and out comes ZZZZZZZRRRRRRRREEEEEEEEEGG GGGGGGGGRRRRRAAAAARRRRRRRRGGGGGGGGGHHH-HHNNNNNNNNNNNNNNIIIIIIIIIIEEEEEEEERRRRRRRRRRRRRR . . . all down the line ebrey one-a-dem egg-zecks past de bucks. "Sure, anything, just get it outta my office!" Right! And into the STREET! From whence it came. Kinda reminds you of Melville, don't it?

Well, I told Lou that I thought *Metal Machine Music* was a *rock 'n' roll* album. "I think so too," he mutters in that peculiar geriatric code of his which passes for speech (perish conversation). "I realized at a certain point that to really do stuff like 'Sister Ray' and 'I Heard Her Call My Name' right, one, it hadda be recorded right, and two, you hadda have certain machines to do it."

"Except it misses certain things," I said. "Like the beat, the lyrics . . ."

"That's not true. If you had a small mind, you'd miss it, but the beat is about like—" and here he verbally mimicked a hammering heart. A *Chorus Line* of hammering hearts. "Very, very fast. And on each side there's a harmonic buildup, whether people believe it or not I don't really give a fuck anymore. It had to be very carefully mastered, because if it was mastered wrong it would all go down the drain because it would go into distortion. It's using distortion but it's not distorted.

"Whether people know it or not, there is a difference between each side, there is a reason why it's 16:01 because I hadda keep it under seventeen. What people don't seem to realize is that you don't listen to it on speakers, because if you do you miss half the fun," he says delightedly. "It should be listened to on headphones because there's left and right but there's no center. It's constantly changing and sometimes one channel goes out entirely. There's infinite ways of listening to it.

"Sometimes I lift the left channel a lot and the right a little and then jack up the left and drop the right almost entirely and it's as though you got whacked in the head! But if you're listening without earphones, you won't get the effect. Each time around there's more harmonics that are added on bass and on treble, and I went as far as you can go without making the needle hop on the record, which is why I kept it at that time. I made it 16:01 to try to get the fact across that I was trying to be as accurate as possible with the stupid thing."

I outlined my feelings re *MetMachMus* to Lou: that as classical music it added nothing to a genre that may well be depleted. As rock 'n' roll it's interesting garage electronic rock 'n' roll. As a statement it's great, as a giant FUCK YOU it shows integrity—a sick, twisted, dunced-out, malevolent, perverted, psychopathic integrity, but integrity nevertheless, to say this is what I think of you and this is how I feel right now and if you don't like it too bad. "Of course," I added, "that's also commercial suicide. Which I suppose is the reason for this phone call."

"It was a giant fuck you, but not precisely the way you're saying it. [The former head of Red Seal] got me curious to see how it would hold up against LaMonte, Xenakis, etc. And I think it held up well against them all, in fact is far better. But I'm not interested in anybody's opinion except my own. When you say 'garage music,' well, that's true to an untrained ear maybe, but there's all kinds of symphonic ripoffs in there, running all through it, little pastoral parts, but they go by like—bap! in five seconds. Like Beethoven's Third, or Mozart . . ."

"Yeah, but that's all by accident."

"You wanna bet? You don't do a note-for-note symphonic thing by accident. No way."

"Well then, how did you get those in there? With a pair of tweezers?"

"No, I had the machines do it. It's very simple for anybody that knows what I'm talking about. Bach and Beethoven both wrote pieces that weren't supposed to be played by people. Now people play them, and I'm sure if they were around now they'd be amazed but they'd also be playing with machines, because nobody can play that thing. But you don't accidentally have part of *The Glass Harp* in there. You don't accidentally have part of *Eroica*."

"Where are these?"

"Well, they keep building up. The thing is, you have to listen for it. But most people get stopped by the initial thing they hear, which is fine by me."

"Well, the initial thing they hear is really not that extreme. It's not so far from, say, 'L.A. Blues' by the Stooges. And that came out in 1970."

"When I was in Japan they liked it. There are about seven thousand different melodies going on at one time or another, and each time around there's more. Like harmonics increase, and melodies increase, in a different combination again. I don't expect anybody with no musical background to get it. I took classical piano for fifteen fucking years, theory, composition, the whole thing, and I'm getting so fucking tired of people saying, 'Oh, it's a rock 'n' roll guy fucking around with electronic music.' That's bullshit. One of these days I'm gonna pull my degrees out and say, 'Does that make me legitimate?' But I don't wanna do that because that's horseshit too. So Neil Sedaka went to Juilliard, so what else is new? But like I told some of the ad people at RCA, they said it's freaky. I said right, and Stravinsky's *Firebird* is freaky.

"As far as taking it seriously, that's an individual thing, but when people start saying 'I have the background,' they're getting in a little over their head, and it's very bad to get in over your head with me when it comes to that because . . . I never pulled a Cale and started talking about studying in a conservatory, but if I ever said what really is my background, a lot of people would have to take their thumbs out of their ass and say, 'He's putting us on!' Well, don't be too sure. I just happen to like rock 'n' roll. But all I'm saying now is that I'm sorry about a kid shelling out that kind of bread for that kind of music when I know they wouldn't like it. But when people start landing on me about their background versus mine, well, I didn't go to college just to beat the draft."

Pomp and circumstance. Fine. What about *Coney Island Baby*?

"They're not what people think of as archetypal Lou Reed songs, but they forgot like on the first Velvets album, 'I'll Be Your Mirror,' 'Femme Fatale.' I've always liked that kind of stuff, and now you're going to have a whole album full of it."

Lou Reed, the Moonlight & You.

"Right. 'The Many Moods of Lou Reed,' just like Johnny Mathis, and if they don't like it they can shove it."

"Are you serious? Is this an album of sensitive songs of love and friendship?"

"Absolutely. What it is, it's gonna be the kinda stuff you'd play if you were in a bar and you didn't wanna hear about it. It's the Brooklyn–Long Island axis at work. Like you know the Harptones' 'Glory of

Love,' doo-wop, I wanted to rip that off them but not use the song, do my own."

I observed that Lou did seem to keep rewriting himself, *Metal Machine Music* to the contrary. "Oh, I've been rewriting the same song for a long time. Except my bullshit is worth most people's diamonds. And diamonds are a girl's best friend. *Sally Can't Dance* is cheap and tedious. Had it been done right . . ."

I noted that the production was very slick. "It was produced in the slimiest way possible. I think that's shit. I like leakage. I wish all the Dolbys were just ripped outa the studio. I've spent more time getting rid of all that fucking shit. I like all the old Velvets records; I don't like Lou Reed records. I like *Berlin* and I positively LOVE *Metal Machine Music*, because that's the idea I had years ago but I didn't have the money or machines to do it. I wasn't gonna put it out except that Clive [*Clive???*] had sent me over to see [appellation deleted], and [ditto, it's Mr. ex–Red Seal again] was outasight. Because he caught all those things and said, 'Ah, what are you doing putting in Beethoven's *Pastoral*,' and it blew my mind that he knew about it. Because like there's tons of those things in there, but if you don't know them you wouldn't catch it. Just sit down and you can hear Beethoven right in the opening part of it. It's down here in, like, you know, about the fifteenth harmonic. But it's not the only one there, there's about seventeen more going at the same time. It just depends which one you catch. And when I say Beethoven, y'know, there are other people in there. Vivaldi . . . I used pretty obvious ones. . . ."

"Sometime we'll have to sit down," I said, "with a tape or the record and you can point these out to me."

"Un-uh. Why?"

"Because I'm not convinced."

"Well, I don't care. Why should I sit down with you and show it to you? It's hard to do, because they occur at the same time. They overlay and depending on your mood which one you hear. I mean like you'll have Vivaldi on top of one of the other ones and that's on top of another one and meantime you've got the drone harmonic building."

Curious image, all those old dead composers stacked atop each other carcass on rotted postpustulant dusty carcass, in layers, strata really, prone yet aligned on a stairway to the stars right there in that old warehouse, the Harmonic Building, next door to the Brill Building. Or do I misinterpret? One must be careful when treading through the rice paddies of the avant-garde, lest a full chute of napalm come slag-screaming down your backbone. R.I.P., John Rockwell.

"There's also some frequencies on there that are dangerous. What I'm talking about is like in France they have a sound gun. It's a weapon. It puts out frequencies which kill people, just like they do operations with sound. It's a very delicate brain operation, they have surgical instruments that are sound. They've had this weapon since 1945. Hitler didn't have it, the French did of all people. Maybe that's why they play such bad rock 'n' roll."

"They like you over there."

"The only one they liked was 'Heroin,' that's because it's the center of it. But anyway, if you check out the rules of the FCC, there's certain frequencies that it's illegal to put on a record. The masterer can't put them on, and they won't, and you can't record it. But I got those frequencies on this record. I tested the thing out at shows during intermission. We played it very softly to see what would happen. Which was exactly what I thought would happen: fights, a lot of irritation," he began to laugh, "it was fabulous, I loved it. People getting very uptight and not knowing why, because we played it very low."

He rambled on for a while after that, mostly about his former manager, Dennis Katz, from whom Lou recently departed rather acrimoniously. ("I've got that kike by the balls," said Lou, who is Jewish himself. "If you ever wondered why they have noses like pigs, now you know. Just like the operators in this hotel—they're niggers, whattaya expect?") Finally we rang off. The highlight for me of this particular conversation with Lou was having JoAnn, a seventeen-year-old friend who positively idolizes the old fraud, listen in for the first ten minutes and ask later: "Lester, why was Lou so *boring*?"

"It's not his fault," I said. "It's just he's like Instant Douse. Like having B.O. or something."

She understood, and I got ready to write my article, when not two days later the phone rang, hot wires straight from RCA-NYC to these plains, it was my faverave publicitous agent, and after we spoke briefly of John Denver he said, "I've got somebody here that wants to talk to you."

Sure enough. And in fine fettle too. "I'm not gonna apologize to anybody for *Metal Machine Music*," the New Old Lou snarled, "And I don't think any disclaimer shoulda been put on the cover. Just because some kid paid $7.98 for it, I don't care if they pay $59.98 or $75 for it, they should be *grateful* I put that fucking thing out, and if they don't like it they can go eat ratshit. I make records for me. Same goes for this new album. I listened to those songs last night, and they're fucking great songs."

"You mean you changed the lineup, and we can expect more sleaze and vituperation?"

"Yeah. The new song titles are 'Kicks,' 'Dirt,' 'Glory of Love,' 'I Wanna Be Black,' 'Leave Me Alone (Street Hasslin'),' and 'Nowhere at All.'" Fuck this Dennis Katz bullshit of 'Oh yeah, sorry kids, the next album'll be songs you'll like.'"

"What about all that stuff you said yesterday, then?"

"Oh, you know, twenty minutes' sleep and a glass of carrot juice and I'm fine. I've never made any bones about the fact that I take amphetamines. Any sane person would every chance they get. But I'm not in favor of legalization, because I don't want all those idiots running around grinding their teeth at me. I only take Methedrine, which most people don't realize is a vitamin. Vitamin M. If people don't realize how much fun it is listening to *Metal Machine Music*, let 'em go smoke their fucking marijuana, which is just bad acid anyway, and we've already been through that and forgotten it. I don't make records for fucking flower children."

I was beginning to feel like Johnny Carson. "Speaking of fucking, Lou—do you ever fuck to *Metal Machine Music*?"

"I never fuck. I haven't had it up in so long I can't remember when the last time was."

"But listen, I was cruising in my car with *Metal Machine Music* blaring the other day, when this beautiful girl crossing at a light smiled and winked at me!" (A true story.)

He cackled. "Are you sure it was a girl?"

Well, yeah, reasonably as you can be these days. And I'm also reasonably sure about some other things having to do with this whole sequence of alleged events. The way I see it, *Metal Machine Music* is the logical follow-up to *Sally Can't Dance*, rather than any kind of divergence. Depersonalization in action: first you make an album that you did not produce (though you got half-credit), played guitar on only one track, used for material either old shit outa your bottom drawers or dreck you coulda scribbled in the cab on the way to the sessions, and do all but a couple of the vocals in one take. The only way you can possibly remove yourself more from what you are purveying after that is to walk into a room, switch on some tape recorders, push some buttons, adjust some mikes, let the static fly, and cut it off an hour later. And the reason for all this is that it simply hurts to feel, anything, so the more distance the better. Also indicative of an artist with total contempt for his audience (and thus, by all the laws of symbiosis *and* parasitism, himself). Note that if we can believe Lou when he says he doesn't like any of his solo albums except *Berlin* and *Metal Machine Music*, he is beginning to let his audience in on the nature of his relationship to them, which is, to put it mildly, slightly askew. Every time he does something *he* really likes or cares about, it bombs; every time he slings out some cheap trough of chintz dimestore decadence, the little scads eat it up. And never the twain shall meet.

Which, actually, is in his favor. Because now, and only now, when everybody in the Western world has written him off as either a bad joke or a drug casualty, is he free to finally *make* a record that feels, that hurts, that might be real and not just more jokes. Because he's kicked up such a dirt storm that everybody's blinded anyway, they're just waiting for the old lunatic to speed himself to death and they positively *would not notice* if he made a record with the depth and sensitivity of his best work for the late Velvet Underground. Now, I hope that *Coney Island Baby*, which as of this writing he has realigned again back into the Valentine's Day package originally promoted, might be that record. Of course, I don't believe it will be, or that Lou will write anything but loony toons ever again, because a few too many brain cells have took it on the lam from that organism that treated them so hatefully. But all that's okay too, because I live for laughs, which is why I love Lou. As far as *Metal Machine Music* goes, I listen to it all the time, but I'll never forget what Howard Kaylan told me Lou said to him after unsuccessfully trying to sell the layers-and-layers-of-sonic-frequencies concept (which was only a speed trip in the first place) to Flo and Eddie: "Well, anybody who gets to side four is dumber than I am." So, slimy critter that he is, we're right back where we started from. The joke's on you, kid. And if I were you, I'd take advantage of it.

Creem, February 1976

Richard Hell
(b. 1949)

*His real last name is Meyers, but Richard Hell seemed better for a student of
the French Symbolist poets and revisionist rocker. He cofounded Television
with Tom Verlaine (another fan of French Symbolists), and when the band
discovered a bar with a good PA system called CBGB they set the tone for a
movement with a jagged beat, spiky hair, and ripped duds. Hell was also writing poetry and published a collaboration with Verlaine under the pseudonym
Theresa Stern. After leaving Television, he briefly joined Johnny Thunders
in The Heartbreakers, then founded Richard Hell and the Voidoids, whose
promising debut was derailed by lifestyle issues or, perhaps, ennui. Hell has
continued to make music on and off, but since the nineties his main focus has
been writing lively poetry, fiction, and essays.*

Blank Generation

I was saying let me out of here before I was
even born. It's such a gamble when you get a face.
It's fascinating to observe what the mirror does
but when I dine it's for the wall that I set a place.

*I belong to the blank generation and
I can take it or leave it each time.
I belong to the _____ generation but
I can take it or leave it each time.*

Triangles were falling at the window as the doctor cursed.
He was a cartoon long forsaken by the public eye.
The nurse adjusted her garters as I breathed my first . . .
The doctor grabbed my throat and yelled, "God's consolation prize!"

(Chorus)

To hold the TV to my lips, the air so packed with cash
then carry it up flights of stairs and drop it in the vacant lot.
To lose my train of thought and fall into your arms' tracks
and watch beneath the eyelids every passing dot.

(Chorus)

1977; *Hot and Cold: Essays Poems Lyrics*
Notebooks Pictures Fiction, 2001

Lynne Tillman
(b. 1947)

*Lynne Tillman came up in the punk/New Wave era but she wasn't a punk,
more a "Pictures Generation" classical novelist (Cast in Doubt, No Lease on
Life, American Genius) adept at exploring the new art world and downtown
paradigms. With her persona Madame Realism (not to be confused with Sir
Realism), Tillman created a feminist narrator who pulls no punches in describ-
ing the chaotic world and maze of mixed signals she finds at Culture Central.*

Madame Realism Asks
What's Natural About Painting?

MADAME REALISM, like everyone else, had a mother, and her
mother had bought and hung two prints by old masters in her
home. One, by Van Gogh—a bearded man sucking on a pipe. One, by
Renoir—a red-headed girl playing with a golden ball or apple. Since
there were redheads in her family, Madame Realism assumed that
the girl was a relative, just as she assumed the bearded man was one
of her grandfathers, both of whom had died before she was born. As
a child Madame Realism thought that all pictures in her home had to
do with her family. Later she came to understand things differently.

With some reluctance Madame Realism went to a museum in Boston to look at paintings by Renoir. By now she felt a kind of despair
when in an institution expressly to look at and judge something which
she could no longer feel or experience as she once had. Boston itself
was a site of contradiction and ongoing temporary resolution. She
knew, for instance, that in Boston the arts were led by the Brahmins,
the Irish dominated its political machine, and the black population
was fighting hard to be allowed anything at all. But in an institution

such as a great museum, where lines of people form democratically to look at art, such problems are the background upon which that art is hung.

Madame Realism was moved along by the crowd, and in another way she was moved by the crowd. "Sinatra is 70 this year," she heard one woman say to another as they looked at a picture on the wall. There's nothing of Sinatra in this picture, Madame Realism thought. Not the skinny New Jersey guy who made it big and for a brief moment was married to Ava Gardner, also thin, then. On the other hand (one has so many hands these days), he did rise like cream to the top, not unlike Renoir, whose father was a tailor. The crowd swelled, especially at the paintings whose labels had white dots on them, as they had been chosen by the museum for special auditory instruction through machines. Madame Realism loitered in the clumps and listened as much as she looked.

In front of a nude, one young woman asked another: "Do you think that's how fat women really were?" Automatically, Madame Realism moved her hand to her hip. She strained to hear the answer, but the crowd advanced, and she completed it as she thought it would be. Women were allowed to be fatter, it was the style. You'd be considered more desirable, voluptuous. There's more of you to love. Diets hadn't been invented. Madame Realism felt self-conscious standing alone, if only for a moment, in front of that nude, her hand resting on her own 19th-century hip. And she thought again of Frank Sinatra and supposed, whatever other troubles he'd had, he'd never had a weight problem. Quite the reverse, she thought, giving the phrase her version of an English barrister's accent.

She didn't like these paintings. They were almost ridiculous when they weren't bordering on the grotesque, and then they became interesting to her. What had happened to this guy on his rise to the top? Was he so uncomfortable that what he painted reflected his discomfort by a kind of ugliness? The women were all flesh, especially breasts, and the faces of men, women and children were notably vacant. Madame Realism imagined a VACANCY sign hanging in front of *Sketches of Heads*, like a cheap hotel's advertisement that rooms were available.

In the middle of her own mixed metaphor, which unaccountably made her think of *The Divine Comedy*, Madame Realism followed a museum instructor, whose students were trailing her with the determination of ducklings after their mother. The woman was saying something about the differences between the 18th and 19th centuries, but became confused as to whether the 18th century meant the 1800s, or the 19th century the 1800s. Madame Realism's heart went out to her on account of this temporary, ordinary lapse, and she wondered how this might affect the students' imprinting. The instructor recovered quickly and said, "You have to look for the structure. The painting, remember, is flat." It wasn't hard to remember that these paintings were flat, she thought, and stood in front of a painting of onions. Renoir's onions are flat, she said to herself. His onions. It's funny that in the language of painting what someone paints becomes his or, sometimes, hers. His nudes. His people. Madame Realism recalled a still life of peaches by Renoir that she'd seen in the Jeu de Paume. Years ago she stood in front of the painting and thought they were perfect, just like peaches. The peaches of Europe, her grandmother was recorded as having said, how I miss them. And there they were. In a bowl. His peaches. Nature at its best. Not vacant like those happy faces. His happy faces.

Two women were deep in conversation, and Madame Realism eavesdropped with abandon. The first woman was saying, "He had an apartment near his dealer's, and his wife didn't know about it, and he had to distort her face so that she wouldn't know who the model was. So he made the faces like penises and vaginas." "The *faces*?" the second woman asked. "Yes," said the first, "like the nose coming out? That's a penis." They were talking about Picasso, Madame Realism figured out, because whatever else you might say about Renoir, his noses didn't look like penises. Although, upon viewing a late painting of nudes, she wanted to rush over to those women and tell them that a Renoir elbow looked like a breast. Or like a peach. Peaches and breasts. Peaches are much more like flesh than apples, or for that matter, onions. A bowl of breasts—a still life. She looked again at the masklike faces of children, the hidden faces of men dancing with women whose faces and bodies were on display. If masks, what were they hiding? she asked herself, moving closer to the painting as if that would reveal something. Instead, she saw brushstrokes. Disappointed, she walked on and thought about D. H. Lawrence and how the flesh and its passion refuse education and class, are, in a sense, used to defy them. She wanted to look at these paintings with something like sympathy rather than indifference. But somehow this evocation of the simple life and its joys, the contented family, the gardens of Eden, did not produce in her pleasure, but she did become aware of how hungry she was. Madame Realism was not one to discount this effect, and couldn't wait to sit down and eat. But there was more to see.

Facing *Sleeping Girl with a Cat* Madame Realism heard two young women agree that the cat looked just like theirs; it was so real, down to the pads on its paws. But, said one, "Doesn't that girl look uncomfortable?" Madame Realism agreed, silently. The sleeping girl had been positioned so that the light would hit her bare shoulders and partially exposed chest. This was supposed to be a natural position, though any transvestite could tell you that naturalness wasn't easy to achieve. Although, according to one of the writers in the exhibition's catalogue, Renoir had "an instinct" for it. Naturalness, that is, not transvestism. Shaking her head from side to side, Madame Realism followed the crowed to *Gabrielle with Jewelry*. Women are home to him, she thought, big comfortable houses. And if representation has to do with re-presenting something, what is it we repeat over and over but our sense of home, which may become a very abstract thing indeed. She imagined another sign. It read: Representation—A Home Away from Home.

Wanting very much to leave and eat, to go home, tired of the insistent flow in front of paintings, of which she was very much a part, Madame Realism was entrapped by another conversation, carried on by two men and a woman. The first man to speak was waving his arms, rather excitedly, saying, "The washerwomen were square. He was painting things as if they were rigid, fixed in a space that wouldn't move." The woman responded, "You can see why his paintings would appeal to the common man and woman. His people are just so unselfconscious." The first man countered, "But his talent was remarkable." The second man asked, "In his notes and letters, is there a more cerebral quality?" The first man answered, "No, and he wasn't a happy person." The woman exclaimed, "But his paintings have such joy." Both men said "vitality" in unison. "It's often true," said the first man. "He was a very cranky guy from a poor family. The sensuality in all his paintings . . . Just wishful thinking." The woman said, "He was like Mozart, a basic talent, but without intellect." The first man threw his arms out again and implored, "But he was a natural flowing talent. It just flowed out." The second man said, "Genius." At genius, Madame Realism walked out of the exhibition to the souvenir shop. He sounds more like a fountain than a painter, or more like an animal who holds a paintbrush. If, according to that same writer in the catalogue, Renoir's brush "was part of him," then maybe he didn't even have to hold it. Madame Realism bought five postcards and thought the paintings looked better in reproduction than as originals, just as a friend of hers told her they would. Maybe that's why he's so popular, she thought.

Back home, Madame Realism surrounded herself with the familiar: her cat, cheese, beer, the television. She turned it on, a public service broadcast which just happened to be about investing in art. She sat up in bed, dislodging her sleeping cat from her lap, and moved closer to the set. The host asked the art-as-investment expert: "The oldest cliché in your business is, 'I don't know anything about art, but I know what I like.' You've suggested that that attitude is a sure loser for an investor in art." "Exactly," answered the expert. "The word is appreciation. I don't care what you like, if you don't learn how to appreciate art, you'll never become a collector." The host smiled and said, "If you don't appreciate art, it won't appreciate for you." "Exactly," said the expert.

Madame Realism switched to another channel and turned the

sound off. Her cat returned to her lap and she fixed the reading lamp as best she could. Often it burned into the top of her head and gave her headaches. Robert Scull had just died, an art collector of some notoriety. When asked, it was reported in his obituary, if "he bought art for investment and social climbing, Mr. Scull responded, 'It's all true. I'd rather use art to climb than anything else.'" Madame Realism put the paper down and the day's words and phrases bounced in front of her eyes. She turned off the light, got comfortable and fell into a deep natural sleep, undisturbed even by the screams in the street.

The Madame Realism Complex, 1992

Cookie Mueller
(1949–1989)

Cookie Mueller first achieved fame (or notoriety) acting in the films of John Waters, whom she met in her native Baltimore. She also acted in films by Amos Poe, Eric Mitchell, and Susan Seidelman, and in my film Downtown 81. *Cookie starred in stills too, and is the subject of Nan Goldin's* The Cookie Portfolio. *Although Mueller spent years in Baltimore and later worked and held court in New York, she often lived an "on the road" lifestyle, with extensive sojourns in San Francisco, Provincetown, and Positano, Italy. She contributed to many magazines, writing fiction, memoirs, and advice. Her "Ask Dr. Mueller" column was a popular feature in the* East Village Eye. *She was also a regular contributor to* Details *before it became a men's magazine. The selection here is from her memoir* Walking Through Clear Water in a Pool Painted Black. *Cookie died of AIDS in 1989, a few weeks after her husband Vittorio Scarpatti.*

Abduction & Rape—
Highway 31—1969

"THEY WERE just three sluts looking for sex on the highway," the two abductors and rapists said later when asked to describe us. This wasn't the way we saw it.

A lot of other people didn't see it this way either, but these were women. Most men who know the facts say we were asking for it.

Obviously you can't trust every man's opinion when it comes to topics like rape. A lot of honest men admit that they fantasize about it and that's healthy but the ones that do it to strangers, unasked, ought to have hot pokers rammed up their wee wees.

The worst part is there's no flattery involved in rape; I mean, it doesn't much matter what the females look like; it doesn't even seem to matter either if they have four legs instead of two. Dairy farmers have raped their cows even.

"It's great to fuck a cow," they say, "you can fit everything in . . . the balls . . . everything."

So I guess it just depends on your genital plumbing as to how you see the following story.

True, we were hitchhiking. True, we were in horny redneck territory, but we hadn't given it a thought.

It was a sunny day in early June, and Mink, Susan and I were on our way to Cape Cod from Baltimore to visit John Waters who had just finished directing us in his film *Multiple Maniacs*.

When we told him we were going to thumb it, he said incredulously, "You three?? You're crazy! Don't do it."

"He's just overly paranoid," I told Susan and Mink. "Hitchhiking's a breeze."

It made sense anyway because we only had about fifty dollars between us and above all we needed a beach.

Mink the redhead was dressed casually as always in a black leather jacket with chains, black fingernail polish and tight black Levis. Susan, the brunette, was dressed as was her normal wont, in a daytime low cut evening gown, and I, the blond, was dressed conservatively in a see-through micro-mini dress and black velvet jacket.

This was not unusual for us, in fact benign, but in Baltimore at this time, the height of fashion was something like lime green vinyl pants suits, or other petroleum-based togs in chartreuse plaid or paisley that melted when the temperature was above 98.6. These clothes became one with Naugahyde car seats on a hot day. So people stared at us. They laughed right in our faces when they saw us.

"I hate to tell ya this," somebody would always take us aside, "but this ain't Hallor-ween."

To this day I can't figure out why we looked so odd to them. What did they see when they looked at their own outfits in their full-length mirrors?

In Susan's thrift store Victorian mirror that was about as useful as looking into a huge silver wrapped stick of Wrigley's, we put on our Maybelline black eyeliner lines and mascara, and were looking much better than any of the other displaced hillybilly beau monde on South Broadway that day.

"FINE MAKEUP, SENSIBLY PRICED" the Maybelline ad on TV said. I thought to myself how true it was. Couldn't beat it for a long trip; water-proof, smudge-proof, it sure held up.

For the twelve hour trip, we didn't forget our two quarts of Jack Daniels and a handful of Dexadrine Spantuals (they were new on the pharmaceutical market), and twenty Black Beauties. Aside from these necessities we had a couple of duffle bags of Salvation Army and St. Vincent de Paul formals and uniwear. We were all set.

On the street, we had no problem getting a ride due north.

The trouble started after about an hour into the journey. We had been travelling in an old green Plymouth with a salesman and his *Gideon Bible*. He had run off the road into an embankment. Trying to follow our conversation, he'd gotten too drunk on the Jack Daniels, so we left him after he passed out behind the wheel.

"I don't think he was ready for us," Susan said, as we tumbled out of his car laughing.

"Let's make sure the next ride is going to Delaware or Connecticut," Mink suggested, "or at least a little further north."

We had no idea that we were standing smack in the middle of a famous love zone, Elkton, Maryland, the quickie honeymoon and divorce capital of the eastern seaboard.

Men whose eye pupils were dilated with goatish desire stopped before we could even free our thumbs. We decided to be selective. Apparently we weren't selective enough.

After a long dull lull in traffic, we hopped right into the back of a burgundy Mach 4 Mustang with two sickos, gigantic honkies, hopped up and horny on a local joy ride. They told us they were going to New York City, the Big Apple, they said.

It is a fact that retarded people do not know they are retarded; they just know that some people do not talk about stuff that interests them.

The conversation we were having in the back was beyond their ken; after a quart of liquor and five Black Beauties apiece, we were a bit hard to follow, even for people who read all the classics.

I suppose they got jealous. They decided to get our attention by going around in circles, north, then south, then north again, passing the same toll booth four times.

Mink, the most astute of us, realized that her instinctive internal migratory compass was awry.

"We're trying to go north," she reminded them.

They just laughed.

"We see that you're playing some kind of circling game with your car." She was trying to make herself heard over the din of some backwoods hard rock bubblegum music that was blaring on the radio.

"Yeah, guys, I saw this same cheesey truck stop whiz by twice already," Susan pointed to a roadside diner that was whizzing by for the fourth time.

"I think they're just trying to get our attention," I said, taking the psychological angle.

"No," said Mink, "these guys are assholes. They're wasting our road time."

She should not have said that, but Mink has never been afraid of telling people about their personality flaws.

"Assholes, huh?" the driver scoffed, and he veered the car right off the highway and into a field of baby green beans and then got back on the blacktop and headed north again. The tires squealed the way they hardly ever do in real life, only in squalid car chase movies

"Round dees parts we don't call nobody assholes," he said. "That's kinda impolite. We call 'em heiny holes." And they laughed and laughed.

"Well at least we're going north again," I said and in the very moment I said it I realized that it was a ridiculous thing to say.

There comes a time when even the most optimistic people, like myself, realize that life among certain humans cannot be easy, that sometimes it is unmanageable and low down, that all people are quixotic, and haunted, and burdened and there's just no way to lift their load for them. With this in mind I wanted to say something to Mink and Susan about not antagonizing these sad slobs, but right then the driver turned to me.

"You ain't going north, honey, you ain't going nowhere but where we're taking you."

These were those certain humans.

"Let's ditch these creeps," Susan said.

"We're getting out at the next truck stop," said Mink and she gathered her duffle bag like a career woman in a taxi with her attache case.

"Shut the fuck up," the driver said as a Monarch butterfly was creamed on his windshield. The wings mushed into his wipers as the blades squeaked over the splattered glass.

"Fucking butterfly guts," he said.

"We have knives," the guy riding shotgun said and he grinned at us with teeth that had brown moss growing near the gums.

"Big fuckin' deal," said Susan, "so do I," and she whipped out a buck knife that was the size of my mini skirt.

The driver casually leaned over and produced a shot gun and Susan threw the knife out the window.

Suddenly the effects of the Jack Daniels were wearing thin and the black reality of a speed crash was barreling in.

Mink began scribbling a note on a Tampax paper, "HELP!!! WE ARE BEING ABDUCTED BY ASSHOLES!!! CALL THE POLICE IMMEDIATELY!!!"

It was a note for the woman at the toll booth.

When we stopped there Mink started screaming and threw it at the woman. The note fluttered back into the car as we sped away.

"Have you ever fucked calves' liver?" Mossy Teeth said.

"How the hell ya supposed to fuck calves' liver?" the driver asked.

"Well, ya buy some fresh liver and ya put it in a jar and ya fuck it. It's better than a pussy."

Now that's disgusting, I thought, almost as disgusting as the popular practice in 17th century France when men took live ducks and placed the heads of the ducks in a bureau drawer, put their dicks in the ducks and then slammed the drawer shut at the moment of their (not the duck's) orgasm. Men will fuck anything.

I suppose they also cooked the duck and ate it too.

They pulled into this long driveway. The dust was rising and matting the mucous membranes of our noses. Everybody sneezed.

I began to realize that for them we were party girls, that this wasn't something unusual, that girls around these parts were game for a good time, a gang bang, and that threats of murder might just be considered all part of the fun.

We bounced full speed down this backroad for quite awhile, passing vast stretches of young corn plants rustling and reflecting the sun on their new green leaves. I remember getting sliced by young corn plant leaves once, the same kind of painful wounds as paper cuts.

Mink and Susan and I couldn't even look at each other; our eyes hurt.

A white clapboard house came up near diseased elm trees in the distance. Some chickens ran away from the fenders. A rusted out pickup truck was growing weeds and a blue Chevy was sitting on four cinder blocks right next to a display of greasy old auto parts and an old gray dog that was trying to bark. We pulled up right to the house and from the front door, screen door slamming, came a big acne scarred man in his BVD underwear, a plaid flannel shirt with a sawed off shotgun.

"I told you once before, Merle, get off my property," the man hollered, "I'll blow your fuckin' heads right off your shoulders."

"My cousin's a little crazy," the driver said to us and he laughed.

"You wouldn't do no such thing," he bellowed to his cousin with the yellowish drawers on.

"Oh yes I would," the cousin said and aimed his gun at the windshield.

"You think he'd shoot us, El?" the driver asked his buddy.

"Sheet," the other one said, "he'd shoot his granny."

The screen door slammed again and then next to the cousin was a woman with dirty blond hair and dirty bare feet. She was wearing blue jean cut offs and a tee shirt that said MARLBORO COUNTRY on it. She looked forty-five but she was probably twenty.

A toddler of about two came to the door, pushed it, and fell out into the dirt. The baby started crying but nobody in the yard noticed. The baby got to his feet and stopped crying when he picked up a piece of car tire and put it in his mouth. He was teething, I guessed.

The woman grabbed the shotgun muzzle. "Put that fucking gun down, Henry," she said.

"Leave goa dis gun, woman," Henry said and shook her off, aimed again. She jumped for it again, and in this moment the three of us, Mink, Susan and I started diving out of the car windows. Mink and Susan got out but Mossy Teeth, El, grabbed my thigh and held me fast. Merle spun the car around and we took off, making corn dirt dust in all the faces of everyone who was standing there in front of the house.

Susan and Mink tried to run after the car, yelling to me to jump. I couldn't now. It was too late. We were burning rubber up the gravel path while Merle and El were pulling me back into the car. They got me in the front seat with them. I was straddling the bucket seats.

I wondered what was going to happen to Mink and Susan, but I bet they wondered more what was going to happen to me.

What happened was this: I began to feel the mood change. As they were talking to each other I noticed that they sounded scared; El even wanted to get out and go home.

After a lot of fighting, Merle finally did let El go. He let him out at a backwoods package store.

Now Merle and his little brain began to wonder what to do with me. His buddy was gone. Who would fuel the fire?

I assumed that he would rape me. He wouldn't let me get away without that at least. Of course I didn't want to get raped, so I began to think of a plan.

I have always been an astute observer of sexy women and unsexy women, and in all my years I've never seen a crazy woman get chased by a man. Look at bag ladies on the street. They rarely get raped, I surmised. And look at burnt-out LSD girls. No men bothered with them much. So I decided that I would simply act crazy. I would turn the tables. I would scare him.

I started making the sounds of tape recorded words running backwards at high speed. This shocked him a bit, but he kept driving further into the woods, as the sun was setting and the trees were closing in.

"What the fuck are you supposed to be doing?" he asked me nervously. "You a maniac or something?"

"I just escaped from a mental hospital," I told him and continued with the backward tape sounds, now sounding like alien UFO chatter.

I think he was believing me, anyway he pulled off into the bushes and unzipped his pants and pulled out his pitifully limp wiener. He tried to get it hard.

For a second I saw him debating about whether or not he should force me to give him a blow job.

"Ya devil woman, ya'd bite my dick off wouldn't ya?"

He tried to force his semi-hard pee-wee rod into me as he ripped my tights at the crotch. I just continued with the sounds of the backward tape as he fumbled with his loafing meat.

This infuriated him. "I'm going to ask Jesus to help me on this one. Come on, sweet Jesus, help me get a hard on. Come on."

He was very serious.

This struck me as deeply hilarious. Praying to the Lord for a hard on was asking for the ultimate Bible text rewrite.

Not waiting to see whose side the Lord was on, I pushed his wiener quickly aside and threw open the door and dove out into the darkness. I ran faster than I'd ever run and I wasn't a bad runner.

As my eyes grew accustomed to the half-moon light, I saw that I was running into very deep woods. Aggressive brambles grabbed at my thighs, poison ivy licked at my ankles and yearling trees slapped me in the face.

After a long time I decided to stop running, so I got under a bush next to a pile of rocks. I felt a bunch of furry things scuttle away. Rats, or possums or raccoons, I guessed.

I laid there for awhile trying to see things in the darkness. And then I heard his voice.

He was far in the distance yelling, "Girl! Girl! Where the hell are ya?"

Did he think I was really going to answer?

As he got a little closer I saw that he had a flashlight and I got scared again. If his light found me there would be no hope. My white skin was very bright in the bluish flood of the half moon.

I had a black velvet jacket on with a black lining, so I ripped out the lining in two pieces and wrapped one around my head and the other on my almost bare legs. Those brambles had shredded my stockings.

No light would bounce off me now.

I was awake for a long time and then I just fell asleep, sure that he had given up the search.

At sunrise, or thereabout, I woke up. I didn't even have a hangover.

I felt very proud that I had melted so well into the underbrush, just like Bambi.

Without too much trouble I found this little dirt road and I started walking to the right.

"All roads lead to Rome," I told myself.

I guess I was walking for almost an hour when I heard a vehicle rumbling up behind me. For a second I thought maybe I better dive back into the woods, maybe it was Merle again but I turned and saw it was a little country school bus, a sixteen seater, a miniature version of the long yellow city buses. I stood in the middle of the road and waved it to a stop.

A woman was driving the bus and there was a load full of kids. I stood in the front of the bus and whispered my predicament; I didn't want to alarm the kids. She drove me to a ranger station and the ranger's wife gave me a cup of Lipton's.

I told my story and they were really peaceful sympathetic people. The ranger called the police station and I found out that Mink and Susan were there.

The ranger's wife liked me, I could tell, and they both drove me to the police station.

When they let me off the wife kissed me and said, "I hope every-thing goes well for ya, honey. That's a nasty thing ta happen. Watch yasself round these parts, there's some hanky panky round every corner here abouts. I know. My husband deals with it everday."

They drove off. I liked her.

Inside the police station the police weren't so nice, but they were patient with my story. They knew the guy. It was a small town.

"He was just released from Jessup's Cut," they said. "He's a bad ass for sure, always in trouble."

"His daddy's a religious man, though, had one hell of a religious upbringin'," one of them said.

Don't I know it, I thought. He believed the Lord would raise the dead even.

It was good to be reunited with Mink and Susan. They told me that they were beside themselves with worry until about ten o'clock. That was about the time I was finally relaxing in the bush, I told them.

The police brought Merle in for questioning. They wanted to hold a kangaroo court right there in the next building. The law is quick in Elkton, Maryland.

In the courtroom I didn't press charges. That would mean lawyers and coming back there and a whole long drawn-out scene. I would lose anyway. I just wanted to leave that town as quickly as possible; anyway Merle was going back to jail for a false insurance claim, or something like that.

The cops then drove us to the bus station and told us that they better not ever see us on a highway again.

While we were waiting for the bus we decided to go to Washing-ton, D.C., to the airport where we could maybe hitchhike a ride on a plane.

"Let's go in style," I said. "No more cheap highways."

At the airport bar we met a marine biologist who was working in Woods Hole, Massachusetts.

"I'm flying back to work. I'm working with endangered bass," he said. "But my buddy's flying right into the P-town airport. He'll take you there. No problem. He should be landing here in about twenty minutes."

In mid-air we told them the story. We laughed a lot.

His friend flew us right into Provincetown.

"Wow, what luck!" Susan said.

I didn't think it was luck. Innocent people are sometimes rewarded.

Anyway, after everything we'd been through, we deserved it.

Walking Through Clear Water in a Pool Painted Black, 1990

Gary Indiana
(b. 1950)

Born Gary Hoisington in New Hampshire in 1950, in New York City he became Gary Indiana, a name with superstar overtones. He has lived up to the star billing, emerging as an important American writer as well an intriguing actor, performer, director, and artist. He has written and directed many plays, and has published seven novels, including the riotously funny Resentment, *loosely based on the trial of the Menendez Brothers; six books of non-fiction, includ-ing* Three Month Fever: The Andrew Cunanan Story *(based on the murder of Gianni Versace); and* Last Seen Entering the Biltmore: Plays, Short Fic-tion, Poems 1975–2010, *from which the monologue "Roy Cohn" is excerpted. He teaches literature at the New School in New York and recently organized a re-enactment of his marathon group reading of the Marquis de Sade's* 120 Days of Sodom.

Roy Cohn

Roy enters, or if stage is set as though it were after dinner at a ban-quet, stands up from his place, reacting to the imaginary applause of the audience after an extensive introduction with the usual gestures of fake modesty "Please, that's enough," and a crooked little smile that says, "Well, I gotta admit, I'm a pretty special guy." Nods, tamps down the applause with his hands, the twisted grin if possible resem-bling the ones of his late performances on *60 Minutes*. Finally, satis-fied that he has everyone's attention, he speaks.

I WANT TO thank Dr. Brenner for that warm introduction and Rev-erend Neville whose work with the victims of child pornography we're all familiar with and Mr., uh, Mr. Jorgenson from the Coors Company for sponsoring this evening's, uh, festivities, to thank them, and you, for the invitation to speak tonight and to say how pleased I am that I could be asked here tonight to talk about the city council hearings on the gay rights bill . . . (*he takes a pen from his inside jacket pocket and holds it in one hand*) among other subjects, and the dangers this bill represents to traditional values . . . I understand that this organization, which is dedicated to upholding family, family rights, protecting morality, that this organization for example has backed up Anita Bryant down in Dade County, reversing the trend towards a, what could you say, a Sodom and Gomorrah atmosphere, which is literally what prevails in every city in this country where the so-called gay rights movement has gained a foothold. These people who want freedom of expression so badly have launched a witch hunt against Anita Bryant to the point that she's losing thousands of dollars in concert fees every week, but this is an old story where the American left wing is concerned. Many of you are here in New York from smaller towns and cities and if time permitted and we all had strong enough stomachs I could escort you on a tour of some places on the West side of Manhattan that would send any decent person into shock, where you would witness the kind of unspeakable behavior that's become part of the Roman Circus of the homosexual underworld . . . and I don't mean in the questionably sacred privacy of people's homes, but right out in the public domain. I won't get into it more than I have to, but to give you an idea of just how low things have sunk, you've got celebrities pulling up to places with names like The Toilet in their limousines in order to observe various sexual rituals that would've been called criminally depraved if not downright satanic in any other period of history except for the late Roman Empire . . . I don't say this for the shock value but only to indicate the irony of these people crawling out of bed after two hours' sleep, having spent the whole night ingesting every drug they could take to heighten their orgiastic revels, some of them involving, and my apologies to the ladies in the audience, but among today's homo set, evidently the most popular sexual practice involves penetration of the rectum with a fist and sometimes an entire arm (*he accompanies this with a gesture of the hand/arm*), unimaginable as this may seem, and I ask the ladies in the audience to forgive the need for graphic detail, but I think we all need to know the extent of what we're talking about, you've got these very shrill inverts that are down there at the hearings every day, screaming their slogans, in their respectable clothes, when only hours earlier they were prancing around the West Village in Nazi uniforms and chains, or hanging from a torture rack in a dimly lit bar . . . believe me, this kind of thing has become so commonplace you can even see it creeping into fashion magazines. Maybe some of you saw that movie *The Eyes of Laura Mars*? Anyway, not so long ago some of the crème-de-la-crème of New York Society showed up at a bar called The Anvil to watch a young man eject pool balls from his rear end, another one who pulled several yards of thick chain out of himself . . . Well, I'm going to spare you more of the details.

This (*holds up pen*) is a pen, ladies and gentlemen. I guess you all can see it. The new Mayor of this city, Edward Koch, is a liberal Democrat from the hub of today's gay world, the West Village. Koch won the primary over a lot of opposition that used the cautionary slogan, "Vote for Cuomo, not the homo." Now, I don't pretend to know the Mayor's sexual orientation, nor do I care about it, but if I had to speculate I'd say he hasn't got any, but I find it symptomatic, either of some type of offbeat personal quirk or his own blind obedience to certain pressure groups, that the first thing the Mayor does, the first signature that goes down on a piece of paper is an executive order, barring, in his words, discrimination on the basis of sex, sexual orientation, race, religion, and national origin, everything jumbled together like peanuts, bananas, and oranges (*gestures with pen, puts it away*), with one stroke of the pen. But. As we know. What with your own experience in Dade County. And as we've seen around the country in recent weeks. One of the primary virtues of a democracy is that when radical measures such as this are imposed on people by fiat, they can also be rescinded when enough people stand up and say, "We're fed up, some things ought to be against the law, enough already." That's democracy and that's what makes us different from Russia.

It's Koch who's dragged up the gay rights bill again, and I have, obviously, some very strong feelings in opposition . . . which I hope to explain to you in somewhat calmer language than I started out with . . . but with your indulgence, and as I've also been asked to say a little bit about me, and maybe you won't mind hearing it since I'm not running for anything . . . well, Dr. Brenner and Reverend Neville asked me to say a word or two about Roy Cohn—(*smirks*) not my least favorite subject, I'll admit—but anyway, to go back a little, when I was first asked to talk to the American Society for the Protection of the Family, I honestly jumped at the chance. I am and always have been a strong believer in Americanism, and the family unit, the strong happy family unit, is the seed at the root of Americanism. At the same time, I thought, "Gee what've I got to tell them? I'm not married, I don't have a family." My sainted mother just died recently, both parents have passed on, no wife, no kids, you know, to tell the truth, I always felt that being a controversial person (*takes out handkerchief or pocket square, wipes his nose swiftly, puts it away*), and being a person that people were always going to be fighting about and over, and always destined to be in some kind of battle or other, that I could go through it better if all I had to worry about was myself, not a wife and kids who are going to have part of the heartache pushed over them.

(*Big smile*) Know what I like more than anything? Birthday cake. A big birthday cake with candles and little kids in party hats with confetti and noisemakers, and parents' faces lit up with the joy leaping in their hearts at the sight of those little ones . . . (*musing*) those little ones. And don't they get adorable when they come into their early teens and shoot up eight or nine inches in a year! I'll tell you something, I don't have a family, not yet anyway, but I do have plenty of godchildren, the children of good friends, and one of the happiest things in my life is what I can give to those kids. Mr. Steinbrenner's a friend of mine, they can always get tickets to the big game. That sort of thing. And when you look at those kids, their innocence, you realize that the family is the basis of everything. And it's facing terrific challenges in the society we live in, the permissive society of 1978.

I mean, to look around today you would start to believe the biggest evil in the world is the idea of having to work for a living. Sorry, that isn't how Roy Cohn was brought up. And here we get to family values. I am rather proud of my family. My grandparents were born in four different European countries, and each chose the United States for a home. My father worked his way through City College and New York Law School at night while teaching during the day . . . Albert Cohn lived long enough to see his name engraved in the rotunda of the state courthouse.

I grew up with the movers and shakers of the Bronx right at the kitchen table. It's true what they say about Roy Cohn, I do know every circuit judge and every minor politician's second cousin twice removed, known them all my life and breathed the air of politics from this high. Frankly, I was not a boy for sports and activities, although I am in good shape. I water-ski (*makes a gesture of holding the towline*), not that water-skiing keeps you in shape, I must have good bone structure or, hey, maybe it's genetics, the old family again, anyway, I was a shy kid, not shy exactly, reticent, whatever, and became interested in the law and the justice system and how it worked behind the scenes—very honestly, from about the age of five. My father would discuss his cases with me. "What do you think about this, Roy? What about that? Is that one out to screw me?" Well, I didn't necessarily have all the answers at that age, but my father always listened to my opinion. My mother . . .

My mother was an intelligent and gracious lady, Dora Marcus (*wipes his nose again with handkerchief*), maybe I was a shy type or, as I say, reticent, the thing is, they both fussed over me a lot to get me out of there, you know, when I was . . . well, in the womb, because she wouldn't, uh, they couldn't, uh, well, they had to blow air up her fallopian tubes to get me out. So she wasn't having any more after that. Unavoidably, I was the star attraction in the family. Dora Marcus of the well-to-do Marcuses of Park Avenue, married a little below her station, so the legend goes, good old Muddy, I called her Muddy, you know. But fuss, I kid you not, she had me at the dermatologist three weeks out of the womb. (*At this point he wipes his nose again.*) Anyway. I learned the value of a close-knit family. In the thirties you learned to stick together, those were hard times, regardless how I look at things now, back then Franklin Roosevelt looked like a savior. I think back to the apartment we lived in on Park Avenue, after we left the Bronx . . . we gave an enormous Passover every year, relatives, ward bosses, the rabbi . . . and Muddy . . . had a slightly hysterical streak when it came to large affairs, you know, she always had to be the queen bee, it came from that rich upbringing, and something always went wrong . . . and one year, my Aunt Libby got there early and wanted to say hi to the cook, and Muddy said No, Libby, I don't want you going in there . . . so later when they got to the part of the Passover service where the question is posed, "Why is this night different from other nights," Muddy answered, "Because the serving girl is dead in the kitchen." She'd keeled over with a heart attack and they had to get the coroner in and that was Passover.

Then every year there were summer camps, this is where all that fussing . . . Camp Menatoma in Maine, Camp Sagamore on Lake George, I'm put in the camp, Muddy checks into the nearest hotel, she comes to the camp every day and tells the counselors, Don't make my Roy walk too far in the woods, the allergies he has, Only allow Roy to swim one half hour, he isn't supposed to exhaust himself, he has weak lungs . . . which I didn't, in fact but I hated those camps anyways, when one of those greasy shtetl Jews that ran Menatoma dropped in on Park Avenue to say what a great camper I was, what was his name, Friedenwalk, Dr. Friedenwalk, and that creep son of his Johnny Friedenwalk the sadist camp counselor . . . drumming up some sheckles for next year, I told that kike he was full of crap . . . pardon my English . . . is anybody here besides me Jewish? (*Pause*) Life is sure full of memories.

I remember afternoons in Mr. Baruth's class at Horace Mann, memorizing Tennyson . . . "Oh purblind race of miserable men / How many among us at this very hour / Do forge a lifelong trouble for ourselves, / By taking true for false, or false for true; / Here, thro' the feeble twilight of this world / Groping, how many, until we pass and reach / That other where we see as we are seen!"

What's striking to me looking back, and I do look back, and others have commented on it too, is when I went down as chief counsel for Joseph McCarthy in 1953, I totally broke with my own background. Here I was, a young Jewish Democrat from New York, supposedly the most liberal, one of the most liberal cities in the United States, going down to become chief counsel for a fellow like Joe McCarthy. Now, you might wonder how that came about. When I was working in the US Attorney's office during the Hiss, you know, espionage business, I didn't believe Alger Hiss had been any kind of Russian spy, neither did my parents, neither did any Jewish liberals at the time, Alger Hiss was a hero, advisor to FDR at Yalta, victim of witch-hunt hysteria, et cetera, and then one spring afternoon in 1949, two FBI agents working on the case took me out to lunch at Gastner's, around the corner from the Foley Square courthouse. You had a choice of Angelo's or Gastner's. And I preferred Gastner's for its corned beef. And I mentioned to these FBI men, I said, Hiss is a scapegoat, and this thing stinks the way herrings stink.

One of the agents smiled and said, "How much do you really know about Alger Hiss and Whittaker Chambers?" I didn't know enough to get through half a bloody mary. Like a lot of people, I couldn't tell reality from fiction. The guy was a brilliant intellectual. He was an editor at *Time* magazine, but then again, he'd also translated Bambi, which made you wonder a little, that maybe he was off among the buttercups and bunny rabbits in never-never-land and it was said that Chambers, who had admitted his homosexual tendencies, had a romantic fixation on Alger Hiss—a handsome WASP, and Chambers, you know, was quite dumpy and fat, with a tendency to, you know, perspire, and Hiss had rejected his advances, which provoked the accusation of spying. Well. Call me irresponsible. I got a crash course in Communism in Gastner's that afternoon that changed my orientation around three hundred and ninety degrees. Boy, did those guys fill me in to what was what, about the Kremlin cells in top secret US federal departments, I was an espionage virgin until that afternoon. After that rude awakening I picked up everything I could get my hands on about Communism.

And here you find the real threat to the American family and our way of life in the great flirtation with Communism that intellectuals like Hiss, and working-class socialists like the Rosenbergs, were swept away by . . . One reason that Jewish families like mine felt embattled during this period was because of a widespread idea associating Jews with a sympathy towards Communism. This is something that has always bothered me, and I've tried in every way I can to make it clear that the fact that the name is Cohn and the fact of my religion has nothing to do except perfect compatibility with my love for America and my dislike for Communism. When the opportunity arose to work on the Rosenberg prosecution, I felt that my overdue moment had arrived. Okay, the prosecution side were not complete strangers, my father put Irving Kaufman on the bench, and I got him the Rosenberg case, which he lobbied for like you wouldn't believe, and once he got it he never stopped complaining. Irving Kaufman was an impossible human being.

Anyway, with the Rosenbergs, you had this idea that Jews would be more willing to betray their country, and we all fought against that idea. Here you had the prosecutor Irving Saypol, me, and Judge Kaufman, all Jews, bringing in a conviction, and imposing the maximum penalty. No one was going to accuse the Jewish judge or the Jewish prosecutors of leniency or lack of vigilance.

Was that a consideration in the trial? Yes and no. It was a scrupulously fair trial, there was a perfect chain of evidence linking Klaus Fuchs with the Rosenbergs, David Greenglass, Morton Sobell, the cut-in-half Jello box—I knew the death sentence would be imposed because Judge Kaufman told me when he got the case that he was going to send Julius Rosenberg to the electric chair. (*Pause.*)

Okay, as far as Ethel Rosenberg is concerned . . . Kaufman always told people he prayed for guidance about the sentences, that's probably true. But. Besides asking God what to do, Irving used to call me from a phone booth next to the Park Avenue Synagogue. (*Ruminative*). In the courtroom, there was a phone I could use, out of sight of everybody walking through—and I told Judge Kaufman, which was certainly true, I said a criminal defendant reveals everything about himself in the courtroom. And if you watched her in the courtroom you could see Ethel Rosenberg was the strong one, Ethel Rosenberg got her brother David Greenglass started with the Young Communist League to begin with. She was the one who kept drilling him full of Communist propaganda. It was as obvious . . . as the nose on her face that Ethel Rosenberg was the queen bee of the whole hive . . . If Judge Kaufman had declined to execute Ethel because she was the mother of two small children, it would be basically a case of reverse sexism not that we had that term back then, saying a woman wouldn't be as much of a traitor, or as guilty as a man.

Well, that's ancient history, and I'm not gonna say now, looking back, I would do everything I did then the same way today . . . blah blah. But I've never felt the slightest qualm about the execution of the Rosenbergs, frankly. But to get back to the point I was getting to, and not to stray too far from the subject of families—maybe the Rosenbergs are an unfortunate example of one, since Ethel's own mother was eager to testify against her—among the Cohns, there was never any family schism during the McCarthy era or later on. As a lifelong bachelor whom luck has eluded in finding the right partner—I'm told the matchmakers have given up, but I haven't; anyway, Barbara Walters and I are going to get married when we're both sixty. At any rate, not having gotten married, I can say that the unconditional approval of my mother and father in those early career days was probably the main thing that kept me in one piece.

I wouldn't mind getting married, by the way, if there's anybody out there—who doesn't mind a halfway attractive guy in middle age—well, young middle age—

It's no wonder that supporters of the traditional family . . . family values . . . like those of us here, in this room . . . feel besieged in this period of women's lib and letting it all hang out, with male and female roles breaking down among the young, more and more couples living together outside wedlock . . . and all the more reason why organizations like yours need to send a message to the Carter Administration and the democratic Congress, and to the city councils of this city and other cities around the country. That message is being sent. In St. Paul, Minnesota, 54,101 against 31,689 voters to rescind the local Gay Rights ordinance. And the same pattern in Eugene, Oregon, and Dade County, as we've seen. In Wichita, Kansas, an overwhelming 29,402 votes against 6,153.

The lesson couldn't be more clear. The vast majority of people in this country are hard-working men and women who get engaged and marry and have children in the traditional pattern, the majority are not the liberal political establishment, the country club set and the martinis and the uh tennis matches on Saturday afternoon and all of that—the majority are the workers and the middle-class, the white-collar people, the blue-collar people, who are fed up with homosexuality and feminist lesbianism being rammed down their throats by the media every 15 seconds. It's a historically proven fact that a decline of masculinity and clearly defined sex roles as well as a tremendous increase in sodomy and other immoral practices always follows in the wake of a humiliating defeat or national catastrophe. The United States has suffered two very dramatic blows in the past years, one right after the other, that have eroded some of the bedrock of American family values. The first was the Vietnam disaster, where American boys were forced to fight in a foreign jungle with their hands tied behind their backs. Undermined by Washington and the TV reporters, the something-for-nothing peaceniks and rabble rousers, the leftist college professors, the Jane Fondas—I saw that god-damned piece of shi—pardon my English, I saw that piece of sleaze coming out of George Steinbrenner's hotel in Tampa in a fur coat, I guess she forgot her black pajamas at home for a change. Hanoi Jane, and her commie husband Tom Hayden. They're both climbing into the back of a stretch Lincoln. Yeah. The Jane Fondas, the Abbie Hoffmans, the flag-burners, the Vanessa Redgraves with their pro-PLO terrorist propaganda, the communist sympathizers all across the board. They won't stoop to support America, but America supports them, in a lifestyle most people can't even dream about. There's Hanoi Jane in her god-damned feature-length mink at the Super Bowl!

The main point is, the war was opposed by people with an unsympathetic point of view towards strong patriotism, and they were able to demoralize the American public through the media.

The second blow was the Watergate brouhaha. Which, partly because of the mass media's enjoyment of playing God after Vietnam, permitted the Democratic congress to railroad Nixon out of the White House for a third-rate burglary he had nothing to do with, and which, on a scale of Presidential transgressions, would have to rank on a par with short-changing the milkman, compared to some of the things every Democratic president from FDR to LBJ has done.

These two blows to America's self-esteem and confidence opened the floodgates to every malcontent with a grudge against this country, from the Symbionese Liberation Front to the bra-burning feminists, the Kate Millet lezzies and the man-eating Ti-Grace Atkinsons and the Gloria Steinems—simple common sense has been chucked out the window.

Today you've got a society riddled with whining, professional victims. Naturally America has got her problems, you don't throw every race and nationality together in a big melting pot without a little friction. But to believe that contentious attitudes can be legislated away, presto chango with some type of magic wand, that's typical of the ultraliberal philosophy of the federal government as everybody's piggy bank.

As I've mentioned earlier, the Gay Rights Bill is unpopular. And more importantly, it's completely unpopular among the people it would affect—employers, landlords, school boards, and so forth. The people of this country don't want to hear about Adam and Steve's honeymoon. People do not want to hear about "lovers" and "longtime companions" and they especially don't want their children exposed to what these people do or don't do as so-called "consenting adults." Where does consent come in when you're acting under a compulsion? We don't talk about consenting psycho killers and consenting necrophiliacs will tell you off the record, homosexuals are basically men who for one reason or another are afraid of women, afraid of sexual relations with women, and afraid of mature relationships generally. In other words they're like children saying, along with Peter Pan, "I won't grow up," yet here they are demanding equal rights, and demanding that other people recognize them as "equal." Go into any neighborhood gathering place, any hardware store, any church basement, in New York any numbers parlor or corner saloon, and ask the common man what he thinks about so-called "gay people" teaching in the public schools and you'll be lucky if you get out of there without your clipboard wrapped around your neck. That's how the people of this country, and this city with all its vaunted liberalism, feel about this perversion of biology and nature. So Mayor Koch thinks he can swish his pen over a piece of Gracie Mansion letterhead and eliminate three thousand years of established sexual morality.

You know, it's personally quite ironic to me that the sob sisters going along with the Gay Rights Bill are the same pinkish Democrats that back in the '50s tried to smear that McCarthy Committee with suggestions that David Schine and myself, that we had some sort of . . . well, involvement, merely because we were both bachelors . . . suggestions about David and me—which were completely ridiculous, David Schine went on and got married to Miss Universe and had eight children. And anybody that knows anything about Roy Cohn knows there is nothing (*series of muffled words*) about me. (*Pause*) Whatever. I'm not afraid of women, I like women. David Schine liked women and still likes women, as for Joseph McCarthy he married his secretary.

There's a moral argument to be made as well. Take this set of facts. For two thousand years Christianity has considered homosexuality an abomination in the eyes of God. It's condemned in Leviticus and in Deuteronomy. I don't recall the exact quotes, but the Bible is explicit in saying if a man lieth with another man as if with a woman he shall be put to death, period, end of story.

Then we return to Jewish law, again, in three thousand recorded years of Jewish teaching, Jewish practice, not one single instance of any provision, any exemption, any suggestion of the legitimacy of a single homosexual relationship. Homosexuality is condemned pure and simple.

So in the moral code of the West, the Judeo-Christian code, we find absolutely no toleration of or excuses for homosexual behavior. It's licentious, it's venal, it's perverted, it's against nature.

You know, one person who was untiring in fighting this thing was Cardinal Spellman, god rest his soul. I had dinner with him last year in Provincetown, and he told me this homosexuality thing just broke his heart. They're sick, he told me, sick in spirit, sad people, and only Jesus himself can really free them from the chains of this perversion, and to see how many of them are turning their backs on Jesus just broke the Cardinal's heart. Now, this was a man of God talking, with all the compassion and wisdom of his cardinalship. He didn't hate the gays, far from it. Neither do I, I feel sorry for them. I sincerely do. Kitty—Cardinal Spellman even counseled these kids, troubled teenagers from broken homes who get mixed up in child prostitution and so forth. Breaks your heart, the way the old ones prey on the young and so on.

This gay lib business can be traced back. 1951, the foundation of an organization called the Mattachine Society. Interestingly and perhaps significantly, this first American homo organization was founded by a Communist named Harry Hay.

June 1969—the vicious Stonewall Riots in which various transvestites or female impersonators upset over Judy Garland's death threw garbage cans at the police and set police cars on fire. Next homosexual groups such as the Gay Liberation Front who made a relentless assault on the American Psychiatric Association, to force them to drop homosexuality as a psychiatric disorder. Which the APA officially did in 1973, after years of intimidation, disruption of its annual meetings, et cetera. This has to be the first and only time in the history of medicine that a disease disappeared from the official vocabulary through the demands of people suffering from it.

Next gay radicals espoused a strategy called coming out of the closet, meaning to make a very dramatic public declaration of their homosexuality, showing off what they do in private, with the female names for men, the limp wrists, the swishery, the various signals by which homosexuals recognize each other, to say nothing about the lezzie girls in their tuxedos and cigars, all the while bringing a lot of pressure on people responsible for public policy.

I can hear howls of protest from the radicals if they ever heard me say this, but in fact, a homosexual who doesn't draw attention to his private behavior in some obnoxious way is not gonna encounter any discrimination. Now that idea comes straight from the *Village Voice*, strange to say, by a writer named Jeff Greenfield who is way to the left of me or you but obviously still has a shred or two of common sense. Gays are not the only people condemned to behave one way in public and another way in private. All of us check some of our habits at the door when we enter the public arena.

Isn't that the whole issue in a nutshell? A black person doesn't choose to be black, a woman is obviously a woman—all right. They can't hide what they are, or change it. So if people discriminate against them—well, it's wrong, a lot of the time. But a drug addict, on the other hand, very much like the gays, the drug addict indulges in behavior abhorred by the majority. So the gays have a responsibility, if they refuse to seek help to change their behavior, which is done, I'm told, with electrical shocks, the gays can be made normal, but okay. If they refuse, the least, the least they can do is act in a way that doesn't draw attention to themselves, or else bring down the wrath of the community.

New York is a melting pot, yes, but let's not forget, it's a melting pot of families. Of Italians and Irish and Jews and Catholics, of Puerto Ricans and Germans and Russians. I think we'd all agree that one place where unusual personal habits have to be checked at the door is the classroom. And there, I really believe, the parents of America have every right to demand that no homosexual phase on their way to maturity, and that's exactly when they're the most vulnerable to seduction by an older person. If the gays can get at our children when they're most susceptible to the virus of homosexuality, we risk an exponential increase of inversion in this country that will amount to a plague-like epidemic.

Only people like you and me, ladies and gentlemen, can stop this obnoxious influence from spreading through and polluting America's school systems, corrupting our young, and ruining the fabric of a great nation.

I'm a New Yorker by birth and as long as there is a Roy Cohn, there's one New Yorker who intends to stand up for American values and American beliefs.

I know you all here feel the way I do, and I hope that now you'll join me in singing my favorite song. I hope it's your favorite song too. Written by Irving Berlin. Let's all sing "God Bless America."

1992; *Last Seen Entering the Biltmore: Plays,*
Short Fiction, Poems 1975–2010, 2010

Richard Prince
(b. 1949)

Born in the Panama Canal Zone in 1949, Richard Prince grew up in Massachusetts, played basketball and golf, and attended college in Maine. As a young artist he worked nights for Time-Life *in the tear sheets department where he began making artworks of re-photographed photography. Prince has been writing as long as he has been making art, and his 1980 exhibition at the CEPA Gallery in Buffalo was accompanied by the publication of his book* Menthol Pictures. *He became a key figure in the "Pictures Generation" group during his time with Metro Pictures gallery. He is famed for his cowboys, joke paintings, celebrities, car hoods, check paintings, and nurse paintings, among many other modes. Prince has written many essays and stories, published numerous books (including* Why I Go to the Movies Alone *and* Wild History*), owned bookstores, and now is a publisher through his company Fulton Ryder. "The Velvet Well" is excerpted from* Why I Go to the Movies Alone. *His* Collected Writings, *edited by Kristine McKenna, was published in 2011.*

The Velvet Well

MAGAZINES, MOVIES, TV, and records. It wasn't everybody's condition, but to him it sometimes seemed like it was; and if it really wasn't, that was alright, but it was going to be hard for him to connect with someone who passed himself off as an example or a version of a life put together from reasonable matter.

He had already accepted these conditions, and built out of their givens, and to him what was given was anything public, and what was public was always real. He transported these givens to a reality more real than the condition he first accepted. He was never too clever, too assertive, too intellectual . . . essentially too decorative. He had a spirit that made it easier to receive than to censor.

His own desires had very little to do with what came from himself, because what he put out (at least in part), had already been out. His way to make it new was to *make it again*, and making it again was enough for him, and certainly, personally speaking, *almost* him.

HAVING FUN? They weren't sure.

IT WASN'T a misunderstanding about the feeling, or difficulty about how it could be appreciated. Nothing about shame, or like, hey, is this allowed, should we really be feeling this good? Nothing like that, or stupid, or anything. Just more like they were so keyed up about having Sex and being Serious that the amount of time funning never seemed sufficient, or quite substantial enough for them to form any kind of reasonable opinion about what fun was supposed to be anymore.

They wanted to be flexible. They wanted to be able to say yes, we've participated, we're acquainted with the emotion and have a pretty fair idea of how and why it exists, but aside from appearing happy, there was, in practice, only a slight commitment, and most of their energy was spent protecting their reservation and skepticism.

They understood, too, though, that if fun was rejected publicly, others might point to them and say their preoccupation with S & S made them dark and square and something to be turned out. So, if they knew they could trust you, that's when they'd come out and just say it, point blank . . . "Okay, out with it. If it was up to us, we'd rather have no part of fun."

They felt the sudden flux, an inflation, transitory . . . like being in love. A kind of swelling from fever. And, if it wasn't too much to ask, all they wanted to do was move at a reasonable pace, sounding along at a nice kind of idle . . . so maybe they could get on with their work and their lives.

For them, funning seemed to be another kind of pressure. An obligation they had come to expect as part of the routine. Something to be taken in doses. Part of the checks and balances. The good with the bad. Another factor to figure in what was prescribed to produce a healthy equilibrium.

It was suggested, too, that fun existed on the same coin as guilt, and if the pleasure of its purpose wasn't occasionally tossed and allowed to be "called" in the air . . . then the game could never begin, and sides could never be taken.

"Lighten up," was what they heard. "Don't be such stones."

They'd hear the dig out doing the shopping. Hear it in the supermarket. Sometimes right in the middle of the week. They would try to smile and sparkle and move down the aisle. One foot in front of the other. They tried. They stepped. They remembered to participate.

They did their bit and acted the part that was called for. Parts of the mood came back, like a view lit up by lightning. Slowly, carefully, as if egged on by some invisible sidekick, they managed to tickle themselves. And, if not exactly to death, then to an acceptable titter and gaffe.

Luckily for them, their having the requisite gullibility, simplicity, and tolerance for repetition made some of life's little jokes impossible to grow out of.

GOING OUT became as private as staying in. Performance became less public, or at least less visible in public, and unless you were a lucky stiff, the witnessing of a natural sequence in light was pretty unlikely. Anything seen in person was probably, at best, received, rumored, or whispered . . . usually by word of mouth (from ear to ear). And, the source of the telling was either confessing under pressure, or bragging and boasting, acting like a big cheese . . . trying to negotiate a brownie point for, say, passage out of the city.

There were two markets. Black and box office. And, if one wasn't, shall we say, discretely camouflaged . . . charged with an ability to adapt by distorting, then the percentage of looking real became cut in half, and the chances of being left out, possibly even terminated, doubled.

What this was about was "watch out." What was real was very real, and it wasn't all that unique to feel terrorized by the real thing. The game was ghost. And whoever became the least recognizable without totally disappearing got to go home.

He was almost there. Near the end. One step away from autonomy. He made sure that everything about him looked the same, and as natural as it had when he first appeared. He was the look generation, and the effect of his appearance was so unreal that his reality began to resemble a kind of virtuoso real . . . a very *real* Real capable of instamatic ambience.

HE WOULD go to the post office and stand in line. When it was his turn to go, he'd let the person behind him, the one second in line, go ahead first (ahead of him), he'd be first in line once again. As long as there was a line, he could be at the head of it, the next one to go.

Allowing those behind to go first was a way of testing his word against theirs. The performance was perfect, transparent, and if properly executed, undetectable. The appearance of politeness without budging an inch. Top dog without the bark. The absence of aggression in a position reserved for a breed apart. An enlightened master? Incredible! What could be better?

Fortunately, he was never perfect, at least when he tried, and on the second day he found himself standing alone just after lunch. When he was called he failed to move. When he was called again he stood firm and refused to step forward. Security was called and he was removed.

Offering himself as a scapegoat was one of the ways he liked to mock and criticize the tradition of romantic silence.

BEING HIP has usually been associated with being new, being "with it," onto something that's in before it's actually *in*, certainly onto something that's in before it's out.

The hipster has usually been associated with being a number, a hot card, something oddly independent, responsive to whatever circumstance he finds himself in, disaffiliated but sovereign to whatever turf he finds himself wise to. Impulsive and nomadic, he's the one without any of the problems that underscore a sudden change, a white shark, so to speak, easily navigating his environment in a smooth and offhanded way.

For him his fashion is more habit than reflex, the cool for the most part always put on, like a well-worn accessory, the play of it often supplemented with an affected and studied style.

Pretending to know anything like this is a terrible strain, but I'm afraid the manner of this thing, this sense of reserve, this type of definition and attitude, got to him early, got to him first through parents . . . *his* parents . . . and later, seconded by an older brother and sister in shifts!

The simultaneous pressures were not, he imagined, unlike spending time in a temporal inferno, a mendactic internment where he found himself being seriously fucked over.

Its anti-commercialism bore a striking resemblance to vows of voluntary poverty, an issue he thought truly emotionless and amoral, and fought hard to undermine.

But his parents and his brother and sister were obsessed by the concoctives of modern living. The canon of their convictions seemed sacred. Their laws, natural ones, instructive and unspoken . . . with rites of passage not to be shrugged off or meddled with.

Early on these conditions were breathed, *mentholated*. It was difficult to do otherwise, its rap was passed around the house like a container of shampoo. There wasn't much one could do, it had always been there, it was there from the beginning, and he was helpless to its charge, being a kid, and impressionable and unformed.

Even after, when he was a teenager, the finer elements of its verse, especially its cynicism, came to be unconsciously absorbed. At times the "cool" seemed unapproachable, as if the particulars were ordained, and only those few who truly sacrificed on all occasions could discipline the gestures into posture.

But mostly, he found its instruction prehistoric, and in time he secretly subverted its registration from imprinting its mark permanently, knowing somehow its brand would burn deep into his hide, and telegraph a sign, the kind of sign they put on cattle and slaves.

It was for shit and it was hard to figure out, but those assholes had given up on the idea of being human, and everything they thought was theirs got hit on to do the same.

THEY WERE never sure why, when the names of the great '50s artists were mentioned, Rod Serling's name wasn't included. To them
it wasn't a question of inclusion, or even nomination: Serling was by
far the most entertaining of the bunch, and it seemed wrong that his
work was not regarded with the respect they felt it deserved.

They hoped that it was just a misunderstanding, a question of time,
that perhaps along with the other so-called "commercial" artists, the
new producers might one day get a good dose of romanticism before
the official fiction . . . what usually came to be called *history*, would
be written.

THEY WERE always impressed by the photographs of Jackson Pollock,
but didn't particularly think much about his paintings, since painting
was something they associated with a way to put things together that
seemed to them pretty much taken care of.

They hung the photographs of Pollock right next to these new
"personality" posters they just bought. These posters had just come
out. They were black-and-white blowups . . . at least thirty by forty
inches.

The photographs of Pollock were what they thought Pollock was
about. And this kind of take wasn't as much a position as an attitude,
a feeling that an abstract painter, a TV star, a Hollywood celebrity, a
president of a country, a baseball great, could easily mix together . . .
and whatever measurements used to distinguish their value would
be done away with . . .

I mean, it seemed to them that Pollock's photographs looked pretty
good next to Steve McQueen's, next to JFK's, next to Vince Edwards',
next to Jimmy Piersall's, and so on . . .

THEY WERE used to seeing things cropped, with the scene or the
image up close and filling up the whole frame . . . making whatever
was there "larger than life" . . . making it a lot more than what it was
supposed to be.

This particular way of looking at what was inside was nothing new, and the effect of this experience was only questioned by those few who still couldn't come to terms with the idea of substitute or surrogate relationships.

Sometimes they found themselves "falling for," and thought maybe what was outside was as good as, or even better than, what was presented inside the crop. It happened, the trip-up did occasionally occur, but when it did, they were the first to admit to their foolish curiosity.

They should have known better, but after they had seen the commercial for the Bronx Zoo they said, "Let's go! It looks incredible!"

There was no hesitation, and looking back it's difficult to determine who to blame for that kind of absence of mind. The "fall" was pretty much like giving in to the temptation of a velvet well, and the "go for it" pitch of the entire advertising industry made sense, that Bud . . . that zoo for them.

Polar bears jumping and splashing in arctic waters. Gorillas swinging from cages and beating chests. The monorail safari train, and the promise of an Arabian night on a Bedouin camel. Bengal tigers prowling around in the open wilds. The tom-tom drama of the African jungle. One began to wonder if Johnny Shefield, the original boy in *Tarzan*, might be tied up somewhere in an unspeakable pygmy punishment machine.

As it turned out, of course, the only punishment was standing in lines with mobs of New York natives waiting patiently to see each attraction. Three to four deep, standing outside the houses of reptiles and birds and fish.

The safari train was filled with families and screaming babies. The elephants were swaying from side to side in neurotic replay. The only large gorilla refused to emerge from his little cement hut, knowing full well that dominance in *Planet of the Apes* was light-years away.

The tiger that had been so beautifully presented in the ad (a nice, tight head shot), was camouflaged and buried under leaves not less than a football field away!

The polar bear looked stuffed, and the lions were locked up. The rhinos moved around with about as much viciousness as a herd of contented cows.

Well, what could they say? An honest mistake? Nobody's fault? Could've happened to anyone? Sure, of course . . . it happens. No hard feelings . . .

They still liked the ad. They still stopped and pointed to it, and joked about what came to mind when it came over the TV . . .

There . . . you see . . . you had to have been there to believe it. You gotta see it to believe it. You should've been there. There's more to it than meets the eye. The naked eye. Ain't nothing like the real thing. Can I get a witness? Show me, I'm from Missouri. Live. *It's Saturday Night*. Wow, I could've had a *V-8* . . .

RECENTLY THERE'VE been a lot of articles and talk about book burnings. Books, pamphlets, periodicals, pornography . . . fuel for the new bonfires. People burning *The Adventures of Tom Sawyer*, burning *Tom Jones*, too. The fear of Tom and Becky, and the fear of the other Tom, his genitals, mostly. The fear of his "equipment" moving slow and subtle, like a real enemy.

Last week when he bought the newspaper there was a *Pleasure Magazine* right next to the paper on the stand. On the cover of the magazine, right out there on the street, out in the open, was a picture of a naked girl with pink breasts, and three titles to articles inside, pasted up over the girl's head.

The titles to the articles were *Ram It Up My Ass*, *Suck My Open Hole*, and *Huge Latex Rod*. They were printed in big, bold, bright yellow letters.

Suck My Open Hole. It startled him. He remembers laughing and saying to himself, *come on* . . .

He didn't know what to think. His reaction was mixed. It took him by surprise. He didn't particularly like what he saw. But he was fascinated by how extreme it was.

He really didn't know what to do, you know? Stand still. Set the fire. Wait. Walk away. *Buy it.* What are you supposed to do with that kind of take?

He thought it was kind of like saying to someone, okay, step over this line if you want to fight, and the someone does, and you step back and draw another line.

ONE OF the things they liked about this place was a particular type of density. The kind of density tempered for the most part by diversity. The source of this fabric was hard to define, but getting to its ingredients was becoming a lot easier, and hopefully, the continued availability of these ingredients would make some conditions less restricted, and maybe even help establish workable redistributions to make things less conflicted and more even.

The best of this place has always been the variety, and, at least up until now, there had existed the possibility of choice; even though the catch to the possibility was mostly a promise.

The promise of diversity had in some ways existed literally, but mostly its existence was a notion, something that looked good on paper. The implications of choice as an availability in reality, of course, could spell disaster for those traditionally desiring, or already in, a position of power. A chicken in every pot was a political ploy, and in a real sense, had as much chance of becoming a reality as fingering a wish on a wishbone. And, up until now, the practice of such a spread happened only in various forms, and only then because they were affordable.

Anyway, they assumed such control was understood, and perhaps, with the tradition of power always shifting about, the fall-out from the technological competition would continue to be available and not become an elected or fixed or licensed privilege.

Access to information, as well as access to the software that sent and received the information, was a concern. The independent, the "mom and pop" brand of business, had suddenly reappeared, and in communications, of all places. Technology, unlike industry, had the enormous advantage of being domestically centered, and the translationships being produced as a result of this access and location would, no doubt, redefine the idea of "home-made."

The new cottage industry probably wouldn't last, but who could say? People in power were always screwing up, and sometimes had a whole lot of trouble keeping a lid on the techy, the science nerd, the gadget man . . . the stranger with the thick glasses . . . making sure they didn't slip away and turn outlaw.

HE LIKED to think of himself as an audience, and located himself on the other side of what he and others did . . . looking back at it, either by himself or with a group, hoping to exchange an emotion that was once experienced only as an author . . . an exchange he willingly initiated for reasons he felt necessary . . . necessary because he knew if he didn't make the switch from author to audience he could never say, "I second that emotion."

Being the audience, or part of one, was for him a way to identify himself physically, and a way to perceive rather than affect . . . a way to share with others what might be described as a kind of impossible or promissory non-fiction. A way to see or realize what essentially was a surface with public image, a surface that was once speculative and ambitious, as something now referential and ordinary. Referential because the image's authority existed outside his own touch, and ordinary because its frequency of appearance could be corroborated by persons other than himself.

"You don't have to take my word for it," he would say, as if defending against a cross-examination . . . "These pictures are more than available, and unless you've been living in an alley, inside an ash-can, wrapped up in a trash liner (with the cover closed), chances are better than even that you've seen them too."

SHE ALWAYS sounded like she actually knew what she was talking about. And this certainly wasn't the kind of presumption he was interested in rediscovering right now. His deal was about almost knowing but not quite . . . preferring not to care to know the little extra, even if he could . . . somehow knowing that that, too, wouldn't be quite true anyway.

She would say something like, "Yes, that sounds generous," and make a little noise, and disappear into a room before he could voice his objections.

She needed clear beginnings and endings, and the idea of feeling reassured with a version of what appeared to be the truth seemed to her almost unfriendly.

What they said to each other about this was, of course, political. And their decision to talk about themselves to each other while talking about "versions" was a big, *monster* mistake. The mistake made it easier to remember that the other (each of them), was a separate person, and that particular fact should have been the other way around. They should've tried to see themselves as almost the same person, and if they couldn't, they should at least deny their differences or try to avoid bringing them up.

They should've been in on this thing together. In collusion. Almost like outlaws, holed-up, waiting for whatever they tried to pull off to die down, disappear, and be forgotten.

"The trouble is this," he said; "some of me is about feeling like I'm somebody else, and about the desires and threats in actually believing I can think about being someone besides what I already think I am." And she would say, right after, "Mine is about my ability to control my identity so I can deliberately undermine what is good for me, so maybe what I see and what I come to know will be too good to be true."

For him, the next best thing was still a condition far from being categorized, and the fidelity of a hands-off sensation. However painful the separation, it not only made sense, but was a way to manage what was always promised, no matter how desperately the promise was made.

She couldn't handle his sense and felt more comfortable qualifying what she received . . . wrapping it up, and sometimes separating what was good from bad with a little gold star.

She was on top of it and he was close. She was faithful and he was sophisticated. Her sense was one of conclusion, and his a shrewd agreement. The two senses were never shared, and the meaning of what that meant to both of them was anything but sensible.

In the end, she would accuse him of being jealous.

"You just don't like it that I'm good at pulling the rug out from under my own feet."

And he'd say, "Not true, I am just as good as you, and if you don't believe me, here, let me show you . . ."

HE's A thief. He steals. But he's generous.

"Without lifting a finger," he says . . . like a slogan, something he repeats so often it sounds like a law.

He goes to church and steals candles. He never panics. He's selective. He knows which ones to take.

"Not the ones already lit. They've been spoken for. Their history has been written by whoever made the flame and their light is to be respected. There are lines that cannot be crossed and this is one of them. Their light is an offering, a kind of ceremonial consultation between an image and its maker."

She didn't steal. She raised her hand and asked permission.

"Would you mind if I steal candles like you do?"

"Not at all," he said.

He hung up the phone and never spoke to her again. As far as he's concerned their affair is over, finished, impossible, and too stupid to begin again. She occasionally calls but he screens the calls. She should have known not to ask. There are things a thief doesn't ask permission for, and two of them are approval and blessing.

It was too bad. She thought the stealing was some kind of party. A birthday. She went to church. She made a wish. She took a breath. And made it dark.

He doesn't pray and he doesn't wish either. But now, every once in a while, he lights a candle for her, hoping it will be the one she takes. It's not what he wanted but it's what he has, and the matter between what he's got and what he doesn't is something that he finds painful to separate.

Perhaps even now his attempt at lighting a candle is more a settlement than a put-down. A coming to terms with cutting her off . . . a gesture for forgiveness. And when he wants to admit it, an effort to share what he steals . . . a way, his way, to stay for her, wanted and remembered.

1993; *Collected Writings*, 2011

Glenn O'Brien

I spent my life at magazines. Almost on arriving in New York I landed a gig editing Interview *at Andy Warhol's Factory. From there I went to* Rolling Stone, *where I too was too humorous, then to* Oui, Playboy's *experiment in new journalism which was too far from New York, then to* High Times *which was too far out, and to* Spin *which was too spun. But I managed to keep the writing going and met a lot of great writers, some of whom are represented here. I also managed to make a living in a world where art was becoming an investment and fashion was becoming artistic. "Beatnik Executives," which first appeared in* Verbal Abuse, *deals with the hipster's place in a corporate world with a "creative department."*

Beatnik Executives

I saw the best minds of my generation
depressed by lawsuits, dieting, sober, all dressed up,
limoing through the negro streets at dawn
looking for an angry member of the Screen Actors Guild.
Angelheaded hipsters renegotiating the social contract,
trying to rewrite the lease on life
and cool a world aflame.

We are beatnik executives and we are just doing our job.
It's the end of the world and we're selling the future
because our pitch is all that's left of it.

We are beatnik executives.
In the face of certain annihilation we say
we're open for business as usual
and the first thirty three customers receive
a complimentary get out of Bardo free card.

Glenn O'Brien

Earth is less than user friendly.
Heaven is closed for repairs.
Hell is overbooked.
So what's the alternative?
We are the alternative.
We are cool beatnik executives
and we are trying to fix the unfixable
and everything is broke.

Hey, let's get this show on the road.
What road?
The interstate?
Interstate is how I feel Jack.
Put her in overdrive and hit the fast lane Dean,
we've got to catch up on old times.
We've got to pass somebody
just to feel like we're standing still
and not backing up into whatever the hell is chasin' us.
We've got to stay ahead of the times
even though the times went thataway. Whichaway? Thataway.

Life is disappearing.
So what can we do about it?
Hey, let's sell it.
Maybe if we sell life itself people will place some value on it.
It's all in the pitch.
And I've got the pitch.
I am a beatnik ad man.
I'm selling a future just in case there is one.
I am young, younger than Pepsi
I am free, freer than Tampax.
I'm live from New York.
I'm a beatnik executive.
I've got bongos in my briefcase and when I wheel and deal

it's a wheel within a wheel and what a deal.
It's Chango that calls the shots
and when we say possession is nine tenths of the law
we mean possession.
And when the spirit enters my body
woe be to the client who tries
to pull the polyester over my eyes.

We are beatnik sales reps marketing fertility in the face of doom,
our expense accounts are deducted directly from our karma.
We are flaunting pleasure in the house of pain,
because if we can sell it maybe, maybe just maybe it will fly.
We are here to fathom the unfathomable and plan around it.
We're selling vision like it was real estate.
Want to buy a picture of the Brooklyn Bridge?

We are beatnik executives
and we are in Gnostic digging distance of the godhead.
I'll show you our flowchart and you'll see
that this corporation has Jah on the board of directors
and our prospectus is without end.

We are beatnik executives.
Lock up your daughters, we are coming to your town with
release forms.
We are beatnik executives.
Our entire organization is free lance.
Our meetings are phantom conclaves.
The jury is always out to lunch.
Don't ask me about my personal business.
I mind my business because my mind is my business.
My database is my art.
Judge me by my product and its reliability.

You have my word. It's the famous word that was in the
beginning, is now, and is backed by our legendary
moneyback guarntee.

We are the beatnik executives.
We wanted to take the easy way out.
And so we did. And here we are. And isn't it fine?
Can we book you into the easy way out?
All it takes is a little hard work.
Inspiration will come later when you least expect it.
Have you met our corporate liaison Cody Pomeroy?
Cody heads up our group of dharma consultants.
Have you met Dr. Benway our man in R & D?
The streets are our laboratory and this week we're test marketing
a condom inscribed with the Mayan Codices.
We believe it might be possible to fuck your way back to 3000 BC.
For the prevention of disease only.

We are the beatnik executives.
Anybody can drop out of society.
But it takes a disciplined organization to drop society out.
And so, blowing gage and roller blading down the corridors
of power, we're getting our kicks on route 666.
We're changing the rules.
We're making business a pleasure.
Stalinist art students may say our advertising is immoral
but we don't want to live in a world without fine Italian
restaurants and firm mattresses.
We are here to change the world from the top to bottom.
We'll start at the top thank you.
We learned that trick from the painters.

We are the beatnik executives.
Step into our private elevator.
No that's not Muzak that's John Coltrane, a Love Supreme.
I want to show you the view from our penthouse headquarters.
I want to outline our plans and show you the bottom line.
We're a corporation with a message.
And the message is crazy, man, crazy.
The message is farout. Dig.

I'm a beatnik executive.
I don't want to drop out. I did that already.
I want to turn on, tune out and drop in baby.
We're the drop in generation.
We can turn this thing around.
We can change the course of history just by switching
the road signs
and that's why our salesmen are always on the road.
What road?
The interstate?
Interstate is our mode of existence.
I'm not comfortable unless I'm in two places at once.

We're beatnik executives.
We've got a finger on the pulse and we're gonna quicken it.
We're going to drop straight to the top.
So maybe he can't inhale.
We're putting the president on an IV drip and teaching him
hard bop straight from the Bird, Charlie Parker appearing
as the holy spirit.
A beatnik president? Why not?
We haven't had one since Lester Young.

We are the beatnik executives.
Our values are visions and our neckties are art.
We can turn this company around like about face Daddy-o.
Let's talk about quality. Let's talk about production.
Let's talk about cornering the market on cool
and putting it in every home in America, can you dig that?

This may be the land of the dead,
but it's a living, man, it's a living.
Hey Buddy, this Buddha's for you.

Verbal Abuse, Summer 1993

Emily XYZ
(b. 1958)

Emily XYZ is a New York poet who lives to perform and I was always delighted by her poetry readings with co-reader, actress Myers Bartlett. Few poets today use the power of voice to make words come alive, and that's what this act is all about. Live, on stage. They tend to bring the house down with two-voice poems such as "Jimmy Page Loves Lori Maddox," "Separation of Church and State," and "Sinatra Walks Out."

Sinatra Walks Out   (for 2 voices)

The bars close and Sinatra walks out	
just a man in a hat and a trenchcoat	
A standing ovation always follows	
He is a terminal delinquent in a bad mood	Because he is such an incredible entertainer
A temper tantrum over three generations	An inspiration to three generations
Age has not mellowed nor time sweetened him	
He is the greatest of them all	He is the greatest of them all
	He is the living embodiment of the fine tradition of macho American overkill
He is the last man I want to	
applaud	sleep with
The opposite of Andy Warhol is Frank Sinatra	The opposite of Andy Warhol is Frank Sinatra
Irredeemably corny	
violent heavy-handed and horny	
He is all/He is nothing at all	
You cannot make jokes about	You cannot make jokes about
Frank Sinatra	Frank Sinatra
	Some say he sings like a dream

and gives
voice to emotions most men
don't even know they have   can never admit to
moved me to tears   that tie up the heart
night I met my first wife   or break it in pieces
Some say he speaks for men   Some say he speaks for men
men unable to speak   men unable to speak
unfortunate men of the 20th century   unfortunate men of the 20th
                                   century
trapped in ridiculous cages   trapped in ridiculous cages
cages they never imagined   cages they never imagined
cages of their own making   cages of their own making
                                   Some say he belongs in prison,
                                   him and his mob connections
                                   You know what they say,
                                   but nothing was proven.
In the 50s, his cloven hooves   In the 50s, his cloven hooves
marked up many a bandstand—Critics said   marked up many a bandstand
QUIT—   QUIT
Hit it!

                                   Who does he think he is?
Sicilian   Overly sensitive
Sicilian   Split personality
Sicilian   Schizy,
Sicilian   scary,
Jilly Rizzo   Jilly Rizzo
                                   alcohol/alcohol
blood/blood alcohol content   alcohol content/alcohol content
blood brotherhood   rat pack
WNEW AM 11–3–0   Radio City Music Hall
Nelson Riddle   Jimmy Van Heusen
Axel Stordahl   Johnny Mercer
Earl Wilson   Harold Arlen
Jule Styne   William B. Williams
Sammy Cahn   Sam Giancana
Sammy Davis Jr.   Cole Porter
Toots Shor—   Toots Shor—
He likes it when people call him a
class act   class act
it confirms his own opinion,

If he is misunderstood,
it is because he is
confusing
This fabulous gift
stored in the case of such a
troubled man—Sad.
Got a telegram from Sinatra/Here's what it says:

don't talk to me baby you're

not in my league, not in my league
where you where you wear you wear you wear

The way you wear your hat/The way you sip your tea

The memory of all that, oh no they can't

take that away from me, the way your smile

just beams/The way you sing off key

The way you haunt my dreams

Oh no they can't take that away from me

We may never never meet again on that

bumpy road to love/Still I'll always keep

the memory of—

TRAMP

(SING:)
Strangers in the night/exchanging glances
wondering in the night
what were the chances

If he is misunderstood,
it is because he is
an asshole
Your fabulous face always
grimacing at reporters—
Don't make me laugh!

Your information stinks lady
broads always think they know
best
don't they don't talk to me baby
you're not in my league,
not in my league
where'd you get that
information you're
a leech, man you're a
parasite just like the
rest of them get it, cunt
C-U-N-T you know
what that who what that is
don't you been
laying down for that two dol
lars all your
life that stench you that
stench you smell is
coming from her! I don't
want to talk to
you go home you go home and
take a bath
let's get the hell outta
here baby you're
nothin but a TRAMP.
In a dream, Sinatra is awakened
by 20-year-old Mia Farrow
as the ghost of his own past.

She comes in the night
praises his phrasing
His voice clear of vibrato

we'd be sharing love
before the night was through

natural as conversation
melodious and cool is restored.
She shows him Pearl Jam
She shows him Nirvana
and he slams them
and when he slams them,
everybody says

WELL, FRANK'S RIGHT!
ROCK N ROLL DOES SUCK

WELL, FRANK'S RIGHT!
ROCK N ROLL DOES SUCK

Somehow the past feels like
a better place/A place where Ava Gardner

a better place/A place where
Ava Gardner

bakes coconut cakes
a place without an Elvis
a world of his own
where all men are equal brutal
insufferable laughable

bakes coconut cakes
a place without an Elvis
a world of his own
where he is the leader
postwar Las Vegas mafia
royalty

childish homophobe RICH

Hollywood underworld RICH
The 60s that the rest of us
remember
are as a little museum to
Frank Sinatra

a small curious place
where Viet Nam and Watts

a small curious place
where Viet Nam and Watts
play constantly in a silent
loop on the video monitor

and there's a box
containing Pink Floyd
Eldridge Cleaver Bernadette Devlin
everything Mark Rudd ever said

and there's a box
containing the Stones, Hendrix
Dennis Hopper Malcolm McDowell
and the whole Stax Volt catalog,
all incomprehensible to Frank.
Only thing in the whole
decade makes any sense to
him is Mrs. Robinson's
stockinged legs—

those he understands.
Back from engagements beyond the grave,
old friends visit Sinatra backstage

those he understands.

Sammy Davis Jr. falls on him weeping/Tells him
Baby you're the Chairman of the Board   Baby you're the Chairman of the Board

Joe E. Lewis is glad to be back
He says Vegas is better than heaven   He says Vegas is better than heaven

Deeper cleavage and lots more booze
Opens a bottle/here's to the boys
They don't notice/the club is closing
They don't notice/the passing of time
because they're drunk   because their wives
because they're has-beens   because their hormones
because they're famous   because their fans
because they're boys   because they're drunk
                                                         but you know somthin
                                                         way I see it

The real problem is mortality   The real problem is mortality
The real problem is nothing lasts   The real problem is you get old and die

Gotta grow up sometime/Life is short   Gotta go sometime/Time is short

songs finish   beauty vanishes
God plays dice in this casino right here   God knows why this world's the way it is

The real problem is body and soul don't mix   The real problem is life doesn't make sense
                                                         WHY DON'T YOU JUST SHUT UP AND SING

The boundaries of good taste and human
decency having been crossed and crossed out
again and again by the bourbon in his
glass,   bloodstream
Frank Sinatra stands and offers a toast:

                                                         To the human race

To the human race
To hell with the human race!   To hell with the human race!
Nancy with the laughing face   Bunch of buck and a half hookers,
what has she ever done for me!   what have they ever done for me!

Emily XYZ

All you mothers are worthless—
There's nobody in my league!

Mr. Sinatra,
how can anyone so wretched
sing so well?

All you mothers are worthless—
There's nobody in my league!
Placing myself on his good side I
raise my hand to ask a question:
Mr. Sinatra,
how can anyone so wretched
sing so well?
Well he says
I'm not the first
and I won't be the last
one born
a walking contradiction,
dead on from the heart
the rest all thrown together,
hitting the same walls
over and over and over—

A person is only a case
A holder for all manner of things
A random arrangement of idiocy and glory
Sometimes a barrage of artistic light
Sometimes an embarrassment,
a dismaying puddle of slush
Sometimes a nobody,
fading into the crowd or the distance
the welfare office
the supermarket
the laundromat, the library
and sometimes
marvelous as a god,
all in one
all in one lifetime
all in one life.

Doo be doo be doo . . .

For Virgil Moorefield

Verbal Abuse, Summer 1993

457

Eric Bogosian
(b. 1953)

In the nineties we found ourselves in a weird place, with poetry as we had known it dissolving before our very ears, morphing into stand-up comedy, often of a faux self-deprecating confessional variety. Quite unhip. We were rescued, however, by of all things performance art and such solo performers as Ann Magnuson, Spalding Gray, Karen Finley, and Eric Bogosian. Mr. Bogosian is also a playwright. His Talk Radio *was made into a movie directed by Oliver Stone and starring the author. He has acted in many films and played one of television's most beloved cops on* Law & Order: Criminal Intent.

America

A silhouette against the back wall of the theater reveals a man speaking into a microphone. We hear a basso profundo radio voice à la Rush Limbaugh.

I WAS SHAVING this morning. Shaving with a disposable razor and suddenly I thought of my *Dad*. I wondered, "What would I be doing right now, if it were forty years ago? If it wasn't 1994, but 1954 and I'm my own Dad?" And I imagined myself going downstairs, and there's my wife and she's not racing to meet the *car pool, no,* she's making me *breakfast*. She's got a gingham apron on, she's making me bacon and eggs . . . which I eat with tremendous pleasure because I've never even *heard* of cholesterol before.

And here are my children sitting at my 1954 breakfast table and they're well-behaved and well-dressed. In fact, my son is wearing a *necktie. I'm* wearing a necktie. I pick up the morning newspaper—all the news is *good*: we've won the war in Korea, they've found a cure for polio, employment's up, housing's up, everybody's *happy.*

I own my own home, I own my own car (which I wash every single Saturday), I love my wife, I like baseball, I believe in the President, and I pray to God in a place called *church*. No drugs. No drugs *anywhere*. Only people doing drugs in 1954 are William Burroughs and Allen Ginsberg!

No one's *complaining*. We're not hearing about women's rights and homosexual *rights* and minorities' rights and immigrants' rights. No *victims*. No sexual *harassment*. No worries about the environment. The environment is just fine, thank you.

No therapists. No twelve-step groups. No marches on Washington. No homeless people. No *AIDS*. Just good old-fashioned values like honesty and hard work and bravery and fidelity. And that's *it*. It's America forty years ago. Everybody's working. Everybody's straight. Everybody's happy.

And I thought to myself, what a wonderful world that must have been, a world without problems. I would love to be there right *now*. And then I remembered a *terrible* nightmare I'd had last night.

Now lemme tell you about this nightmare: It's the middle of the night, I'm in bed, of course, who shows up in my bedroom but *Bill Clinton*. As I said, it's a nightmare. He takes my hand and he says, "Come with me." And we float out the window and into the night air, and down to the street and we drop into this open manhole.

And we're walking around in the sewers, Bill and I. I'm thinking, I never trusted this guy, where's he taking me?

We walk and we walk and we come to this big cave and in this cave there are all these people lying around on mattresses, smoking things: pot, crack, hashish, opium. Whatever these people smoke.

And through the haze, I see all these familiar faces! Oh, there's Whoopi Goldberg reading the *Communist Manifesto*. And there's Ralph Nader bitching about something. And Susan Sarandon and Tim Robbins leading a peace rally. And Roseanne Arnold having sex with Madonna. And Ice T and Ice Cube and Vanilla Ice and all the other pieces of ice and all the other *troublemakers* and *commies* and *lefties* and people with green hair and tattoos and goatees and rings through their noses and rings through their nipples and rings through their penises.

And some of them are marching around protesting something ... there's another bunch of them counting their food stamps and *welfare checks*. Right in front of me a bunch of idiots are watching *Beavis and Butt-head* on MTV.

And I'm horrified. And I turned to Bill and I said, "Bill, where are we? I'm frightened." And he said, "Don't you know?" And I said, "No. Hell?" And he laughed and he said, "No, of course not! This isn't Hell. Look around you. Don't you recognize the place? This is America, 1994! Better get used to it."

Let's go to a commercial.

Pounding Nails in the Floor with My Forehead, 1994

George Carlin
(1937–2008)

It seems appropriate to end with a comedian. Comedy has always represented the front lines. It doesn't just sit there in its comfy coffee shop, it gets up in front of louts, drunks, and hecklers and challenges them to a mental fight. Well, great comedy like that of Lord Buckley, Lenny Bruce, and Mort Sahl did. It picked up where the poets left off, with the facts. In 1966 Lenny Bruce was arrested for using nine specific words. Seven of them appear in George Carlin's "Seven Words You Can Never Say on Television" routine, which wound up figuring prominently in a test case before the Supreme Court. As a result of that decision you will hear "motherfucker" on the radio only between 10 P.M. and 6 A.M., unless it's a hip-hop station that the FCC can't understand.

A Modern Man

I'm a modern man,
digital and smoke-free;
a man for the millennium.

A diversified, multi-cultural,
post-modern deconstructionist;
politically, anatomically and ecologically incorrect.

I've been uplinked and downloaded,
I've been inputted and outsourced.
I know the upside of downsizing,
I know the downside of upgrading.

I'm a high-tech low-life.
A cutting-edge, state-of-the-art,

bi-coastal multi-tasker,
and I can give you a gigabyte in a nanosecond.

I'm new-wave, but I'm old-school;
and my inner child is outward-bound.

I'm a hot-wired, heat-seeking,
warm-hearted cool customer;
voice-activated and bio-degradable.

I interface with my database;
my database is in cyberspace;
so I'm interactive, I'm hyperactive,
and from time to time I'm radioactive.

Behind the eight ball, ahead of the curve,
ridin' the wave, dodgin' the bullet,
pushin' the envelope.

I'm on point, on task, on message,
and off drugs.

I've got no need for coke and speed;
I've got no urge to binge and purge.

I'm in the moment, on the edge,
over the top, but under the radar.

A high-concept, low-profile,
medium-range ballistic missionary.

A street-wise smart bomb.
A top-gun bottom-feeder.

I wear power ties, I tell power lies,
I take power naps, I run victory laps.

I'm a totally ongoing, big-foot, slam-dunk
rainmaker with a pro-active outreach.

A raging workaholic, a working rageaholic;
out of rehab and in denial.

I've got a personal trainer,
a personal shopper,
a personal assistant,
and a personal agenda.

You can't shut me up;
you can't dumb me down.

'Cause I'm tireless, and I'm wireless.
I'm an alpha-male on beta-blockers.

I'm a non-believer,
I'm an over-achiever;
laid-back and fashion-forward.
Up-front, down-home;
low-rent, high-maintenance.

I'm super-sized, long-lasting,
high-definition, fast-acting,
oven-ready and built to last.

A hands-on, footloose, knee-jerk head case;
prematurely post-traumatic,
and I have a love child who sends me hate-mail.

But I'm feeling, I'm caring,
I'm healing, I'm sharing.
A supportive, bonding, nurturing
primary-care giver.

My output is down, but my income is up.
I take a short position on the long bond,
and my revenue stream has its own cash flow.

I read junk mail, I eat junk food,
I buy junk bonds, I watch trash sports.

I'm gender-specific, capital-intensive,
user-friendly and lactose-intolerant.

I like rough sex; I like tough love.
I use the f-word in my e-mail.
And the software on my hard drive
is hard-core—no soft porn.

I bought a microwave at a mini-mall.
I bought a mini-van at a mega-store.
I eat fast food in the slow lane.

I'm toll-free, bite-size, ready-to-wear,
and I come in all sizes.

A fully equipped, factory-authorized,
hospital-tested, clinically proven,
scientifically formulated medical miracle.

I've been pre-washed, pre-cooked, pre-heated,
pre-screened, pre-approved, pre-packaged,

post-dated, freeze-dried, double-wrapped
and vacuum-packed.

And . . . I have unlimited broadband capacity.

I'm a rude dude, but I'm the real deal.
Lean and mean.
Cocked, locked, and ready to rock;
rough, tough and hard to bluff.

I take it slow, I go with the flow;
I ride with the tide, I've got glide in my stride.

Drivin' and movin', sailin' and spinnin';
jivin' and groovin', wailin' and winnin'.

I don't snooze, so I don't lose.
I keep the pedal to the metal
and the rubber on the road.
I party hearty, and lunchtime is crunch time.

I'm hangin' in, there ain't no doubt;
and I'm hanging tough.
Over and out.

When Will Jesus Bring the Pork Chops?, 2004

Sources & Acknowledgments

Lester Bangs. How to Succeed in Torture Without Really Trying: *Psychotic Reactions and Carburetor Dung,* Greil Marcus, ed. Copyright © 1987 by The Estate of Lester Bangs. Used by permission of Alfred A. Knopf, a division of Random House, Inc.

Amiri Baraka (LeRoi Jones). The Screamers: *The Moderns: An Anthology of New Writing in America*; reprinted in *Tales* (New York: Grove Press, 1967). Used by permission of SLL/Sterling Lord Literistic, Inc. Copyright © 1967 by Amiri Baraka.

Eric Bogosian. America: *Pounding Nails in the Floor with My Forehead* (New York: Theatre Communications Group, 1994). Used by permission of Eric Bogosian.

Richard Brautigan. The Kool-Aid Wino: *Trout Fishing in America* (San Francisco: Four Seasons Foundation, 1967). Copyright © 1968 by Richard Brautigan. Used by permission of Houghton Mifflin Harcourt Publishing Company. All rights reserved.

Chandler Brossard. From *Who Walk in Darkness* (New York: New Directions, 1952). Used by permission of The Estate of Chandler Brossard.

Anatole Broyard. A Portrait of the Hipster: *Partisan Review*, June 1948; reprinted in *The Scene Before You: A New Approach to American Culture,* Chandler Brossard, ed., (New York: Rinehart and Co., 1955). Used by permission of The Estate of Anatole Broyard.

Lenny Bruce. Pills and Shit: The Drug Scene: *The Essential Lenny Bruce,* John Cohen, ed., (New York: Random House, 1967). Copyright © 1967 Douglas Music Group. Used by permission. All rights reserved.

Lord Buckley. The Naz: *Hiparama of the Classics* (San Francisco: City Lights Books, 1960). Used by permission of City Lights Books.

William S. Burroughs. Last Words: *Nova Express.* Copyright © 1964 by William S. Burroughs. Used by permission of Grove/Atlantic, Inc.

George Carlin. A Modern Man: *When Will Jesus Bring the Pork Chops?* Copyright © 2004 by Comedy Concepts, Inc. Used by permission of Hyperion. All rights reserved.

Neal Cassady. Letter to Jack Kerouac, March 7, 1947: *The First Third & Other Writings: Revised and expanded edition* (San Francisco: City Lights Books, 1981). Used by permission of City Lights Books.

Del Close. Dictionary of Hip Words and Phrases: Del Close and John Brent, *How To Speak Hip*, Mercury Records, 1961.

Gregory Corso. Marriage: *The Happy Birthday of Death*. Copyright © 1960 by New Directions Publishing Corp. Used by permission of New Directions Publishing Corp.

Miles Davis with Quincy Troupe. From *Miles: The Autobiography*. Copyright © 1989 by Miles Davis. Used by permission of Simon & Schuster, Inc. All rights reserved.

Diane di Prima. From *Memoirs of a Beatnik* (Paris: Olympia Press, 1969); reprinted by Last Gasp in 1988. Copyright © by Diane di Prima. Used by permission of Last Gasp.

Bob Dylan. From *Chronicles: Volume One*. Copyright © 2004 by Bob Dylan. Used by permission of Simon & Schuster, Inc. All rights reserved.

Babs Gonzales: From *I Paid My Dues: Good Times No Bread, A Story of Jazz* (East Orange, NJ: Expubidence Publishing Corp., 1967).

Brion Gysin. From *The Process* (New York: Doubleday, 1969). Copyright © 1969 by Brion Gysin. Published in 1987 by The Overlook Press, Peter Mayer Publishers, Inc., New York, NY. www.overlookpress.com. All rights reserved.

Bobbie Louise Hawkins. Frenchy and Cuban Pete: *Frenchy and Cuban Pete and Other Stories* (Bolinas, CA: Tombouctou, 1977). Used by permission of Bobbie Louise Hawkins.

Richard Hell. Blank Generation: *Hot and Cold: Essays Poems Lyrics Notebooks Pictures Fiction* (New York: powerHouse Books, 2001). Words and music by Richard Hell. Copyright © 1977 (renewed) Warner-Tamerlane Publishing Corp., Quick Silver Music, and Dilapidated Music. All rights administered by Warner-Tamerlane Publishing Corp. All rights reserved.

John Clellon Holmes. The Pop Imagination: *Nothing More to Declare* (New York: E. P. Dutton, 1967). Copyright © by John Clellon Holmes. Used by permission of SLL/Sterling Lord Literistic, Inc.

Herbert Huncke. Spencer's Pad: *The Evening Sun Turned Crimson* (New

York: Cherry Valley Editions, 1980). Used by permission of The Estate of Herbert Huncke.

Gary Indiana. Roy Cohn: *Last Seen Entering the Biltmore: Plays, Short Fiction, Poems 1975–2010* (New York: Semiotext(e), 2010). Used by permission of Semiotext(e).

Joyce Johnson. From *Minor Characters: A Beat Memoir.* Copyright © 1983, 1994 by Joyce Johnson. Used by permission of Penguin, a division of Penguin Group (USA) Inc., Joyce Johnson, and Irene Skolnick Literary Agency.

Bob Kaufman. Walking Parker Home: *Solitudes Crowded with Loneliness.* Copyright © 1965 by Bob Kaufman. Used by permission of New Directions Publishing Corp.

Jack Kerouac. The Origins of the Beat Generation: *Playboy*, June 1959. Copyright © 1959 by Jack Kerouac. Used by permission of SLL/Sterling Lord Literistic, Inc.

Seymour Krim. Making It!: *Views of a Nearsighted Cannoneer* (New York: Excelsior Press, 1961). Used by permission of The Estate of Seymour Krim.

Fran Landesman. The Ballad of the Sad Young Men: *The Nervous Set*, lyrics by Fran Landesman, music by Tommy Wolf, Columbia Records, 1959; reprinted in Fran Landesman, *The Ballad of the Sad Young Men and Other Verse* (Sag Harbor, NY: The Permanent Press, 1982). Used by permission of The Permanent Press.

Norman Mailer. The White Negro: Superficial Reflections on the Hipster: *Dissent*, Spring 1957; reprinted in *Advertisements for Myself* (New York: G. P. Putnam's Sons, 1959). Copyright © 1957 by Norman Mailer. Used by permission of The Wylie Agency LLC.

Gerard Malanga. Photos of an Artist as a Young Man: *Chic Death* (Cambridge, MA: Pym-Randall, 1971). Used by permission of Gerard Malanga.

Richard Meltzer. Luckies vs. Camels: Who Will Win?: *Gulcher: Post-Rock Cultural Pluralism (1649–1993)* (San Francisco: Straight Arrow Publishers; reprinted Carol Publishing Group, 1990). Used by permission of Richard Meltzer.

Mezz Mezzrow and Bernard Wolfe. If You Can't Make Money: *Really the Blues* (New York: Random House, 1946). Copyright © 1946, 1974 by Milton Mezzrow and Bernard Wolfe. Used by permission of Milton H. Mesirow, Miranda Wolfe and Jordon Wolfe.

Henry Miller. Soirée in Hollywood: *The Air–Conditioned Nightmare*. Copyright © 1945 by New Directions Publishing Corp. Used by permission of New Directions Publishing Corp.

Cookie Mueller. Abduction and Rape—Highway 31—1969: *Walking Through Clear Water In a Pool Painted Black* (New York: Semiotext(e), 1990). Used by permission of Semiotext(e).

Glenn O'Brien. Beatnik Executives: *Verbal Abuse* number 1, Summer 1993. Used by permission of Glenn O'Brien.

Frank O'Hara. The Day Lady Died: *Lunch Poems* (San Francisco: City Lights Books, 1964). Used by permission of City Lights Books.

Iris Owens. From *After Claude* (New York: Farrar, Straus and Giroux, 1973). Copyright © 1973 by Iris Owens. Used by permission of New York Review of Books.

Art Pepper and Laurie Pepper. Heroin: *Straight Life: The Story of Art Pepper* (New York: Schirmer Books/Macmillan Publishing Co., 1979). Used by permission of Laurie Pepper.

King Pleasure. Parker's Mood: Recorded 1954, Prestige Records; EMI Music Publishing Ltd.

Richard Prince. The Velvet Wall: *Richard Prince: Collected Writings*, Kristine McKenna, ed. (New York: Foggy Notion Books, 2011). Copyright © Richard Prince. Used by permission.

David Rattray. How I Became One of the Invisible: *How I Became One of the Invisible* (New York: Semiotext(e), 1992). Used by permission of Semiotext(e).

Ishmael Reed. From *Mumbo Jumbo* (New York: Doubleday, 1972). Copyright © 1972 by Ishmael Reed. Used by permission of Scribner, a division of Simon & Schuster, Inc., and Lowenstein Associates, Inc. All rights reserved.

Annie Ross. Twisted: Words by Annie Ross, music by Wardell Gray; on *King Pleasure Sings/Annie Ross Sings*, Prestige Records, 1952. Copyright © 1952 by Orpheum Music.

Mort Sahl. The Billy Graham Rally: *The Future Lies Ahead*, Verve Records, 1958; reprinted in *Breaking It Up!: The Best Routines of the Stand–Up Comics*, Ross Firestone, ed. (New York: Bantam Books, 1975). Used by permission.

Ed Sanders. Siobhan McKenna Group-Grope: *Tales of Beatnik Glory* (New York: Stonehill Publishing, 1975); expanded edition (New York: Carol Publishing Group, 1990). Used by permission of Ed Sanders.

Delmore Schwartz. Hamlet, or There Is Something Wrong With Everyone: *Vaudeville for a Princess and Other Poems*. Copyright © 1959 by Delmore Schwartz. Used by permission of New Directions Publishing Corp.

Jack Smith. The Perfect Filmic Appositeness of Maria Montez: *Film Culture* 27, Winter 1962–63. Used by permission of the Anthology Film Archives and of the Gladstone Gallery, New York and Brussels. All rights reserved.

Carl Solomon. A Diabolist: *Mishaps, Perhaps* (San Francisco: City Lights Books, 1966). Used by permission of City Lights Books.

Terry Southern. You're Too Hip, Baby: *Esquire* 1952; reprinted in *Red-Dirt Marijuana and Other Tales* (New York: New American Library, 1967). Used by permission of the Susan Schulman Literary Agency.

Hunter S. Thompson. From *Fear and Loathing in Las Vegas: A Savage Journey to the Heart of the American Dream*. Copyright © 1971 by Hunter S. Thompson. Used by permission of Random House, Inc. and The Wylie Agency LLC. Artwork: "Crap Table" by Ralph Steadman. Used by permission of the Ralph Steadman Art Collection.

Lynne Tillman. Madame Realism Asks What's Natural About Painting?: *The Madame Realism Complex* (New York: Semiotext(e), 1992). Used by permission of Semiotext(e).

Nick Tosches. From *Dino: Living High in the Dirty Business of Dreams*. Copyright © 1991 by Nick Tosches. Used by permission of Doubleday, a division of Random House, Inc.

Alexander Trocchi. From *Cain's Book* (New York: Grove Press, 1960). Copyright © 1960 by Grove Press, Inc. Used by permission of Grove/Atlantic, Inc.

Andy Warhol. From *a: a novel*. Copyright © 1968, 1998 by The Andy Warhol Foundation for the Visual Arts, Inc. Used by permission of Grove/Atlantic, Inc., and The Random House Group Limited.

Rudolph Wurlitzer. From *Nog* (New York: Random House, 1968). Used by permission of Rudolph Wurlitzer.

Emily XYZ. Sinatra Walks Out: *Verbal Abuse* number 1, Summer 1993. Used by permission.

Lester Young and François Postif. Lesterparis59: *The Jazz Review* 2/6, July 1959. Used by permission of Scribner, a division of Simon & Schuster, Inc., from *Jazz Panorama: From the Pages of The Jazz Review*, by Martin Williams. Copyright © 1958, 1959, 1960, 1961, 1962 by The Jazz Review, Inc. All rights reserved.